SCHOOL OF
ORIENTAL AND AFRICAN STUDIES
UNIVERSITY OF LONDON

HENRY BURNEY

A Political Biography

D. G. E. HALL

*Professor Emeritus of the
History of South East Asia
in the University of London*

LONDON

Oxford University Press

NEW YORK   KUALA LUMPUR

1974

Oxford University Press, Ely House, London W. 1

GLASGOW NEW YORK TORONTO MELBOURNE WELLINGTON
CAPE TOWN IBADAN NAIROBI DAR ES SALAAM LUSAKA ADDIS ABABA
DELHI BOMBAY CALCUTTA MADRAS KARACHI LAHORE DACCA
KUALA LUMPUR SINGAPORE HONG KONG TOKYO

ISBN 0 19 713583 8

© D. G. E. Hall, 1974

All rights reserved. No part of this publication may be reproduced, stored in a retrieval system, or transmitted, in any form or by any means, electronic, mechanical, photocopying, recording or otherwise, without the prior permission of Oxford University Press

*Printed in Great Britain
by W & J Mackay Limited, Chatham*

Contents

Acknowledgements		vii
Preface		ix
List of abbreviations		xv

PART ONE	PENANG AND SIAM		
CHAPTER 1	Introducing Siam and Henry Burney		3
CHAPTER 2	John Crawfurd and Robert Fullerton		16
CHAPTER 3	The Bangkok Régime and the Burney Mission		31
CHAPTER 4	The Burma War and the Deportees		54
CHAPTER 5	The Raja of Ligor enters the Contest		74
CHAPTER 6	The Negotiation of the Treaty		99
PART TWO	THE CONTROVERSY OVER THE TREATY		
CHAPTER 7	Governor Fullerton's moves		129
CHAPTER 8	The Ratification		140
CHAPTER 9	Burney and the Raja of Ligor		148
PART THREE	BURMA		
CHAPTER 10	Burma and the British		171
CHAPTER 11	Burney moves in		192
CHAPTER 12	Tenasserim, the Kabaw Valley, the Indemnity		209
CHAPTER 13	Burney and the Court of Ava		231
CHAPTER 14	Burney changes his mind: the Kabaw Valley, the Residency		242
CHAPTER 15	The Assam-Burma Frontier		263
CHAPTER 16	The Coup d'Etat of 1837		270
CHAPTER 17	The End of a Diplomatic Career		290
EPILOGUE	Burney the Orientalist		309
Bibliography			320
Index			323

Maps
(at end)

Burma
Malaya

Plates

	facing page
Bangkok from across the river Maenam Chao Phraya	1
Suffolk House, Prince of Wales Island, the residence of the Governor of Penang	127
Rangoon in 1825	169

Acknowledgements

The cost of production of this volume has been met by the School of Oriental and African Studies, University of London, and to it and its Publications Committee I wish to express my sincere gratitude for their generosity. I also thank the India Office Library and Records, London, for their permission to reproduce the three illustrations from originals in their possession.

Preface

No one can have contributed more to the East India Company's records, and no one in what he wrote for them can have been more reticent about his private life than Henry Burney. But though deficient in the more intimate personal information needed by the biographer, his writings are a rich mine of materials for the historian. Thus it was as a student of South-East Asian history that I first made their acquaintance, and through them that of Burney the diplomatist and orientalist.

In the history books Henry Burney appears in two different settings; first in that of Penang seeking to contain Siamese expansion into the south of the Malay Peninsula, and of Bangkok, whither he went as British envoy; secondly in that of Burma, recoiling into self-imposed isolation after defeat by British India. Each of these two phases of his career has been recorded from the original sources, the earlier by Professor L. A. Mills, the later by Professor W. S. Desai, entirely separately and simply in the context of the country with which each was concerned, Malaya in the one case, Burma in the other. It was almost as if he were two different people.

It seemed worthwhile therefore to join up the two disparate pieces and take a look at the whole. And, as I had come to expect, there emerges one of the most noteworthy servants of the East India Company of his time, one who in serving it came to play a markedly important part in the histories of two South-East Asian kingdoms, Siam and Burma. Siam he influenced to take a tentative, though as it turned out, decisive, step towards a policy of co-operation towards the West which proved to be a turning-point in its history. In Burma's case he strove against the greatest odds, not without success, to develop satisfactory relations between its government and that of British India; and though finally failing in his contest with the forces of isolation, he maintained over a period of years a closer personal relationship with the Court of Ava than any foreign envoy had ever done before. In both cases his own contribution to the study of their languages and cultures by Europeans was notable, though nothing to what it could have been had not his untimely death prevented him from completing the work he was preparing for publication.

In one sense therefore this present book represents a belated attempt to give Burney his rightful place, not among the great builders or administrators of British India, but among the great ambassadors sent to establish understanding between it and its neighbours, men who through their studies of the languages of the lands to which they were sent sought to improve their own understanding of their peoples, primarily in order to carry out their duties efficiently, yet ultimately because they developed an interest in such studies for their own sake.

The main sources for the study of Henry Burney's diplomatic career are his own journals and other writings and their collateral documents in the East India Company's records. Those for the Siam period, which are to be found in the many volumes of Factory Records, Straits Settlements, were printed in extenso in 1908 for private circulation by the Vagirañāṇa National Library at Bangkok. A reprint of this collection with an Introduction by Professor David Wyatt of Cornell University was published by Gregg International Publishers Ltd in 1971 in five volumes. Those for the Burma period are to be found in the Bengal Political Proceedings, the India Secret Proceedings and the India Political Proceedings, and have not been printed.

The Burney private papers were presented in 1921 to the then Royal Colonial Institute, now the Royal Commonwealth Society. Among them are bound copies of his Siam and Ava journals. Both journals were written daily and copies despatched at intervals to the authorities he served, Penang and Calcutta in the case of his mission to Siam, Calcutta in the case of his residency in Burma. There are two copies of his Ava journal in the India Office records, one, in instalments, in the Bengal Secret and Political Proceedings, vols. 358, 361–3 and 366, and the other bound in seven separate MS volumes, in vol. 4 of which are also Dr. Richardson's journal of his journey from Ava to Kindat and Burney's 'Observations on the Currency of Ava'. The Ava journal covers only the first two years of his stay in the country. His subsequent reports do not take the form of a diary until the outbreak of Tharrawaddy's rebellion in February 1837 when they revert to the form of a detailed journal of events up to the removal of the residency from Ava. Among the Siam papers are his valuable 'Report concerning the Commerce of Siam' (Burney Papers, II, 4, 79–121). The India Political Proceedings contain his long and detailed 'Account of the Burmese

Mission which resided in Bengal from December 1830 to July 1833, compiled from the Reports sent by the Envoys to the Court of Ava and other Burmese documents'.

The Royal Commonwealth Society's collection contains for the most part materials connected with Burney's official activities. There is, for instance, his report on the insurrection at Tavoy and Mergui in 1829, and the letter from the Chief Secretary at Calcutta conveying the Government of India's 'high approbation' for his part in putting it down. I have omitted the story of this incident since it was outside Burney's diplomatic activities. There is also his 'Memorandum regarding the Singphos'. These documents, like a good many others in the collection, are merely duplicates of documents in the India Office records. Of those that are not the more notable ones are his 'Hints regarding the characters of the principal persons at the Court of Ava and the conduct to be observed towards them' (B XV), an annotated edition of which I published in the *Bulletin of the School of Oriental and African Studies*, XX, 1957; his 'Account of the Trade, etc. of Rangoon' (B XXVII); and the correspondence concerning Captain Lake's challenge to a duel (D XXVIII). In addition there are chronolgical tables of the kings of Siam (C XXI) and Ava (B VI), a table of correspondence between the Christian and Burmese eras from A.D. 1538 to 1838 (B XVI), notes on Buddhism in Burma, a description of 'Pictures of Boodh' and a list of the books of the Tripitaka (B IX), and translations of extracts from the Burmese chronicles B XIII, XIV). There is almost nothing of a really private nature. The nearest approach to it is in one or two letters from correspondents who ask him to convey their 'best respects' to Mrs. Burney.

My former colleague at Rangoon University, Walter Sadgun Desai, worked with great thoroughness through the India Office records relating to the English residency in Burma and has used them with scrupulous faithfulness in compiling his book to which I make frequent references in the Burma section of this volume. I gratefully acknowledge my indebtedness to it as well as to his articles in the *Journal of the Burma Research Society*. I appreciate the empathy with Burney which he seems to have developed in the course of his study. Burney charms those who approach him through his own writings. And it seems significant that in his own day some of those with whom he clashed strongly, such as the Prahkhlang at Bangkok and King Tharrawaddy of Burma, betrayed a genuine regard for him. It is difficult not to take his side even when he was wrong, as in his advocacy of the views of the Raja of Ligor regarding the Kurau incident, and his recommendation to Lord Auckland of military action against Tharrawaddy for disowning the treaties with British India.

One important document of which Professor Desai makes no use is R. B. Pemberton's graphic account of his journey from Manipur to Ava in 1830 to join with Burney and the Court of Ava in the discussion of the Kabaw Valley question. I came across it while reading Burney's journal in the Bengal Secret and Political Proceedings, and found it so interesting that I published an annotated edition of it in the *Journal of the Burma Research Society*.[1] It provides a welcome supplement to Burney's own record of Pemberton's visit. Another source not consulted by Desai is Burney's published account of the Ava revolution of 1837 in the *Colonial Magazine and Commercial Maritime Journal*.[2] It follows very closely the reports he made to the Government of India dated 3 March and 26 May 1837.[3] It adds nothing of any significance to the accounts contained in those two despatches. He must have hoped to contribute a further article on the subject of his relations with King Tharrawaddy and the withdrawal of the residency from Ava, for at the end of the article are the words 'to be continued'. In it he would have defended his actions which Lord Auckland so strongly criticized. So far as I know it never appeared and one would like to know what went on behind the scenes in the matter. The Royal Commonwealth Society's Burney collection contains nothing on the subject. Apparently Burney was not permitted to defend himself in public.

I am much indebted to a number of friends for very generous help. Professor David Wyatt, now of Cornell, the writer of the Introduction to the 1971 reprint of *The Burney Papers* by Gregg International relating to Henry Burney's mission to Siam, produced some identifications of people mentioned in the text for the use of students in a course which he, and later I, conducted at the London School of Oriental and African Studies. These I have drawn upon freely in writing the first nine chapters of this book. He has also read the whole of the book in typescript and provided me with

[1] XLIII, ii, Dec. 1960.   [2] Vol. VII, 1842.
[3] India Political Proceedings, vols. 35 and 41.

many valuable criticisms and suggestions. Professor Hla Pe of London University, whose friendship I have enjoyed for close on forty years, gave me many hours of his time taking me through the parts of the *Konbaungset Chronicle* dealing with the period of Burney's connexion with Burma. At Cornell Mrs. Margaret Aung Thwin gave me much appreciated help also with that source. To these three in particular, and to Professor C. D. Cowan and Professor O. W. Wolters, who read the original typescript, I wish to express my gratitude, as also to Mr. S. C. Sutton and his staff at the India Office Library, whose assistance in exploring its MS sources of the Burney period was vital, when long ago I began to collect the materials which have made possible the writing of this book. Finally, a special word of thanks to Mr. Oliver B. Pollack, who discovered Burney's article on the Burmese revolution in the *Colonial Magazine and Commercial Maritime Journal*, 1842, and made a copy of it for me.

List of Abbreviations

BP	Burney Papers, Bangkok edition.
BPC	Bengal Political Consultations.
BSOAS	Bulletin of the School of Oriental and African Studies.
BSP	Bengal Secret and Political Consultations.
IPP	India Political Proceedings.
ISP	India Secret Proceedings.
JASB	Journal of The Asiatic Society of Bengal.
JBRS	Journal of The Burma Research Society.
JRAS MB	Journal of The Royal Asiatic Society, Malayan Branch.
JSS	Journal of The Siam Society.

Bangkok from across the River Menam Chao Phraya

Part One

PENANG AND SIAM

Chapter 1

Introducing Siam and Henry Burney

ONE of the key developments on the mainland of South-East Asia in the fourteenth and fifteenth centuries was the expansion of Tai power. From the last years of the thirteenth century the Siamese, the most adaptable of the Tai-speaking peoples, having gained command over much of the Menam Chao Phraya basin, were pushing their control southwards into the Malay Peninsula; indeed, after the foundation of the Kingdom of Ayuthaya in 1350 Siam sought to make good claims to suzerainty over all the Malay states of the Peninsula. Her real power in the area must have varied considerably from time to time. During the course of the fifteenth century, for instance, the Malay maritime state of Malacca was able to expand its dominion over the whole of what is today mainland Malaya, together with the island groups immediately south of it, as well as over much of the east coast of Sumatra. It flouted Ayuthaya's claims and signally defeated her attempts to assert them by force of arms. When in 1511 Don Affonso de Albuquerque conquered Malacca for the King of Portugal, the dispossessed Sultan Mahmud re-established his capital in Johore, and laid effective claim to the allegiance of all the states previously under Malaccan suzerainty.

Siam's claims during the remainder of the Ayuthaya period were never effective over the part of the Peninsula south of the state of Pattani on its east coast and of the island of Puket (Junkceylon) on its west coast. Pattani was a vassal kingdom, as also was its neighbour on the west coast, the then large kingdom of Kedah. Northwards of them the whole of the rest of the Peninsula, including the Malay states of Nakhorn Sithammarat, once a powerful kingdom, and Songkhla, was fully incorporated in the Kingdom of Ayuthaya. Malacca during its period of greatness had been a main diffusion-centre of Islam. The Malays, differing from the Siamese in race and language, now developed a strong religious antagonism towards the Buddhist power which claimed their allegiance, even though the acknowledgement of it might amount to little more in practice than the periodical presentation by their rulers of the Bunga Mas, the traditional tribute of gold and silver flowers from a vassal to his overlord.

In 1767 Ayuthaya fell before the armies of King Hsinbyushin (Lord of the White Elephant) of Burma and Siamese control over the peninsular states vanished for the time being. Burmese armies overran the Peninsula as far as Nakhorn Sithammarat, and the vassal states ceased to pay homage. But the Malay world was by this time hopelessly fragmented: the Johore empire was no longer a reality and there was no nucleus around which the Malays could have grouped themselves, had they wished to. Hence when King Taksin, in the course of freeing his country from the invader, drove the Burmese out of the Peninsula, Siamese authority there revived, and pressure was put upon Pattani and Kedah once more to send the *Bunga Mas*. Neither, however, responded.

In 1782 Taksin was dethroned and the king known today as Rama I took his place. Two years later the Burmese, this time under King Bodawpaya, launched another full-scale invasion of Siam. It failed ignominiously, but in 1785 and again in 1786 peninsular Siam suffered serious inroads by large Burmese forces. The intruders were decisively defeated by a rapidly reviving Siam, and as a result, even stronger pressure was brought upon the Malay states of the area to toe the Siamese line. Pattani refused, but fell before the forces of the Siamese Maha Uparat, who had been specially entrusted with the task of bringing the Malay sultanates back into the Siamese fold. In the face of this display of Siamese strength Kedah submitted and, a little later, the east coast sultans of Kelantan and Trengganu followed suit.

The Sultan of Kedah had hoped for the assistance of the English East India Company to maintain his independence, and encouraged in that hope by Francis Light had permitted the Company in 1786 to occupy the island of Penang. But the Directors in London, though accepting the island, took refuge in the doctrine of non-intervention, enjoined upon the Company by the British Government, and left the Sultan in the lurch. In any case they were only concerned with the place's potential value in the sphere of maritime commerce and strategy. The last thing they wanted was to become

Introducing Siam and Henry Burney

involved in the internal politics of the Malay Peninsula.

As to Penang itself, for some years there was much doubt as to whether it was worth retaining, notwithstanding the rapid growth of its population and trade. There were pirate villages all around it on the mainland and in the neighbouring islands; its harbour at night was unsafe from their raids; while their fleets until as late as 1830, when returning from their annual cruises, would sail right past its harbour between the island and the mainland.

There was scepticism as to its potential value as a naval base until in 1797 the expedition designed for the conquest of Manila in the Philippines assembled there, and it was reported on in the highest terms for the facilities it offered for refitting ships.[1] The writer of the report was Arthur Wellesley, later to become Duke of Wellington. His elder brother, Lord Mornington, became Governor-General of India in that same year, and during his regime the climate of doubt regarding the island switched to one of the rosiest optimism. So, instead of being abandoned, the settlement was strengthened by the acquisition of the strip of territory opposite to it on the mainland from the Sultan of Kedah. By this new agreement the Company was to pay him ten thousand dollars a year in respect of its occupation of Penang and Province Wellesley, as the newly-acquired mainland territory was dubbed. The object of this additional acquisition was to safeguard Penang's food supply, which was dangerously dependent upon Kedah. Nothing was said in the new agreement about a defensive alliance, but the Sultan undoubtedly made it in the hope that he was thereby binding the British more closely to his cause.

This exaggerated belief in Penang's importance reached its climax in 1805 when the settlement became a fourth Indian presidency along with Bengal, Madras and Bombay. Judged in the clear light of history it was a quixotic move. But Britain was engaged in the great struggle against Napoleon, and the Indian Ocean was seen as a vital area of conflict. Penang commanded the Straits of Malacca and was expected to become a naval base. From the Coromandel Coast it was only a week's sail in any weather. It was a port of refreshment for ships engaged in the China trade. The hope was indulged in that it would become a trading centre for the islands of the Malay Archipelago, and even that spices and

---

[1] The expedition was called off and the fleet brought back to India for operations against Tipu Sultan of Mysore.

pepper could be grown there to free the British from dependence upon the Dutch.

Then came disillusionment. No dockyards could be built there and no suitable timber for ship repairs was available locally: it had to be imported from Rangoon. So the plan for a naval base had to be abandoned. Moreover, native shipping from the archipelago dared not approach it through the pirate-infested Straits of Malacca. And although pepper cultivation succeeded, spice cultivation was a complete failure. The naval situation also began to change as a result of the battle of Trafalgar, the capture of the French naval base in Mauritius and the British conquest of Java (1811). The French danger receded into the background, and, as it did so, the realization grew that Penang with its host of officials was an unnecessary drain upon the Indian treasury. Raffles's occupation of Singapore in 1819, and the Anglo-Dutch treaty of 1824 delimiting the spheres of interest of the two powers, put the final touches to the disillusionment, and in 1830 the presidency was abolished. The Straits Settlements of Penang, Malacca and Singapore became a residency, a mere offshoot of the Bengal presidency. And in 1832 Singapore supplanted Penang as its capital.

Henry Burney's connexion with Penang from start to finish fell within the period when it was a presidency. Its official designation was Prince of Wales Island. Its governor was President of the Straits Settlements with his headquarters in Fort Cornwallis. Burney went there with his regiment, the 25th Bengal Native Infantry, after serving with Lord Minto's expeditionary force which in 1811 wrested Java from the Dutch. He served there in a purely military capacity for two short periods, from 1811 to 1814 and from 1816 to 1818. In that last year he was seconded from regimental duties to become Military Secretary to its governor, Colonel John Alexander Bannerman, notorious in history for his pathetic opposition to Raffles's moves leading to the acquisition of Singapore. In June of the same year he married the governor's niece Janet.

Henry Burney belonged to the third generation of a family distinguished beyond most of its time for contributions to music, literature, art and scholarship. His grandfather was Dr. Charles Burney, the 'Great Doctor Burney' of Percy Scholes's biography,[1]

[1] Percy A. Scholes, *The Great Dr. Burney*, London, Oxford University Press, 2 vols, 1948.

Introducing Siam and Henry Burney

a leading musician of his day and the author of a famous *History of Music*.[1] Charles Burney was the brother-in-law of Arthur Young, he was also the intimate friend of Edmund Burke, David Garrick, Sir Joshua Reynolds, Dr. Johnson and the Thrales, and numbered Handel, Haydn, Rousseau, Horace Walpole and Samuel Wesley among his close acquaintances. His elder brother James, a naval officer, was a writer of histories of voyages and discoveries, which brought him the friendship of some of the literary elite of his time, Lamb, Hood, Southey, Wordsworth, Coleridge and Crabb Robinson. Two of Charles's daughters were novelists, the famous Fanny, Madame d'Arblay, and Sarah Harriet, of lesser fame. His son Charles became Prebendary of Lincoln and a Chaplain to the King, but was chiefly known for his library, which after his death was bought by the British Museum. Dr. Burney's nephew Edward Burney, his brother Richard's son, achieved renown for his water colours and drawings, which may be seen today in the National Portrait Gallery, the Victoria and Albert Museum and the British Museum, where his pencil portrait of David Garrick is of special interest.

Henry Burney's father was Richard Thomas (1768–1808). Dr. Burney's youngest son by his second wife. Dr. Scholes records that as a child Richard was the pet of the family and a general favourite.[2] But at Winchester College, where he was educated, he received 'monitory letters' from Mrs. Thrale because of his propensity for 'playing the buffoon', whatever that may have meant. There is, however, little about him in the family papers, and Dr. Scholes poses the question whether his going to India was the result of some minor scandal about which 'the Burney tribe', as they were sometimes dubbed by contemporaries, kept scrupulously silent. Whatever the reason, 'Bengal Dick', as his family came to call him, left home, and in due course became Master of the East India Company's Orphanage of Kidderpore. And there he established a reputation for extreme piety. The Burney Papers in the Royal Commonwealth Society's collection include a printed brochure of the sermon preached at his memorial service in Calcutta

---

[1] *A General History of Music from the Earliest Ages to the Present Period. To which is prefixed a Dissertation on the Music of the Ancients.* 4 vols., I, 1776; II, 1782; III and IV, 1789. See Percy A. Scholes, *op. cit.*, I, pp. 289–315, II, pp. 333–6.
[2] *Op. cit.*, II, p. 30. A miniature of him by George Chinnery, painted in India, is reproduced in Vol. II, plate 44, p. 244.

on 15 May 1808 by the Senior Chaplain at the Presidency of Fort William, Rev. David Harvie.[1] It records that on the sabbath he would not allow 'any token of levity to appear such as thoughtless whistling, or any sort of play, however innocent in itself'. He wished his children to be brought up strictly religious, we are told.

Henry was his second son, and was born in Calcutta on 27 February 1792. His mother's maiden name was Jane Ross, but of her and her background Dr. Scholes's compendious record has nothing to say. His elder brother Richard like him pursued a military career in the East India Company's service, and, also like him, interrupted it to develop special interests. Richard went to Cambridge to study, and took his degree. Henry represented the Company in two South-East Asian capitals and seized the opportunity to study their languages and cultures. Both brothers achieved some distinction in their respective fields. Richard founded the Burney Prize at Cambridge, and there is a memorial to him in Christ's College chapel. Henry presented a valuable collection of Burmese manuscripts to the East India Company's library, and after his death a Pali dictionary with explanations in Sanskrit and Bengali, compiled for him at the Court of Ava, was deposited in the Bodleian Library at Oxford. Moreover, the Royal Asiatic Society printed a lengthy obituary notice of him in its Proceedings, giving an outline of his career and a list of his contributions to the Journal of the Asiatic Society of Bengal, and describing him as 'an excellent scholar in several oriental languages'.[2]

'Bengal Dick's' health broke down in August 1806, and after a 'long and severe illness' he died on 8 March 1808 in Rangoon, whither he had gone on a sea trip hoping it would aid his recovery. He arrived in Rangoon on 28 February, and recorded in his journal, 'Hallelujah, Hallelujah, Bless the Lord, O My Soul; and all that is within me bless His holy name, for evermore'.[3] He died there just over a week later in the Baptist Mission House, headquarters of the mission opened there by J. B. Chater and Felix Carey, the eldest son of William Carey of Serampore. His eldest son Richard seems to have accompanied him from Calcutta and together with Felix Carey nursed him during his last night.[4]

[1] Document A1.
[2] Proceedings of the 23rd Anniversary Meeting, 16 May 1846.
[3] Document A, p. 16.
[4] The incident is mentioned by B. R. Pearn in 'Felix Carey and the English Baptist Mission in Burma' JBRS, Vol. XXVIII p. 20 note 20. Pearn gives as his

On 14 August of that same year Henry arrived in India, having been appointed in the previous year, 1807, to a cadetship in the East India Company's service.[1] Of his life up to that point the sources so far available to us have nothing to say. He himself in his manifold writings preserved in the East India Company's records maintains the most discreet silence regarding his own domestic life, as indeed one would expect of a public servant writing in an official capacity. It is very tantalizing and would be extremely frustrating were one attempting to write anything more intimate than his political biography. He and his younger contemporary Arthur Phayre share this quality of extreme reticence regarding their private lives. It is almost as if both men had hardly any existence outside their work. This may well have been true of Phayre, who was a bachelor and, judging by such of his private journals as have survived, was completely absorbed in the official tasks he had to perform. But Burney was a married man with a family whom he took with him to Bangkok, as we know indirectly from his Siam journal, since he has to record that the king invited him to bring his young son, aged six, to Court to receive a present of Siamese toys.

The writer of the obituary notice in the *Proceedings of the Royal Asiatic Society* tells us that 'from the moment of his arrival in India' Burney became a marked man because of his 'application to study'. He first qualified as interpreter in Hindustani to his regiment. Then, while in Penang, he learnt Malay and endeavoured to learn all he could about conditions in the Malay-speaking world of both the Peninsula and its adjacent islands. As Military Secretary his duties were to conduct the Governor of Penang's relations with the various states into which what was then termed the 'Peninsula of Malacca' was divided; and since Siamese pressure upon them had become a dominant factor in Malayan politics, Burney soon decided to add Siamese to his repertoire of oriental languages.

The East India Company, let it be again emphasized, was strongly averse to becoming a participant in the politics of the Peninsula. It had its hands full in India. Its main interest in the

---

authority the Periodical Accounts relative to the Baptist Missionary Society, London 1800 onwards, and refers to Richard's wife as 'Janet Ross of Bengal'.

[1] *Bengal Army List.*

Malay world arose out of its geographical position on the trade route to China. But in 1818 the situation which faced Henry Burney was both complex and in a state of rapid change. Britain, having assumed control of much of the Dutch eastern empire during the Napoleonic wars, had been handing it back to its previous owners under the Convention of London of August 1814. The returning Dutch, however, showed obvious signs of a determination to revive their monopolistic policy and keep out British trade from what they regarded as their own area. In 1818 they frustrated Bannerman's moves to negotiate trade treaties with the rulers of the old Johore empire and of the West Coast of Borneo. In the following year, however, Sir Stamford Raffles, who had reappeared on the scene as Lieut.-Governor of Bencoolen, the Company's pepper port in western Sumatra, unable to win over Calcutta to his schemes for expanding British commercial influence in that island, neatly outwitted the Dutch, his own employers and even Bannerman of Penang by taking possession of Singapore island.

Then, when the tumult died down and the Company decided to retain possession of Singapore, negotiations began for a settlement involving the definition of mutual spheres of influence. The solution, embodied in the Anglo-Dutch Treaty of 1824, was for Britain to abandon any influence in Sumatra or the islands south of Singapore and for Holland to abandon any influence in the Malay Peninsula and claims to Singapore. The corollary was, of course, that Britain could now proceed to make herself the paramount power in the Peninsula. But such was far from being the intention of the Supreme Government in Calcutta, East India House in London or the British Government itself. So far as the Peninsula was concerned the principle of non-intervention laid down in Pitt's India Act must prevail. There must be no intervention in the affairs of the Malay states, no treaty with a Malay ruler with political implications, and no increase in British territorial responsibilities. Political alliances, the Government of India well knew from its own experience nearer at hand, would involve constant intervention under the anarchical conditions in the Peninsula. Worse still, they could lead to war with Siam, and this Calcutta was determined to avoid.

That such a policy was quite unrealistic in terms of the actual situation in the Malay world only the men on the spot were in a position to understand. For one dominant fact was, in the words of

Lennox Mills, that the Malay states were 'hard at work committing political hara-kiri'.[1] Wars and feuds between sultan and sultan, disputed successions resulting in civil wars, and piracy flourished on a scale that indicated a widespread breakdown of political authority; these were the great evils. They horrified Europeans who came into contact with them. The Penang records of Henry Burney's time are full of references to piracy. Penang's own food supply, which largely depended upon the mainland opposite, was threatened. Hence there was intervention, notwithstanding the thunders of Calcutta and Leadenhall Street. Some of it was unavoidable, but not all, as the activities of John Anderson and James Low were to demonstrate. It was directed to the furtherance of peaceful conditions of trade, which were threatened by Siamese attempts to expand their control southwards. The methods they used created disorder and chaos in the Malay lands within Penang's commercial orbit. Moreover, if successful, it meant the substitution of Siam's very restrictive policy towards *Farang* trade for that of rulers who welcomed Penang's trade.

One may detect a further factor in the situation, the pro-Malay sentiment of British officials at Penang. They saw clearly that Siam aimed at taking advantage of the fragmentation of the old empire of Johore to extend her sway over the whole peninsula, acting on 'the time-honoured principle of Asiatic monarchies that the stronger has the right to subdue the weaker power'.[2] But Siam was not strong enough to pursue a policy of outright military conquest. She relied upon keeping the Malay states in a state of turmoil, upon troubling the waters in order to fish in them, and upon making use of Malay factions to help carry out her designs.

At Nakhorn Sithammarat, the chief provincial centre in the south, the governor, called the 'Raja of Ligor' by the British, was a man of ability with immense influence at the Siamese court. He was Chao Noi, an actual son of King Taksin, the hero of Siam's recovery from the Burmese conquest of 1767, and an adopted son of his predecessor in office, Chao Phat, whom he had succeeded in 1811. His mother was a daughter of a previous Chao Phraya of Sithammarat. Two of his own daughters became royal concubines of King Rama III. He it was who was responsible for the rather acute anxiety regarding Siamese designs which the Penang government began to feel in 1818. Under him Siamese policy in the

[1] *British Malaya, 1824–1867*, p. 171.   [2] L. A. Mills, *op. cit.*, p. 128.

Peninsula took a new turn, one of increasing Bangkok's control over existing Malay vassals and of asserting it over hitherto independent Malay rulers.

In 1818, that key year in Henry Burney's career, when he was seconded from his regiment to become Military Secretary to the Governor of Penang, a series of events began, which drew him more and more deeply as a participant in the diplomatic moves made by the British Indian authorities because of the repercussions of this new turn in Siamese policy. In that year Siam ordered the Sultan of Kedah to invade the neighbouring state of Perak and force its sultan to send the *bunga mas* to Bangkok. Perak was an independent state owing no allegiance whatever to Siam; yet for some years previously Siam had sent repeated demands, transmitted through the Sultan of Kedah, for an acknowledgement of her suzerainty. These had one and all been rejected by the Sultan of Perak. He argued that his authority as an independent ruler was of longer standing than that of any neighbouring Malay ruler. The Sultan of Kedah, however, feared lest the wrath of Siam would be visited upon his own state, if Perak persisted in rejecting the Siamese demands. When therefore the order came for him to invade Perak, he did so, though according to John Anderson's account, with the utmost reluctance and, as he put it, 'only to avert mischief from my country'.[1]

Only a month before the invasion took place the East India Company had concluded a commercial treaty with Perak. For centuries Perak had been famous for its tin exports. The Dutch had planted a factory there in the seventeenth century. When the armies of the French revolution overran Holland and Britain had taken over the Dutch settlements in the Peninsula by agreement with the exiled Stadthouder, Perak's tin trade had fallen into British hands. That was in 1795, and since then it had increased considerably. Those who knew the country estimated that its tin industry was capable of great expansion, given peaceable conditions. Hence the disorder created by the Kedah invasion, and the threat of further Siamese moves in the future, caused the deepest

---

[1] *Political and Commercial Considerations relative to the Malayan Peninsula and the British Settlements in the Straits of Malacca,* 1824, pp. 86–7, quoted in P. J. Begbie, *The Malayan Peninsula,* Kuala Lumpur, Oxford in Asia Reprints, 1967, p. 92 originally published in Madras, 1834. Anderson's pamphlet was suppressed soon after publication, but a facsimile reprint of it with an introduction by J. S. Bastin appeared in JRASMB, vol. XXV, part 4 (Dec. 1962).

concern to the Government of Prince of Wales Island, fettered as it was by the policy of non-intervention. The opinion was firmly held that the mere threat of intervention would suffice: Siam would never risk any action likely to bring her troops into collision with those of British India. But so long as she was convinced that there would be no British reaction to her moves, she would go ahead with them, carefully and systematically. This was all the more galling since it had long been clear that the Malay rulers believed that a British guarantee would be enough to assure their independence of Siam, and successive sultans of Kedah never ceased pressing for the defensive alliance which they held to be the price owed them by the British for the cessions of Penang and Province Wellesley. The latest argument used by the Government of India in Kedah's case was that it could not interfere between a vassal and his suzerain. Penang was forbidden to take any measures for Kedah's protection; the Governor was told, however, that if a suitable opportunity presented itself, he might negotiate with the Bangkok authorities for a mitigation of their pressure upon the Sultan.

When he did negotiate on the latter's behalf, he was a fugitive in Penang and thousands of his subjects had poured over the frontier into Province Wellesley fleeing from the atrocities of a Siamese army led by the Raja of Ligor. One of his sons together with his chief minister had fallen into Siamese hands and the latter had been deliberately killed despite a request from the Governor of Penang that his life be spared. This happened in 1821. The Sultan had failed to comply with a number of demands for supplies and money made on him by the Government of Siam. He contended that they were in excess of what was customary. He was accused of having intrigued with Burma and ordered to present himself before his suzerain in Bangkok to answer for his conduct. Fearing the worst, he refused to go. Therefore in November 1821 a Siamese fleet, secretly assembled in the Trang River, appeared in the Kedah River and began the work of invasion and destruction. The Raja of Ligor, as soon as he learnt that the Sultan had escaped, wrote a letter to the Government of Prince of Wales Island demanding in peremptory terms the surrender of the fugitive. His demand was summarily rejected, and a Siamese attempt to enter Province Wellesley easily repulsed by a small party of Bengal Native Infantry.

At the same time the fallen sultan's request that the British reinstate him was flatly rejected. Thereupon he sent envoys to the Court of Ava and a number of Malay states in the hope of persuading them to stage a combined attack upon Siam. But these moves came to nothing. For one thing the Penang authorities got to know of them and reported them to the Raja of Ligor. For another, the Burmese at the time were concentrating all their efforts upon expanding their control over Assam and the other states on the north-east frontier of India, and were in no position to interfere effectively in Siam, much as they might have wished to.

Nevertheless, the Penang Council wanted the deposed sultan to be restored. It feared that the Siamese in Kedah might threaten Penang's food supply, and, despite the repulse of the Siamese force in Province Wellesley, it appears to have much overestimated Siam's military capacity. And although, in reporting the matter to Calcutta the Council warned that Siamese 'haughtiness and pride' could only be checked by force, with Governor Phillips in control the chief emphasis was upon friendly relations in the interests of commerce.

Siam's experience of the Dutch and the French in the seventeenth century had taught her to prefer Asian to European traders. Hence she imposed highly discriminatory duties on European trade in striking contrast to her treatment of Chinese shippers and traders. Penang wanted to expand trade with metropolitan Siam, where sugar and, it was hoped, rice could be obtained in return for Indian piece-goods and opium. It was also much interested in the tin trade, not only of Perak, but also of the island of Junkceylon (Ujong Salang), where Francis Light had once operated, and of other Malayan dependencies of Siam. In 1818 and again in 1819 the Penang Council had sent letters and presents to the Siamese Government at Bangkok asking for some relaxation of the harsh conditions of trade. These, however, proved ineffective. The foundation of Singapore in 1819 made Penang, scenting rivalry, all the more anxious to expand its trade with mainland South-East Asia, and in 1821 Governor Phillips sent a Singapore merchant named Morgan to Bangkok to collect information and make contacts with members of the government. But he failed to make any headway at all. It was obvious, therefore, that only action on the part of the highest authority stood any chance of receiving serious attention at the Court of Bangkok.

This was what Penang had been pressing for since its first

approach to the Siamese Government in 1818. So the Governor-General of India decided to send a full-scale diplomatic mission to the Siamese Court with John Crawfurd of the Bengal Medical Service as its leader. And not only to the Siamese Court, for it was also deputed on a similar errand to the Government of newly-united Vietnam at Hué.

Chapter 2

John Crawfurd and Robert Fullerton

JOHN Crawfurd, like Stamford Raffles his senior, had begun his career as an orientalist by learning Malay. During Raffles's Lieut.-Governorship of Java he had served as Resident at the Court of the Sultan of Jogjakarta, and had subsequently published his *History of the Indian Archipelago* (1820), which established his reputation as an authority on his subject along with Marsden, John Leyden and Raffles.

The chief object of the Crawfurd mission was commercial. In his instructions Lord Amherst wrote that Crawfurd himself was well aware that among the states of farther Asia 'a very general fear and distrust of Europeans' predominated to the serious detriment of commerce. It was the result of their 'violence, imprudence and disregard of national rights'. Hence the Envoy's first object must be to remove it. He must make it clear that the East India Company was 'seeking a renewed connexion' solely for purposes of trade, and that he was forbidden to ask for privileges such as 'the establishment of forts and factories, exemptions from municipal jurisdiction and customary imposts, monopoly of favourite articles of produce, and exclusion of European rivals'.[1] In this context he was directed to try to obtain better conditions of trade through the substitution of a 'fixed duty upon tonnage or measurement' for the existing method of payments in kind based upon a rough examination of the cargo by revenue officers whose irregular exactions were impediments to trade. In addition, he was to stay long enough in the country to enable him and his staff to collect adequate information about 'the character of the Court, the manners of the people, and the resources of the country'.

On the subject of Kedah Crawfurd's instructions made it clear

---

[1] Governor-General of India's Instructions to John Crawfurd in Crawfurd's *Journal of an Embassy to the Courts of Siam and Cochin-China*, 1828, pp. 589–90.

that the Government of India did not wish 'anything of a political nature' to complicate the negotiations. Nevertheless the Envoy must study the causes of Penang's anxiety regarding the security of the states of Perak and Kedah so that if an opportunity presented itself he might take the matter up in the negotiations. But this must depend upon the possibility that such an overture would be favourably received.

The Government of India asked the Penang Council for its views regarding the objects of Crawfurd's mission. The latter in its reply made three points: firstly that the mission's primary object must be to improve Penang's trade with Siam, notably in tin and food supplies; secondly that the restoration of the Sultan of Kedah was a minor matter compared with trade; and thirdly that the most important matter to be settled was the question of Penang's own status, since Kedah's cessions of territory had never been confirmed by Siam as its suzerain.

It was rather late in the day to raise this matter, and obviously, had the Sultan of Kedah not been deposed, neither Penang nor Calcutta would ever have considered doing so. The sultan, who had made the original treaty with the Company in 1786, had been regarded by it as an independent ruler, and treated as such. Penang had been in the Company's undisputed possession for thirty-six years, and Siam had never challenged the Company's right to it. But in 1821, when the Siamese forces conquered Kedah, the Raja of Ligor laid claim to the annual subsidy of ten thousand dollars paid by the Company in respect of Penang and Province Wellesley. This had been rejected, and there the matter stood when Crawfurd arrived in Siam.

Crawfurd's stay in Siam lasted from 24 March to the end of July 1822. He found that the dominant party in the government, headed by the Phrakhlang and Prince Chetsadabodin, whom he calls Prince Kromchiat, was opposed to any relaxation of the handicaps under which European trade laboured, and even more so to any change in the state trading system which would reduce the very large profits that fell to them personally. A commercial treaty seemed quite out of the question. All that he was able to extract from the ministers was a written promise that the duties paid by English merchant-ships going to Bangkok would not be increased, and that the Superintendent of Customs would afford English merchants every assistance in dealing with those of Siam.

The document ended with 'Let the English merchants come to Siam to sell and buy in conformity to this agreement'.[1] It was far less than the mercantile community had hoped for, and less than the objective set forth in Crawfurd's instructions. But it was something: the door was no longer so firmly closed. And Crawfurd was a better scholar than negotiator.

On the Kedah question he was up against a brick wall. The ministers rejected any suggestion of mediation. They wanted him to promise that the Sultan would be handed over to them, and his annual pension transferred to a Siamese nominee. This, however, he refused even to consider: he declared emphatically that the Company would continue to protect the Sultan and pay the subsidy. On the subject of the East India Company's right to Penang no direct reference was made. The Court's silence, Crawfurd wrote in his *Journal*, 'could only be accounted for by its fears, which prudently induced it to abstain from making a claim which it had not the power to enforce'.[2] When the Siamese had to refer to Penang in the discussions, they spoke of it as a British possession. Crawfurd took this as an indication of their acceptance of British sovereignty over the place, and the Government of India concurred with his view.

Crawfurd's account of his mission has been described as its most valuable result.[3] The information contained in it was of immediate use to the Government of India in framing a Siamese policy. It became, when published, a statesman's handbook to a country about which no information had been available since the spate of French writings at the end of the seventeenth century; and great changes had taken place in it since then. In manuscript form it was to be a *vade mecum* for Henry Burney when he went to Bangkok in 1825; he makes frequent mention of it in his own Journal.

Crawfurd dispelled a number of illusions regarding Siam. Its military strength, he said, was 'very contemptible'. The presence of Siamese in Kedah did not menace the safety of Penang; indeed, the Court of Bangkok was secretly in dread of British power. His own opinion was, he said, that had the Company used military force when the Siamese invaded Kedah, they would have with-

---

[1] Crawfurd, *Journal*, p. 174. [2] *Ibid.*, p. 160.
[3] See J. Kennedy, *A History of Malaya* (1962), p. 108, and L. A. Mills, *op. cit.*, p. 133.

drawn and given no further trouble. One must therefore avoid writing off Crawfurd and his mission as 'unsuccessful'.[1] Crawfurd himself, as David Wyatt puts it in his Introduction to the 1967 reprint of the *Journal*, saw his mission as 'a useful exploratory probe which others might later follow with more substantial results'.

The Sultan of Kedah's invasion of Perak on behalf of Siam in 1818 had placed Siamese and pro-Siamese Malays in control over the state. This situation lasted six years. Then the Sultan of Perak turned for aid to his one time suzerain, the Bugis ruler of Selangor, Sultan Ibrahim, and together they expelled the Siamese. Sultan Ibrahim's price for his aid was the recognition of his suzerainty and the payment of a tribute of tin. But the force he left behind made itself so much disliked by plunder that Perak now wished to free itself from its liberators. And as the Raja of Ligor was preparing to move against both states, he welcomed the opportunity to do so on the pretext of helping Perak against Selangor.

The imminent war, however, was prevented by the action of Robert Fullerton, who became Governor of Penang in October 1824. He learned early in 1825 that the Raja was preparing a fleet in the Trang River for the invasion of the two states. He therefore sent a warning to the Raja that if he did attack either state, the East India Company, having inherited the previous Dutch treaty rights with both, would be likely to take action such as might involve hostilities with Siam herself. He followed up his warning by sending gunboats to watch the mouth of the Trang River, where they found three hundred war boats waiting to sail. The expedition was cancelled, and later in the year the Raja agreed to accept British mediation with Selangor.

Fullerton's bluff succeeded, but he had clearly exceeded his powers. His excuse was that he believed he had evidence that an attack upon Penang was intended. Later this proved to be erroneous. Only the opposition of his Council had prevented him from attacking the Raja of Ligor's fleet at Trang. The fact of the matter was that he was itching to put a stop to Siam's southward progress, and John Anderson's pamphlet[2] had become his textbook for dealing with Malayan affairs. On becoming governor he had written a full statement of his views to Calcutta.[3] He accepted

[1] See Walter Vella, *Siam under Rama III* (1957), p. 63.   [2] See above p. 12.
[3] *Straits Settlement Records*, vol. 96, Oct. 19th 1824, summarized in L. A. Mills, *op. cit.*, pp. 137-8.

Anderson's argument that the Sultan of Kedah had been an independent ruler, and advocated his restoration, by force if necessary. Siam, he said, must be made to renounce all claims over the Malay states south of Pattani and Kedah: a Siamese conquest would destroy British trade with the Peninsula.

The Supreme Government in Calcutta rejected his proposals: they would amount to a British protectorate over the Malay states, he was told, and this was not expedient. For one thing the 'arrogant and haughty' Court of Bangkok would not abandon its claims. Political relations with Siam were to be avoided since they might too easily lead to war. Hence two things were needed, an agreement reconstituting Kedah as a buffer state and a commercial treaty which would offer free and fair trade with Siam.

Nevertheless Fullerton remained on the alert. He had won the first round of his contest with the Raja of Ligor. He awaited the opportunity for another. It arose out of the Anglo-Burmese war which had begun in the February before he became Governor of Penang. One of the subsidiary operations of the war had to do with Burma's Tenasserim provinces, Martaban, Tavoy and Mergui, stretching down the Malay Peninsula. Originally conquered in the eleventh century by the Burmese empire of Pagān, they had become a bone of contention between Siam and Burma after the fall of Pagān in 1287, and had changed hands several times. Siam had held them for about 160 years when Burma finally recovered them in 1759. Therefore the Government of India conceived the idea of sounding Siam regarding possible co-operation. In September of 1824 Sir Archibald Campbell, the Commander-in-Chief in Burma, had deputed Lieut.-Colonel Snow of the Madras Army to discuss with the Penang authorities plans for Siamese armed co-operation in the conquest of the Tenasserim provinces and for obtaining draught animals for the use of the British army. The suggestion was that Tavoy, Martaban and Mergui might be handed over as a temporary measure to Siam pending the conclusion of peace, when some equivalent, satisfactory to the Bangkok government, might be given in exchange. This quite unrealistic proposal had to be dropped because Tenasserim had fallen into British hands while Snow was at Penang and he drew a complete blank in his attempts to contact any Siamese local authorities beyond the Tenasserim border.

Faced thus by an uncomfortable impasse, and worried by their ignorance about Siam's attitude towards the Burma war, the British authorities turned to Henry Burney to help them out of their difficulties. He was accordingly appointed Political Agent to the Siamese States in the neighbourhood of Penang in January 1825 and instructed to contact the Raja of Ligor and other local chiefs.

Burney was already personally acquainted with the Raja as well as with his son who had been placed in charge of Kedah. In March 1822, when there had been alarm in Penang about the Raja's further intentions after his conquest of Kedah, Burney had visited him and received assurances from him that the British had no cause for alarm. Burney had paid the Raja a second visit in the following May to ask for the release of the ex-Sultan of Kedah's family and personal servants. This request, however, had been refused. The Raja told him that he was only doing what the British had done in India when they captured the family of Tipu Sultan of Mysore.

In his new capacity Burney got busy at once making contacts with local Siamese officials. During January, February and March of 1825 he went to Kedah and on northwards to Phangnga, the seat of a governor who ruled also Junkceylon, Takuapa and Takuathung. In Kedah Burney learnt that the Raja of Ligor was convinced that he was about to be attacked by forces from Penang and was accordingly refusing to receive British envoys or entertain friendly overtures. Had this anything to do with the Trang incident? What was more to the point was the news that the Raja's sons were in control of the output of paddy, timber, tin, birds' nests and beche de mer in Kedah, and he himself had appropriated all the state revenue to the estimated value of 30,000 dollars. So it was obvious that he would strongly oppose the restoration of the ex-sultan.

The Governor of Pangnga gave Burney a most friendly reception. He said that as the nearest Siamese officer to Mergui he had been ordered by the Bangkok government to transmit correct information about British activities there, since it could not trust the accounts it had received. Burney gathered that Siam would welcome the retrocession of her former territories in Tenasserim, but in reporting this he added his comment that in such a case its Burmese inhabitants would receive 'the most inhuman treatment'.[1] The Governor wanted Burney to guarantee the immediate

[1] Burney Papers, II, 4, p. 18.

restoration of the Siamese deported by the Burmese in 1809 when they had occupied Junkceylon. He also urged him to accompany him to Bangkok to attend the funeral ceremonies of King Rama II, who had died in the previous July. Both requests were somewhat embarrassing and Burney had to give diplomatic answers to them. The Governor went so far as to renew the invitation in the letter he entrusted to him for delivery to the Governor of Penang, with the offer that he would leave his son behind at Pangnga to conduct Burney to the capital in case permission were given him to go there. Before leaving Burney gave his host a written account of the progress of the Burma war for transmission to the government at Bangkok, and letters addressed to the British officers in charge of the towns of Martaban, Mergui, Tavoy, Tenasserim and Ye for the use of the chiefs of the nearest Siamese towns in each case in order to promote friendly contacts.

In reporting all this Burney explained that the Siamese chiefs of the states on the Isthmus of Kra were under the close control of the central government, and, moreover, the co-operation of those in the neighbourhood of Penang was essential if an approach to Bangkok were to stand any chance of success. The Governor of Pangnga, he said, had warned him that the Raja of Ligor, as the uncle of the Wangna, possessed great influence at Court, and that the latter received most of the pickings from the occupation of Kedah. Hence, if the ex-sultan were to be restored, it would be necessary to offer these two officers suitable compensation, or the Court of Siam some equivalent 'calculated to make the general advantages to be derived by it in other quarters outweigh the more immediate views of those two Chiefs'.[1]

Junkceylon, Burney reported, had once had a population of about 12,000 and produced 400 tons of tin annually. The Burmese raid of 1809, however, had been so devastating that the seat of government had had to be moved to Pangnga on the mainland; its male population was now as low as 800 to 1,000, and most of their women and children spent the wet monsoon every year at Pangnga. Now, with the British in possession of Mergui, the neighbouring Siamese territories were enjoying a degree of security such as never before, and the Siamese were considering improving Junkceylon. Commercial regulations both there and at Pangnga were said to be liberal. Moreover, it would not be difficult, he

[1] Burney Papers, II, 4, p. 19.

thought, to open a navigable communication across the Isthmus of Kra between the Pakchan River flowing into the Bay of Bengal and the Chumphon River flowing into the Gulf of Siam.

Governor Fullerton was deeply impressed by this report. It convinced him that a further mission to Bangkok had become indispensable and that Henry Burney was the man to lead it. He accordingly deputed Burney to Calcutta to submit to the authorities there the information he had collected, and present Penang's views on the policy to be followed. Fullerton's two main proposals, namely that a new direct approach should be made to Bangkok, and that the conquered Tenasserim provinces should be placed under the superintendence of the Government of Prince of Wales Island, were readily accepted by the Government of India. To a third proposal, however, made by him to the effect that a part of Tenasserim might be offered to Siam in exchange for the restoration of the ex-sultan of Kedah it raised what turned out to be an insuperable objection. Penang was asked to provide full and accurate information regarding the new acquisitions on the Tenasserim coast and indicate how much of it should be annexed permanently and how much relinquished, having regard to the claims which the inhabitants might have established to British protection.[1]

Burney had arrived in Calcutta in May 1825, and by this time Calcutta had completely changed its mind on the subject of Siamese co-operation in the Burma war, and consequently on the cession question. Both John Crawfurd and the Penang Council itself had contributed to this change of mind by representing that Siamese co-operation might prove an embarrassment, since their troops were inferior to the Burmese and their methods of warfare cruel and barbarous. In 1825 too the whole complexion of the war had changed in favour of the British, so that the object now became that of keeping Siam out of the war, or, if that were not feasible, keeping her troops as far away from British operations as possible.

Actually, the Siamese had cooked their own goose. Early in 1825 a Siamese detachment composed of 500 Mons under a Mon chief, referred to by the British as 'Ron Rov',[2] had turned up in

[1] *Ibid.*, p. 22.
[2] He was the General Chaophraya Mahayotha, a Mon in the Siamese service, whom we shall meet often later on. Information supplied by Professor David Wyatt.

the vicinity of Martaban and got into touch with Sir Archibald Campbell at British army headquarters offering co-operation against 'their inveterate enemies' the Burmese. It styled itself the army of Dvaravati, after the old Mon empire of the Menam valley before the coming of the Thai. Accordingly Colonel Henry Smith was deputed to discuss matters with the chief. His enquiries, however, led him to suspect that Ron Rov's real object was simply to gain possession of Martaban and establish himself there as its ruler. In any case he and his force suddenly disappeared after announcing that they had been recalled by orders from Bangkok because of the imminence of the wet monsoon. Presumably Ron Rov had found the situation at Martaban inauspicious for his plans. There was a small British holding force there.

At roughly the same time another Siamese detachment had raided the Tavoy area deporting some of its inhabitants. Major Balmain, the British commander at Tavoy, had made contact with its leader who had replied to his complaints with 'professions of friendship', he reported, and 'specious assurances' that the captives were being well treated at Bangkok and were at liberty to return home. From Mergui came a much grimmer story. Early in February the Siamese had plundered the town of Tenasserim and several neighbouring villages, and carried off a considerable number of people. A British officer with a body of sepoys had chased after the raiders in country boats and attacked their flotilla, capturing six armed boats and 124 Siamese. The commander of the flotilla had escaped. He turned out to be no less a person than the Governor of Chumphon, who in the previous month had visited Mergui as the guest of the British. It was reported that he had cut his visit short, to leave for home, it had been thought, but, as it turned out, to raid Tenasserim, and there had pulled down the British colours 'with insult'.[1] He claimed that he was acting on orders from the king.

These examples of Siamese 'co-operation' had their due effect upon the minds of the British. So also did a letter from the foreign minister, the Phraklang, to John Crawfurd, then Resident at Singapore. The minister explained that in the past the Mon general Chaophraya Maha Yotha had been operating in Siam's northern provinces 'to seize all the Burmans that might fall into his hands'. Because of the British invasion of Burma he had received

[1] Burney Papers, II, 4, pp. 23–5.

large reinforcements with orders to protect the frontier. He had gone to the neighbourhood of Martaban and found the city in British hands, so had remained nearby. The minister had sent him a letter for transmission to the British commander at Rangoon, but had had no reply. Then he went on to deal with the deportations. All the people from Tavoy and Pegu, who were in Siam, he claimed, had returned home on hearing that the British were in control; and, he added, 'All those that wish to go back the King permits to do so, and provides them with money, etc. as well as with an escort that they may reach their country in safety'.[1] Henry Burney was later to nail these specious falsehoods when he was in Bangkok. The Government of India had come to the opinion that the last thing it wanted was Siamese military co-operation. At the same time it was equally convinced of the need for another mission to Bangkok: in its view positive action to establish a better understanding with the Siamese must be taken.

Burney's mission therefore was described in his instructions as experimental in nature. Its proclaimed object was to be primarily to compliment King Rama III upon his accession to the throne, to assure him that Siam had nothing to fear from British operations in Burma, and to offer his government the fullest information regarding them. Beyond that Burney was to demand on behalf of the Government of India the repatriation of all the deportees carried off by Siamese raiders, and to offer in exchange the prisoners made by the Mergui garrison in chasing away the raiders from Tenasserim town together with such of the Siamese prisoners of the Burmese raid on Junkceylon in 1809 as could be identified. He was, of course, to strive for an improvement in the regulations regarding British trade with metropolitan Siam. As for the Sultan of Kedah Burney was strictly enjoined not to offer any cession of territory in order to secure his re-instatement. The utmost he might offer would be a British guarantee that if restored he would pay an annual tribute of 4,000 Spanish dollars and present 'the customary gold and silver flowers' every third year. Burney, under no illusions as to what the Siamese view of such an offer would be, summed up the situation in a nutshell when he wrote: 'the Supreme Government . . . virtually gave up the Raja of Quedah.'[2]

Finally, the instructions touched on the delicate subject of Siamese co-operation. It was plainly described as undesirable. If

[1] *Ibid.*, p. 26.   [2] *Ibid.*, p. 32.

the Siamese wanted to attack Burma from their north-west frontier they were, of course, free to do so, but no attack might be made on territory occupied by British troops or under British protection. Burney might, however, if it seemed practicable, make an offer for draft and carriage cattle.

The question may well be asked why Calcutta at this stage had decided to hold on to the Tenasserim provinces. The answer seems to be that they were seen as a potential future base of operations, should one be needed, against either Burma or Siam. The naval strategists on their part remembered that their harbours had been used by French commerce-raiders against British shipping in the Bay of Bengal during the Revolutionary and Napoleonic wars.

Burney arrived back in Penang shortly after Governor Fullerton had bluffed the Raja of Ligor into abandoning his projected expedition against Perak and Selangor. During his tour of Kedah and Phangnga Burney had written to the Raja asking for permission to visit him. The Raja's reply inviting him to come, went to Penang, and was awaiting him there when he returned from his tour at the end of March. There was no time to fit in a visit to Ligor before his journey to Calcutta, but as soon as he returned to Penang he decided that a meeting with the Raja was urgently necessary. In the light of what he had learnt about the Raja's influence at Court he had come to the conclusion that the best approach to that Court would be through the Raja. His aim therefore was to negotiate a provisional treaty with him for submission to Calcutta. Then, if it gained the approval of the Government of India, it could serve as a basis for negotiations at Bangkok, provided that the government there would be willing to receive him. And this is how matters turned out.

Burney's meeting with the Raja of Ligor took place in July 1825 and resulted in a provisional treaty agreed to on the last day of that month. In the discussions the Raja intimated that he had not given up the idea of attacking Selangor; his intention now was to send three thousand men by land to help Perak against Sultan Ibrahim. In reply to this Burney stressed that Perak was not a Siamese dependency, that the East India Company could not be indifferent to such an operation, and that a quarrel with it over such a matter could lead to war. The warning was sufficient: in the provisional treaty it was laid down that Siam would not send a force to either Perak or Selangor by land or sea. Burney on his part pledged the Company not to interfere with the government of Perak, but to persuade the Sultan of Selangor to refrain from disturbing the peace of Perak. In addition, the Sultan of Perak was not to be forced against his will to send the *bunga mas* to Bangkok, and the Raja of Ligor's quarrel with Selangor was to be submitted to the mediation of the Governor of Prince of Wales Island.

Regarding Kedah Burney declared that the Company had no desire to interfere with its government, and if the King of Siam restored the ex-Sultan to his throne, the Penang Council would ensure that he paid three thousand dollars annually and the *bunga mas* triennially by way of tribute. The Raja of Ligor on his part promised that if the ex-Sultan were restored, he would not attack Kedah either by land or by sea. Moreover, if the Governor-General of India approved the treaty, which Burney was to submit to him, the Raja would accompany him to Bangkok and 'join with him in submitting to the King of Siam a proposition for the restoration of the King of Queda on the terms and footing suggested by the Government of Prince of Wales Island'.[1] The treaty also contained clauses providing for mutual assistance in suppressing piracy and for the negotiation of a commercial treaty at Bangkok.

Armed with this document Burney returned to Penang. In discussing it with the Council he admitted that it was not strictly non-interventionist in character, but argued that the alternative would be to permit Siam to overrun Selangor, turn its inhabitants into pirates, and disturb native trade for many years. The most important point about the provisional treaty, he claimed, was that it prevented the 'extension of Siamese dominion to the vicinity of Malacca' and at least postponed the Siamese occupation of Perak and Selangor, thereby giving the British authorities time in which to decide how to deal with 'Siamese aggrandisement'.[2]

Governor Fullerton welcomed the treaty warmly, and while Burney sailed off to Calcutta with it, seized the opportunity to act upon it by sending John Anderson to mediate between Perak and Selangor while assuring both sultans that the East India Company had no political designs whatever upon their states. Both received him gladly and accepted his advice for the settlement of their dispute. Sultan Ibrahim of Selangor, in a treaty signed on 20

[1] Burney Papers, II, 4, p. 27; L. A. Mills, *op cit.*, p. 142. [2] *Ibid.*, p. 28.

August 1825, promised to remove his henchman, Tuanku Hassan, the cause of all the trouble, from Perak, abandon his claim to suzerainty, and accept the Bernam River as the boundary between the two states.[1] With Perak Anderson made a similar treaty on 6 September by which the Sultan accepted the Bernam River as the boundary and undertook to keep the peace with Selangor and refrain from all interference. The Sultan was in such fear of Siamese intervention that he proposed that the Company should annex his state. Since that was out of the question, he asked for Governor Fullerton's advice on whether, as a matter of precaution, he should send the *bunga mas* to Siam. He wanted to avoid the fate of Kedah. His fears were indeed justified, for the Raja of Ligor, prevented by his agreement with Burney from using the method of direct military occupation, was now resorting to that of internal subversion by means of a so-called diplomatic mission sent to assist the Sultan in ruling his state. It was a veiled form of military intervention, and Fullerton, claiming that it was an infringement of the Burney agreement, demanded the mission's recall. The Raja, however, played for time by using all the arts of prevarication, of which he was a master, and while the argument was proceeding Henry Burney returned from Calcutta, bringing with him the ratified provisional treaty and the Government of India's authorization to proceed to Bangkok as British Envoy.

Governor Fullerton, as we have seen, welcomed Burney's provisional treaty with the Raja of Ligor; but he and the Penang Council pressed the Government of India to go a long way further in dealing directly with the Court of Bangkok. They recommended four objects for negotiation in addition to the restoration of the Sultan of Kedah. The first was in no uncertain terms the disavowal by Siam of all her claims to the Malay states south of Pattani. The second was the grant of full trading facilities in the Siamese states of the Peninsula subject to fair transit and export duties. The third was the free import of provisions needed at Penang from all the Siamese ports on the west coast of the Peninsula. The fourth was the cession by Siam of the island of Junkceylon, or Puket, as the Siamese called it.

The Government of India's response showed how widely its view of the mission's objects differed from Penang's. It rejected outright the first and the last proposals. It contended that the

[1] Mills, *op cit.*, pp. 143–4; Aitchison, *Treaties*, I, pp. 413–14.

'haughty and arrogant' Court of Siam was most unlikely to waive its claims to the Malay states of the south, while the retention of Mergui would bring the same benefits as were looked for from Junkceylon. Even such matters as the restoration of the Sultan of Kedah or the improvement of commercial relations were not indispensable: they were to be introduced into the discussions only if circumstances were favourable. The primary object of the mission, Calcutta reminded the Penang authorities, was to maintain harmony between the Company and Siam. Nevertheless, it would be in order for the Government of Penang to add to the Envoy's instructions any special items such as 'the actual state of affairs on his arrival at Prince of Wales Island might render necessary'.

It did so, and with a vengeance. The restoration of the Sultan of Kedah was laid down as Burney's first objective, the withdrawal of the Siamese 'mission' from Perak as his second, the prevention of further conquests by the Siamese over the Malayan states on either side of the peninsula and the maintenance of their independence as his third, and the improvement of conditions of trade in the Peninsula as his fourth. That was all: Penang was not concerned with such things as harmony or even co-operation. It wanted results.

No envoy can ever have gone to seek a treaty with more contradictory instructions; or with less to offer. As he himself described it, he had to prove to 'a jealous, vain and ignorant race' that the realization of the objects adumbrated in his instructions would be for the mutual benefit of both sides. Moreover, having no equivalent to offer for the restoration of the Sultan of Kedah, he would have to make it his great aim to conciliate the two people most concerned in the matter, the Raja of Ligor and the Wangna, so that if he failed over the Kedah question, 'he might at least secure their cordial co-operation towards effecting the other objects of the mission'.[1] This was how things appeared to him in retrospect when writing his final report. How unpropitious were the circumstances at the outset he was to learn from the Raja of Ligor, when they met during the mission's voyage to Bangkok. His host said that he had been assured that when Captain Burney paid his visits to Kedah and Phangnga, at the beginning of the year, and had been so anxious to meet him at Ligor, it had been 'for the

[1] Burney Papers, II, 4, pp. 32–3.

express purpose of collecting information respecting the state and condition of his dominions, to enable the British Government to possess itself of them'.[1] But that was nothing to the sort of rumours he had to deal with while he was actually in Bangkok. What he did not say in his reply was that he learnt one thing in particular from his visit to Ligor: it was so poverty-stricken compared with Kedah that he was convinced that no inducement could be offered that would lead the Raja of Ligor to surrender Kedah.

[1] Burney Papers, II, 4, p. 34.

Chapter 3

The Bangkok Régime and the Burney Mission

THE Siam to which Henry Burney was deputed was in the process of recovery after one of the greatest disasters in its history, its defeat by the armies of the Lord of the White Elephant, King Hsinbyushin of Burma, in 1767, and the destruction of its old capital, Ayuthaya. Far greater damage to its political and social system might have ensued, had not Burma needed all her troops to repel a series of large-scale Chinese invasions beginning in that same year and continuing until the end of 1769. Burma had effectively stopped the Chinese, though at the price of decisively weakening her forces in Siam, so that the Siamese, under the leadership of the half-Chinese Phraya Taksin, were able within a comparatively short time to drive out their enemies and begin the work of national reconstruction. Taksin first of all devoted himself to the task of reunification. He had to crush the various local leaders who had taken advantage of the fall of the central government to set up independent régimes, and did so with such success that by the time the Burmese were in a position to renew their attacks, he had established himself as king, with a new capital at Dhonburi, close to modern Bangkok, and with control over much of the territory previously forming the dominions of Ayuthaya.

The renewed Burmese attacks failed so signally that in 1776 a new king, Singu, called a halt to the war. When this happened, Taksin had gained possession of the northern kingdom of Chiengmai, which had been under Burmese suzerainty since the sixteenth century, and was about to assert his dominance over the two Laos kingdoms of Vientiane and Luang Prabang. He was also profiting from the eclipse of the power of the Nguyen of Hue, because of the Tayson rebellion, to revive Siam's claims to suzerainty over Cambodia. Thus, when he fell a victim to the revolt in 1782, which placed General Chakri on the throne, a new Siam was arising, which had recovered politically and militarily from the disaster of 1767.

What was now needed was a statesman rather than a war lord, and this the new ruler showed himself to be. A recent writer has used the term 'restoration' to describe his achievement.[1] He sought to restore the pattern of Siamese life of the Ayuthaya period, though not the burnt and looted city itself. He chose Bangkok as the site of a new Ayuthaya, a 'City of the Gods ... most precious of all the gems of Indra'. The danger from Burma was again becoming acute, with an ambitious new king, Bodawpaya, upon its throne. Taksin's capital, Dhonburi, was exposed to land attack from Burma. Military considerations therefore dictated the choice of a more defensible site inside the great bend of the Menam Chao Phraya, which covered it from the west and the south, and in such a way that a canal could easily be constructed around its exposed northern and eastern sides. There he built a palace of traditional type, using bricks from Ayuthaya and Dhonburi in the construction of its defences. And he furnished his new capital with temples named after, and resembling those of the old one.

Long before it was finished the new capital was threatened in 1785 by the most comprehensive plan of invasion ever launched by Burma against Siam, and under the supreme direction of King Bodawpaya in person. But he was no general, and the enterprise ended in complete disaster. One more attempt in the following year was stopped by the Siamese at Kanburi. It proved to be the last serious threat by the Burmese to the heartland of Siam. Fighting continued still for many years in the north, where the Burmese strove, without success, to recover control over the Laos states. In the peninsular region of the south also the war flared up from time to time with the Siamese striving to regain possession of the districts of Tavoy, Mergui and Tenasserim, and with the Burmese attempting to seize and exploit a *pied-à-terre* south of the Isthmus of Kra and on the island of Puket. Their biggest attempts were between 1809 and 1811. After defeating them the Siamese replied by carrying out slave-raids in the Tenasserim region. These, as we have seen, were still going on when the British occupied the area during the first Anglo-Burmese war. They formed a major subject for discussion when Henry Burney went to Bangkok in 1825.

[1] Klaus Wenk, *The Restoration of Thailand under Rama I, 1782-1809*, Tucson, Arizona, 1968.

The rage to restore the essentials of the Ayuthaya kingdom showed itself in every phase of public life, in the administration both central and provincial, the system of taxation, the legal system, the Buddhist establishment, and, not least, in efforts to restore Siamese suzerainty over vassal states, which had been lost when Ayuthaya fell. In the cultural sphere too great efforts at reconstruction were made by the founder of the new dynasty.[1] The first of these, in order of precedence, was the thorough reform of the Buddhist Order by the revival of the study of the Tripitaka, its scriptures, the revision of its texts by committees of learned monks, and by measures to raise its moral level instituted by the king as its patron and protector. The next was to show the coronation as a contract between sovereign and people for the welfare of the kingdom. In addition, a new codification of the law was carried out, not in order to revise it, but to recover it, since we are told that when Ayuthaya perished, nine-tenths of the legal materials there perished with it. Finally, in an effort to stimulate a literary revival the king himself composed literary works and translated foreign writings.

In the state the king was technically omnipotent, all power being concentrated in his person. Nevertheless, as a Buddhist ruler, he was bound by the prescriptions regarding royal duties contained in the accepted Buddhist writings, notably the *Phra Thammasat*. Then also, his life was hedged in by a mass of Brahmanic and Buddhist ceremonial, which he must perform because of the general belief that they were essential to the material well-being of the kingdom. In Brahmanic ritual he was given a quasi-divine status, notwithstanding the fact that Theravada Buddhism, which he and his subjects officially professed, was atheistic in its fundamental concepts. But everyone from the lowest to the highest accepted the existence of supernatural powers, and looked to the king to act as intermediary with the divine world in order to ward off calamities such as defeat in war, the failure of the monsoon rains or dangerous epidemics. Thus he was the chief actor in an annual round of spectacular ceremonial, much of it public, in celebration of the great national festivals, royal funerals and dedications of temples, and usually involving displays of fireworks, music, dancing and drama, and distributions of royal largess.

The government of the country was carried on through a variety

[1] Prince Dhaninivat, 'The Cultural Reconstruction of Rama I', JSS, XLIII, p. 1.

of departments staffed by a hierarchy of officials. All were appointed by the king, all were responsible to him, and in theory he directed and controlled their efforts, and could review any decision made in the courts of law. Much, of course, depended upon his knowledge, industry and strength of character. But Siam possessed a large and powerful aristocracy, and the writ of the central government hardly ran below provincial level save for the maintenance of peace and order. Even then it had to depend largely upon the loyalty and co-operation of the local officials. And the great princes and nobles usually knew how to defend themselves against excessive royal ardour in going over their heads to deal directly with the people.

Closely associated with the king were the seven officers of state superintending the principal *krom* (departments). All were princes of the blood, and each received a name indicating the department over which he was titular head. Their duties, however, were nominal, for the real control was exercised by nobles entitled Senabodi, of whom there were six. They were the Mahatthai in charge of the regional ministry for northern Siam, the Kalahom in charge of the regional ministry for southern Siam, the Phraya Yomarat in charge of the internal security and safety of the capital, the Phrakhlang in charge of foreign affairs, the Bhonlathep in charge of the Krom Na or department of lands, and the Thammathikoranathibodi in charge of the Krom Wang or department of Court affairs. The ranks of nobility held by officials began with Chaophraya, the highest, held by the Senabodi. Below it in descending order of importance were Phraya, Phra, Luang and Khun.

Besides the princely supervisors and the noble heads of the central *krom* the king might appoint an official known as the Uparat, or Krom Phraratchawangborworn Sathan Mongkhon. He held the highest rank next to the king in the kingdom. His title has been rendered in English as Heir Apparent, and by some Western writers as Second King. In his account of Rama III's reign Walter Vella questions the correctness of the latter term on the grounds that the literal translation of Uparat is 'Vice-King', not 'Second King', and that his function was really that of heir apparent.[1] Rama III, on coming to the throne, appointed one of his uncles Uparat. He was the person Burney always refers to as Wangna. He was Krom Mun Sakdiphlonlasep, the new ruler's

[1] *Siam under Rama III*, p. 6.

closest personal friend, whose support had helped him to secure the crown, though of lower royal rank than his half-brother Prince Mongkut. Under the Palace Law Mongkut, as a Chaofa, i.e. son of Rama II by his queen, took precedence for the succession over Chetsadabodin, who, although Rama II's eldest son, was only a Phra-ongchao, a son by a lesser wife. When their father died in July 1824, Prince Chetsadabodin was a man of 37 with a distinguished career behind him, while Prince Mongkut was under twenty years of age, had had no political experience, and was serving his time as a Buddhist monk. The elder brother was therefore considered by the leading statesmen of the country to be the more suitable candidate; and since the Heir Apparent had died some years earlier, and Rama II had given no indication of his wishes regarding the succession, they proceeded to place their candidate upon the throne. Mongkut himself let it be known that in the interests of internal peace he would not challenge their decision. It was not a case of usurpation, as some writers have tried to make out, since in the past the rules of succession had never been rigidly adhered to. And the general feeling at the Court in this case was that with the dynasty so recently established, and with Burma and Vietnam potential sources of danger, a man of tried experience was to be preferred to a mere boy. The historian, with the advantage of hindsight, cannot but be aware that the young prince, passed over on this occasion, was later to prove one of the great figures of Siamese history. But in the eighteen-twenties no one could have foreseen such a possibility and after meeting Rama III personally, Henry Burney was to write in his Journal that he was 'infinitely superior in judgement and ability' to Prince Chao Fa.[1]

Before his accession as Rama III Prince Chetsadabodin had led an active life. He had been the military commander of the Siamese defence force on the Burmese border. He had also been in charge of the shipbuilding occasioned by Siam's booming trade with China. In Burney's day these vessels were Chinese-style junks. The king and his ministers directed the state-trading enterprises. Later in his reign, because of the competition of European-style square-rigged vessels, Rama III was to patronize the construction of such ships in the Menam shipyards. Long before his father's death this capable and intelligent man had become the real director

[1] Burney Papers, I, p. 50.

of the government. He was also a pious Buddhist and a patron of religious and historical literature. As a prince he himself had shown literary tendencies; as king his collected writings in official decrees and letters, since published by the Royal Institute at Bangkok, are thought to be excellent examples of Siamese prose.[1] To Henry Burney he appeared as the 'most enlightened and moderate man of the Court'.[2] And whenever the British envoy felt himself up against a brick wall of official obstruction, he would seek ways and means of having the matter at issue laid before the king.

The mission left Penang for Bangkok on the brig *Guardian*, Captain George Sutherland, on 25 September 1825. It was composed of the Envoy, Captain Henry Burney, the medical officer, Mr. Sub-Assistant Surgeon Harris and an escort of thirty sepoys under the command of Captain Hugh Macfarquhar, who was also appointed Assistant to the Envoy. On its way it touched at Malacca, Singapore, Trengganu and Ligor, arriving there on 28 October. It is noteworthy that at Trengganu it met with a ship belonging to the King of Siam which was halted there because of a rumour that a British naval expedition was fitting out at Singapore to sail against Bangkok. At Ligor the Raja was awaiting the mission with a flotilla of boats intending to accompany the *Guardian* to the capital. But his youngest, and favourite, son was suddenly taken ill and his departure was accordingly delayed. While they were held up there the north-east monsoon began to blow. This meant that the Siamese craft must abandon the voyage, and created difficulties even for a square-rigged ship like the *Guardian*. The Raja begged Burney to wait until his son was well enough to permit him to depart, and he accordingly delayed for ten days. Then he decided that he must go on without him, since further delay might make the sea journey to the Chao Phraya River impossible, and it was discovered that the Raja's retinue was more than the ship could accommodate. So, notwithstanding the Raja's 'urgent entreaties' for the ship to await him, he was left behind to make the journey overland in due course. And Mr. Harris and the interpreter, Mr. Leal, were also left behind to accompany him. Instead of the Raja it was agreed that one of his sons and a commissioner from Bangkok should travel up by the *Guardian*. When, however, they arrived at the ship at the head of no less than twenty-seven followers, twelve of these had to be left behind for lack of accom-

[1] Vella, *op cit.*, p. 53.   [2] Burney Papers, II, 4, p. 57.

modation. As it was, the newcomers caused some little embarrassment by bringing on board provisions obnoxious to the escort and the Envoy's personal servants, who were Mohammedans. Happily there was no trouble and Burney put this down to the fact that the men of the escort belonged to his own regiment.[1]

The question of the Raja's bona fides naturally arises. Illness in the family was a serious matter in Siam, and was accepted as a genuine reason for postponing even important official business. But with the north-east monsoon about to break when Burney arrived at Ligor, the temptation to enlist its aid so as to delay him as long as possible must have been very strong, especially since suspicion regarding his real objects ran so high. Even leaving as it did before the wind reached anything like its full force, the *Guardian* experienced great difficulty in making the bar of the Menam Chao Phraya, taking twelve days over the short trip from Ligor.

The ship came to anchor outside the bar on 20 November and Burney sent off a letter to the 'Chief of Paknam' announcing his arrival, and with it a packet of papers for delivery to the Phrakhlang. They contained a statement of the object of the mission, a copy of his own credentials as Envoy, a list of the crew, passengers and warlike stories on board, and a detailed description of the presents brought for the King, the Wangna and the Phrakhlang himself, all written in Siamese, to avoid misrepresentation by the official interpreters on shore, who were native Christians with a reputation for untrustworthiness.

In response to the letter a pilot and two interpreters arrived on the next day, but they had to wait until the 28th before the ship could cross the bar, although drawing only eleven feet of water. At Paknam they were met by a peremptory demand to unship and deposit the brig's six guns. It was useless to argue, Burney was assured, since it had been the established custom of the country ever since the French had been expelled in 1688 from what had then been the village of Bangkok. Moreover, the king had made up his mind, and he had an inflexible will. Burney, on the other hand, knew that John Crawfurd had gone up to the capital without unshipping his vessel's guns, and that the regulation had not been enforced in the case of the Portuguese consul. He was told by Robert Hunter, a British merchant residing in Bangkok, that the authorities there were in a state of intense alarm because the story

[1] Burney Papers, I, 1, p. 22.

of a projected British expedition to attack the city had reached them, and the defences of Paknam and Paklat were being repaired and strengthened. Nevertheless he refused the demand. He suspected that there was a catch somewhere, and, although the ship was detained day after day at Paknam, with messages constantly passing between the Phrakhlang and himself, he maintained an attitude of stubborn refusal.

Finally, after a week's delay, he sent the Raja of Ligor's son to the Phrakhlang to announce that if within twenty-four hours the ship were not permitted to pass up the river with her complement of guns, the Mission would withdraw from the country. The effect was immediate: his demand was accepted, and on 4 December the brig sailed up the river and was met by a high-ranking deputation 'with a fleet of war-boats with colours, streamers and bands of music', sent to convey the Envoy and his official letter from the Governor-General of India in state to the capital.[1]

What had happened, he found, was that the Phrakhlang had been responsible for the hold-up; but Burney's threat to leave the country had forced him to submit the matter to the King, who had at once passed orders for the ship to be allowed to proceed and for the Mission to be received with every mark of distinction. So the story of the King's inflexible will had been mere make-believe. Burney wondered whether the delay had been a ministerial ruse partly to prevent the Mission from arriving too far ahead of the Raja of Ligor, and partly because the accommodation that was being built for it in Bangkok was not ready for occupation. He himself welcomed it, for it afforded him the opportunity to make a firm stand at the outset, and to impress upon the ministers 'that the British Government was not courting an alliance with Siam'.[2] He noted with interest that the boats sent to receive the Governor-General's letter exactly resembled those illustrated in de Chaumont's and La Loubère's books recording the reception of Louis XIV's letters.[3] And, not to be outdone by the French, he delivered the letter 'with all possible parade. The Escort presented arms to it, whilst the Drum and Fife struck up, and the Brig fired a salute of 19 guns'.[4]

[1] Burney Papers, II, 4, p. 36.   [2] Ibid., I, 1, p. 24.
[3] Chaumont, de, *Relation de L'Ambassade de Mgr. Le Chevalier de Chaumont a la Cour du Roi de Siam*, Paris, 1687 La Loubère, Simon de, *A New Historical Relation of the Kingdom of Siam, by M. de, L. L, Envoy Extraordinary from the French to the King of Siam in the years 1687 and 1688*, 2 vols., London, 1693.
[4] Burney Papers, I, 1, p. 26.

Burney's first discussions after landing were with the Phrakhlang, who explained that as the official accommodation for the Mission was not yet ready for occupation, the Mission would be housed by Robert Hunter until its completion. As soon as he took up residence in his temporary quarters, however, he found to his embarrassment that he had again to take a firm line with the Phrakhlang. A sealed despatch from the British Commissioner of Tenasserim, Mr. A. D. Maingy, was delivered to him from the Phrakhlang. He learnt, however, from an informant he does not name, that another letter from Mr. Maingy addressed to him had been opened by the Phrakhlang and its contents translated. Burney at once sent a message enquiring about the detained despatch, explaining that it was referred to in the one just received. In due course he received it with an excuse from the Minister that he had opened it by mistake, thinking that it was from a Burmese. It was too serious a matter to be allowed to pass; and on the next day, while in conference with the Minister, Burney made an opportunity to take it up with him. He handed him a Siamese translation of one of the letters which he had previously delivered to him. The Minister fell into the trap. How was a translation possible, he asked, seeing that the original had been sealed? Burney replied that he had been supplied with a copy of the sealed letter, and went on to say that he would never venture to break the seal of any letter directed to the Minister or anyone else, since in England it was an offence for which a man might be hanged. At this the Phrakhlang, looking grave, began to make excuses for his own action, but Burney cut him short by saying that fortunately there was nothing to be concealed in any of his letters, since the sole object of his mission was to improve friendship with Siam. Nevertheless opening the letters of an Envoy, he continued, was considered outrageous in Europe under the law of nations. But he would take particular care to report to his government that the letter had been opened entirely by mistake. Some days later a third despatch from Maingy was, immediately on arrival, delivered to him unopened. The incident provides an eloquent example of the supreme tact that Burney knew how to employ in order to gain an essential point without hurting the other man's feelings. One wonders how Crawfurd would have behaved under the circumstances.

Another matter, however, which came up in their early discussions, could not be smoothed over. The Phrakhlang enquired what Maingy was writing about, and the Envoy replied that it had solely to do with the cruel and unjustifiable conduct of the Siamese officers who had invaded the districts of Tavoy and Mergui after their takeover by the British: they had burnt and destroyed many villages and carried away a large number of Burmese as prisoners, whose immediate release as British subjects he must now demand. The Phrakhlang then said that according to his information they had voluntarily come over when Mergui and Tavoy fell to the British because they had friends and relatives in Siam. But Burney pointed out that this did not tally with Maingy's reports of towns and villages plundered and burnt, and of hundreds of refugees in the greatest distress. He had evidence, he said, of such outrageous conduct on the part of the 'Pya of Chumpon', that had the Governor-General not been confident that the Siamese Government would take appropriate action, war between Britain and Siam might well have resulted. Mr. Maingy, he went on, had released ten of the raiders who had been captured, and sent them to Bangkok with his despatch of 8 October. He was willing to release the remainder, if the Burmese deported from Martaban, Tavoy and Mergui since the British occupation were returned. He would also permit all the Siamese previously deported by the Burmese to return to their homes, if this were done. Those carried away from Junkceylon alone numbered at least five thousand.

The Phrakhlang was obviously much disturbed by what Burney had to say. The reason for this became apparent only a good deal later in Burney's stay in Bangkok. It transpired that the captives—there were many hundreds of them—had been allotted as slaves among the ministers and other officials, and that he himself was employing a large party of them in the construction of a 'splendid temple' on his behalf. He never forgave the British for putting a stop to the work, Burney noted in his final report on his mission.[1] He told Burney that the king entirely disapproved of the conduct of the Governor of Chumpon, and that he had been placed in confinement in the palace. He seems to have forgotten rather quickly what he had said when the subject first came up. But at a later conference on 11 December he lamely asserted that the King had not put the captives in irons, but had given permission for any who wished to return home.

Such palpable nonsense drew from the Envoy the scornful

[1] Burney Papers, II, 4, p. 39.

rejoinder that it was absurd to tell poor men that they might return home, when they were hundreds of miles away and completely destitute. He went on, however, to assure the Minister that in the Government of India's eyes no better proof of Siamese goodwill could be given than the return of the captives to Burma. To which the Phrakhlang rather pointedly replied that as soon as the British conquered Burma all would be released. Burney's keenly alert mind interpreted this to mean that the Burmese king's vaunt, made in a letter to the King of Siam, that he would drive the British into the sea, might not turn out to be an empty one; therefore why be in a hurry to lose so much free labour? Nevertheless he was relieved to hear that the Phrakhlang had put the matter up to the King and the latter had asked the Wangna to give it his attention.

In his final report on his mission, written after his return from Bangkok, Burney explains that it would have been useless to propose an exchange of the Siamese raiders captured at Mergui for the Burmese deportees. The Court would not believe that the British would really return their prisoners, and in any case considered the Burmese more valuable. They were performing nearly all the public work in Bangkok, including the most menial tasks and the heavy labour. They were allowed only half a *chupa* of paddy a day without clothing or living quarters. And because their food was inadequate, they were allowed to prey upon the boats plying the river with foodstuffs. 'We repeatedly saw two or three Burmese prisoners in a boat chasing and plundering the boat of some old Siamese woman,' he writes.[1] A large proportion of the deportees were women and children, and conditions had been so bad on the journey that at least half of them had died.

In the course of their preliminary skirmishes the Phrakhlang told Burney that the commander of the Siamese army on the Siamese frontier, Chau Phraya Maha Yotha, had been instructed to inform the British commander at Martaban that Siamese co-operation would depend upon their being permitted to occupy Tavoy and Martaban as bases. He showed Burney a letter written in Burmese by the British officer in charge of Martaban to Maha Yotha which, he claimed, indicated that he hoped the Siamese would arrive there quickly. This put Burney very much on his guard. For one thing it turned out that permanent occupation of

[1] *Ibid.*, II, 4, pp. 71–2.

the two places was what the Siamese really had in mind; and in any case with the British army hundreds of miles away advancing on the Burmese capital, their occupation as bases was quite inconsistent with the military situation. He therefore pointed this out to the Phrakhlang, saying that under the circumstances a reference to army headquarters in Burma would be necessary before such a move could be carried out, and moreover, that the Government of India had instructed him to point out to the Court of Siam that its troops might attack any part of the Burmese dominions from Siam's north-west frontier, but that the two places in question were much too far away from the scene of operations to be used as bases.

When the letter was examined by the Mission's interpreters, they reported that it did not bear the meaning attributed to it by the Phrakhlang. Far from being in the slightest degree perturbed by this news, however, that gentleman then said that when the Burma war began, the Siamese government had decided to take possession of Martaban, but the British had got there first. In reporting the incident Burney wrote that the Siamese considered Martaban 'the most valuable place on the Western Sea'.[1] He was convinced that their co-operation would never go beyond quietly seizing what they wanted should the opportunity arise. They hated the Burmans, but were not anxious for the British to win the war. They refused to believe in a British victory, and when reports of British successes came in, Maha Yotha 'was sent towards Martaban with two sets of despatches, to be used according as he might find the Burmese or the English the victorious party'.[2] The King of Burma had written twice to the King of Siam, and in his second letter had begged him to remain neutral, because, although the English had occupied parts of his dominions, they would never reach his capital, and would ultimately be expelled.

On 13 December the conferences with the Phrakhlang and his assistants were switched from the discussion of issues to that of the ceremonial to be observed at the Mission's official presentation to the King, which was to take place three days later. As he had expected, Burney had to stand up to tremendous pressure to accept the Siamese customs regarding unshoeing and prostration in the royal presence, but with de Chaumont's and Crawfurd's books as guides he was firm in his refusal. He was then requested

[1] Burney Papers, I, 1, p. 36.   [2] *Idem*, p. 37.

to put down on paper his own proposals regarding the forms to be observed by the members of the Mission, and did so. These were agreed to without difficulty, with only one important change, which he readily accepted. It was that they should imitate the Siamese form of obeisance in the way Crawfurd had, by joining their hands and raising them three times to the forehead. When next they came to discuss the composition of the British party that was to appear before the King and its means of conveyance to the palace, the Phrakhlang introduced a pleasant domestic note by asking Burney if he would care to bring his small son, aged six, with him. He said that it was a personal invitation from the King. Burney accepted it with very real gratification; it was a gracious gesture indicative of the much greater degree of urbanity shown by the Thai in dealing with representatives of the West than any other South-East Asian rulers in those days. It helps to explain why Siam retained its independence at a time when all the rest came under European domination.

For the royal reception on 16 December Burney was at pains to make the procession to the palace as imposing as possible. The crossing of the river from the Mission's residence was made in four boats, with the sepoys of the guard and their drum and fife in the first, a Siamese band in the fourth and the members of the deputation in the second and third. This consisted of Burney himself with his interpreter, Captain Macfarquhar, his assistant, Captain Sutherland of the *Guardian*, and Robert Hunter, the merchant. Their small flotilla was followed, Burney writes, by between two and three hundred small boats carrying Siamese officers and sight-seers. On landing, the Envoy and his assistant made the rest of the journey on litters, the other gentlemen on horseback.

Inside the palace they were conducted to a large ante-chamber with a number of state elephants standing outside, and inside the senior members of the Phrakhlang's staff waiting to escort them into the royal presence. After about half an hour word came that the King had taken his seat upon the throne in the Hall of Audience, and thither they were conducted through a guard of Siamese troops to the sound of solemn music by drums and gongs. They entered, with their Siamese attendants moving before and on each side of them on knees and forearms. The King was seated at the far end of the hall about ten or twelve feet above floor level.

On seeing him they halted and made three profound bows, while their crawling attendants bowed their heads to the floor the same number of times, raising their clasped hands to their foreheads. Then, moving forward twenty paces, they stopped and made the same obeisances again three times before sitting down on the carpet which covered the floor. In front and to their left the official presents from the Governor-General of India were arranged, and, nearer the throne, the gold vase for the receipt of the official letter.

At a given signal from the head of their escort, the Phrakhlang's deputy, Phraya Phiphatkosa ('Pya Phi-phut'), Burney rose to his feet and deposited the letter in the vase. Then, taking out an address, which he had prepared on the previous evening, he read it in a loud voice in English, and placed it, together with a Siamese translation, in the vase beside the official letter. Having done so, he walked backwards with his face towards the throne and rejoined the other members of the Mission, whereupon all raised their clasped hands three times to their foreheads. The King invited them to move closer to him, and when they had complied Phraya Phiphatkosa read out a list of the presents and a short complimentary speech of his own composition on behalf of the Mission. The King then began to ply Burney with a number of questions. The method of interrogation must be described in Burney's own words. 'The questions were repeated by Pya Phi phut to Pya Chula, who repeated them to Jose Pediada [the official interpreter], who interpreted them to me in English. Having my own interpreter behind me I often understood the King's question long before it reached me through the official channels. My replies were taken in the same manner to Pya Phi phut, who made them much longer by first repeating all the King's titles stating that his great and excellent and infallible Majesty had been pleased to ask such a question, to which I begged with all humiliation to submit such an answer.'[1]

The King asked whether Burney had been deputed by the Governor-General who had sent John Crawfurd to Siam, and how long he had been in India. He next asked what was the object of the Mission. Burney replied that its object was in the first place to congratulate him on behalf of the Governor-General upon his accession to the 'great throne of Siam', secondly 'to cement

[1] Burney Papers, I, 1, p. 41.

friendship between the Siamese and the English nations', and thirdly 'to submit propositions for improving the wealth and commerce of both countries'. Then, in case the King might not have realized that his own address had a Siamese translation attached, he picked it up and placed it in Phraya Chula's hands, telling his majesty that it explained the objects of his mission. The King voiced his thanks to the Governor-General and directed that the paper should be handed to the Phrakhlang. The address itself and the special attention drawn to the Siamese translation were a manoeuvre aimed at circumventing a possible attempt by the Phrakhlang and his associates to feed the King with their own version of the Mission's objects. The address ended with a strong appeal for the liberation of the deported Burmese, and Burney was particularly anxious that the King should be made aware of it. He had even hoped that the King might order the Siamese translation to be read aloud.

The King next asked what was the cause of the Burmese war. Burney's reply was that the Burmese had made incursions into British territory, burning and destroying places on the Chittagong frontier, and carrying away British subjects. A question so apposite to the Tenasserim affair was indeed welcome. 'I took care to shape my reply so as to bear on the subject of the Burmese captives,' he notes in his Journal.[1] The King commented that the Burmese were old enemies of the Siamese and he was glad to hear of the war. Was it a difficult war, he asked; and Burney replied that it was difficult because of the use the enemy made of woods and swamps. The King then requested the members of the Mission to come still closer to him, and went on with his questioning. Some of his questions were conventional ones, enquiries after the health of the Governor-General and of the King of England. He asked the Phrakhlang which officer was higher in rank, Crawfurd or Burney, and that worthy replied with supreme adroitness that Crawfurd was a captain of merchants whereas Burney was a captain of soldiers. He also paid special attention to Burney's small son, who was with him, asking how old he was and where he had been born; and at the end of the audience a present from the King 'of toys and other articles' was delivered to the boy by the Phrakhlang.

It was a highly satisfactory audience. The King was particularly

[1] *Ibid.*, p. 45.

pleased that Burney had not answered his question about the
Burma war in an evasive manner, but had freely admitted that the
British had difficulties to contend with. Burney was pleased because
of the honour done him by the King in twice asking him to move
closer to the throne. The Phrakhlang assured him that it was most
unusual. He was, however, a little disappointed in what he calls
'the *tout-ensemble*' of the display. The 'finery' in the Audience Hall
he thought looked second-hand, the body-guard were poor, thin
and ill-kempt, many wearing old sepoy's coats, and their muskets
were old and rusty. 'Nothing can be more contemptible than the
appearance of the soldiers,' he wrote in his Journal.[1] Nevertheless
the general treatment of the Mission was most gratifying. There
was a monthly allowance of money from the King and the Wangna
to cover the cost of its food. In addition rice and fruit were often
sent for the escort and servants, and Siamese dishes came regularly
from the King and Wangna, 'tokens of royal favour and consideration', as Burney put it, 'that were said to excite the surprise and
envy of every Siamese who witnessed them'.[2] And, besides the
house specially built for its accommodation, a boat with ten boatmen was allotted to the Mission.

Immediately after the royal audience Burney and his colleagues
were taken on a round of ceremonial visits to the royal White
Elephant and the principal temples of Bangkok. Then, beginning
with the Wangna, another round of visits to the chief ministers.
These included the two princes of the blood royal who superin-
tended respectively the foreign and judicial departments, Krommamun Surin and Krommamun Rakrannaret, both sons of Rama
I and hence uncles of the reigning monarch. Then came the two
principal ministers, Chao Phraya Chakri, or Aphaiphuthon, the
head of the Mahathai department, and Chao Phraya Akka Mahasena, the Kalahom, and lastly a group of their subordinates.

The procedure at the Wangna's court was an exact repetition
of what had taken place in the King's presence, even to the reading
of a brief address by Burney, at the Wangna's special request.
Before the ceremony the British merchants, Hunter and Malloch,
told him that the Wangna, who was a brother of the previous king,
Rama II, was married to a sister of the Raja of Ligor and exercised
special superintendence over the southern part of the kingdom.
Malayan affairs were thus his particular concern. Burney noted

[1] Burney Papers, I, 1, p. 47.　　[2] Final Report, Burney Papers, II, 4, p. 37.

that during the audience he smoked a cigar, whereas the King had chewed betel.

Krommamun Surin, it transpired, had only nominal authority, and the attendance at his reception was small.[1] His nephew, the Phrakhlang was the real wielder of power. The latter's brother and assistant, Phraya Si Phi-phut, were in attendance upon the envoy and his colleagues, and also two officials of his department, Phraya Chula and Ratchasethi. They were father and son. Phraya Chula was a Tamil from the Coromandel Coast, who had worked his way up in the Siamese governmental service, married a lady of the powerful Bunnag family whose father had held office in the Phrakhlang's department, and succeeded his father-in-law. His son, Ratchasethi, whose name Burney spells Radsithi, was closely associated with him. Between them they largely controlled the port at Bangkok. They were strongly opposed to any relaxation of the discriminatory practices against British trade there, fearing that their own power would be undermined. Burney learnt that they had in their hands the appraisal of the presents made by foreign merchants to the King and of his return presents to them, carried it out with such glaring unfairness that the Phrakhlang himself had on occasion to intervene and even double the price fixed by them. When, for instance, John Crawfurd had sent two emerald rings as a present to the Phrakhlang, they had given him to believe that the jewels were only glass imitations.

When the arrangements for the Mission's reception by the King were under discussion, the two Indians did their utmost to introduce into the procedure prostrations and other acts contrary to what Burney had already agreed upon with the Phrakhlang. Even in the royal presence he had sternly to check Phraya Chula's efforts in this direction. And when Ratchasethi told him to keep his head down and not look at the King, he laughed and asked him if he had never heard of the English proverb, 'a cat may look at a king'. The climax came at Krommamun Surin's reception. Ratchasethi, who was interpreting, grossly misrepresented what Burney was saying about the Raja of Ligor. He therefore stopped in the middle of what he was saying and stood in silent protest. 'This created as strong a sensation among the prostrate Courtiers as if a Pistol had been fired at the Prince,' he wrote in his Journal.[2] The native Christian interpreters present were too scared to open their mouths, while

[1] See infra p. 101. [2] Burney Papers, I, 1, p. 56.

Burney's own interpreter, who understood the cause of his silence, was refused a hearing. Luckily, he himself was able to muster enough Siamese to tell the prince in his own language that Radsithi was not repeating what he had been saying. To his great relief the prince was not offended with him for taking this stand. The Raja of Ligor's son, who was present with some of his followers, was shocked by the Indian's conduct. After the ceremony, however, Burney felt it necessary, as he puts it, to expostulate mildly and in a friendly manner with Radsithi and his father about the incident.

The next in the series of ceremonial calls was made on Krommamun Surin's brother Krommamun Rak. Burney noted with some amusement that the Phrakhlang went ahead of him to call upon each prince, but was not present at the audience, since it it would have been improper for the members of the Mission to see him prostrate before anyone save the King and Wangna. These ceremonial calls upon the highest in the land went on, with brief intervals between each, until early in January. The last two were upon Chao Phraya Chakri and Chao Phraya Mahasena on 4 and 5 January respectively. The former, who was head of the Mahathai Department, was generally considered to be the first minister of Siam, Burney was informed. The new king, however, on coming to the throne, had given as much power as possible to four members of his own family, Krommamun Surin, Krommamun Rak, Chao Phraya Phrakhlang (Dit Bunnag) and his brother, Phraya Si Phiphat (That Bunnag). Nevertheless, as Burney saw it, all of them together were barely a match for the Chakri in ability and influence, and though an old man, he was obviously far more intelligent than the Phrakhlang. Burney therefore seized the opportunity to broach with him two matters which he regarded as of immediate concern, namely the release of the Burmese deportees and Siam's position in regard to the war in Burma. The Chakri told him that he would be happy to submit his views on these subjects to the King. This, of course, was exactly what the Envoy had hoped for, and the two of them accordingly got down to a thorough discussion of the two issues which Burney reports on at length in his Journal.

This decision to go beyond the purely formal type of interview and introduce main issues for discussion was due to a growing feeling that it was necessary, wherever possible, to seek to enlist the support of the King. The Phrakhlang was obviously unfriendly to the Mission and could not be relied on to report the points brought up in conversations with him to the other ministers of the group Burney refers to as the 'Cabinet'. For another thing, his knowledge according to Burney was only about the level of that of a 'common native shopkeeper'.[1] Although acute and cunning in matters of trade he was no more fit to be foreign minister of Siam than a *banya* of the Calcutta bazaar.

In his final report on his mission he explained that there were two parties at Court headed respectively by the King and the Wangna, the one intelligent, moderate and anxious to cultivate friendly relations with the British, the other characterized by conceit and ignorance. The latter was dangerous, because the Wangna was in special charge of the southern part of the kingdom and at the head of the military establishment; dangerous also because the Court was in a state of alarm concerning British intentions, with all sorts of mischievous rumours being circulated by interested scaremongers.[2] Hence, in view of the Phrakhlang's inadequacy, it was highly desirable to transfer the oversight of the Mission to ministers such as the Chakri and the Kalahom, who were concerned with the great questions of war and peace, and frontiers.

When with the greatest tact Burney made a suggestion along these lines to Phraya Wisset, who was acting-Phrakhlang to the Wangna, he was naturally told that for a foreign envoy to deal with any minister other than the Phrakhlang was entirely without precedent. His reply to this was that the custom of putting the Phrakhlang in charge of foreign envoys was simply because previous ones had come with commercial objectives. Nevertheless, interviews were fixed for him with the Chakri and the Kalahom.

Burney told the Chakri that although he had been promised an early release of the deportees from Tavoy and Mergui, nearly a month had gone by and nothing had happened. To this the minister made what was obviously a diplomatic reply: he must not worry, the King had ordered their release and in due course they would be brought before him so that he might ascertain which of them wished to remain in Siam. Burney, normally the most patient of men, retorted hotly that many British officers under such circumstances would not have waited five days, let alone nearly a month; and he followed this up by the threat that unless there were soon some

[1] Burney Papers, I, 1, p. 71.   [2] *Ibid.*, II, 4, p. 42.

sign that the government was going to comply with his request, he would consider it his duty to quit Siam. The Minister replied that it took some time to collect and register all the deportees, but he promised to tell the King personally what Burney had said and to urge him to expedite matters; and with this they passed on to the war in Burma.

Before dealing with this it is necessary to go back a few days. One of the special tasks laid upon Burney by the Calcutta Government was that of keeping the Government of Siam as well informed as possible on the progress of the war, and on 27 December he had delivered to it a note containing information he had just received from the British officer commanding at Martaban. It showed that the main British force under Sir Archibald Campbell had left Prome, and was advancing up the Irrawaddy towards the Burmese capital, while to the east of it another force of five thousand men under Colonel Pepper had left Pegu and was marching on Toungoo in the Sittang valley. Siamese co-operation with Colonel Pepper's force was invited, should the Court of Bangkok be disposed to give orders to this effect to Chao Phraya Maha Yotha and his Dvaravati army. Burney went on to say that according to information received from the same source the British Government planned to revive the old Mon kingdom of Pegu 'as a barrier between the Burmese, the English and the Siamese', and hoped that Siam would welcome such an arrangement. This harebrained project will be discussed later. Finally Burney said that the British forces in Burma needed draught animals, elephants and horses, and he was ready to negotiate their purchase.

Four days later he followed this up by recommending that Maha Yotha be sent at once with four or five thousand men to Martaban to act in conjunction with Colonel Pepper's force and that the most profitable operation for the Siamese main army would be to advance into Burma from Chiangmai as a diversionary manoeuvre. Posterity, he said, would then be able to claim that under the present King Siam had punished Burma for past aggression by sending an army to march in triumph through the capital of Ava. This all reads very strangely in the light of the Government of India's instructions regarding Siamese co-operation, and makes one feel that Burney's tongue was firmly fixed in his cheek. He knew perfectly well that what he was asking was outside the bounds of possibility, that the sort of thing that the Siamese were out for was demonstrated by their raids into Tenasserim and their talk of the need for a base at Martaban. What he does not seem to have learnt until later was that there was no Siamese army capable of taking the field against the Burmese, for whose fighting capacity they had a very healthy respect; though he probably suspected that this was the case.

The ministers, however, could match his bluff. Invasion of Burma by the Chiangmai route, they assured him, was impossible for a large force because of the nature of the terrain and the difficulty of obtaining provisions. The only practicable route was by Martaban. Hence that place and Tavoy should be handed over to Siam. Such a plan would render victory 'most certain'.[1] Since they already knew that there was not a hope that these places would be handed over to them this was tantamount to a rejection of military co-operation, and as such Burney interpreted their reply when he discussed the matter with the Chakri. That being the case, he said, the Siamese forces ought to be withdrawn from the Tenasserim frontier, where their presence could lead to trouble. The Chakri, however, merely repeated and confirmed the condition laid down by the Ministers as the price for co-operation, and there the discussion ended. Burney made it abundantly clear that such a condition was quite unacceptable, and the Chakri promised that he would inform his colleagues of what he had said.

The Chakri had kept the British delegation waiting for rather longer than they considered proper before being ushered into his presence. Hence on the following day, 5 January, before going to his promised meeting with the Kalahom, he sent him notice that he would not submit to so long a delay this time. To his delight he and his colleagues were received by the minister immediately upon their arrival and found him 'the most polite and good-natured Siamese' they had so far encountered. Burney was therefore encouraged to make a further stand, this time about seats. The story must be told in his own words.

> I had hitherto avoided in my visits to the different Siamese Officers to enter into petty discussions as to the forms or manner in which they might receive me. But I found the more I yielded on such points the more a Siamese assumed. Pya Wisset is the only person who presented us with Chairs. The rest obliged us to sit upon the Carpet as far distant as possible from their own seat, and with our own feet thrown back in

[1] Burney Papers, I, 1, p. 130.

the most irksome position. They omitted to furnish us even with a separate cushion, or pillow upon which to lean, which two Articles are always offered to men of any rank. I learnt that Pya Phiphut had placed Chairs for us on the day we were to visit him, but that Radsithi had advised him to remove them. On this night therefore I took no notice of the signs which the attendants made to us to sit down at our usual distance from the seat of the Chief, but moved on and sat close to the Kalahom. I then noticed the absence of a separate cushion and pillow. The Kalahom apologised for not having had them in readiness, and presented me with one of his own cushions, with such true politeness and kindness as to disarm me immediately. Another cushion was brought for Captain Macfarquhar.[1]

The conversation began with the subject of the Burmese deportees and the Kalahom gave exactly the same assurance about their delivery as the Chakri had given on the previous evening. Burney then raised the question of boundary demarcation: now that the British had taken over the Tenasserim coast, he said, a boundary commission was needed to demarcate and establish the frontier between the territories conquered by them and the Siamese dominions. The Kalahom, however, thought that such a matter could stand over until it was certain that the Burmese would not return. To this Burney retorted crushingly that the Burmese could as easily come to Bangkok as return to the coast. To his surprise his words shocked his hearers. It turned out that the interpreter, unable to translate what he had said accurately, conveyed the notion that he had uttered a threat. He had therefore to save the situation by explaining the real meaning of what he had said. Then good humour was restored; indeed, the old Kalahom—he was about seventy—appeared to be rather amused at the misunderstanding. And in clearing it up Burney was able to show that he had raised the boundary question in the interests of good relations in the future between the two countries. He emphasized that it was his duty as British envoy to provide against any misunderstanding arising thereafter; to all of which the Kalahom replied that it was perfectly just and proper, and that he would recommend the matter to his colleagues for early consideration.

He concluded his remarks with a gentle admonition as from an older to a younger man, saying 'that he feared I was sometimes too

[1] Burney Papers, I, 1, p. 85.

warm in my language, and that he would advise me as a father to take things more coolly and patiently; that if I did so, he was certain my Mission would in time be the means of establishing between the Siamese and English nations the most advantageous relations'.[1] Burney thanked him for his good advice, explaining that he spoke with animation because he feared that otherwise the Siamese would not believe he was in earnest. When they rose to take their leave, 'the old man ... gave us his blessing and good wishes in the most affectionate terms, and we returned home full of regret that so fine an old gentleman as the Siamese Minister really is has not more influence'.[2]

[1] *Ibid.*, p. 87.   [2] *Loc. cit. supra.*

Chapter 4

The Burma War and the Deportees

ONE matter Burney was not prepared to take coolly and patiently was the repatriation of the deportees. His humanitarian instincts were strongly aroused by the callousness shown by the Siamese towards these unfortunate people. He was well aware that the Government of Ava had started the trouble in the first place by raiding parts of Siam with the utmost cruelty and deporting all the people its forces could round up, that this was the time-honoured method of warfare used by both countries, and that under the circumstances Siam considered herself, as the victim of Burmese aggression, to be more than justified in pursuing a tit-for-tat policy when the Burmese were on the defensive against a British invasion. Nevertheless, he could not bear to remain passive under the circumstances. In his own country it was the age of the humanitarians, of the Protestant missionary societies and the agitation against slavery. His father, an ardent Anglican evangelical of saintly character, had been charged with the care of orphan children in Calcutta. These were potent influences upon his outlook.

To the Siamese authorities, however, Burney's outlook was incomprehensible. As Buddhists they believed that what happened to these unfortunate people was dictated by their karma, and was the result of actions in previous existences. It speaks much for Siamese diplomacy that his protests and pleadings did not fall on stony ground. The King and his ministers could not grasp Burney's point of view on this matter, but they were intelligent enough to perceive that it would be to their advantage, in the new and unfamiliar situation created by the British occupation of Tenasserim, to accede to this request, though not without much dragging of feet. Thus on 8 January Phraya Wisset, one of the Phrakhlang's assistants, came with the request that Burney would not insist upon the release of all the Burmese, but allow those in Bangkok to be retained until the end of the Burmese war: the ministers, he said, were so strongly averse to releasing them that if they had to give way, they might refuse to accept any further proposal from him. In his Journal[1] Burney commented that 'indefatigable lying' was an essential part of a Siamese statesman's duty, and, unfortunately, they believed that the same was true of the British. He can never have heard the pun on the Elizabethan Sir Thomas Smith's definition of an ambassador as a statesman sent 'to lye abroad' on behalf of his country.

He became very worried when he was shown a draft of a letter from the Phrakhlang to A. D. Maingy, the Commissioner for Tenasserim, which contained no assurance of an early release of the deportees. Accordingly on 10 January he addressed a memorial to the ministers asking them to settle the matter as soon as possible and convince the British that their desire to cultivate good relations with them was genuine.[2] This had its effect, for on the next day Phraya Phi-phut brought along a number of the deportees to show Burney and invited him to interrogate them. He brought also with him Phraya Thep, the official charged with compiling the list, who promised to supply him with a complete list of all those in or near Bangkok. Burney refused to question any of those paraded before him: he feared they might be made to suffer for anything they might say. Actually he was receiving visits from some of them and had learnt that with the arrival of the Mission their treatment had much improved; nevertheless, their one desire was to go home. One of them told him that he would rather go home and live on rice and salt than remain in Siam with a basketful of gold.

The truth of the matter was that South-East Asian governments such as that of Siam dreaded any diminution of population in the states they ruled. All had abundance of unoccupied land and an inadequate labour supply. One of the essentials of statecraft was the maintenance of population. It was prescribed by Kautilya's *Arthasastra*, which had been studied for centuries at South-East Asian courts. Wars were fought for the acquisition of people rather than territory, and were accompanied by large-scale deportations. And Burney well knew that when he urged the release of the deportees as a proof of Siam's desire for better relations with the British, the ministers, before taking any decision, would have carefully weighed in the balance the consequences of not doing so,

[1] Burney Papers, I, 1, p. 92.   [2] *Ibid.*, p. 134.

and decided where the course of safety lay. The Portuguese consul at Bangkok told him that as recently as 1821, when an agent of the Netherlands government at Batavia was in Bangkok, and a party of Javanese, who had been forcibly deported, appealed to him for protection, his request to be allowed to take them back home with him was not only refused, but so strongly resented, that when he went a second time to present his demand, he took a loaded pistol in his pocket for self-defence in case of attack. The minister with whom he had dealt was the present king.

On 14 January Phraya Phi-phut and Phraya Thep came bringing with them some four hundred deportees, men, women and children, but still with no authenticated list. They told him that the Ministers were against supplying any such list. The reason for this, he learnt, was that Maingy, the Commissioner of Tenasserim, claimed that no less than 1,600 people had been deported, and they could not account for more than 800. Nevertheless, he was told, the Phrakhlang was writing to Maingy promising the immediate release of all the deportees. On the other hand he learnt that the Wangna, who had been allotted a share of the deportees, was refusing to hand them over. And, although large numbers of these people had been brought to his residence and left there, more or less as his responsibility, the Ministers had sent no reply in writing to his memorial of 10 January. He therefore decided to get tough with them. He wrote a very stiff note to the Wangna and a brief curt one to the Ministers. Days went by without any response. The Mission's residence was almost in a state of siege being surrounded by hundreds of deportees without food or shelter while the Siamese authorities were allegedly collecting boats for their transport homewards. Burney describes them as 'lying about in all directions around my house, many afflicted by smallpox; with no food save what I give them; with no other shelter than the Trees, and a few loose Attaps, and with scarcely any Clothing, while the thermometer during the nights and mornings has been so low as 60 degrees'.[1]

On 19 January he sent another memorial to the Ministers saying that he was convinced that the King himself could not be aware of the miserable condition of the deportees, and he sincerely hoped he would not have to report to the Governor-General something that would 'lower the character of the Siamese Nation in the eyes of the English'.[2]

[1] Burney Papers, I, 1, p. 99. [2] *Ibid.*, p. 136.

The Burma War and the Deportees

This time he received what he accepted as a suitable reply. The Ministers dealt item by item with the points he had raised. They said that about 480 of the deportees had so far been collected, others from more distant places would be delivered to him as they arrived, and all who were at Chumphon were to be released. An enquiry was to be made as to the number of those who had been brought to Siam, of those who had died on the journey, and those remaining, all of whom would be allowed to return home. They were all to be sent home together, not in smaller parties at different times. The route proposed by Burney was impracticable during the season of strong north-east winds; therefore he must enquire from the deportees themselves which of the other routes was the safetest. Meanwhile, those who were parked around his house must be registered and sent back to their former dwellings, where they would receive food and clothing until all had been collected and were ready to start away. The veiled threat in Burney's note to report to the Governor-General things that would lower the Siamese national character in British eyes obviously touched a tender spot: it was referred to more than once in the letter. But, the Ministers reminded him, the Burmese were enemies, and no pity could be felt for them; they did not care whether he reported their sufferings to Calcutta or not. That was his affair. Phraya Phi-phut Kosa, who had drawn up the reply on behalf of the Ministers, told him personally that while his government would release all its Burmese captives, it would not insist upon the return of all the Siamese prisoners held at Mergui. On which Burney commented in his Journal that although he was sure that the Court of Bangkok was indifferent to the fate of the Mergui prisoners, he was equally sure that it was essential to the good name of Britain that all of them should be released immediately the Burmese deportees arrived there.

He was by this time able to draw upon adequate sources of information though rarely mentioning them in his Journal. His interpreters were his intelligence officers. The following paragraph from the Journal[1] gives a graphic picture of what he was up against:

It would be irksome to attempt to describe the disgraceful and cruel treatment which the Burmese Captives have experienced in Siam. They have been dispersed in every direction. Five or six are daily brought to us, and several are said to be in the interior and at the old

[1] *Ibid.*, pp. 100–1, Journal, para. 82.

capital Yothya [Ayuthaya]. No list of the whole was ever taken, and we learn that when the late Pya of Champohun found that the King disapproved of his proceedings, he secretly distributed many of the Prisoners among his friends in different parts of the Country between Champohun and Bangkok. The King of Siam has ever been desirous of sending back these Captives but his Ministers and petty servants deprecate the loss of so many laborers, and are still striving to evade the execution of His Majesty's liberal orders. We have set some of the Prisoners to find out what Officers are detaining them, and through this means we have obtained the release of several more men and women. A woman came to us yesterday in great distress, stating that she and her husband and three children had been secretly removed to Paklaat by Belat Khun Thon, the moment he received the orders for their release, and that she had just escaped to us leaving her husband and children at Paklaat. We reported the circumstances to Pya Wisset, and I threatened to make a public complaint against Khun Thon, if the whole party were not immediately released. I was assured that this should not only be done, but that Belat Khun Thon should receive a severe punishment.

A few days later Phraya Wisset handed over not only the husband and children but also seventeen others who had been employed upcountry by the Wangna.

From the man appointed as the headman of the deportees by the Siamese Burney learnt that the best route for them to take was by junk from Bangkok to Muang Mai on the western coast of the Gulf of Siam near the Sam Roy Yot hills.[1] Its sailing distance from the capital was estimated at two days. Thence there was said to be a very good carriage road by which women and children could reach the Burmese border in four days, arriving at a place named Sing-khon or Tha-phi, situated on a tributary of the Tenasserim River. This stream could be navigated on rafts in four days to its junction with the main river, where boats could be procured which would do the journey to Tenasserim Town in one day. Twelve days was the estimated over-all time for the journey.

When on the strength of this information Burney applied to the Court for junks and provisions for the 450 deportees collected at his residence he was told that the approach to Muang Mai was dangerous at this time of year. But the headman assured him that this was not so. Then he was told that a royal order for the delivery of the junks had been issued, and the Phrakhlang told Captain

---

[1] This seems to be the place shown in Crawfurd's map at 12 degrees north latitude on that coast.

The Burma War and the Deportees

Macfarquhar that they would arrive on 24 January. No junks, however, appeared either on that day or the next. So on the 26th he sent his messenger to Phraya Phi-phut Kosa to ask when they might be expected. Positively on the next day was the Phraya's reply, and alongside the Mission's quarters. But again no junks, although his messenger waited daily on the Phraya. On the 29th he sent a request for the Phraya to come and see him 'for a few minutes'. Whereupon that officer lost his temper: he sent a rude reply to the effect that he could not be bothered to call on the Envoy, let him do the calling, if he had anything to say. Shortly afterwards he pointedly sent a messenger of the lowest class to announce that one of the junks would arrive that very day.

Such a gratuitous insult Burney decided, with great reluctance, could not be allowed to pass. He sent a message to say that he was addressing a complaint against him to the King. This evoked the haughty reply asking who would dare to carry his complaint to the King. The upshot of these exchanges must be told in Burney's own words.

> Judging that I ought not to submit to such impertinence, I wrote a short note to the King, and carrying it to Prah Klang on the following day, desired it might immediately be laid before His Majesty. The Prah Klang, considering that Pya Phi-phut is a Siamese and his own deputy, behaved much better than I had expected. He made many excuses for his friend, and strove much to prevent matters proceeding to an extremity—and when he found me resolute, he made Pya Phi-phut declare his regret for what had passed, and his readiness to wait upon me on the following day, and whenever I pleased to require his attendance.[1]

Phraya Phi-phut's taunt was not without substance; and Burney wisely accepted the Phrakhlang's mediation. No bones were broken. And in due course, on 2 February, six junks anchored outside the Mission's house, and Burney reported to the Ministers that 585 men, women and children had been delivered to him, though of that number 17 had died and a further 21 were too ill to be moved for the present. Among the dead was the headman himself, who had succumbed to cholera. His loss was a grievous one, Burney noted, because of his proficiency in the Siamese language and general intelligence.

There was still a good deal of trouble before the junks could set

---

[1] Burney Papers, I, 1, p. 105.

out from Bangkok. Embarkation could not take place until 13 February because of the delay in supplying provisions and water, and when they did arrive they were 'of the most disgusting quality' notwithstanding the abundance and cheapness of rice in the country. Then difficulties were raised over the issue of passes, and Burney had to use 'strong and decisive language' or the junks would never have sailed, he tells us. They left on 15 February, six junks escorted by the Brig *Guardian* and with Burney's interpreter in charge of the deportees, since they were afraid to travel by themselves across Siamese territory. On the 19th the whole fleet crossed the bar of the Menam River.[1]

The *Guardian*'s departure with the junks caused the utmost alarm at the rumour-ridden court. On the 20th, Captain Sutherland reported back to the Mission that Paklaat and Paknam were being feverishly prepared to meet an expected hostile attack. Burney hurried off to the Phrakhlang to ask what was the matter. The latter denied that anything of the sort was happening, but complained that the captain of the brig had not reported to the Governor of Paknam before crossing the bar. Burney replied that the captain had not been aware that he had to stop at Paknam; he offered to recall the brig to Bangkok as a proof that no breach of port regulations was intended. He went on to say that he had heard from a number of sources that a rumour was circulating to the effect that the *Guardian* was returning to Penang in order to head an expedition against Siam, and that this was causing much alarm. He asked how could he possibly believe that the Mission would remain in Bangkok if such a report were true, and would he let the King and Ministers know that if they had the slightest doubt regarding his intentions, he was prepared to recall the *Guardian*. The stiff little breeze dropped as suddenly as it had arisen. The Phrakhlang went to the Palace, and in the evening Burney received a message saying that the King and Ministers would not insist upon the recall of the vessel nor object to the Envoy sending her wherever he pleased. Three days later a worse storm blew up. The deportees, however, were not involved, and their story must be rounded off first.

[1] Among the unpublished Thai documents among the Burney Papers at the Royal Commonwealth Society, London, is what amounted to a pass for the *Guardian* dated 19 February in the form of a letter of an official to the governor at Paknam. (Information supplied by Professor David Wyatt.)

It must suffice to say that all were landed safely on the west coast of the Gulf close to their objective, Muang Mai. One of the junks became separated from the rest through stress of weather, and reached the little village of Sam Roy Yot, where its 80 passengers insisted on landing and going on foot to what Burney describes as the 'high road' at Bangnarom. Its nakoda then sailed on to Bangnarom, where he found the other junks empty. There were no passengers in sight: all were on their way towards Mergui. How many of them actually reached home is not recorded. Probably all.

These, however, were not the only Mergui deportees held in Siam. Assistant-Surgeon Harris and Leal, the Mission's interpreter, whom the Raja of Ligor had sent on ahead by sea from Chumphorn, so that they should have no opportunity of learning the overland route to the capital, which he proposed to take, reported that some 700 had been taken there. And as A. D. Maingy, the Commissioner of Tenasserim, had declared that the total number deported was not less than 1,600, even allowing for a high percentage of deaths, there were obviously many more still to be sought out for repatriation. Indeed, the Chaophraya of Chumphorn, the leader of the raid, as soon as he heard of Burney's demand for the surrender of deportees, had apportioned his own batch out among his friends in southern Siam. The assiduous Burney, however, secured an order for their release from the Kalahom to Pya Kray Kosa, who assumed control at Chumphorn, when the Chaophraya was recalled in disgrace to the capital. The new governor was instructed to draw up a list showing how many had died, and how many were living. Those who opted to return home were to be provided with suitable food for the journey, and none was to be 'troubled, or dragged and brought to Bangkok, or concealed in any place'.[1] Eventually 237 were released and sent to Mergui under the charge of the British officer who had had the task of repatriating the 109 Siamese prisoners captured by the British when chasing after Phraya Chumphorn's raiders.[2]

That was in April 1826, and the ministers at Bangkok sought to assure Burney that no more deportees remained unaccounted for. But only a month later his sleuth hounds discovered a large party of Mons from the Martaban area who had been captured by Maha Yotha's force. Maha Yotha himself was of Mon origin and the

[1] Burney Papers, I, 1, p. 142.   [2] Ibid., I, 2, p. 212.

deportees had acquaintances among the many Mon immigrants settled in Siam. Hence they were treated much less harshly than the Burmese deportees had been. Nevertheless, they were just as anxious as the latter to return home.[1] 'To effect their release', Burney reported, 'the Mission had to go through the same vexatious discussions as on the former occasion, before the Siamese Court was prevailed upon, in the latter end of June, to forward in the same manner to Mergui, another party of 640 men, women and children under charge of another of our interpreters'. Finally, after that batch had been sent off, eight more of the Mon deportees were surrendered by the Siamese and five 'native Christians'. These latter were Indian seamen whose vessel had been captured and burnt by the Siamese off the coast of Tavoy while conveying a party of Burmese officers some four or five years earlier. No arrangements could be made for sending them by the route across the peninsula to Mergui. They were accordingly brought away in the Mission Brig when Burney departed from Siam at the end of July 1826.

Thus ended the affair of the deportees. It was, of course, unprecedented for a South-East Asian government to surrender such spoils of war by negotiation. Moreover, when the British invaded Burma in 1824, Siam and Burma had been at war—on and off—since 1759. Burma was the aggressor, and had inflicted dreadful wounds upon her neighbour including deportations of Siamese subjects far worse than those with which Burney was concerned. His success may be contrasted with the failure of the British post-war negotiators to obtain the liberation of the thousands of Manipuris and Assamese carried off by the Burmese during the period leading to the Anglo-Burmese war. The Treaty of Yandabo, which ended that war in February 1826, while Burney was struggling to secure the repatriation of the Burmese and Mon deportees in Siam, provided for a return of all prisoners. This was interpreted as including not only those taken during the actual fighting in Burma but also all deportees from the territories on the north-east frontier of India, the invasion of which by the Burmese had been the main cause of the war. The Burmese surrendered all prisoners taken during the war, but successfully evaded all British efforts for the repatriation of the others. In Siam's case there can be no doubt that the success of British arms in Burma next door

[1] Burney Papers, II, 4, p. 73.

was a decisive factor, whereas in Burma's case the rather too speedy withdrawal of the British forces down the Irrawaddy played into the hands of the intransigents at the Court of Ava. Nevertheless, it was Burney's crusading zeal in the cause of humanity and his unremitting efforts that broke through the opposing ministerial phalanx at Bangkok. Every member of the Mission, he proclaimed to Calcutta, would feel 'great and lasting satisfaction that he was instrumental in rescuing upwards of 1,400 of his fellow creatures from a most intolerable slavery'.[1]

Some time later, after the conclusion of his mission to Bangkok, it was his great pleasure to meet many of them at Mergui. 'They crowded round the Mission with presents and tokens of gratitude in the most pleasing and gratifying manner,' he records. 'No instance had ever before occurred of the return of captives from Siam, and the arrival of these prisoners at Mergui was as astonishing and embarrassing as the return to life of the dead. The British authorities there were required to decide upon the claims of husbands for their wives, masters for their slaves, and owners for their lands and other property, that had all undergone alienation according to ancient custom, upon the abduction of the prisoners by the Siamese. The small party of Siamese which Major Frith had detained, were released the moment these prisoners arrived at Mergui. The conduct of the inhabitants of Mergui towards these Siamese prisoners formed a striking contrast to that their townsmen received in Siam. They repeatedly requested the permission of the British authorities at Mergui to be allowed to deliver to the Siamese in confinement supplies of fruit, clothing and other articles, which they voluntarily brought to promote the comfort of people who, they said, although enemies were in adversity. It is unpleasant to relate that the Mission did not see or hear of a single instance of a Siamese showing kindness or even commiseration towards a Burmese prisoner at Bangkok.' They hated the Burmese, the Ministers told Burney. The horrors of repeated invasions were not to be forgotten.

The Government of India had decided against soliciting Siamese co-operation in the war with Burma before deputing Burney to Bangkok, and he had been directed to abstain from raising the matter. Yet the idea had apparently not been completely abandoned at Sir Archibald Campbell's army headquarters in Burma, for at

[1] BP, II, 4, p. 74.

the end of December a message came to Bangkok from it inviting Maha Yotha's 'Army of Dvaravati' to join the British forces in their advance into Upper Burma. It arrived on 27 December when Burney and his staff had gone up the river by invitation of the King to witness the ceremony of bringing to Bangkok one of the oldest Buddha images in the kingdom. It was to be housed, he writes, in one of the Bangkok temples, but he gives no precise details of either the image or the temple. When his boat met the flotilla conveying the image downstream, the King sent a message inviting him to join in towing it, but he refused. He writes rather contemptuously of the scene he witnessed, and one feels that his Anglican conscience was offended by this exhibition of idolatry. Afterwards, while returning to his headquarters, his boat was stopped by the Phrakhlang, who delivered him a private letter from the British commandant at Martaban, and earnestly requested him to let him know as soon as possible what news it contained.

Two items in the missive were of such importance that Burney at once composed a note on the subject which he translated into Siamese and sent to the Ministers. The first concerned the war in Burma. The Burmese attacks had been beaten off at Prome, Burney was informed, and the British army, heavily reinforced, was advancing towards the capital. At the same time another force under Colonel Pepper was about to march on Toungoo from Pegu, and the British commander-in-chief invited the Dvaravati army under Maha Yotha to join it. The second item was an announcement, which seems to have taken Burney completely by surprise, that the British government had decided to revive the old Mon kingdom of Pegu as a barrier between the Burmese, the British and the Siamese. 'Such an arrangement,' went on the despatch, 'will, it is hoped, be highly satisfactory to the Court of Siam, and urge it to the most prompt and decisive co-operation with the English.'[1]

Long before this document arrived to complicate his discussions with the Ministers Burney had made up his mind that to expect anything of the nature of co-operation in the Burma war from the Siamese was a complete delusion: all that he had ventured to ask for had been a supply of draft and carriage cattle for the British forces. His application for these had been fruitless. Various excuses had been proffered, one being that it was against Buddhist

[1] BP, I, 1, pp. 125–6.

tenets to supply animals for the troops to eat. Burney replied to this one that the British did not eat elephants; but he soon realized that he was up against a brick wall and dropped the matter. Hence it was embarrassing to find it raised once again in the final paragraph of Captain Fenwick's despatch. He suspected that the general tenour of the despatch would encourage the Siamese to believe that the British forces in Burma were actually in need of their help.

The Ministers' response to the invitation was immediate. The price of Siam's assistance, they said, was the cession of the Burmese provinces of Martaban and Tavoy, and they must be handed over before any Siamese would march against Ava. Burney countered this with a firm refusal. He explained that in any case nothing could be done in the matter without the sanction of the Governor-General, and that by the time that his reply could be received, the opportunity for the Siamese to be of any use in the war would have been lost. There the matter ended. But a short time later Burney's interpreter, Mr. Leal, passed through Maha Yotha's headquarters while carrying despatches from him to Sir Archibald Campbell and Commissioner Maingy. He reported that not only had the generalissimo no draft or carriage animals to spare, having only 20 elephants and 150 horses all told, but that his total force numbered no more than 1,200 men, and they were engaged upon cutting sappan wood and cultivating cotton.[1] The only largish force on the frontier, Burney discovered, was one of eight or nine thousand men, assembled at Chumphorn as a precaution against possible British reprisals from Tenasserim for the late Phraya's raid. In his final report Burney includes a careful estimate of Siam's military potentiality showing it to have been far lower than the Government of India had been led to believe. He points out also that the Siamese mode of warfare was entirely different from that of a disciplined, well-organized British force. 'Pillage and plunder,' he writes, 'are the regular parts of the Siamese mode of warfare, which the Court could not attempt to forbid.' And it was aware that the British would not tolerate such practices. Moreover, besides these two reasons for the failure of the Siamese to co-operate was the further one that they were 'most unwilling' to pit their forces against those of the Burmans: they considered them invincible.

[1] BP, II, 4, p. 49.

The Government of India's quixotic notion of reviving the Mon kingdom of Pegu, which King Alaungpaya of Burma had destroyed in 1757, came no nearer practical realization than the equally quixotic one of Siamese military co-operation in Burma. The Mon peoples of the Irrawaddy delta, and of the valleys of the Sittang and the Menam Chao Phraya, had played an important role politically and culturally long before the arrival of the Burmese and the Siamese in the countries now named after them. The Burmese empire of Pagān, founded in 1044, absorbed the Mon states of Hamsavati (Pegu) and Sudhammavati (Thaton) and held on to them until its conquest by Kublai Khan's Mongols at the end of the thirteenth century enabled Pegu to regain independence and make good its control over Lower Burma until the middle of the sixteenth century. The Siamese, who absorbed the Mon kingdom of Dvaravati in the lower Menam valley into their kingdom of Ayuthaya in the fourteenth century, incorporated its name in the official designation of the kingdom. Both Burmese and Siamese were strongly influenced by Mon Theravada Buddhist culture.

The Mon kingdom of Pegu lost its independence to the Burmese under the leadership of the Toungoo Dynasty. The Burmese rulers sought to expand their control over the Tai states beyond their south-eastern borders, and hence made the city of Pegu their capital. But after nearly half a century of attempts to hold the Ayuthaya kingdom in subjection the Burmese were finally driven out during the sixteen-nineties and their kingdom in its turn suffered the horrors of invasion. The Mon country bore the brunt of the struggle, being invaded not only by the Siamese, but also by Burmese armies from the north and an Arakanese sea-borne expedition with Portuguese mercenaries as its shock troops. From this holocaust those Mons who could trekked away to take refuge in Siam. The plight of those who could not was described by a Jesuit priest who was with the Portuguese. 'It is a lamentable spectacle,' he wrote, 'to see the banks of the rivers set with infinite fruit-bearing trees, now overwhelmed with ruins of gilded temples and noble edifices; the ways and fields full of skulls and bones of wretched Peguans, killed or famished and cast into the river in such numbers that the multitude of carcases prohibits the way and passage of any ship.'[1] The once-prosperous land, which had supplied Malacca in the days of its greatness with abundance

[1] Boves in Purchas, *His Pilgrimes*, 1625 ed., II, p. 1748.

of rice and teakwood junks, was reduced to destitution from which it never recovered under Burmese rule. The Burmans shifted their capital far up the Irrawaddy to Ava near modern Mandalay, foreign seaborne trade was discouraged, the Delta region relapsed into jungle and its ports stagnated.

In 1740, when Burmese leadership was in a state of near-collapse because of Manipuri raiding, the Mons made a desperate bid to regain independence. At first it succeeded, because of the weapons they were supplied with by European traders, and French assistance came to them from Pondicherry, where the ambitious Josef Dupleix was looking for opportunities to increase French influence in the lands around the Bay of Bengal. The Mons fought their way up the Irrawaddy as far as Ava, which they captured. There, however, their progress ended. Under a new leader, a local headman calling himself Alaungpaya, 'Embryo Buddha', the Burmans staged a series of counter-attacks with mounting success, which brought them once again down the Irrawaddy into the Mon country, which they finally subjugated in 1757. This disaster caused another large Mon exodus to Siam, and the failure of further risings in 1773 and 1783 swelled the numbers fleeing from the Burman terror. Siam, herself the victim of repeated Burmese invasions, one of which had destroyed her old capital Ayuthaya, received them with open arms. John Crawfurd in 1822 was told that there were no less than 43,000 Mons from Burma settled in Siam. Burney noted that they were some of the most useful subjects of the King of Siam, and that many were employed by the Court in positions of great trust.

The scheme to resurrect the Pegu kingdom was of such concern to Siam that the presence of a Siamese delegation at the peace talks in Burma was considered essential, and Burney was instructed to invite the Court to appoint someone of ministerial rank to confer with the British authorities there on the subject. He was also asked to make enquiries about any members of the old Mon royal family, who might be living in exile in Siam or, failing them, any Mons of distinction who might be suitable candidates for the Pegu throne.

Burney's first reaction to the news was to warn the Government of India that the Court of Siam had not received it with the satisfaction it had expected.[1] In particular the proposal that an

[1] BP. I, 1, p. 70.

agent should be deputed to carry on negotiations with the British Commissioners in Burma, a procedure which Burney had repeatedly recommended in the case of the frontiers, was totally rejected. 'No Siamese Ministers would ever dream of proceeding upon such a mission,' he explained, 'and if one had been deputed, he would have received no powers to act on the spot.' In his Journal he describes with amusement the Phrakhlang's reaction to his suggestion that he might himself go to the frontiers of Martaban or Tavoy to confer with the British on the spot. 'The Minister rolled his large body round, stared at me, and seemed as much startled as if I had proposed to him to take a trip to Europe.'[1] In some vague way the Ministers feared that any subject proposed for discussion, such as the Tenasserim boundary or the revival of the kingdom of Pegu, would be merely a trap to cause their country to lose its independence to the British. In any case the British had not yet conquered Burma; whether they could do so had yet to be seen. So nothing was done, and throughout the month of January Burney's attention was mainly directed to the negotiations for the repatriation of the Burmese deportees. The talks also regarding his own treaty proposals had never got beyond their preliminary stage, and it was clear that the Court of Siam would commit itself to nothing until the situation in Burma cleared up.

Then suddenly two things sparked them off to a real start. On the last day of January news came from the British political agents at Martaban that peace was about to be concluded with the Court of Ava. Three days later the Raja of Ligor, with whom Burney had made his preliminary treaty, at last arrived at the capital.

The news about the Burma peace treaty was premature. To clarify the situation it is necessary to look back a few months. The main British army marching up the Irrawaddy valley had spent the wet monsoon at Prome. When it resumed its northwards march with the coming of the dry season in November 1825, the Burmese had proposed an armistice for peace talks. Their real object, however, was simply to gain time in which to raise fresh armies to replace those which had retired in disorder after the death of Generalissimo Maha Bandula in the previous April. The ruse failed, the Burmese attacking forces were completely defeated, and on 9 December the British were again on the march towards the

[1] BP, I, 1, p. 54.

capital. On 29 December, when they reached Pantanaw, a truce was again sought by the Burmese, this time with a view to serious negotiations, and though staggered by the British terms, the Burmese commissioners accepted them, a treaty was signed, and sent up to the capital for royal ratification. It was news of the Pantanaw agreement that Burney received on 31 January. What he did not hear until much later was that King Bagyidaw had summarily rejected the treaty and that the British had resumed their march on the Burmese capital.

As soon as he heard of the Pantanaw parleys Burney drew up a brief statement of suggestions regarding Siam for the British commissioners in Burma, and asked the Phrakhlang for a messenger to take it immediately for delivery to the British political officers at Martaban. Soon afterwards Phraya Phiphatkosa, the Phrakhlang's deputy, called to tell him that news of the peace talks had been received through Maha Yotha, who had forwarded to the Court letters addressed to him by the political officers at Martaban as well as one addressed directly to the Ministers by the British Commissioners. Burney gathered from his visitor that the Ministers were doubtful of the credibility of the news, but at the same time were annoyed that they had let slip the opportunity to derive advantage from the situation through their refusal to co-operate with the British. He told him that he would try to obtain what advantages he could for Siam in the peace treaty. The latter replied that Siam required no territory from the British, and that Burney's mission was not concerned 'with such minor matters' as cessions of territory. Burney at once took him up on this point, asking whether these were the sentiments of the Ministers. But the other refused to be drawn: they were his own sentiments, he said, and the Envoy had better address the Ministers themselves on the subject. Accordingly he did so, in a brief memorial which must be given verbatim so that its full flavour may be conveyed. It runs:

> Captain Henry Burney has the honour to apprize the Ministers of Siam that he has received letters containing intelligence that the Burmese have been so severely and completely defeated by the English Army in a battle which lasted for three days near Prome, that they have sent Envoys to the English General to sue for peace, which is about to be concluded on the following terms. Namely—The Cession of Assam and other states in that quarter, the four provinces of Ye, Tavoy, Mergui and Tenasserim to the English Government, besides a large

sum of Money towards indemnifying the English for the expenses of the war

The issue of this war will, therefore, now augment the honour and glory of the English Government, and Captain Burney appeals to the Ministers of Siam, whether since his arrival in Bangkok he has not used every possible exertion to induce them to move Chow Pya Maha Ayothia's army towards Martaban and to secure for the King of Siam a portion of this honour and glory.

Captain Burney was unfortunately unable to win the confidence of the Ministers, and the customs of the Country prevented his addressing directly the King of Siam, whom Captain Burney considers as not only the greatest but the most enlightened personage at Bangkok.

Captain Burney is still actuated by the most friendly dispositions towards Siam, and in proof of this assertion he now proposes to the King and Ministers of Siam to depute immediately to Martaban some Siamese Officer of rank and character, in company with Captain Burney or Captain Macfarquhar for the purpose of conferring with the British Commissioners in Ava, of ascertaining whether Martaban or any other territory can now be ceded in favour of Siam, and of making the necessary enquiries in view of the future settlement of boundaries between the Siamese dominions and the British Possessions of Tavoy and Mergui.

Captain Burney requests the Ministers will once more peruse the letter which he presented to the King of Siam from the Governor-General, and then determine whether the proposition which Captain Burney now makes is not of the most friendly character, and one likely to prove highly advantageous to the interests of Siam.[1]

Burney's advice to the British commissioners charged with the negotiations in Burma, which he sent off with such haste to the British officers at Martaban, cannot have been received by them before the signature of the Treaty of Yandabo on 24 February 1826; nevertheless it is too interesting a document to be passed over, if only as an example of Burney's grasp of the main issues involved. He begins by laying down the two fundamentals, that Siam must abandon all claims to sovereignty over the Malayan states, and that she must permit unrestricted trade with her territories. Siam, he explains, wanted Martaban and Tavoy, but she had not fulfilled her promises to co-operate with the British. This was partly because she had been doubtful of the result of the war, and partly because of her fear that Britain intended to attack her. He then proceeds to consider the Siamese case on its merits,

[1] BP, I, 1, pp. 143-4.

and to demolish it. The Burmese, he says, were far superior to the Siamese militarily. Siam's strongest defence against Burma was the 'mountainous waste' of several days journey on both sides of the frontier, and it would be well to keep it between Siam and whatever parts of the Tenasserim coast Britain might retain. If it were proposed to cede a part of Tenasserim to Siam, two questions must be considered: firstly could she defend it, and secondly would the inhabitants accept Siamese rule? Tavoy, Mergui and Tenasserim were inhabited by Burmese whom the Siamese would enslave and treat with the utmost inhumanity. Much of the population of Siam was Mon, the descendants of immigrants from Pegu. Martaban therefore in Siamese hands could be made very strong; but it would bring the Siamese closer to the Burmese, with inevitable disputes as a consequence. British posts at Tavoy and Mergui, however, would enable the British to keep peace between them. The danger was that when the terms of the treaty began to press upon the Burmese in the north and west, they would try to move southwards and eastwards. They had learnt much in fighting the British, and unless the Siamese were given a post of advantage on the Burma borders, they would have all the more inclination, as well as the ability, to strike at Bangkok from Martaban. Next to that place perhaps Ye might be acceptable to the Siamese together with parts of Tavoy and Tenasserim. But the Burmese inhabitants of these places would have to be moved. Martaban, however, he stresses, was in Siamese eyes the most desirable acquisition, and to offer it to the Court might perhaps be the best way of obtaining from Siam all the objects of the mission.

Burney concludes by stressing Siam's great apprehensions of British power. Unless some proof of Britain's friendly disposition were 'unequivocally' offered, he insists, there would be no trading concessions and no ratification of his provisional treaty with the Raja of Ligor regarding Kedah and Perak. Free trade was unknown to the Siamese, and to obtain it the negotiator would have to be able to prove to the Ministers that it would be 'of great present advantage' to themselves personally.

It is a strange document. One is struck by its unreality. Martaban was not mentioned in the list of territories to be ceded by the Burmese. What was under consideration was the revival of the Mon kingdom of Pegu, of which Martaban would naturally form a part. Was Burney attempting to substitute a Siamese Martaban for the Pegu project, which he knew to be chimerical? He obviously hoped to use Martaban as a bargaining counter. As events turned out, however, he had much overestimated Martaban's desirability in Siamese eyes. The Ministers replied to his memorial that in the King's view Martaban was 'far from the country of Siam', very difficult to protect and certain to involve the Siamese in war with the Burmese. 'Now the English are not to fight with the Burmese,' they continued, 'but they are respectively to live in peace and friendship. Do not take any more trouble about Martaban.'[1]

Actually this was the second of two letters on the same subject. The first conveyed the Ministers' own sentiments on the subject, and was in all essentials the same as the second, but they had told him that it had been unnecessary to submit his memorial to the King, who had already heard from 'the English General' about the truce with the Burmese. It was a very cordial letter: he was told that the Siamese were extremely pleased with what he had come to perform. Nevertheless he decided to stand upon his diplomatic dignity. He called upon the Phrakhlang to demand why his memorial had not been submitted to the King. It had been written, he said, under the authority of the Governor-General, and under Siamese law it was the King, and not the Ministers, who should issue orders on so important a matter. If the Ministers declined to submit his letters to the King, he explained, the Governor-General might be led to think that they wished 'to do mischief between him and the King'.[2] He refused to accept any of the Phrakhlang's excuses, but went home and repeated what he had said in a note to the Ministers. This is what elicited the second reply, which came on 10 February. He was right to make his stand, but he was not guiltless himself, as he well knew; for in his Journal he expresses the opinion that the Ministers had been reluctant to lay his Memorial before the King because he had complimented His Majesty at their expense. Did he realize that to them he might seem, to use his own phrase, to wish to do mischief between them and the King? In English the wording of the sentence in the third paragraph of the memorial, in which the King is described as the 'most enlightneed personage in Bangkok', is clearly provocative. In Thai it was probably toned down in such a way as to deprive it of any arrière pensée. It was undoubtedly

[1] BP, I, 1, p. 154. [2] BP, I, 1, p. 112.

aimed at the Phrakhlang, through whom all Burney's dealings with the Government had to be conducted. Burney considered him stupid in matters of politics as well as hostile to the Mission's objects. The latter, of course, adversely affected his own personal interests, and in defence of them he was thoroughly astute. He professed to believe all the rumours of a British naval attack upon Bangkok and was frantically attempting to put Paknam in a state of defence. He professed also to believe that the principal object of Burney's mission was to establish a British Resident and factory at Bangkok; and when at this time in conversation with his deputy, Phraya Phiphatkosa, Burney tried to disabuse him of such a notion, since it was completely erroneous, he appeared to be surprised and asked the Envoy to declare this to the Ministers in writing. Since nothing of the sort appeared in the official documents connected with the Mission one wonders how such a notion could have arisen. It could, of course, have originated with the Phrakhlang himself.

On 27 February news came through that the Court of Ava had repudiated the peace treaty agreed to by its commissioners early in January at Pantanaw, and the war had been resumed. The Phrakhlang's pleasure that the Siamese estimate of Burmese faithlessness had been confirmed was unconcealed: it provided an excellent excuse for refusing to engage in talks with the British commissioners in Burma. Among the orders issued by the King in reply to Burney's memorial of 2 February was one rejecting the invitation to joint talks regarding the frontiers between British Burma and Siam; the British, it was naively suggested, could get all the necessary information from the local inhabitants. The Siamese on their part were forbidden 'to infringe on the frontiers of the English' and Siamese officers strictly prohibited from crossing the frontiers to 'seize men'. Traders, however, might cross over safely if provided with passes. In the Siamese view this sort of thing was adequate to meet the situation.

By this time, however, the repudiated treaty had been signed at Yandabo, and this time there was to be no going back.

Chapter 5

The Raja of Ligor enters the Contest

WHEN Burney's little set-to with the Phrakhlang over his memorial occurred, a new actor had just arrived upon the scene who was largely to supplant the Minister in the conduct of the negotiations. This was the Raja of Ligor, and on 7 February Burney received a message from him requesting that he pay him a visit. He found the Raja in very shabby quarters and in what appeared to be a state of considerable alarm. He told Burney that he was accused at Court of sacrificing the interests of his country by cultivating too great an intimacy with the English. The basis for these charges was apparently the information contained in the letters from Tavoy directed to Burney, which the Phrakhlang had opened and caused to be translated, an action which had led to the Envoy's first major tussle with him. The Raja explained that this was why he had not brought Harris and Leal with him overland: the Court had forbidden it. Now, he said, he had to satisfy the Court of the propriety of his conduct and of the sincerity of Burney's friendly declarations regarding Anglo-Siamese relations.

Burney gave him a detailed account of what had happened since his arrival in Bangkok. 'It was really some relief,' he writes, 'to converse with a person who listened with attention and intelligence, two qualities which no Minister or Officer at Bangkok ever betrayed at any conference with me.'[1] When he went on to tell the Raja that the Ministers were labouring under the error that the Mission was deputed to establish a British consul or resident and a factory at Bangkok, the latter asked him to report that such a notion was quite unfounded. Burney did so, and emphasized his own absolute conviction that such an establishment would run the risk of bringing on war between the British and the Siamese within six months. This, he added, was also the opinion expressed in Craw-

[1] BP, I, 1, p. 114, Journal, para. 104.

The Raja of Ligor enters the Contest 75

furd's report on his mission. The Raja seemed to be greatly relieved at this. He had started to tell the Envoy not to be uneasy because the Ministers had not shown his memorial to the King when they were interrupted. The arrival of two Siamese officials was announced. Burney asked the Raja to send a message to excuse himself from seeing them, and he did so. But the attendant returned with a further message which caused the Raja to go into another room to meet them. After a few minutes he returned, saying that they came from the Palace and he must admit them. 'The Raja,' writes Burney, 'carefully put his apartments in order, begged me not sit down too near him, or show too great an intimacy, but to adopt as much as I could the customs observed in my visits to other Siamese Chiefs. The two visitors, Pya Ram and Pya Ram Kamheing, then came in. They crawled towards the Rajah and made him the most abject obeisances, but I soon saw they had been deputed as spies to see what passed between the Rajah of Ligore and myself.' They asked Burney if the treaty with Burma had been actually signed and whether the English put any trust in Burmese assurances of peace. He replied that the British would probably not evacuate their troops from Burma until all the stipulations of the treaty had been carried out. But they remained sceptical regarding Burmese intentions: the negotiations, they were convinced, were merely a ruse to gain time and deceive the British. The Raja asked him for the names of the territories the British were to annex and the amount of the indemnity to be paid by the Burmese, and wrote down his answers. Burney expressed the view that next to the possession of the Burmese capital the payment of an indemnity was the clearest proof of the British victory, but Phraya Ram showed by his manner that he was completely unconvinced; and when the Envoy protested that this accorded with what the British Commander-in-Chief had written 'from the seat of the negotiations', the Siamese unabashedly commented: 'The story comes from a great distance.'[1] Burney's own comment in his Journal was that the Siamese believed that he had been instructed by the Commander-in-Chief to utter falsehoods in exactly the same way as in the case of their own government and its officers.

After returning home Burney received a message from the Raja expressing his great happiness at their meeting and saying that he

[1] BP, I, 1, p. 116, Journal, para. 106.

was about to wait on the King with a full report of their talk. Next day one of the Raja's servants, whom Burney had found 'very useful' when he was in Kedah three years earlier, told him that the King had sent for the Raja on the very night of his arrival at Bangkok, and had transferred to him the conduct of the negotiations with Burney. One wonders how this tied up with the Raja's own description of his position at his meeting with the Envoy. He was an immensely astute man. In any case, having negotiated the preliminary treaty with Burney, he was the obvious choice for going ahead with the consideration of the matters with which it was concerned. But had he been putting on an act designed to enable him to escape from the commitments he had entered into with Burney when they had made their provisional treaty in the previous July? He had, it will be remembered, promised to join with Burney in recommending to the King that the Sultan of Kedah should be restored?[1] Or was he truly in semi-disgrace on account of this promise, which, presumably, he had never intended to keep, and had now to convince the Court that he fully accepted its absolute veto of the Sultan's restoration?

Burney's informant also told him that the two spies had been sent to the Raja's house by the King personally as a result of his having seen him pass by the Palace on his way thither. The King had instructed them to report to him the substance of Burney's replies to their questions.

That same evening a message came from the Raja asking him for a definitive statement, for the King's private information, of the views of the Government of India with regard to trade and the Malayan states. Burney had drawn up such a statement as soon as the news of the opening of peace talks in Burma had reached him. It had been intended for the Ministers, and had been secretly translated into Siamese by one of the royal officers. This he sent to the Raja, asking him to make a copy of it. He added a brief note to explain British views regarding the Malayan states. Regarding Kedah, Selangor and Perak he said, the Governor-General had indicated that he would ratify the treaty made between Burney and the Raja. Regarding Kelantan and Trengganu all that was required was for Siam to engage not to 'visit them with her armies or to molest them and disturb the peace and commerce of the neighbouring English Settlement'.[2] He also asked the Raja to

[1] *Supra*, p. 29.   [2] *Ibid.*, I, 1, p. 117.

The Raja of Ligor enters the Contest 77

assure the King that he could prove 'every syllable' in the document.

It is a masterly exposition of British requirements. Burney begins with a general statement of the British position in relation to the Malayan states. Next he adumbrates his three proposals regarding them. Then he passes on to a detailed account of the regulation of British trade at Bangkok. Finally he submits eight proposals for its more liberal treatment.

The British, he says, do not require territory; nor do they want a factory or consul at Bangkok. A consul would bring war within six months. They do require Siam to grant more liberal trading terms and to refrain from molesting the Malayan states. They do not intend to take possession of any Malayan states, and will engage not to do so if Siam will make the same engagement on her part. If on the other hand Siam refuses, and overruns Malayan countries, driving their people into the British settlements of Penang, Malacca and Singapore, friendship with the British will very soon be disturbed. All that is needed is for the King of Siam to settle the matter, and that should be quite easy. The British will see that the inhabitants of the Malayan states do not disturb the peace of Siam.

Then, coming to his three proposals, first of all with regard to Perak and Selangor, these two states, he says, previously had treaties with Dutch Malacca. The Dutch, however, had resigned that settlement, and all rights and claims connected with it, to the British. Hence the latter could not permit the Siamese to interfere with those states. His second proposal is the restoration of the Sultan of Kedah, the release of his family and the evacuation of his territories. In such a case the British would engage not to take possession of Kedah, and would ensure that the Sultan would send the Bunga Mas and 4,000 dollars in annual tribute to the King of Siam. Thirdly, with regard to Kelantan and Trengganu, if the Siamese would engage not to molest them, the British would promise not to occupy them or prevent their sultans from sending the *bunga mas* to Bangkok.

Burney begins his account of trade regulations at Bangkok by asking for the immediate removal of all impediments and delays. In Singapore, Malacca and Penang, he says, Siamese ships pay no duties. Chinese junks visiting Siam pay only one measurement duty. The Portuguese, with so little trade, pay only a 6 per cent import duty. The English, he explains, do not ask for exemption, but to have regular fixed duties, and to be permitted to buy and sell anywhere in Bangkok. At present no one can buy from an English merchant without the Phrakhlang's permission, and this is never given if he or his officers have anything to buy or sell. This means that sugar, which is 8 to 9 ticals per pecul (including 1½ peculs duty) in the market, has to be bought from the Phrakhlang at 10 to 11 ticals per pecul; that pepper, which in the market sells at 14 ticals per pecul (including 3 ticals duty), is sold by the Phrakhlang at 18 ticals per pecul; and that sappan wood, the price of which (including 1 tical duty) is 2 ticals per pecul, has to be bought from the Phrakhlang at 4 ticals per pecul.

An English or Surat Merchant, [he writes,] can sell no part of his cargo before the Prah Klang, his petty Officers or the King's Merchants have selected whatever they please, and for which they will not settle a fair price, keeping the Merchant waiting day after day for a month or six weeks, until they either force him to submit to their terms or lose the chance of selling his Cargo to any advantage. While the Prah Klang and his petty Officers are settling a price in this extraordinary manner, the English or Surat Merchant cannot transact business with anyone else, and if he refuse to accept their offer, it is well known and cannot be denied, that no inhabitant of Bangkok dare make any other offer, for what these officers desire to possess. Yet Captain Burney knows that upon the accession of the present King of Siam, His Majesty was pleased to declare that the trade of his Kingdom should be henceforth made free to all persons.[1]

Then, turning to shipping, there was no fixed rule for port and anchorage duties, he declared; charges were made by guesswork. The total alone was given to the merchant: there was no statement of particulars. In addition to a general import duty of 8 per cent, and heavy export duties ranging from 20 to 50 per cent, a three-masted vessel paid 2,357 ticals and a brig 1,726½ ticals in port and anchorage duties. Moreover, the Governor of Paknam, had increased his fee from 80 to 124 ticals, without explaining why, or by what authority. Ships had to pay the same scale of duties upon each visit, whereas elsewhere in the world the full rate was payable only once in six months or a year. In addition an English merchant had to pay 28½ ticals (sometimes more) for a pass for every Siamese junk hired in order to lighten the load of his ship to enable it to cross the bar. If he bought rice, paddy or salt, he had to pay half

[1] BP, I, 1, p. 170.

a tical a day each to 40 clerks to see the article measured, although only one of them actually turned up, and for only two hours each day. Burney invited the King to appoint appropriate officers to examine the truth of these statements. Because of the delays imposed upon English and Surati ships, he says, many English and American traders had left Bangkok. His closing comment is that the Phrakhlang's Chulia officers were the cause of all the mischief; the Siamese and Chinese merchants behaved fairly.

Burney's proposals for the reform of the regulations begin with the recommendation that the measurement charge on a vessel should be rated so as to include anchorage and port dues, presents and import and export duties. This was the Chinese method, he explains, and a charge of 1,500 ticals per fathom according to the breadth of the vessel made in lieu of all other charges would be readily paid. In consequence, the number of English vessels resorting to Siam would much increase. This charge should be reduced for a second, third or forth visit within twelve months.

Having paid this charge, the merchant should be free to sell and buy wherever he pleased. The King himself, he urges, should buy or sell in the market. He had the most, and the best, goods for sale, the earliest information and the greatest command of money. Hence his merchant would buy and sell to a greater advantage than any private merchant. The existing system, he says, was the greatest grievance experienced by merchants at Bangkok. Burney then makes two proposals that to a European must have represented ordinary common sense. Measurers of rice, paddy and salt should be remunerated according to the amount measured, he suggests, and ships should deposit only their powder and shot at Paknam, not their guns. The removal of their guns was troublesome and expensive, and in Western eyes, *infra dignitatem*. His last two proposals deal in general terms with procedure in case of debt and the amenability of British subjects to established Siamese law while living in the Siamese dominions. They call for no comment here.

One of the document's concluding paragraphs runs:

The world is grown older and wiser, and the trade of the Siamese as well as of the English is infinitely greater than what it was when the rules now in force at Bangkok were established. No nation can supply the Siamese with many articles required by them so well or so cheaply as the English, and the present enlightened Monarch need not be told that the prosperity and happiness of his subjects will increase in proportion as the resort of trade and shipping to Siam increases.[1]

But the Siamese were not impressed by the doctrines of Adam Smith. They were to show quite clearly that they much preferred Chinese vessels, and the trade they brought, to Western ones with the political complications that could follow in their wake. In the explanatory notes which he appended to the copy of the document which he forwarded to the Governor-General, Burney has some interesting observations to make on this subject.

The Chinese pay a small duty upon their junks, [he writes] and an export duty of half a tickal per pecul upon sugar. The rest of their exports and the whole of their imports are free of duty. The British merchant who pays an import duty of 8 percent and heavy export duties, cannot compete with the Chinese.

The latter, he adds, had actually flooded the Bangkok market with British cottons and merchandise from Singapore and other parts of the East; the trade between China and Siam was very extensive and valuable, and the King and his courtiers had a share in it. The Chinese formed a large proportion of the population of Bangkok, and were immigrating into Siam at the rate of two thousand a year.[2]

Burney knew that the difficulties encountered by Europeans in Siam sprang from Louis XIV's attempt to gain control over that country in the late seventeenth century and the fear of the *farang* which it had aroused. But he seems to know nothing of the stranglehold on Siam's foreign trade imposed earlier by the Dutch, which had caused King Narai to seek the help of France. The Siamese had never forgotten these experiences. And, to complete the picture, when Siam freed her foreign trade from the Western incubus, it was the Chinese who reaped all the advantages.

Regarding the political recommendations in Burney's statement his notes contain some interesting comments. Most of the chief people at Bangkok, he says, shared in the plunder of Kedah, and about a thousand Malays were sent up to the capital as slaves for the King, the Wangna and the Ministers; but, he declares emphatically, this conquest would never have occurred if the Court of Siam had expected British intervention. He adduces historical evidence—not very convincingly—of Kedah's relations with Siam when Ayuthaya had been the capital, and asserts, correctly, that at the time of the Burmese conquest of Siam in 1767 Kedah had

[1] BP, I, 1, p. 174.   [2] BP, I, 1, pp. 178–9.

The Raja of Ligor enters the Contest

behaved as an independent state. Then, in 1771, when King Taksin was in the course of asserting his control over all the states over which Ayuthaya had claimed suzerainty, Kedah had begun to seek protection from the British in India, and in that hope had ceded the island of Penang in 1786. The revenue derived by the Raja of Ligor from Kedah, he says, was 30,000 dollars a year. Hence, if the Sultan were restored, his present stipend of 10,000 dollars from the British could be discontinued.

In Perak's case his provisional treaty with the Raja of Ligor 'yielded somewhat', he now thinks, to the Siamese demand for the Bunga Mas. What he had since learned at Bangkok had induced him to assume a higher tone and claim for Britain the right of protection over both Perak and Selangor because of their earlier connexion with Malacca. Trengganu and Kelantan had submitted so often to Siamese claims that he had deemed it prudent to yield the point of the Bunga Mas in their cases. By so doing he hoped to stop the Court from sending two junks bearing a deputation to Trengganu. He is referring, let it be explained, to a practise used by that Court to bring a recalcitrant Malay ruler to heel.

Burney's notes contain much supplementary detail about the treatment of European ships at Bangkok which need not concern us here, but some of his illuminating comments are worth noting. He explains that he had gone into such detail regarding charges at Bangkok because the King was unaware of the amount embezzled by the Phrakhlang and the officers made a practice of denying any charge not accounted for to the King. The heavy rate of port dues ought to be made known more widely, he insists, since shipowners in London were chartering vessels for Siam at only £1 per ton higher freight than to Singapore. Much of the royal revenue, he explains, was in kind. The troops were employed cutting timber and sappan wood; the Lao people paid tribute in sticklac, ivory, benjamin, etc.; the people of the Siamese portion of Cambodia sent gamboge, pepper and cardamums. Thus the King was a merchant, and his officers sold to foreign merchants on the highest terms. And, our last selection from this very informative document, the tonnage duty, which Crawfurd had recommended in substitution for the existing measurement duty, on ships, was rejected by the Siamese, Burney writes, because they refused to credit any registers or ship's papers.[1]

[1] The notes are printed in BP, I, 1, pp. 176–84.

The lengthy document, which Burney sent to the Raja on 8 February so that it might be copied and shown to the King, was submitted by him in person to the Phrakhlang six days later as a memorial for the consideration of the Ministers. In his Journal he says that they had considered his previous one too short, 'but the present Memorial, I regret to state, in consequence of the tautalogical structure of the Siamese language, and their custom of pasting the sheets to one another, was 10 feet long'.[1] Two days later the English version of it was forwarded by him with his progress report and other papers to Calcutta.

The report, which must have cost him untiring labour, goes over all the points dealt with in its ancillary documents, and adds a number of items of information of special interest. Siam, he writes, never intended to co-operate against Ava, but Maha Yotha was ordered to deceive the British in his communications with their officers at Martaban. When news came of the termination of hostilities, the Court of Siam, hoping to profit by the situation likely to be caused by the evacuation of the British forces from Burma, had issued an order that when that occurred Siamese troops were to invade the country, lay it waste and deport the inhabitants. This had caused Burney no little worry until on 9 February Phraya Philphatkosa had let him know that news had come to the Siamese government that a special clause had been inserted in the peace treaty by which the Siamese, as allies of the British, were to be admitted to the benefits of the peace, if they cared to avail themselves of them. Burney had immediately seized on this to move the Raja of Ligor to persuade the King to rescind the order. Thus the Ava treaty, he wrote, by demonstrating the friendly disposition of the British Government towards Siam, had been helpful to him.

He adds a postscript to his report. He had been privately assured by the Raja of Ligor, he writes, that all the proposals in his Memorial were likely to be accepted save that for the restoration of the Sultan of Kedah. In any case the annual payment of 4,000 dollars by him as tribute that had been offered was too insignificant. Then, with the warning that the Raja's interests were too much involved for implicit faith to be placed in his word, and the comment that his proposals did not offer a clear equivalent for the restoration of the Sultan, Burney throws the ball to the Govern-

[1] J, para. 117.

The Raja of Ligor enters the Contest

ment of India. 'It will rest with my Superiors.' he writes, 'to determine whether I shall sacrifice, the claims of Kedah, and accept whatever the Siamese Ministers are now described to be willing to grant, or offer to them any other advantage besides an augmentation of the proposed sum of 4,000 Dollars to induce them to concede that point also.'[1]

The more hopeful turn in the discussions which Burney had so ardently striven for, proved to be illusory. There was first the storm over the Brig *Guardian*'s departure from the Menam on 19 February without reporting to the Governor of Paknam.[2] No sooner was this settled, when it was succeeded by a fresh one, equally unexpected. The Brig *Guardian*'s serang, or boatswain of its lascar crew, absconded when the vessel left Bangkok. He was arrested and brought before the Wangna on 23 February. Questioned as to the real object of Burney's mission and furthermore of the *Guardian*'s return to Penang, he asserted that the vessel was on its way to join the British fleet which was coming from Singapore to attack Bangkok. The Envoy himself, he declared, was collecting information likely to be of help to the attackers, and had made a secret pact with the Raja of Ligor to place him upon the throne with British assistance.[3] He rather spoilt his case, however, by offering his services against the British in return for the post of shahbundar of Bangkok, 'a proposition', Burney records, 'which made the Wangna laugh heartily, and which threw doubt upon the whole of his alarming tales'. At almost the same time stories were brought in of a fleet of sixty ships near Mergui and of an expedition ready to sail from Penang.

The Raja of Ligor, naturally, was very worried. Troops were summoned to the capital, and the forts at Paklaat and Paknam were manned. 'All was war and bustle,' comments Burney in his final report.[4] 'Not a word uttered by any of us received credit. The boatmen allotted to us were removed and we were evidently viewed with indignation as well as distrust. The renewal of hostilities with Ava also, accounts of which arrived at this very time, threw back our negotiations, the whole of which we found we had to begin again.'[5] When on 11 March Phraya Phiphatkosa brought Burney a despatch from Captain Williamson at Martaban regarding the proposed re-establishment of the Pegu monarchy, he

[1] BP, I, 1, p. 162. [2] *Supra*, pp. 90–1.
[3] BP, I, 2, pp. 195–6; II, 4, p. 40. [4] II, 4, p. 41. [5] *Ibid., loc. cit.*

showed complete lack of interest in its contents; and a few days later, when he delivered further despatches from the same source, his visitor showed clearly that he did not believe a word of their contents, which Burney translated for him.

On the contrary, the Court preferred to listen to the absurd stories purveyed through Maha Yotha from his watch on the frontier opposite Martaban and Tavoy. Here is Burney's description of them in his final report on his mission:

Once, the Burmese had succeeded in blowing up the whole English army with gunpowder. Another time in drowning it by flooding the whole country, another time by destroying it by poisoning all the wells and streams in its neighbourhood. Three several times accounts were brought of the Burmese drawing the English into an ambuscade upon pretence of meeting them to treat for peace, and completely destroying them. Another time, during the negotiations for a peace, the King of Ava had, according to custom, sent down to each person of the English army a lady, who had risen at night and slain her companion. Just before the close of the war, a tale was brought that the Burmese had succeeded in cutting a ditch in rear of Sir Archibald Campbell's army, which could neither advance or retreat, and some time after the treaty of peace was signed, Phya Ratnachak, who had been for a long time at Martaban, brought a circumstantial story of the Burmese having attacked and overwhelmed our army whilst evacuating the country, and of 30 ships full of wounded having sailed from Rangoon. The ready credit which these absurd tales received from the court of Siam too clearly manifested its real feelings towards us, while such accounts had a most mischievous effect upon our proceedings, by unsettling the public mind at Bangkok, augmenting the spirit of procrastination which characterizes the Siamese at all times, and adding to the difficulty of bringing our negotiations with the Siamese ministers to a close.[1]

Late in March a report came from Maha Yotha, that the British were besieging Amarapoora, the Burmese capital. It was untrue, but news from the front in Burma took so long to reach Bangkok that no one knew that the war was over already, and the peace treaty agreed to at Pantanaw and subsequently repudiated had been accepted by the Court of Ava while the invaders were still five days' march from the capital. The story, however, caused such a sensation in the highest quarters that Burney decided to seize the opportunity of coming to grips with the Court over the objects of his mission.

[1] BP, I, 4, p. 54–5.

The Raja of Ligor enters the Contest 85

His decision was strengthened by an incident which must be described in his own words.

On the 27th [of March] the Ship *Hunter* arrived from Singapore.... The moment the Prah Klang received intelligence of her Arrival he hurried down to Paknam, expecting as I was assured, that the vessel was the first of the English Expedition against Siam. Fortunately the Commander Captain Johnstone has been here twice before in command of Mr Hunter's Vessels, and his presence disappointed the Prah Klang, and now renders him doubtful of the tales which have been brought to him of our hostile preparations.[1]

Burney accordingly decided that the moment had come for a decisive move. On the evening of 29 March he sent Captain Macfarquhar to deliver to the Phrakhlang the draft of a treaty embodying his proposals and a memorial explaining them. A day or two later he forwarded copies of these documents to the Governor-General of India asking him to strengthen his hand by writing to the King to assure him of the friendly intentions of the British Government and the falsehood of the various stories to the contrary which were being circulated at Bangkok.

The proposed treaty was a short document of fifteen clauses accompanied by a schedule of commercial regulations. There was to be perpetual 'peace, friendship and good understanding' between the British and the Siamese (Art. 1) and an undertaking by both sides not to invade or occupy any of the Malayan Peninsular States, or disturb their peace in any way (Art. 2). The Sultan of Kedah was to be restored, and all Siamese troops and subjects withdrawn from his territories (Art. 3). The British Government engaged not to take possession of Kedah or disturb its peace, and stipulated that the Sultan should pay to the King of Siam four thousand Spanish dollars annually and the *bunga mas* of gold and silver flowers triennially (Art. 4).

The remainder of the document dealt with commerce and shipping. British and Siamese subjects were to have freedom of intercourse with all the Malayan Peninsular states, and the local officers of both nations were to take common action against piracy. The ships of both nations were to have access to each other's ports on a most-favoured-nation footing, those of the British subject to the regulations and rates of duty in the annexed Schedule. Article 8 specifically provided for free trade between the Straits Settlements

[1] BP, I, 2, 200-1

—Prince of Wales Island, Malacca and Singapore—and all the adjacent Siamese states by sea, overland or by river. Article 9 accorded the same facilities to the newly annexed British possessions of Ye, Tavoy, Mergui and Tenasserim, and any other places which the British might annex from the Kingdom of Ava; it also provided for joint meetings between Siamese and British officers to fix proper boundaries between the British and Siamese possessions.

Articles 10 to 12 were clearly inspired by the desire to clear away the notorious and longstanding difficulties experienced by Western merchants in Siam. They were tactfully worded in reciprocal terms. Merchants from both countries were to be permitted to rent houses and godowns in each other's territories, to be subject to the laws and jurisdiction of the country in which they were residing, and to be able to depart from that country with their property without obstruction. No special privileges were sought: reciprocity was to be the guiding principle. There were also provisions for assistance to damaged ships of the one in the ports of the other, and for equitable salvage regulations in the case of wrecks. The final article stressed again the principles of perpetual peace, friendship and good understanding.

The suggested treaty was rather of the nature of an experiment with the object of pacifying the Court's alarm, Burney explained to the Government of India. But he entered a significant caveat regarding Kedah. He believed, he said, that he could ultimately rescue that state from Siamese domination by perseverance and intimidation, but at the expense of good relations with the Siamese Government. He even went so far as to express his personal opinion that the arguments used by the Ministers against restoring the Sultan had 'some truth and force'.[1]

Burney's draft treaty must be seen against the background of his memorial of 28 March which accompanied it.[2] This in turn was written as a commentary upon a reply by the Ministers to his previous memorial of 13 February written upon receipt of the news of the Pantanaw peace talks, and in the belief that the Burma war had ended[3]. It is a wearisome document, a verbose attempt to justify the actions which Burney had complained of and to refute his arguments. Regarding Kedah, however, while complaining

[1] BP, I, 2, p. 257. [2] BP, Appendix no. 24 in I, 2, pp. 244–9.
[3] *Supra*, pp. 116–23.

The Raja of Ligor enters the Contest

that the English favour 'this criminal', the Ministers make a new assertion. The crimes of the 'Governor of Kedah', they write, were fully known by the 'great men' of that state, all of whom had sent an address 'stating that he was not a fit and proper person to be its ruler, having transgressed against the ancient customs and laws of the Country', and that they did not wish him to be reinstated.[1] They accordingly begged Burney to drop the matter, 'and do not let the Captain be uneasy about it'. With regard to the other four states, about which Burney had submitted proposals, what they had to say amounted to a complete rejection of them. Kelantan and Trengganu were faithful to Siam, they said; what therefore would Siam desire to do to them? Perak had supplicated Siam 'to live under its orders and to send it the tribute of the Golden and Silver Flower in the same manner as Calantan and Tringano'. Selangor, 'insolent and without respect for Siam', had invaded Perak; but when Siam raised an army to deal with Selangor, the English opposed their action, claiming that Selangor was 'subject to their orders' and promising not to allow it to molest Perak. If that were possible, the Siamese would refrain from military action; but they would deal with Perak just as with all their other subject states.

The Ministers were equally uncompromising on the subject of trade regulations. They brushed aside Burney's complaints concerning the treatment of British merchants by the Phrakhlang's officers with the observation that 'the whole business of superintending Trade' was in his hands. They noted his proposal for a comprehensive measurement charge of 1,500 ticals per fathom, but told him that this was something to be settled with the Phrakhlang. Regarding his eight propositions they reminded him that there was a great difference between English and Siamese customs, but thought that in the interests of friendship between the two countries some remission of the regulations, 'where proper', might be made. They totally rejected his plea for merchants to be free to buy and sell in the open market, and also his request that powder and shot only, and not guns, should be deposited by ships at Paknam. It would infringe an ancient custom, they said, and because Siam was a great country, she must conserve such customs. Moreover it was a matter affecting the whole country and had nothing to do with trade.

[1] *Ibid.*, p. 232.

Burney's memorial of 28 March opens with the remark that having read with great care the Ministers' reply to his letter of propositions he found it 'very unsatisfactory'. He feared that his ignorance of Siamese customs had given offence, but hoped they would realize that his sole desire had been to establish true friendship between the two nations. Nevertheless he believed that they had not fully understood what he had written; hence he had drawn up the accompanying treaty to prove that the English did not wish to take possession of any Malayan states, but were entirely concerned with persuading the Siamese 'to join them in the bonds of Peace and friendship'.

He then goes on to stress points dealt with in his former memorial, about which he tells them, there were inaccuracies in the Ministers' reply. In the cases of Trengganu and Kelantan he repeats that Britain would not interfere if Siam would refrain from interference. He knew full well that this was tantamount to asking Siam to relinquish all her claims over these states and that, to the Court of Siam, this was out of the question. In the same category, of course, was his plea for the restoration of the Sultan of Kedah. Nevertheless he renews it and adds that unless it were conceded, a situation could arise which would endanger the continuance of Anglo-Siamese friendship. As to the reported Malay petition to the King not to allow the Sultan to return, those who had joined the Raja of Ligor might have reason to fear his return, but the British would 'oblige him to engage' not to punish anyone on such grounds; and on this point he could assure the Ministers that the refugees from Kedah numbered not just a hundred or two, as they asserted, but at least twenty thousand. He rounds off this discussion by reminding the Ministers that the Raja of Ligor himself had yielded to English representations to the extent of agreeing, in his treaty with Burney, to ask the King of Siam to forgive the Sultan.

On the subject of Perak and Selangor he knew that he was on much stronger ground. Both states had been dependencies of the Dutch, but twelve months earlier the Dutch had ceded Malacca and all its dependencies to Britain. This meant that the rajas of these two states became connected with Britain. Therefore the Ministers' proper course was to complain to the British Government, not to seek redress in an unfriendly manner. Perak, he emphasized, had been a dependency of Malacca for 180 years, yet Siam now wanted to force it to pay tribute to her.

Having submitted a schedule of regulations for trade and shipping together with his draft treaty Burney goes into no details in his memorial. He does, however, pass a few comments upon items in the Ministers' reply to his previous memorial. He would not press his point about the unshipping of its guns by a merchant vessel, he says, because of the strong feeling on the subject on the part of the Court of Siam; but he begs the Ministers to bear in mind that the greatest grievance complained of by English merchants was not being permitted to buy and sell where they pleased in Bangkok. Having to report to the Phrakhlang before doing any business caused great loss of time and money. In the final paragraph he writes: 'The English have now established themselves in extensive contact with the Siamese, and they desire to live with the Siamese as friends and good neighbours and not on the same terms as the Burmese did. A more extensive intercourse than formerly must now take place between the Siamese and the English, and if the Ministers of Siam desire this intercourse shall be so settled and conducted so as to prevent all chance of dispute between the two Nations, they will approve of the Treaty which Captain Burney now forwards to them in the name of the Right Honorable the Governor-General of British India.'

The time was ripe for Burney's move. The Phrakhlang read over the documents carefully and said he would lay them before the King and Ministers. He offered only one comment: why, he asked Macfarquhar, were the English so pertinacious in their demands for the restoration of the Sultan of Kedah? Later that same evening Burney saw the Raja of Ligor, who had apparently already learnt the main items of the draft treaty. The Raja went so far as to warn him that unless he dropped the proposal for the restoration of the Sultan, all the other objects of his mission might be lost. The King's mind, he said, 'was fixed against such a measure.' This does not quite accord with what Burney was to write later in his final report.[1] He well knew from experience how ready a minister was to make such an assertion merely to give additional force to an argument. The Raja also described the difficult position he was in because on certain matters, as he expressed it, Burney's views differed from those of the Ministers. He explained that he could not be as intimate with him as he would have liked because, if he were suspected of encouraging Burney to press these views,

[1] BP, II, 4, p. 42.

it might cost him his own life. Soon afterwards, however, the Raja sent him the comforting message that the King and the Ministers considered his draft treaty and the memorial accompanying it much more satisfactory than any previous documents he had addressed to them.

At this point treaty discussions dropped into the background for nearly three weeks, and although the impatient Envoy pressed almost daily, as he tells us, for a reply, none was vouchsafed until 19 April. 'No argument,' he commented, 'can urge a Siamese to greater activity or exertion than what he has been used to.'[1] In this case the celebration of the Siamese New Year during the first fortnight of April was largely to blame. Burney gives us no description of what took place: he seems to have had little interest in such festivities. Partly, however, his mind was preoccupied with other things, among them a contretemps with the Phrakhlang over a matter of etiquette. The Minister had not returned his ceremonial call, when he had made his round of calls on the Court dignitaries after the royal reception.

The Phrakhlang had promised to do so, but had failed to keep his promise. In January Burney had sent Captain Macfarquhar with a note reminding him of his promise, and pointing out that as the Minister had paid ceremonial calls upon John Crawfurd and the Portuguese Consul, he must insist upon him carrying out his promise. The latter then made what Burney describes as a frivolous excuse, and repeated his promise. Time, however, passed and nothing happened, and Burney was privately informed that having been promoted to the rank of Senapati with the title of Chao Phraya since calling on Crawfurd and the Consul, he considered it derogatory to his enhanced dignity to return the Envoy's official call. He had also, as we have seen, deprived the Mission of its officially allotted boatmen, and they had been unable to hire others, presumably through his influence. Accordingly at the beginning of April Burney prepared an address to the Ministers complaining of the Phrakhlang's disrespect to the representative of the Governor-General of India and his negligence in failing to pay 'those little attentions' which the King of Siam had ordered to be paid to him.

When Burney presented this document to Phraya Phiphatkosa for delivery to the Minister, the latter, having read it carefully,

[1] BP, I, 2, p. 209.

said he dared not deliver to his superior a letter in which he was so severely complained of, and handed it back to the Envoy. Later, however, Burney heard that he had repeated its contents to the Phrakhlang, the King, and the other Ministers. This actually suited his purpose better than the delivery of the missive, and four days later, on 6 April, the Raja of Ligor sent him a message beseeching him not to deliver the letter, and assuring him that if he would call upon the Phrakhlang, he would return the call and restore the boatmen to the Mission.

The sequel must be told in Burney's own words.

On the 10th I called upon the Phrakhlang, who appeared at first a little out of humour, alluding to the letter of Complaint which I had prepared against him. I assured him that it was my sincere wish and intention to cultivate the most cordial good understanding with him; that with this view I had submitted to several instances of a want of proper consideration on his part, that I had delayed as long as possible from taking notice of his neglect to return my visit, but that I had a duty to fulfil towards the exalted personage whom I had the honour to represent, and that I was determined to fulfil it. The Phrakhlang stated that I ought to have given him time to return my visit, which he assured me he would now soon do; and he told it was not the Custom to supply Envoys at Bangkok with Boatmen, and that no such persons were granted to Mr Crawfurd, but that nevertheless, if he and I were friends, of course the services of ten or twelve men could be no greater object to grant me. After some further conversation the Minister and I parted on apparently very friendly terms.[1]

In due course the boatmen made their appearance, and on 15 April the Phrakhlang together with his brother, Phraya Si-phi-phat, paid an official call on the Envoy. Burney reported that he was as conciliatory and agreeable as it was in his power to be. So honour was satisfied. But Burney learnt that it had been accomplished only by the King's special direction.

Burney, as we have seen above, had been asked to make inquiries regarding possible suitable candidates for the Pegu throne among the Mons in Siam, yet the Pantanaw peace terms, news of which he received at the same time—31 January—were silent on the subject. The only annexations from Burma in the south named in the treaty were the four provinces running down the Tenasserim coast, Ye, Tavoy, Mergui and Tenasserim. Moreover,

[1] BP, I, 2, p. 204–5.

all his efforts to persuade the Court to depute someone to discuss frontier questions with the British commissioners in Burma were fruitless: the Ministers refused to show the slightest interest in the matters at issue. Then on 27 February came the news of the renewal of hostilities. The natural inference was that the final word had not yet been spoken on the subject of peace terms, and Burney accordingly penned his 'Additional Suggestions respecting Siamese Negotiations' for submission to the commissioners. He dealt first and foremost with the Pegu project.

There were no descendants of the Pegu royal family in Siam, he said. The Burmese kings had done their utmost to extirpate it, and if any still survived, they would only be found at the Burmese capital. Chao Phraya Maha Yotha Bonnarong had 'no drop of royal blood in his veins'. He was the son of a 'respectable land-holder' who had migrated from Martaban some forty years earlier, and achieved distinction in the Siamese military service. Maha Yotha and his 'Army of Doorawuddee' (i.e. Dvaravati) were more anxious to make Siam powerful than to restore Mon independence. If, however, the Government of Siam were only to hear that the British contemplated placing him on the throne of Pegu, he would most probably be immediately recalled and put to death. He had probably in his correspondence with British officers in Burma conveyed a false impression of his power and influence. He could act only under orders from the Court. There were indeed Mons in Siam of greater rank and more ancient lineage than his, notably Phraya Phiphatkosa, the Deputy Phrakhlang, and his elder brother, the King's Treasurer, but like Maha Yotha they had no real power nor 'the capacity or spirit to form an opinion contrary to what they know their Siamese masters entertain'.

As to the project for reviving the Pegu Kingdom, it could not, Burney thought, maintain itself against the power of either Siam or Burma unless 'placed under the absolute pupillage of the British Government'. And if the Siamese were unwilling to lose the services of a few hundred poor Burmese prisoners, they would never be induced to permit the repatriation of many thousands of people as valuable as the Mons. Siam would probably not object to the restoration of the Mon kingdom if it were made completely dependent upon her. Such an arrangement, however, would be certain to draw the British Government into 'a labyrinth of Indo-Chinese politics', for it would increase the arrogance of the Siamese and revive old quarrels between them and the Peguers. It would be better for the British to keep control over the whole Mon kingdom rather than place Maha Yotha on its throne. On the other hand, if that were not feasible, Maha Yotha would be the best candidate for the throne, if the Siamese Government could be persuaded to agree to his elevation. He was decidedly the best military commander in the service of Siam, and had made himself feared by the Burmese in operations against them.

Burney seems to be bending over backwards in an effort to treat the proposal seriously though quite obviously in his opinion it was impracticable and absurd. Was he taking it too seriously? The Treaty of Yandabo, already concluded when Burney composed this minute, merely confirmed the territorial provisions of the Pantanaw document. But he was not to know that, for the news had yet to reach him. Nevertheless, when he came to write his final report on his mission several months later, he devoted a long paragraph to a recapitulation of the points made in his minute of 1 March. One suspects that he felt there was still a possibility that the project was not quite dead, and wanted to make sure that those in authority were sufficiently warned of the dangers involved in any attempt to resuscitate it. No attempt was ever made, and it may be that what Burney wrote merely helped to confirm a decision already taken before it reached those concerned in the matter. However, that may be, the historian is in his debt for valuable information unavailable elsewhere.

Burney's own treaty negotiations, which seemed likely to make real progress as a result of the news of the Burma cease-fire and the arrival in Bangkok of the Raja of Ligor, had come almost to a complete halt as a result of the defaulting serang's accusations. How seriously he saw the situation shows in the following entry in his Journal: 'It is hard that such a worthless character should be able to destroy in a few minutes, and with so much ease, the whole fabric of confidence and good will which had cost me an unremitting exertion of three months to raise.'[1]

Yet it was the Burma war, more than anything else, that dominated the situation. The news of the breakdown of the Pantanaw peace talks, which arrived on 27 February, had a much bigger real influence than any alarmist rumours in causing procrastination. Even the delivery of the draft treaty on 29 March,

[1] BP, I, 1, p. 199.

although it helped to clear the air, brought no immediate resumption of negotiations: the Ministers took three weeks to consider it before sending their reply. Then an outbreak of cholera at the capital provided an excuse for further delay, but with a difference: discussions would be resumed as soon as it abated, Phraya Phiphatkosa told the Envoy on 26 April.

News of the signing of the Yandabo Treaty must have arrived well before that date, but Burney is silent about it, probably because, as he writes in his final report, the termination of the Burma war had less effect than he had anticipated upon his negotiations. Copies of the treaty first reached Bangkok on 3 May.[1] They were brought by the Brig *Guardian*, and in Burney's view it was her arrival with the same number of guns and firearms as she had had when previously leaving Bangkok that finally exploded the myth of the expected British attack upon Siam.[2] For it was soon after this that the Ministers at long last and after repeated requests invited Burney to attend upon them in full session for the discussion of his treaty proposals. It was his fixed impression that it was the explosion of the myth of an impending British attack that was responsible for this turn of events. And it was a decisive change of direction, as we shall see. There were to be no further setbacks.

But the question naturally arises whether in this connexion one should not also take into consideration the possible effect of the arrival of the actual text of the Treaty of Yandabo, which the Brig brought with her. Burney at once delivered a Burmese copy of it to Phraya Phiphatkosa, who took it away for a Siamese translation to be prepared. The statement regarding the King of Siam's inclusion in the treaty seems to have puzzled the translators, for the Phraya referred it back to Burney for elucidation: was it, he asked, 'hereafter to receive good or bad'? Burney does not quote his reply to this, and one can easily imagine what he said, and how he said it. But he records further signs of Siamese mistrust. On 7 May Phraya Phiphatkosa called to say that the Court was instructing Maha Yotha to send 'trusty officers' to confer with Captain Fenwick, now transferred to the new British settlement at Amherst, not on the subject of boundaries, as Burney had so often urged, but to ask whether the war had really ended, and in accordance with the terms of the treaty. Burney felt sure that the Court confidently expected the Burmese to seize some opportunity of

[1] BP, I, 2, p. 275.   [2] BP, II, 4, p. 41.

The Raja of Ligor enters the Contest 95

committing 'some foul treachery' against the British. To his thinking therefore even the receipt of a copy of the treaty had little effect upon the Court's attitude. But was he right? The facts are that before the Court had received its copy it had made use of every excuse to postpone decisive talks around the conference table, but that quite soon after studying the document it had invited the Envoy to a meeting of Ministers on 13 May. Was this the last straw that broke the back of the opposition? Burney believed that it was the victory of fact over fantasy with the arrival of the Mission Brig alone and not at the head of an invading armada that was responsible for the subsequent turn of events. But was the Court as credulous as he was prone to think? He may well have been the victim of a campaign of delay to enable it to postpone committing itself in any way before it knew what the outcome of the Burma war would be. After all, although Burney never even suggests it, his *bête noire* the Phrakhlang could have instigated the serang and the more obscure rumourmongers to tell their stories.

In his final report Burney interprets the situation at the highest level as a struggle between two parties led respectively by the King and the Wangna.[1] The King's party he describes as 'intelligent, moderate, and really well disposed to cultivate friendly relations with the British Government'. Walter Vella, on the other hand, quotes a Siamese chronicle to the effect that the greatest obstacle to Burney's success lay in the opposition of Rama III himself, and that he was persuaded to change his mind by the Uparat, the Phrakhlang, the Governor of Nakorn Sithammarat (i.e. the Raja of Ligor) and Prince Surinthorarak, who argued that since the British by defeating Burma had come to occupy territories on Siam's frontier, a treaty of friendship with them had become essential.[2]

Burney, however, even goes so far as to say that the King was thought to favour the British demand for the reinstatement of the Sultan of Kedah. The Wangna, he says, who had 'special superintendence' over the southern part of the kingdom and hence received the revenues of Kedah, was so bitterly opposed to the Sultan's restoration that the subject 'irritated and exasperated'

---
[1] BP, II, 4, p. 42.
[2] In *Siam under Rama III*, p. 119, quoting Chaophraya Thiphakarawong, *The Royal Chronicle of the Third Reign of the Bangkok Dynasty* (in Siamese) written at the request of Rama IV, but unpublished until 1934.

him, and indeed to such an extent that he was said to have even proposed to the Ministers that Burney should be hanged for his presumption in plaguing the Court in the matter without authorization from the Governor-General. He adds that when the story first reached him, he ridiculed it, but that he mentioned it because it came from a normally trustworthy source. Unfortunately he gives no indication as to the composition of the two parties, and one is left with the impression that he is describing tendencies rather than parties in the strict sense. It is perhaps significant that his discussion belongs to the part of his report in which he is explaining that he had had to abandon the Sultan of Kedah's cause in order to save his treaty, an action, which he well knew at the time of writing, was strongly condemned by Governor Fullerton of Penang.

Was Burney as wrong in his assessment of the King, the Wangna and the Phrakhlang as the treatment of his mission in the Thiphakorawang chronicle would appear to indicate? One would hesitate to think so. His journal and its appended papers inspire confidence in his understanding and integrity. He seems to have had abundant sources of information, and his command of the language gave him unusual insight for a Westerner into Siamese thought processes. On the other hand Chao Phraya Thiphakorawang was Kham Bunnag, the son and ultimately the successor of Dit Bunnag, the Phrakhlang with whom both John Crawfurd and Burney had to deal. He wrote four chronicles, one for the reign of each of the first four Chakri kings. They are more concerned with the greatness of the Bunnags than with the other aspects of the reigns they deal with. The doings of the Bunnags are shown in the most favourable light.[1] To the people of Chulalongkorn's reign the Burney treaty of 1826 must have appeared as the first step in the new direction successfully pursued by Mongkut and his successor. How appropriate that a Bunnag should be shown as helping to persuade an unwilling king to take it. Later on in his reign the King did indeed become anti-Western in his attitude, so that it would be natural for a chronicler familiar with only the latter part of his life to assume that this had always been his attitude. The truth of the matter may be impossible to ascertain, but one would think that Burney's version of the story is preferable to the Bunnag one.

---

[1] On this subject see Constance M. Wilson, *State and Society in the Reign of Mongkut, 1851–1868: Thailand on the Eve of Modernization*, a Thesis presented for the degree of Doctor of Philosophy of Cornell University 1970, pp. 35–6.

Just before the opening of official treaty talks a little contretemps suddenly arose out of the activities of the Mission's interpreter, Mr. Leal. He, as we have seen above, had been left behind with Assistant Surgeon Harris at Ligor to accompany the Raja on his overland journey to the capital.[1] The Raja's party did not leave until 18 December and the long procession of some 4,000 men and 70 elephants made very slow progress through country which had to be cleared ahead of it by an advanced party. The route followed the coast and the two Englishmen were able to check up on Crawfurd's chart of that coast, which Burney had left with them for that purpose. Their activities caused both the Raja and the Court, to which he reported them, some apprehension. At Chumphorn he received orders which led him to impose some restraint upon them. Finally, on reaching Putti-hew, he sent them on by boat under the charge of the son of the local governor. That was on 27 January. They arrived at Bangkok on 31 January, three days ahead of the Raja himself.

Leal proved himself to be a man of parts. Burney speaks of his exceptionally good knowledge not only of the Siamese language but also of the customs of the country. He seems also to have carried out excellent survey work while accompanying the Raja of Ligor's party, and it was he and Harris who brought news of the large number of deportees for whom the Governor of Chumphorn had been responsible. After his arrival at Bangkok Leal had acted as Mate of the *Guardian*. The Ministers evidently saw him as a man to be reckoned with, and Burney was agreeably surprised when they accepted his proposal to place him in charge of the repatriation of the first batch of deportees to leave Bangkok. He had feared lest their belief that the British would take any opportunity that offered to discover overland routes into their country would lead them to refuse.

Leal accompanied the repatriated deportees to Mergui. On 20 March Burney received a letter from him written at Bangnarom describing their disembarkation there before making their way overland to their homes. Then he disappears from the Burney Papers until 8 May when he unexpectedly turned up at Bangkok bearing despatches from Mr. Maingy, the Commissioner of Tenasserim, and Captain Fenwick, the British Intelligence Officer at Martaban. The despatches he brought complained that the

[1] *Supra*, p. 36.

Siamese authorities at Chumphorn had sent back to Mergui only a very small number of the Burmese deportees under their charge, and Burney had to address a long memorial on the subject to the Phrakhlang. This, however, caused little trouble. What did cause real heartburn was firstly that Leal had inspected the whole line of the new Anglo-Siamese frontiers from the Mergui area northwards, and compiled a journal on the subject, and secondly that he had made the journey from Martaban to Bangkok in only 15 days, 'and found the route by no means difficult', according to Burney.[1]

On the very next day Phraya Phiphatkosa called on the Envoy with 'many complaints' against the inquisitive interpreter. He had refused to wait at Menam noi and again at Ratburi when requested to do so in order that due notice of his arrival could be sent to Bangkok, complained the official. 'The truth is', wrote Burney in his Journal, 'The Court is extremely vexed at Mr. Leal's having seen and travelled over so much of the interior of Siam, and if he had waited at Menam noi until accounts of his Arrival there had been received here, there is no question that he would never have been suffered to pass down.' (BP, I, 2, pp. 279–80.) Burney sent his apologies to the King for the interpreter's conduct, explaining that it was due to his haste to deliver the despatches with which he had been entrusted. He promised to warn Leal 'against offending again in the same manner'. One further point in Leal's report he noted with interest: he was emphatic that it would be extremely easy to open a navigable passage across the Isthmus of Kra between Pakchan and Chumphorn. This was a theme that in one form or another was to tantalize British and French prospectors in the latter part of the century. Burney, however, made no suggestions as to a possible follow-up of Leal's report, though he did note that he would consider later, when he had had time to study his Journal of his peregrinations, whether to forward a copy to the Governor of India. With his apology to the King the Leal incident closed. Very soon afterwards, on 13 May, Phraya Phiphatkosa called on him again, this time to invite him to the first of the formal treaty talks at the residence of Krommamun Surinthararak,[2] the King's uncle, who was in charge of the Krom Tha and the Mahatthai, and, as Burney puts it, exercised superintendence over the commercial and foreign relations of the kingdom. So to the treaty talks we now turn.

[1] BP, I, 2, p. 279. [2] *Supra*, pp. 46–7.

Chapter 6

The Negotiation of the Treaty

THE invitation to attend the full session of the Ministers to discuss the treaty was brought by Phraya Phiphatkosa on the afternoon of 13 May. The meeting was to begin at 8 p.m. at the residence of Prince Krommamun Surin on the following day. In anticipation of such a summons the Envoy had prepared a revised draft of his proposed treaty together with a memorial defining his attitude with regard to the matters at issue. These documents he handed to the Phraya for consideration by the Ministers before the opening of the talks. He also asked for a copy of their treaty proposals, which he understood had been revised. There were to be seven of these meetings, the early ones lasting long into the night and not ending until three o'clock in the morning. There was very hard bargaining, and Burney was forced to give way on a number of important points, though only after putting up a very hard fight. Sometimes tempers were frayed, and there were hot exchanges. But things never came to breaking point, and the credit for this must go largely to Burney, who could have quitted the conference table and sacrificed all the goodwill he had so patiently built up in the face of so much difficulty, but decided that the larger issues of Anglo-Siamese relations demanded a negotiated settlement rather than one dictated by threats, even though it meant abandoning the Sultan of Kedah and facing the wrath of the Penang authorities. The Siamese themselves showed great skill in negotiating, and this coupled with their immense caution tested Burney to the utmost. As he commented in his final report:

It is extremely difficult to persuade such a capricious and mistrustful Court as that of Siam to disclose its real views and feelings, and it is scarcely possible for a British negotiator to form any rational conjecture respecting grounds and motives of action which are not founded on the same modes of reasoning as would govern the conduct of a European Court.[1]

[1] BP, II, 4, p. 65.

It was perhaps to his advantage that he was too far away from Calcutta to be able to refer any matter to it for a decision; but it must have cost him untold anxiety. The main points upon which he took his stand in his memorial were first of all that Britain did not admit that the Malayan states of Trengganu and Kelantan were subject to Siam in the same way as Ligor and Singora were and therefore did not recognize Siam's right to invade them. She did recognize Siam's right to receive the bunga mas from them every three years, and was ready to engage that the troops of neither party to the treaty should invade or occupy these states.

Next, he made it clear that, notwithstanding all that had been said on the subject, he could not drop the Kedah question: the Brig *Guardian* had brought letters instructing him to represent the Sultan's case still more forcibly. Moreover, while at one time there were no disputes between the Penang people and the Kedah revenue farmers, now there were frequent disputes, and indeed the farmer at Kuala Muda had seized the property and boats of British subjects. The English would not submit to interference of such a kind. The Raja of Ligor, he said, had made a treaty to assist Burney in negotiating for the restoration of the Sultan. This had been ratified by the Governor-General of India. If it were not carried out, the effect on relations between the Raja's followers in Kedah and the people of Penang would be disastrous. The Government of India urged the King of Siam to put relations between Penang and the local Siamese officials beyond risk of collision. If the Sultan of Kedah were allowed to return home, Burney would see that he solicited forgiveness and that the annual stipend paid by Kedah to Siam were increased by a thousand or two thousand dollars.

Finally he turned to trade at Bangkok, which, he declared was more oppressed than before, so much so that the commander of the American vessel recently there had proclaimed that he would not return there and would spread abroad the misconduct of the Siamese officers. Foreigners, said Burney, spoke well of the Phrakhlang and Phraya Phiphatkosa but blamed their subordinates for all the trouble, and particularly Phraya Chula and his son Khun Rachasethi. These officers gave 'infinite trouble' and did all the mischief that caused foreign vessels to avoid a second visit to Bangkok. He had received, he went on, a detailed list from the Phrakhlang of the port and anchorage charges levied on the ship

The Negotiation of the Treaty

Hunter. 'In this list many Clerks, Godown Keepers, Weighmen, Letters, Interpreters and their Clerks, and about 10 passes are charged for; while Mr. Hunter never saw more than two Clerks and one Weighman, and they attended for scarcely four hours a day, and he was often obliged to go and call them himself.'[1] Hence, after seeing this list, how could he possibly raise his offer of 1,500 ticals per fathom of breadth for each English ship? He had, however, abandoned his proposal for a reduction to 1,000 ticals for the second, third or fourth visits within the same year. On the other hand, he had added a clause to the eleventh article permitting English merchants to go to certain districts where sugar was manufactured and buy what they required, and inserted a twelfth article to the Regulations for facilities to be granted for British subjects to engage in shipbuilding in Siam.

Shortly after 8 p.m. we repaired to the Palace of Krom Meun Surin, where every preparation appeared to have been made for an important debate. On either side of the Prince were seated the Chakri, Kalahom, Tharama and Prah Klang, and a little below them were Phya Kray, Phya Si-Phi Phut, the Rajas of Ligor and Singora, and several other Officers. We sat down in the middle of the Hall of Audience near Phya Phi-phut, who was the channel of communication between my Interpreters and the Prince and Ministers.

In such laconic terms does Burney describe the opening of the treaty talks on the evening of 14 May. The list of Ministers present shows that they were at the highest possible level, and thus a token of the importance attached to them by the Court of Siam. Krommamun Surinthararak, who presided over them, was the twenty-ninth child of King Rama I, the founder of the dynasty.[2] He was thus uncle to the reigning monarch, but also through his mother, who was a Bunnag uncle to the Phrakhlang and Burney noted that the conversations were carried on with him almost entirely by the Prince, the Phrakhlang and the Raja of Ligor.

The Kedah question was the first topic of discussion and Burney at once found himself—as indeed he must have expected—up against a brick wall of opposition. As he puts it:

I used every Argument in my power to persuade the Ministers of the justice, humanity and policy of restoring our Ally, the Ex-King. I pointed out the great mutual benefits which such an arrangement would

[1] BP, I, 2, p. 302.　　[2] See *supra*, p. 47.

afford to both the Siamese and English Nations; the certainty of our friendship remaining unbroken and the security and cordiality which such a concession on the part of Siam would give to our future intercourse. I argued, flattered and even threatened, but I am sorry to say I made no impression.

It was, of course, useless to argue: the Sultan had committed the unforgivable sin. He had engaged in treasonable correspondence with the Burmese. The Ministers on their part tried to assure Burney that they would settle the future government of Kedah so as to ensure friendly intercourse with Penang, and they asked whether he was prepared to throw away all the other advantages they were prepared to grant merely for the sake of the Sultan's restoration. The argument went on and on for a long time, with growing irritation on both sides. At last, when it was obvious that an impasse had been reached, it was decided to shelve it for the time being.

Next came the question of Siam's relations with the Malayan states. Burney refused to discuss Perak's case, maintaining that Siam had no right to interfere in that state. On the other hand there was much argument over Kelantan and Trengganu. Burney was willing to accept that they belonged to the category of states which sent the *bunga mas* to Siam as a token of respect and in order to secure her goodwill, but argued that this did not involve any loss of independence. And he warned that the British Government 'could not possibly view with indifference' any attempt Siam might make to treat these states in the same manner as she had dealt with Kedah. There was naturally a great deal of argument about Siam's rights over these states with Burney seeking to give his government the right to protect them from any arbitrary interference by Siam and the Ministers insisting upon Siam's supremacy over them. No agreement seemed possible, but Burney uttered a firm warning that the British Government would not admit the right of Siam to occupy the two states.

One further matter was discussed at this first meeting, the form of the treaty itself. There were two documents on the table, one composed by Burney in English and translated into Siamese, the other composed by the Ministers and, of course, in Siamese; not, however, the first draft that they had served on Burney, but a revised one. He describes both drafts as 'very curious documents'. Nevertheless, although he considered his own draft treaty 'accorded more with what was necessary to be done', and told the Ministers so, he agreed to accept their version as the basis for the treaty. He records no argument on the subject; his decision was made because he was of opinion that they 'would place more confidence in a document which they themselves had drawn up'. He relied upon being able to persuade them to accept very considerable amendments, and in this he was not mistaken. He made literal translations of both ministerial drafts, adding to the second notes of the revisions he managed to get the Ministers to accept, and sent them to Calcutta 'in order to afford my Superiors the best possible conception of the character, views and feelings of the Court of Siam'.[1]

In the long fruitless discussion of the Kedah question Burney became aware that, as he puts it, his 'most sturdy opponent' was the Raja of Ligor, who even went so far as to deny categorically the facts which he mentioned regarding the numbers of refugees who had left Kedah and the 'mischievous interruptions' to the trade between Penang and Kedah occasioned by his own officers. The indignant Envoy accordingly on the following day sent a message to the Raja warning him that his conduct would ruin him in the estimation of the Government of India, and that at the next conference he, Burney, would not hesitate 'to expose the whole of his proceedings at Queda'.

The second session of the conference therefore promised to be a stormy one, as indeed proved to be the case. It opened at 8 p.m. at Krommamun Surin's residence and the Ministers at once opened the attack on the subject of Siam's relations with the Malayan states. They handed Burney an article on the subject which they proposed to substitute for the one which he had proposed at the previous session. It restated Siam's 'most arrogant pretensions' in a way that he found not only most objectionable but even ludicrous; for one of its points was that these states must not treat Siam with disrespect. Who was to decide 'what the Siamese chose to consider as disrespect'? he asked, and he rejected the proposed substitution.

They then went on to read through the rest of the treaty, and Burney proposed a number of additions and alterations. The Raja of Ligor, he noticed, was avoiding as much as possible participating in the discussions, but was prompting the Phrakhlang instead. He therefore seized a convenient opportunity for carrying out his threat. To savour the piquancy of the scene Burney's own description

[1] BP, I, 2, p. 284.

of it is essential. He pointed out to the Ministers, he tells us,

> in very strong terms, the serious collision His Highness had nearly brought on with the British Government, by refusing to apprize Mr. Maingy, when deputed by the Honourable the Govenor of Penang to enquire, the object of the armament which had been collected at Queda, and the mischievous proceedings of his Emissaries at Penang, where the name and character of the Raja of Ligor, I stated, I was sorry to declare, were held in such terror by the Native and such abhorrence by the European inhabitants, that I feared the relations between Penang and Queda could never be placed upon a quiet and satisfactory footing, so long as His Highness or any of his family governed the territory of Queda. I urged the Ministers to recommend to His Majesty to appoint some Malayan Chief to rule Queda, if the ex-King could not be restored. The Raja of Ligor seemed to feel keenly the severity of my animadversions. The Ministers declared, that His Majesty would send persons to enquire of the principal inhabitants of Queda, whom they would prefer for their future Govenor, in lieu of the ex-King. I recommended that the Officers deputed to make this enquiry at Queda, should be sent via Penang and not via Ligor. I pressed the Ministers again to restore our Ally the ex-King, and it was not until the discussion became angry on both sides, and I was satisfied of the impolicy of further perseverance that I yielded the point, upon condition that certain facilities should be stipulated in the Treaty to be given to the trade and intercourse between Penang and Queda, and that His Majesty of Siam should make such an arrangement with respect to the future government of Queda, as to preclude all chance of collision of disturbance between that country and Penang.[1]

Burney's strong outburst must have made quite an impression upon his hearers, though to get the record straight it must be borne in mind that it was whispered in English to the interpreters who in turn whispered its translation in Siamese to the Ministers and that their replies were subject to the same procedure. In the highest circles in Siam no one ever raised his voice. The Ministers seem to have listened to his strictures on the Raja of Ligor's methods with remarkable restraint. Burney himself gives the highest credit for this to Krommamun Surin. 'He showed an intelligence and moderation that surprised us all,' he writes. 'He repeatedly saw and acknowledged the fairness and justice of a proposition made by me, when no other Siamese in the room could apprehend it; and whenever the discussion was becoming irritating, he strove to

[1] BP, I, 2, pp. 285–6.

The Negotiation of the Treaty

restore all parties to reason and quiet.' (*Ibid.*, p. 287.) But seeing the fairness of a proposition was quite a different thing from accepting it; it was part of the technique of bending before the wind so characteristic of Siamese diplomacy. It was the Ministers, not Burney, who were negotiating from strength. They knew pretty well how far they intended to go with him, which means to say that they were just as aware as he was of the weakness of his bargaining position. One might hazard the guess that the uppermost thought in the Raja of Ligor's mind, when Burney was exposing his methods, was that in order to succeed next time he must devise less obvious ones. When Burney finished what he had to say the Phrakhlang rounded off the discussion with the remark that if he would only stop pressing the Ministers on the Kedah issue, he could have all that he wanted in the case of the commercial clauses of the treaty, even to the fixed payment of 1,500 ticals per fathom of breadth on English vessels. Then the atmosphere cleared and Burney was asked which language should be used for the official version of the treaty. He proposed both Siamese and English; but the Ministers were opposed to an official English version. The Phrakhlang said that none of them would know what Burney might write in the English version, and Burney sensed that they did genuinely fear lest later on the British might put 'unwarrantable constructions' upon parts of the treaty. Accordingly, he gave way, and it was agreed that the document should be written in three languages, Siamese, English and Malay. This pleased the Ministers much, he writes, and it was also agreed that he should in due course call upon the Phrakhlang to draft the new set of port regulations to go with the treaty. The latter assured him that these should be in accordance with his wishes. So at 3 a.m. after seven hours of argument and recrimination goodwill was restored and the weary contestants dispersed to their various abodes.

The third session of the conference was not held until 26 May. This was largely because of the arrival of a Vietnamese envoy bringing with him a number of Siamese who had been shipwrecked off the coast of Cochin-China. The Phrakhlang had to hurry away to Paknam on 17 May to meet the new arrival and detain him there until his business was completed. Burney learnt that he was not to be permitted to come to the capital, partly for fear lest the British mission might get into touch with him. He was very busy at the time dealing with deportee matters. He also took advantage of the break to send off another chunk of his Journal and duplicates of other papers, including the second draft of the Ministers' treaty proposals with his notes, to Singapore for transmission by the Resident to Governor Fullerton at Penang.[1]

Also during this period Burney paid a visit to Maha Yotha and found him much to his taste, though the old soldier refused to be drawn on a number of questions about his failure to co-operate with the British when he was in the neighbourhood of Martaban in the previous year. He made no reply when Burney made the somewhat puerile remark that had he joined the British he might now be the head of a restored kingdom of Pegu; but he was willing to give details of his family history, mentioning that his father had been governor of Martaban under the last Mon dynasty, and that after its overthrow by the Burmese his father had lived for some time at Martaban privately before migrating with his whole family to Siam. When that happened he himself had been thirteen years old; he was now nearly sixty. Burney noted with appreciation his very animated manner of speaking, quite different from that of a Siamese. Captain Macfarquhar, who accompanied Burney, said he reminded him of Sir David Ochterlony, famous for his campaigns against the Gurkhas in Nepal in 1814–16, who had died in the previous year. On the next day they learnt that two members of the treaty conference, Phraya Kray and Phraya Thep, had listened in to the conversation concealed in an adjoining room. Hence his wary refusal to be drawn when twitted with his failure to co-operate with the British.

When the third session of the treaty conference assembled at the usual time on 26 May it at once became obvious that the negotiations had reached a critical stage, and that the Kedah question had to be resolved before any further decisions could be taken. In his despatch of 31 March he had turned the matter over to the Government of India. But Mr. Leal had met the messengers carrying the missive at Ratburi as late as 5 May on their way towards Martaban, and Burney calculated that at the rate they were travelling they would have only reached that place by the time he had expected to receive the Government of India's reply. So now he was faced with the responsibility of making the decision himself. He writes in his Journal: 'After much discussion and altercation, I found I should not be justified in a perseverance to effect the

[1] BP, I, ii, pp. 237 and 310–19.

removal of the Siamese from the territories of Kedah.'[1] It was a very hard decision to make, and was taken only after what he calls 'unceasing meditation for many days.' He indicates that he was influenced by the fact that a year earlier the Government of India had expressed the view to the Penang authorities that unless it could offer to cede Tavoy or Mergui the Siamese would never be persuaded to give up Kedah, and that it was not prepared to offer such an inducement. As we have seen above (p. 25) he was under no illusions as to what this meant; and now he was painfully aware that he had 'no equivalent to offer the Ministers in lieu of Kedah'. The alternative, which he considered and rejected, was to be prepared to abandon the conference and leave the country, in the belief that the Court of Siam would give in to his demand for the reinstatement of the Sultan rather than let him depart. He was inclined to think that it would do so, but was uncertain; and since his instructions contained no express authorization for such action, he decided that the risk was too great. And he felt that even if he did prevail upon an unwilling Court to give way in the matter, it would be so dissatisfied that the improvement in commercial relations envisaged in the treaty would prove ineffectual.

Therefore, as he puts it, he was obliged to propose that his government should permit Kedah to remain in Siamese hands and prevent the Sultan or any of his supporters from disturbing the country. He laid down a number of conditions. The Sultan's family and personal servants were to be released and sent to Penang; intercourse between Penang and Kedah was to be unrestricted; the export of supplies from Kedah for the population of Penang and the shipping there was to be subject to no duties or other charges; and the evil system of farming out the rivers of Kedah, that had been introduced by the Siamese, was to be abolished and instead fair import and export duties on the transit of merchandise substituted.

There was strong opposition on the part of the Raja of Ligor and the Phrakhlang to the free export of supplies from Kedah to Penang. They called upon the Governor of Singora to join them in assuring Burney that for many years the Sultan had charged the British authorities a heavy duty on grain. But Burney knew he was on safe ground in this matter, and he refused to budge. The third article of the British treaty with Kedah stipulated that there should be no

[1] BP, I, 3, p. 322.

duty of any kind on provisions exported for the use of Penang or of British warships or East India Company's ships there. On the following day he sent a copy of the treaty to the Raja of Ligor. He was equally firm in insisting upon the insertion in the treaty of a clause prohibiting the opening of mail addressed to British subjects in Siam; he brushed aside the objections raised by the Ministers.

Then he turned to the article in the Treaty of Yandabo in which the King of Siam, subject to his consent, was included in the peace made with Burma. He reminded the Ministers that if the King wished to avail himself of the benefits offered by this article, he must let the British Government know as soon as possible; moreover, he must give orders to his frontier officers against committing any sort of aggression against the Burmese. The Ministers, however, were against doing anything in the matter; he was up against a brick wall. He sensed that now that Burma was so much weaker through her defeat by the British, they felt disposed to avail themselves of opportunities to attack their old enemy; he learnt, indeed, that a party of Siamese had already raided the Sittang district and carried away some prisoners. So that matter had to be dropped.

Just before the meeting ended the Phrakhlang brought up the matter of Perak; he asked for a British guarantee that the Raja should send the *bunga mas* to Siam. Burney flatly refused to discuss any such matter, and with that the session ended. Not so, however, the Phrakhlang's efforts over the Perak issue, though for the moment they were held up by the death of the mother of the previous king, which brought all public business to a halt for a few days. 'The principal Officers of the Court have entirely shaved their heads,' Burney noted in his Journal, 'and an order has been issued for the whole of the female population of Siam to do the same.'

On 30 May the Phrakhlang returned to the attack. He sent an invitation to Burney to meet the Ministers again on the following evening but at the same time indicated that unless the Envoy was prepared to give way on the subject of Perak there would be no point in holding the meeting. In face of such a clumsy attempt at intimidation Burney returned a reply in the most forcible terms that occurred to him. If any Siamese went to Perak to interfere in its government, he wrote, he would do his utmost to persuade the Raja to hang him. On the next day, when he saw the Phrakhlang, the latter seemed 'unusually sullen and discontented'; he told Burney that he had broken his heart by sending such a reply to his message. Burney, quite unabashed, told him that the message had been an attempt to bully him, which was quite the wrong method to use with an English envoy. He advised him not to try it again. The Phrakhlang then said that the Ministers had postponed their next session with Burney until 2 June.

Burney was now thoroughly allerted to the Court's determination to challenge him on the subject of Perak. He therefore took the initiative by sending a message to the Raja of Ligor 'urging him as a sincere well-wisher' to abandon all designs of interference in Perak. The Raja replied that it was the Ministers who were unwilling to relinquish Siam's claims to Perak: he himself had no particular feelings in the matter, and in order to prove this would absent himself from the next session of the conference. This, of course, proved nothing, and subsequent events, one may remark, were to give the lie to his protestation.

When the fourth session opened at the Krommamun Surin residence, the Raja was duly absent when the Phrakhlang opened the expected attack by calling upon the Envoy 'to make some concession to Siam' regarding Perak. Burney's reaction must be told in his own words.

I observed that if the Rajah of Perak had sent the *Boonga Mas* to Siam in former times, or that if he wished even now to send that token of respect to Siam, the British Government would not think of forbidding him. But that since my arrival in Siam I had discovered, that the attack which the Rajah of Kedah had made upon Perak by orders from Siam, was one of the most wanton and unjustifiable acts I had ever heard of, and that Mr. Anderson, the gentleman who had been deputed last year to Perak and Salengore, had satisfactorily ascertained, that the Rajah of Perak had no desire whatever of sending the *Boonga Mas* to Siam, or of continuing any relation with the Rajah of Ligore. When this last fact was doubted, I produced the letters which Luang Packdee Sombat wrote to Perak by order of the Rajah of Ligore, and after explaining them I enquired whether the Rajah of Perak, if he had desired to live under Siam, would ever have delivered letters of such a tenor as these were to the British Agent. I commented on the impertinent language of these documents, and upon the improper conduct of the Rajah of Ligore in sending such letters to Perak after he had concluded the Provisional Treaty with me.

These letters I saw, produced a great impression upon the Prince and

Ministers. They asked me if we possessed the originals, and upon my answering in the negative, the Prince and Ministers recovered themselves, and when they further learnt that the letters were in the Malayan language, they declared, that they had no doubt the translations were incorrect, and that the phrases used in them were evidently not Siamese.

The tone of this last paragraph is delicious. Burney describes the scene to perfection, and with an economy of words which reveals the literary skill he was able to command. It surpasses that of any other British envoy to a South-East Asian court. His stand over Perak was successful: the Phrakhlang dropped the matter and passed on to the next item on the agenda. Burney makes no further mention of it in his Journal. His victory, however, was not a complete one, as a glance through his translation of the fourteenth, and last, article of the treaty serves to show. Both sides engage that the Raja shall govern his state 'according to his own will'. Should he desire to send the *Bunga Mas* to Siam, the English will not prevent him from doing so. All that is quite in accord with Burney's stipulations. But the next part of the article, which Burney had to accept, had dangerous implications. It runs:

If Chao Phya of Ligor desire to send down to Perak, with friendly intention, forty or fifty men whether Siamese, Chinese or other Asiatic subjects of Siam, or if the Rajah of Perak desire to send any of his Ministers or Officers to seek Chao Phya of Ligor, the English shall not forbid them. The Siamese or English shall not send any force to go and molest, attack or disturb Perak.

Did Burney realize the kind of use the Raja could make of a loophole such as this? He makes no comments on the subject. Luckily for the independence of the Raja of Perak, however, Governor Fullerton of Penang saw quite clearly what was to be expected from Ligor and took effective measures to prevent it, more than effective as it turned out; and he claimed that his actions were entirely within the limits of the Burney Treaty, for if the British were not to forbid parties of Siamese subjects being sent into Perak with friendly intention, the natural corollary was that, if the intention was not friendly, they were no longer debarred from action of that kind. This, however, will be dealt with in due course. Now we must return to the treaty discussions.

When Burney showed that he would not yield on the Perak issue, the Phrakhlang next took up the question of Trengganu and

[1] BP, I, 3, pp. 328–9.

Kelantan. He said that the King wanted the Envoy either to accept the Ministers' proposal regarding them or modify his own proposal so as to make it more precise. Their obligation to send the *bunga mas* to Siam was not in dispute. What Burney was concerned about was whether Siam had the right to interfere in their internal affairs. It was, of course, hopeless to expect the Ministers to accept any denial of that right. Burney therefore sought to achieve his objective indirectly through an agreement regarding commerce. He proposed that Siam should engage not to interrupt British commerce with the two states, that British subjects should trade with them in the same manner as in the past, and that the British should not attack or molest them in any way. It was an astute move. The Ministers 'after some consideration' accepted the proposal. Burney himself thought it a better solution to the problem than the one he had suggested when the talks began.[1] A Siamese attack upon either state would clearly interrupt British commerce and would therefore constitute an infringement of the article; so he argued. Later, when the vagueness of the article was strongly attacked by Governor Fullerton, Burney was to defend its wording on precisely those grounds.

That was the end of the political discussions regarding the Malayan states. Two more sessions, on 6 and 16 June respectively, dealt with the commercial clauses and the remainder of the treaty. At the first of these strong exception was taken to the Sultan of Kedah being allowed to continue to reside in Penang, and Burney agreed that the East India Company should pledge itself that he would not be permitted to remain there, or to take up residence in Province Wellesley, Perak, Selangor or 'any Burmese country'. This was only reasonable, for since the proclaimed object of the treaty was to establish friendly relations between the East India Company and Siam, it was essential that the deposed sultan should not be allowed to abuse the protection accorded him by the British by making Penang a base for attempts to recover control over his former state. And this, one presumed, is precisely what Burney had in mind in accepting the Ministers' proposal. Unfortunately, however, he had earlier agreed that the British should prevent the sultan or any of his supporters from disturbing Kedah, and in the thirteenth article of the treaty this stipulation appears without any reservation as to where the sultan might be residing

[1] *Supra*, p. 100.

when making an attempt to regain power. And although Burney, when challenged, declared that it meant that the British were pledged to assist Siam against an attempt by the sultan to liberate his state only if it were made while he was living in British territory[1] this was not the view of Governor Fullerton and the Penang authorities, who roundly denounced him for so complete a surrender to the Siamese. Without doubt he had slipped up rather badly in failing to realize the full implications of what he had agreed to, for that must be what had happened. It was a regrettable oversight, and, unfortunately, had regrettable consequences in terms of British obligations to Siam over Kedah as interpreted by the Penang authorities subsequently. One may question, however, whether they would not have been better advised to have accepted, and acted upon, Burney's own version of those obligations.

Having won their point regarding the ex-Sultan's place of residence, the Ministers returned to the subject of the free importation of grain to Penang, about which Burney had made his stand at the third session of the conference after he had abandoned the cause of the ex-Sultan of Kedah. They had proposed a duty of 16 dollars on each 'coyan' or cartload of 80 baskets exported from Kedah. Burney had told them that this was very exorbitant, and, more important still, that the unrestricted importation of supplies to Penang was one of the chief motives of the British in pressing for the restoration of the Sultan. They now offered him various concessions all of which he rejected. Things then reached an impasse, and the Phraklang again disappeared from the scene to travel down to Paknam 'to dismiss finally' the envoy from Vietnam. He, it seems, was using every possible argument to be permitted to come to Bangkok, ostensibly to indulge in some private trade on his own account, but really, according to Burney's information, to find out all he could about the British mission.

After his departure the Raja of Ligor assumed the task of mediator. He sent a message to Burney to say that the Phraklang had been ordered by the King to stay only two days at Paknam, and to advise him to ask for another meeting of the conference as soon as he returned. The King, he went on to say, was 'really well disposed' towards the British Mission and had determined to let Burney have his way regarding the duties on grain from Kedah and upon British shipping at Bangkok. A few days later, on the day

[1] Burney MSS, D, IX, in Mills, *op. cit.*, p. 153.

The Negotiation of the Treaty

before the next session, which was fixed for 16 June, the Raja essayed to take the softening-up process a stage further. He sent another message 'entreating me to soothe and flatter the Prince and Ministers as much as possible, at our next meeting, and advising me to address them myself in the Siamese language as much as possible. He stated that they are much pleased to hear my attempts to speak their language, and that nothing but a few compliments were now necessary for me to secure all that I desired.'[1]

When the conference re-assembled on the following day, Burney not only carried out his instructions to the full, paying 'the handsomest compliments' to the Prince, but went on to preach a little homily in the style of Adam Smith, on the virtues of reducing the duty on ships to 1,500 ticals per fathom of breadth, and asking whether it were not better for ten ships to come annually at the reduced rate than the present two or three at the existing much higher one. He rounded it off by 'extolling the virtues and enlightened character' of King Rama III. 'My address appeared to soften even the Phrakhlang', he wrote in his Journal. Yet, when he took up the argument, he showed himself able to bargain just as sturdily as ever. He told Burney that his calculations had not taken into account Indian vessels sailing under English colours which also would benefit from his plan, and insisted that 1,500 ticals represented too great a reduction under such circumstances. The argument went on for two hours, and Burney had finally to accept the figure of 1,700 ticals, where a vessel flying English colours brought an import cargo, and 1,500 where it did not. So the Raja of Ligor's prediction that 'with a little soft language' in Siamese he would get all that he desired proved somewhat illusory. He comforted himself with having secured agreement that these amounts were to be in lieu of every other charge.

The Raja himself also joined in the game of whittling away Burney's proposals. He proposed the reduction of the previously mooted duty on the importation of grain from Kedah to Penang to 8 ticals per *coyan* on milled rice and 4 ticals on paddy, and again Burney was forced to give way. In this case the outcome was a compromise whereby the duty was to be levied while the ex-Sultan of Kedah remained in Penang, but would cease upon his removal.

It was a long session, lasting until 4 o'clock in the morning.

[1] BP, I, 3, p. 333.

They went through the schedule of forms and regulations to be observed by British vessels visiting Bangkok. Most of them were in the schedule attached to Burney's draft treaty: he had accepted them as being the established practice of the port. Of the additional ones Burney strongly opposed one making British subjects liable to the death penalty or whipping for offences which carried such penalties under Siamese law. He contended that since British subjects were quite ignorant of Siamese law the clause should specify the actual offences carrying the death penalty, and this was agreed to. With regard to whipping, he said it was not the English custom to flog ships' officers or merchants, but to fine them. This amendment was also accepted subject to the proviso that a seaman or lascar should be whipped or imprisoned in accordance with the requirements of Siamese law. The age of extraterritoriality had yet to come, one may note. It is interesting also that nothing is said of the old system, which held in seventeenth-century Ayuthaya, whereby foreign merchants lived in communities the chief man of which was responsible to the Phrakhlang for their internal discipline, and for assisting the authorities in cases involving any of their members.[1]

There was one offence, said the Phrakhlang, that in Siamese eyes was even worse than murder, and that was speaking disrespectfully of the King. Burney, bearing in mind Alexander Hamilton's account of his narrow escape from such a charge for saying that the King of Siam had been imposed upon, replied that he had no power to engage that British subjects should incur the death penalty for such an offence, adding, however, that he could not imagine anyone speaking disrespectfully 'of so great and enlightened a prince as the present Monarch of Siam'. The matter was settled by his agreement that the Governor-General of India should forbid British subjects going to Siam to speak disrespectfully of any of the great officers.

Then, having referred to the provision in the treaty for British subjects to buy and sell freely, the Phrakhlang intimated that this included the right to send natives of the country to the sugar districts to purchase sugar. He also held out the prospect of British subjects being permitted to engage in shipbuilding at Bangkok 'when the new relations between the Siamese and the English

[1] The matter is referred to in G. William Skinner, *Chinese Society in Thailand*, pp. 13–14.

The Negotiation of the Treaty 115

became well established'. These points were not specifically laid down in the treaty, and Burney decided not to press for their inclusion. His main attention, he writes,[1] was directed to the task of making the phraseology of the paper of forms and regulations, which he had received from the Ministers, as clear and precise as possible, for he found he could not rely upon either his own or the Court interpreters to do so. And in this task his own knowledge of Siamese, little though it was, he confesses, proved invaluable.

Finally it was arranged that the treaty document should be written in three columns in Siamese, Malay and English respectively and sealed with the seals of each of the Ministers and of Burney, that Burney should take one copy to Calcutta for ratification by the Government of India and return within five months to deliver it to the Raja of Ligor's son in Kedah, in exchange for another ratified by the King of Siam and bearing his seal, and, when the exchange had been carried out, the Raja of Ligor would release the family and servants of the ex-Sultan of Kedah.

This, however, was far from the end of the negotiations. In his covering letter of 19 June to the Government of India when forwarding an instalment of his Journal covering the period from 31 March onwards, he wrote that a perusal of that document would enable them to realize how much patience and perseverance were still requisite before a treaty could be concluded, and warned that until the document was actually sealed it would be imprudent 'to consider any object as attained'.[2] On that same day a further difficulty did, indeed, arise. A message came from the Phrakhlang asking him to call on him, and on arrival he found him struggling with the difficulty, as he saw it, of his king, a sovereign ruler, making a treaty with the East India Company, a non-sovereign body. He insisted that the King of England's name must be inserted in the treaty. Burney, however, tried to explain that as he had not been deputed to Siam by the king, he could not make a treaty in his name. The East India Company, he said, governed British India under the authority of the King and Parliament of England, and made war, carried out negotiations and concluded treaties in India in its own name. Hence, he suggested, the treaty should be shown as having been made between the King of Siam and the Honourable East India Company who governed British India under the authority of the King and Parliament of England.

[1] Journal, para. 206, BP, I, 3, p. 337.   [2] BP, I, 3, p. 371.

This seemed far from satisfactory to the Phrakhlang, and he kept Burney arguing for some hours about the British constitution and the powers and duties respectively of the monarch, parliament and the East India Company. He annoyed Burney by asking what the latter considered to be frivolous questions such as what kind of carriages did the various people in authority use,[1] and showed 'with his usual arrogance and ignorance' that he did not believe what the other was trying to explain to him. 'The Phra Klang', wrote Burney in his Journal, 'in all his conversations with me never hesitates to let me see his belief that I am telling untruths, whenever I attempt to describe anything of which he has never heard before.'[2]

Stymied on this front, the harassed Envoy accordingly went straight to the Raja of Ligor and explained the difficulty. The Raja took down in writing all that he had to say and promised to report it to the King and Ministers. Burney then went home and on the following day wrote out in Siamese a brief account of the British constitution and sent it to the Phrakhlang. Soon afterwards the Raja sent some of his officers to ask Burney a number of questions, which he was given to understand were posed by the King himself. They were of a quite different nature from the Phrakhlang's. 'His Majesty asked whether the Office of East India Director is hereditary, whether a Member of Parliament possesses any power individually or only when he is joined with the other Members and seated in Parliament, whether the East India Company pays any revenue or tribute to the King of England and whether the succession to the Crown is hereditary.' Burney jotted down the comment that next to the Raja of Ligor he considered the King to be the most intelligent man in his dominions, and certainly the one most anxious to establish friendly relations between the Siamese and the British.

The difficulty was eventually disposed of in the preamble to the treaty by the King and Wangna being described as having commanded the Ministers to assemble and frame a treaty with Captain Henry Burney, the English Envoy, on the part of the English Government. He, in turn, was shown as having been deputed by

[1] Professor Wyatt comments that these questions were not frivolous, but the kind of questions Thai would ask to determine the rank and status of a ruler. 'Thai society was heavily laden with such sumptuary restrictions and privileges.'
[2] BP, I, 3, p. 343.

The Negotiation of the Treaty

the Honourable East India Company, who governed the English possessions in India under the authority of the King and Parliament of England, and by Lord Amherst, Governor of Bengal, and other English officers of high rank. Thus the English translation of the treaty, but in his Journal Burney substitutes 'the Right Honourable the Governor General in Council' for Lord Amherst and the officers of high rank.[1]

It was next the Raja of Ligor's turn to embarrass Burney by suggesting additions to the treaty which he found highly undesirable. He asked that a clause be inserted to forbid British troops, in future warfare with the Burmese, from destroying or plundering religious edifices, and a second one permitting him to purchase arms and warlike stores at Penang whenever he needed them. With regard to the first he said that the King and Court viewed with 'the utmost horror' the treatment of temples and images in Burma by British troops. Burney was acutely aware that the Siamese, professing the same form of Buddhism as the Burmese, had been easy victims to stories of this kind just as they had been earlier to stories of impending British attacks upon their country. He replied that such a clause would tend to cast unjust reflection upon the British troops in Burma and the British Government itself, seeing that it had always been its custom in wars in India to show the greatest respect for the religion and religious buildings of the enemy. He begged the Raja to assure the King and Ministers that the stories they had heard must be gross distortions of the facts.[1]

With regard to the second matter Burney, knowing well how troublesome it had proved to his predecessor, John Crawfurd, was most unwilling to commit himself in any way. He argued that there were serious objections to the inclusion of such a stipulation in a treaty of friendship, and suggested an innocuous clause to the effect that should the Raja of Ligor need to purchase arms and warlike stores, he should apply to the Governor of Penang, who would let him have such supplies as might seem right and proper. To Burney's relief both proposals were dropped. In the case of the second, however, he found himself in agreement with Crawfurd's view that if British merchants were prohibited from selling arms to the Siamese, they would acquire them from the Americans or other foreigners, who would thereby gain not merely greater

[1] BP, I, 3, p. 349.

commercial profit, but also a warmer welcome from the Siamese.

The treaty discussions were now at an end, and on 25 June Burney called upon the Raja of Ligor to hear the Siamese version read over preparatory to its translation into Malay. He was then requested to scrutinize the Malay version. It was a very troublesome task, for in the articles relating to Kedah and Perak he found what he describes as gross inaccuracies. One may guess their nature, of course, though he offers no clue to it. When he pointed them out to the Raja, the latter accepted his corrections in nearly every case. He is very scornful of the methods of the Malayan interpreters.

I insisted upon the whole of the King and Wangna's Bali titles being put down in the same words, [he writes in his journal] for the Malayan Interpreters made sad trash [sic] of them in their language, and one or two other Siamese words, the precise meaning of which these Interpreters would not give, which is down in the Siamese language in their Copy of the Treaty, were set in many places a spurious and Ligor dialect of the Malayan tongue, arising principally from the anxiety of Translators to give a corresponding word for every word and for the component parts even of every derivative and compound word, in the Siamese original.[1]

One slight amendment, proposed by the Raja and accepted by Burney during this discussion, extended the period from five to seven months within which he was to obtain the Governor-General's ratification of the treaty, and return with the document to Kedah. They also agreed to add a clause to the treaty by which the Siamese stipulations regarding Kedah and Perak were to be carried out when the Raja returned from Bangkok to Ligoi. He expected to be detained some weeks after Burney's departure from the capital. The delay, it may be mentioned, had vital effects quite unforeseen by the Raja, upon the situation of the west coast of Malaya, for it provided the ever-alert Governor Fullerton of Penang with the opportunity to make a decisive move which completely, and finally, upset the Raja's carefully laid plans for the subjection of Perak.

The trouble which the scrutiny of the Malay version of the treaty cost Burney was nothing to the embarrassment, as he describes it, of preparing the English version. His dilemma must

[1] Ibid., p. 349.

be expressed in his own words, even at the expense of a long quotation from his Journal.

The whole of the Treaty had been discussed and originally written in the Siamese language, a language full of repetitions and pleonasms. Were I to make a translation of it with reference to the idioms of the English language, and such a translation as would bear the criticisms of Europeans, I should have to retrench nearly one half of the original Siamese, and as this Court, jealous and suspicious at all times, would I knew, submit my translation to its Interpreters, to the Portuguese Consul, or to any other persons who may hereafter visit the Country, any omission or reduction of sentences in the English version would appear to have been made with some evil intention, and would tend to destroy the whole value of the Treaty. I had provided myself with Siamese and Portuguese versions of the public Letters which I brought, but the Court, notwithstanding, had other translations made here both in the Portuguese and Siamese languages. Whilst discussing the Treaty I attempted repeatedly to reduce the length of each Article, and often proposed, that instead of setting down that 'the English should not go and intrude' &c, &c, and then that 'the Siamese shall not' &c. in the very same words, the Article should say at once 'Neither the Siamese nor the English shall intrude' &c. But the Ministers objected decidedly to such a construction of the sentences, stating that it was contrary to Siamese custom and that it could not possibly render the meaning of the Articles so clear and precise as to put down separately what either party engaged. After some hesitation I determined at length upon annexing to the Treaty as literal a Translation as I possibly could make from the original Siamese, and although such Translation appear verbose and quaint, I hope my Superiors will consider my determination as judicious with respect to the peculiar character of this people, their jealousy at all times, but of late so much excited by our conquests in Ava, and by the mischievous reports of incendiaries, and their profound ignorance of all the principles of international law, and the form even of drawing up a Treaty.[1]

The next stage in the proceedings was the formal sealing of the treaty by the six ministers concerned in the negotiations and Burney himself. This was fixed for the evening of 8 July at Krommamun Surin's residence. Again Burney decided to go ahead with the matter rather than incur the long delay of seeking instructions from Calcutta. It was a case of striking while the iron was hot: a delay of several weeks, he was convinced, would give time for the impression caused by the British success in the Burma war to

[1] Journal, para. 220, *ibid.*, pp. 353-4.

wear away to a point which would enable the opposition of the Phrakhlang and his party to prevail. Were this to happen, he believed, nothing short of a declaration of war would be required in order to secure the objects gained by the treaty. He was naturally only too conscious of the difficulties with which he had been faced at each stage of his stay at Bangkok, and of the concessions he had had to make in order to obtain even this imperfect document; but one wonders whether he allowed himself too easily to speak, and possibly to think in terms of war or the threat of war as likely to be the only efficacious means of resolving a situation such as this. Can it have been more than a façon de parler, which must have been common among military men in his own day? Yet he wrote this in a report to the Government of India. Surely he must have known that to the Government of India war with Siam was unthinkable. This is not the only example of loose thinking of this kind to be found in his Journal. Frustration, or the threat of it, was the cause of this attitude of mind on each occasion when Burney gives expression to it. One would hardly take note of it on this occasion were it not for the fact that years later when faced by King Tharrawaddy's defiant attitude over British treaties with Burma Burney's advocacy of military sanctions against him was to cause the then Government of India to bring his career as a diplomatist to an abrupt and unsatisfactory termination.

In his Journal Burney describes with amusement the fixing of the ministerial seals.

To the Chao Phya of Ligor the Prince allotted the task of applying the Seals which, being cut in relief and used with paint, could not make a good impression on English paper without its being previously moistened with water. The Raja took at least a quarter of an hour to make each impression, and it was ludicrous to observe the childish interest and delight with which most of the Siamese, and particularly the Phra Klang watched his progress and success.[1]

At the end of the ceremony he notified the Ministers that he proposed to make his departure from Bangkok at the coming spring tides and asked them to apply to the King to grant him a farewell audience. At once the Phrakhlang replied with a blunt refusal; it was not the custom, he said, and Mr. Crawfurd had not had one. But Burney took him up on this. The present King, then Prince Krom Chiat, had apologized to Crawfurd, he said, because of the

[1] BP, I, 3, p. 356.

The Negotiation of the Treaty

late King's inability to grant him a farewell audience owing to family distress, and had said nothing about it not being the custom. Furthermore, seeing that a treaty of peace and friendship had now been concluded, while previously the public mind at Bangkok had been disturbed by reports of the British Government's hostile intentions, for him to take proper and public leave of His Majesty would have beneficial results. He would be seen to leave the country in the most friendly manner, and he himself would feel satisfied that His Majesty would confirm what had been agreed to by his ministers. The Phrakhlang, however, remained obdurate: the Ministers, he said, dared not submit such a request to the King. Whether this were true or not, the matter was nevertheless clinched over their heads by Prince Krommamun Surin, who 'with his usual politeness, agreed to represent the matter to His Majesty', as Burney puts it.[1]

In due course, on 16 June, Phraya Phiphatkosa called on Burney and announced that the King would grant him an audience of leave on the evening of the next day, and Burney at once set to work to draft an address to the King in Siamese. It must have afforded him rather more than usual satisfaction to hand it to the Phrakhlang with the request that it be considered by the Ministers and permission be granted for it to be read. He records that they made only a few purely verbal changes. The brief summary of it in his Journal demonstrates his ability to compose the fulsome expressions that such an occasion demanded; but one detects a note of genuine sincerity in his encomiums paid to the King, for whom he had great admiration. Yet when in extolling that monarch's many virtues he says they are of such a nature as to make everyone realize that the Almighty has conferred a blessing upon the Siamese people in appointing him to rule over them, he must have forgotten that he was addressing the head of a Theravada Buddhist state, whose religion did not recognize an Almighty Person and whose succession to the throne was governed by the law of Karma. He made a special point of thanking the King for the release of the Mergui and Martaban prisoners; it was a well-conceived gesture of recognition both of an unprecedented act of statecraft and of the part played by the King in the matter. In his reference to the treaty he made a pointed remark to the effect that if the Siamese governors and customs officers would carry out its stipulations

[1] *Ibid.*, p. 357.

honestly, Bangkok's commerce would greatly increase and excellent relations be maintained between the English and Siamese nations.

The audience began at 10 p.m. It lasted much longer and was much less formal than Burney's first one. The King and court were not in full dress and the King did not occupy the throne. It was an extremely friendly meeting: the less formal procedure had been decided upon by the King, Burney was told, so that the English deputation could be treated as friends. The King asked many questions and passed many comments. When, for instance, Phraya Phiphatkosa read out the list of jewels which were presented as a parting gift by the Mission, the King at once said, 'What, presents when you come and presents also when you are departing?' When Phraya Phiphatkosa read out Burney's address, the King was obviously pleased with it, but appeared to be for some time at a loss as to how to reply. Then he said, 'The treaty which you have concerted with my ministers I will take care shall be strictly fulfilled, but you see that the English receive and respect it properly, and if they do so, you will have a very great name in every Siamese country.' He asked Burney what sort of employment he would be given upon his return from Siam, and the latter replied that it would depend upon the will of the Governor-General. He was then asked to describe the various territories acquired by the British from Burma in the recent war. This led to further conversation in which the Raja of Ligor and Maha Yotha were invited to join. The King questioned them regarding the date of the Burmese conquest of Arakan: he thought Burney was wrong when he said it was only forty to fifty years earlier, because there had been 'Ye-Kains' in the Burmese army which had captured Ayuthaya [in 1767]. Maha Yotha confirmed that 'Ye-Kain' was the Burmese word for Arakanese, but no one present seems to have known the actual date of King Bodawpaya's conquest of Arakan, which was 1785; so that Burney's estimate was reasonably close.

Finally the King wanted to know how long Burney's voyage via Singapore, Malacca and Penang to Bengal would take. He hoped it would be safe and pleasant, and that on arrival in Calcutta Burney would convey his good wishes to the Governor-General 'for the health and happiness of his Lordship and of his Family'. On the termination of the audience Siamese dresses of silk and gold cloth were presented to Captain Macfarquhar and Burney by the

Phrakhlang on the King's behalf. Afterwards they were assured that the King was much pleased and had shown them 'extraordinary kindness and consideration'. In diplomatic courtesy the Siamese outshone all other South-East Asian courts, notably the Burmese and Vietnamese, who were past masters in the art of humiliating foreign envoys.

On the following day the Wangna accorded Burney and Macfarquhar a farewell audience. It was similar in every detail to the one given by the King. 'His Highness put precisely the same questions, without seeming to understand their purport or to care whether any answer was made to them,' wrote Burney in his Journal; but, of course, he disliked the Wangna. This was followed by the ceremonial reception on board the Brig *Guardian* of the public letters from the King and Phrakhlang to the Governor-General. They were conveyed to the ship by a procession of large war boats with music playing and streamers flying, and were received on its quarter deck with the Mission's escort presenting arms. Finally, in the evening, Burney went to say farewell to the Phrakhlang himself. 'The Minister,' he writes, 'was full of friendly professions, requested me to forget all the disputes which we had had, and engaged me to write to him and let him know where I may hereafter be employed.'[1] He sent his eldest son to escort him back to the ship.

When the treaty talks had begun in the middle of May, deliveries had also begun of the return presents from the King and Ministers to the Governor-General. According to the prescribed custom they had to be in products of the country, sugar, aguila wood, elephants' teeth, sappan wood and tin. The proceedings began with the appraisal of the value of the presents brought by the Envoy from the Governor-General. This was carried out by the King's merchants, whose custom was to place as low a value as they dared upon each item, and treat the thing like a business transaction with the value of the return presents representing roughly the estimated value of the ones received. It was an old established custom arising from the fact that the King was the chief merchant of his country taking what he required of the goods brought into his country by foreign merchants and making them a return 'present' of equal value. When Burney was made aware of what was happening, he told the Phrakhlang that he would receive

[1] BP, I, 3, pp. 335–6.

whatever return presents the King and Ministers wished to make, but he would have nothing to do with any appraisal; he would not condescend to treat presents as a matter of barter. The immediate effect of his declaration, he writes not without amusement, was that the Phrakhlang was 'shamed' into raising the value of the British presents and consequently the amount of the 'returns'.

Even then there was no guarantee that the articles delivered were according to specification in weight and quality. Burney therefore had to resort to the method used by the private merchant of weighing and examining each article received on board the Brig *Guardian*, assigning this duty to Captain Sutherland, her Master with a commission of $2\frac{1}{2}$ per cent upon the value of the goods, for his trouble. The Siamese officers responsible for the deliveries played every kind of trick that they were accustomed to play on the private merchant, he tells us. 'Day after day the same boats with bad sugar were brought to the Vessel and declared to be other boats newly arrived from the sugar districts, and the most impudent attempts were made to induce Captain Sutherland to receive sugar of an inferior quality, or with short weight.' Being confident that neither the King nor the Wangna knew of these malpractices, Burney asked the Raja of Ligor to report them to the latter. The effect was immediate: the officers in charge of the deliveries took back a number of articles and brought better ones in exchange.

Shortly before the ship's sailing date the Phrakhlang made the embarrassing request to be allowed to send four or five of his followers with 200 piculs of sugar on board in order to travel to Calcutta to sell the sugar and buy emeralds with the proceeds. Burney deemed it 'prudent and politic' to consent, but it went against the grain to do so. The man in charge of the party was an Indian Christian 'in favor of whose appearance or information', he wrote, 'little can be said'.[1]

The *Guardian* set sail from her moorings at Bangkok at 11 p.m. on 18 June and arrived at Paknam at midday on the following day. Burney and his colleagues had an opportunity of examining the defences against a possible English attack that the Phrakhlang had been so assiduous in superintending. They were agreeably surprised at their strength, but thought that the force of the Menam's current would soon dispose of the piles driven into its bed. Burney decided that the actual design was the same as the one used in

[1] *Ibid.*, p. 359.

1688 when the French were besieged in the then village of Bangkok. In face of a strong southerly wind they suffered considerable delays before being able to cross the bar, and were able to do so only because of a change in the wind and the commander's decision to cross at a place much to the westward of the one indicated by the Siamese pilot. He did so because the previous experience had led him to suspect that the Siamese pilots had been instructed to take foreign vessels through the worst channels; he proved to be right. That was on the night of 24 June. But there was further delay for the reloading of the part of the cargo that had had to be put on board junks in order to lighten the ship sufficiently for it to cross the bar. Not until 31 June did they sail away southwards towards Singapore.

On the way they anchored off Trengganu and Burney sent a message to the sultan that although he had been unable to liberate him from Siamese suzerainty, the treaty laid down that the Siamese might not interrupt commercial intercourse with his state. If they did so, he should immediately notify the Governor of Prince of Wales Island. The sultan sent a message thanking him 'in the strongest terms' and begging him to call on him personally. This he did on the afternoon of 12 July, and found him dangerously ill and unlikely to survive long. He was given a notably warm reception, and repeated to the sick man the points he had made in his earlier message, asking him to send to his neighbour in Kelantan a copy of the article in the treaty relating to their two states. The sultan introduced his two sons to Burney, who later learnt that the old man intended to make the younger of the two his successor, and noted down in his Journal his apprehension that the elder would not accept exclusion and the country would pretty certainly be thrown into confusion.

Then on to Singapore, which was reached on 25 August, and, after a stay of four days there, the slow voyage through the calm waters of the Straits of Malacca to Penang which they reached on 9 September. And there Governor Fullerton began a study of the Burney treaty which produced his minute of 20 September 1826, highly critical of its three main political articles, numbers 12, 13 and 14, and speedy action to save Perak from the clutches of the Raja of Ligor.

Suffolk House, Prince of Wales Island, the residence of the Governor of Penang

Part Two

THE CONTROVERSY OVER THE TREATY

Chapter 7

Governor Fullerton's moves

GOVERNOR Fullerton wrote an extremely critical review of the treaty. In particular the articles dealing with Trengganu and Kelantan (12), the ex-king of Kedah (13) and Perak (14), came under hostile scrutiny.[1] The commercial clauses, he thought, were to the mutual advantage of both sides, but in the case of a despotic and arbitrary government such as that of Siam what hope of fair dealing was to be expected? He had grave doubts, he said, about recommending their ratification. These views were transmitted to Burney in a letter of 23 September 1826 from the Penang Council over the signature of John Anderson its secretary. Article twelve, he wrote, was very ambiguous: it conveyed by implication that Siam was supreme over the two states, whereas an express disavowal of this was the Penang Government's object. The undertaking by the Siamese not to interrupt the trade of these states could be taken to preclude any interference on their part. If this was the meaning of the article, then it appeared to be unobjectionable. If, however, it left undisputed power to Siam and precluded British right to interference, it was opposed to his government's line of policy.

Article thirteen, wrote Anderson, dropping all contemplation of the ex-king's restoration, and, in fact, involving a British guarantee for his final renunciation of all future claims on his kingdom, was quite contrary to the expectations of his government in deputing the mission. Moreover, while the Siamese had the right to insist that while the ex-king was living under British protection, no hostile attempts or preparations should be made against them, the Raja of Ligor had acquired by the treaty a right he had never before possessed, in that the Penang Government was pledged to take an active part against the ex-king 'to prevent his seeking elsewhere that assistance which we have refused'. As to his residence,

[1] BP, I, 3, pp. 438–51.

since he had not been a party to the treaty, the Penang Government could not ratify a treaty for his forcible removal elsewhere. Every attempt would be made to persuade him to reside at Malacca, but his forcible removal would violate every principle of justice. If on the other hand he left British territory, no promise could prevent him from attacking Ligor.

Article fourteen, Burney was informed, 'was so far satisfactory that it confirmed the Preliminary Agreement' regarding Perak. By declaring the king independent, it presumably gave the British the right to support his independence; but the latent objects of the Raja of Ligor were betrayed by the provisions about sending the *bunga mas* and 'receiving certain persons in a friendly way'. They were a cover for 'the exercise of every trick which cunning and deceit can devise' to evade adherence to the spirit of the article. The treaty did indeed give them the right to interfere forcibly, but that was a negative advantage, since the objects of treaties were to promote amicable understanding and not the disagreeable alternative.

In conveying to Burney the governor's refusal to discuss the commercial articles Anderson wrote that the suggestion for such negotiations had come from Singapore, and that the Penang Government thought that Singapore's trade with Siam could be infinitely better carried on through the native junks frequenting its harbour. Praise was bestowed upon Burney for his 'unremitting exertions' to bring about Siamese co-operation in the Burmese war. Equally favourable comments were made on his success in preventing trouble between the Siamese frontier forces and the very small British forces holding Martaban and the Tenasserim coast. And there was high approval of his 'recovery from slavery and misery' the Burmese prisoners taken by the Siamese from the territories under British protection. His efforts under trying circumstances, he was told, had removed potentially dangerous matters of dispute between the two governments.

But, the letter continued, candour obliged the Governor and Council to confess that in all matters connected with the Malay Peninsula the mission had, in some degree, failed. In his negotiations Burney seemed to have relied too much upon the influence of the Raja of Ligor.

Now considering that the Raja of Ligor was the aggressor and is now in actual possession of Quedah, deriving all the advantages therefrom:

that he is moreover the person directing all the interference and aggression in the states of Perak and Salengore; that he is, by far, the most intriguing and ambitious of all the Siamese Chiefs,—it was not likely that his influence would ever be exerted towards the completion of the objects in which this Government were interested. The very reverse might safely have been presumed. The counteraction and the destruction of this man's influence ought therefore to have been the first object of your arrangements.

On the contrary, however, by asking and accepting his advice on some occasions, and by making him the principal medium of his most important communications Burney had caused the Raja's influence to be increased rather than diminished. Hence the Raja must now be considered the only one in the Bangkok government 'fit to meet an European opponent'. He had been the Penang government's main enemy all along. Now he would return to Kedah with 'extended views of conquest', which would have to be met by steady and unremitting opposition.

During the Burmese war, the letter continued, Burney had had to adopt a conciliatory policy; but when it was won, he could have adopted a higher tone. Had he done so, all the objects of his mission, even the restoration of the king of Kedah, would have been achieved. This section of the letter then ended with an assurance that the Penang government fully recognized the difficulties Burney had had to contend with and an invitation to explain 'the true intent and meaning' of the particular provisions in the treaty to which it took exception.

The rest of the letter was devoted to the Perak question. As soon as the provisional treaty with the Raja of Ligor had been executed, Burney was told, the Raja had sent nearly 200 people to Perak, who 'on the plea of demanding the Boongah Mas actually assumed the complete management of the country'. Now, however, seeing that the present treaty virtually confirmed the previous one, action had to be taken to counteract Ligor's plans against Perak. It was quite clear that the King of Perak did not wish to submit to Ligor. Hence it had been decided to depute Captain Low to explain to him what had been negotiated with Siam about his state, and in particular to let him know that he was an independent sovereign and could rule his country without interference from either Ligor or Selangor. Hence he could decide whether or not to send the Bunga Mas to the king of Siam. Under the treaty both the Siamese and the British engaged not to attack Perak. If therefore the Siamese interfered with his government, he could rely upon the British to protect him, should he decide to declare his independence. In addition, Burney was told, letters were to be sent to the son of the Ligor chief and to his father warning them not to interfere in Perak, and saying that if they sent people into that state, the British also would have to send people there. Burney was to deliver these letters to 'the young chief' at Kedah on his way to Bengal to convey the Siam treaty to the Supreme Government for ratification.[1]

Burney defended his treaty and the negotiations leading to it in a document running to over five thousand words dated 3 October 1826. In answer to the complaint that after the Burmese war he ought to have assumed a higher tone in dealing with the Bangkok government, and should have endeavoured to destroy the Raja of Ligor's influence, he quoted his instructions from the Governor-General emphasizing that conciliation was to be the leading feature of his mission. Had he been guided by his personal feelings, he said, he would have left Bangkok before staying there a month. Had he taken the wishes of the Penang Council to be his sole guide, he would have urged the matters concerning the Malay Peninsula upon the Court of Siam 'to the last extremity'. But the Governor-General had other views, and he quoted passages from the Government of India's official letters to the Penang Council to show that his mission had been defined as being purely complimentary and conciliatory, that he was empowered to seek some improvement in commercial relations, and the restoration of the king of Kedah if conditions were favourable. In any case, he said, the Governor-General entertained the strongest doubts whether it would be worth while to make any attempt to induce the Court of Siam to waive its claims to supremacy over the Malayan peninsula south of Pattani. Nevertheless, as his reports would show, he had mooted this last matter at Bangkok. Yet, having no power to pledge the British Government to protect the Malay states, all he could do was to warn the ministers that it would not permit the Siamese to invade or oppress those states. The argument he had used was that if the Siamese did molest them, British commerce with them would be interrupted and this would bring British intervention on their behalf.

[1] BP, I, 3, pp. 451–60.

He himself, he explained, had drafted the twelfth article and translated it into Siamese, flattering himself that it was worded in precisely the terms which the situation demanded. It did not commit his government 'to ulterior procedures', but left it free either to wait and interfere if the Siamese encroached upon Trengganu or Kelantan, or, when ratifying the article, make a declaration that it would adopt the course he had described to the Siamese government, namely that the British would not permit the Siamese to invade or oppress them.

To the criticism that Article thirteen gave the Raja of Ligor rights over Kedah 'tacitly allowed but never hitherto distinctly admitted' Burney replied that four years earlier John Crawfurd had admitted in writing the complete right of Siam over Kedah. Moreover, there was intense feeling at the Court of Siam against the king of Kedah because of his treasonable correspondence with Ava. Hence the ministers to a man were opposed to his restoration. By giving in over his restoration, Burney pointed out, he had taken advantage of the party benefiting from his removal, the Raja of Ligor and his nephew the Wangna, to effect the other objects of his mission. They had given him their strong support in matters in which they were not immediately interested. Without it he would have left Siam without even securing the release of the Burmese prisoners.

The termination of the war in Burma, he said, did not place him in the strong position imagined by the Penang Council. The abortive negotiations at Pantanaw gave the Siamese ministers a very great advantage over him, and the fact that the British did not capture the Burmese capital much reduced the effect of their success in Siamese eyes. Even after a copy of the Treaty of Yandabo reached Bangkok, reports of some foul act of treachery by the Burmese came in daily, and were believed by the Court. 'At my distance from, and with my limited communications with the Seat of War,' he wrote, 'these reports, at the same time that they impaired the effect of our successes in the minds of the Siamese Ministers, obliged me to found arguments upon the successful termination of the War with more caution and hesitation than what I had used after the peace signed at Pantanago.'

And, he continued, he was up against the party at Court led by the Wangna, who was very influential since he was in special charge of the southern part of the kingdom and was also head of the armed forces. To have upset such a personage could have laid the foundations of war. Had he adopted a high tone over the king of Kedah, and had it succeeded, they would have been obliged to maintain a military force in Kedah and assume charge of the country. They would have lost ten thousand useful subjects, who had settled in Province Wellesley. By creating bad relations with Siam they would have seriously endangered trade with both upper and lower Siam; worse still in his opinion, by restoring the king of Kedah on such terms the British 'would soon have been drawn on to Ligor and even to Bangkok, whilst the resources of Kedah would not have met a hundredth part of all the expense'. There was an added reason for not adopting a high tone in dealing with the Court, he continued. It was constitutional practice for the ministers to approve what should be shown to the king. Early on they had refused to show two of his memorials to the king because he had refused to alter their wording in the way they required. The only way to get through to the king, who was the most intelligent and moderate man in the government, was to couch one's arguments in moderate language.

Burney roundly defended the undertaking in the treaty to remove the king of Kedah from Penang and not to permit him or his followers to attack Kedah or any other Siamese territory. The understanding on both sides, he explained, was that the pledge held good only while the king continued to live under British protection and at their expense. The ratification of the treaty, he suggested, might be accompanied by a declaration of the extent to which the British Government would consider itself pledged to prevent such attacks. Subsequent events, it may here be remarked, were to show that Burney much underestimated the difficulties that were to arise in this connection. The Straits authorities were to be called upon again and again, particularly in the eighteen-thirties, to assist the Siamese to repel attacks by supporters of the ex-king, and co-operate, howbeit unwillingly, in the hateful task of preventing Malays from recovering control over a Malay state, until at last they served notice upon the Court of Siam that no further assistance would be forthcoming. At the same time they persuaded the ex-king to offer his submission to Bangkok, and in due course he was permitted to return, though to a much reduced patrimony.

Burney next turned to the objections raised by the Penang

Council regarding the fourteenth article dealing with Perak. He explained that while he was well aware of the king's sentiments on the subject of his independence, he had been helpless because of the assurances given to the ministers by Malay chieftains in Siamese pay that he wished to send the Bunga Mas. They belonged to the weaker party in Perak, and hence were responsible for calling in the Siamese about whom Governor Fullerton had protested. He had now learnt that upon receiving the governor's letters on the subject, the Raja, who was still in Bangkok, had given orders for them to leave Perak. If Captain Low were to procure a public statement by the king of his wishes concerning his relations with Siam, the British would then have sufficient grounds for supporting his independence, and thus preventing the extension of Siam's conquests to the vicinity of Malacca. Thus a long-desired object of the British Government 'would be satisfactorily and quietly accomplished'.

The Penang Government's view of his negotiations regarding commerce, Burney said, occasioned him 'much mortification'. He did not expect the present treaty to change a system which had lasted for centuries, but it had been freely negotiated, not dictated, and it was to the interest of the Siamese to keep it. So he hoped its commercial provisions would be respected. Failure to ratify them would greatly increase Siamese distrust of the British, whereas 'at no period of our history in India could we so well afford, as at the present moment, to conciliate the Siamese by giving them proof of our moderation and forbearance.'

These were wise words, as any student of nineteenth-century Siam will realize, and Burney followed them up with a percipient explanation of his treatment of the Raja of Ligor. To have attacked him, he said, would have been the best possible way of raising him in the estimation of the Court of Siam. The Raja lived in apprehension of being charged with cultivating intimacy with a European, an imputation dreaded by every Siamese. The best way to destroy his influence would be 'to draw him on at Quedah into such close and friendly relations with us, as he is disposed, I know, to maintain, when distant from his jealous and distrustful Court'. But did he underestimate the Raja's ability to play the diplomatic game?

Then referring to the letters he was to deliver from the Penang Government to the Raja enquiring about the military preparations going on in Kedah, he said he believed them to be purely defensive and due to the threats of the ex-king to attack the Siamese. Then, as if unaware of the contradiction, he said it was the ambitious schemes of the Wangna and his party that had brought the Raja to be the neighbour of Penang. He was bound implicitly to obey their dictates. Their object was to bring not only the southern Malay states, but also the kingdom of Achin in Sumatra under the Wangna's authority. 'This extensive plan of conquest,' he wrote, 'has now, I hope, met with a decided check, and although we may not make the Wangna retreat, we can certainly put a stop to his advance, and of this the King of Siam is well aware.'

Burney concluded by expressing the hope that his letter would induce the Governor and Council to relieve him of some of the distress caused him by learning their views on the results of his mission. 'I could not wish to set my worst enemy a more difficult task than to send him to Bangkok, to negotiate matters connected with the Malay Peninsula, without authority, or means of employing effectual intimidation.'[1]

Governor Fullerton's reactions to Burney's arguments were no less hostile than his original reception of the treaty had been. With total disregard for the instructions given by the Government of India to Burney as its envoy he insisted that the main object of the mission had been to restore the king of Kedah. In this it had failed, and, having regard to the views expressed by Captain Burney, it was a pity, from Penang's point of view, that he had ever been entrusted with the negotiations. His government's failure to protect the king had caused it a material loss of reputation. Had Burney carried out his threat to break off negotiations in order to force the Siamese to give way over the restoration question, he was convinced that he would have succeeded. He could not understand, he said, what had been gained by refraining from intimidation in that matter when it had succeeded in the case of the repatriation of the Burmese captives.

He was equally unconvinced by Burney's interpretation of the thirteenth article of the treaty dealing with the position of Trengganu and Kelantan. He quoted Crawfurd's opinion that while the Court of Siam would never agree to a treaty securing the future independence of the Malayan states, nevertheless, if the British assumed that they were independent, they would be allowed to act on that principle 'without any serious demur'. Captain Burney, he

[1] BP, I, 6, p. 512.

said, was fully aware of this and it was therefore regrettable that he had permitted the insertion of an article 'so exactly calculated to preclude the future resort to it.' The proposed declaration to be attached to the article would not alter the fact that it acknowledged Siam's overlordship over the two states.

Article fourteen, he said, he had already admitted to be favourable in that it halted the progress of the Siamese in the direction of Malacca. This was the only point on which Captain Burney had succeeded. It had long been his government's belief that some barrier must be imposed to the further progress of Siam. The Burney mission had not achieved this object, and he feared that the time for intervention was past and the fate of the peninsula irretrievably decided. For judging by Burney's reports of the war party's ascendancy and other information, extensive views of conquest were entertained. It would have been better to have kept the matter of ratification open until the opinion of the home authorities could be sought regarding the policy to be adopted. But this would take too long. Hence he was disposed to think, after the most deliberate reconsideration, that the best course under present circumstances would be to ratify the treaty. He was satisfied that no possible good could come from further negotiation.[1]

Those words were penned on 5 October 1826. In it he said that the time for intervention was past. His agent Captain James Low was, however, at that very time engaged in activities in Perak which could hardly be defined by any other term. Their object was to free its ruler from Siamese influence to which he was said to be unwillingly submitting. Fullerton suspected, not without reason, that the Raja of Ligor was looking for ways and means of sabotaging the provision in the treaty by which the king of Perak was declared to be free to decide whether or not to send the Bunga Mas to Bangkok. Ever since the signature of the preliminary treaty with Burney on 31 July of the previous year he had been sending missions and small detachments of troops on the pretext of assisting the king to govern his state, and bribing members of the court to support the Siamese interest. The king had appealed to Penang for protection, and Penang had protested to the Raja of Ligor, but without avail. So in September 1826 Fullerton resorted to the method of sending an agent to explain article fourteen of the Bangkok treaty to the king. His agent, Captain Low, very naturally,

[1] BP, I, 3, p. 521.

for he was going on a dangerous journey, sailed off in a small armed vessel with a well-armed escort of forty sepoys to the Perak capital. There the grateful ruler assured him that he was absolutely opposed to sending tribute in any shape to Siam. He made it quite clear, however, that he must have a guarantee of British protection, in case of need, against Siam. Low's instructions permitted him to assure the king of British support in case of aggression, and it does not seem to have occurred to him that all that was necessary was for him to obtain from the king a document stating that he wished to be independent of Siam. Instead, fearing a Siamese invasion of Perak as soon as he left, he executed an 'engagement' with the king promising British support in such an event. And it was a thorough-going instrument which defined the types of aggression, against which help was to be afforded, political embassies, whether Siamese or Malay, and, of course, armed parties, even should they consist of no more than thirty men. It was signed on 18 October. Furthermore, Low's presence enabled the king to deprive the pro-Siamese heir-apparent and nobles of office and replace them with loyal Malays.[1]

Low's action was decisive, but embarrassing, and Governor Fullerton in reporting it to Calcutta had to admit that it went far beyond his instructions and was open to the charge of contravening Burney's treaty. At the same time, he claimed, the measures adopted by the Raja of Ligor were also a distinct breach of that treaty. He had further to report that Captain Low had brought with him from Perak a token of its monarch's gratitude in the form of a grant of the island of Pangkor and of the Dindings, though, of course, no steps would be taken in that matter without the sanction of the Board of Directors in London 'unless the future perseverance of the Chief of Ligore in his views against Perak should render that measure indispensable'.[2]

The energetic governor also followed up Low's return by writing to the Raja of Ligor warning him against further interference in Perak since it could lead to war with The East India Company. Then he made a further move of even more decisive significance. It was to put an end to a pirate stronghold up the Kurau River a little south of Penang within the territory of Perak, from which raids were being carried out on coastal shipping, sometimes into

[1] Low's Report, BP, II, 6, pp. 1–15, Engagement, *ibid.*, pp. 20–3.
[2] BP, II, 6, p. 49.

the Penang harbour. Nakhoda Udin, the chief of the place, was known to be an ally of the Raja of Ligor, and was suspected of being used by him in his efforts to destroy Perak's independence. Again it was Captain Low who carried out the enterprise. At the head of a body of Indian sepoys he stormed the place, capturing many of the pirates; and when the chief himself went to Penang to complain, he was arrested and sent to the Raja of Ligor for punishment.

Despite the fact that four years earlier the Raja had denounced Nakhoda Udin as a pirate, he now claimed him as a dependent, declared that the Kurau River was in Kedah, and charged the British with violating Siamese territorial rights.

Chapter 8

The Ratification

BURNEY was no longer in Penang when this happened; he had left on 17 October, before Low's return from Perak, to take his treaty to Calcutta for ratification. He arrived on 2 December, and in reporting his arrival, apologized for the fact that the collateral documents detailing his 'proceedings and sentiments' on the subject of the king of Kedah and the Malay states were so voluminous. The reason for this, he said, was the dissatisfaction with his mission expressed by the Government of Prince of Wales Island. This had imposed upon him the need for a full examination of the questions at issue.

Lord Amherst was away on a tour of the 'Upper Provinces'; so the documents were first considered by the Vice President in Council before being forwarded to him. In their covering letter they expressed their agreement with the Penang Government that the treaty should be ratified, and recorded the opinion that 'in the circumstances detailed by the Envoy in his clear and very able report' he had acted with great judgment and address, and had carried every point which the Court of Siam could have been expected to concede. This is not surprising for right from the start, it will be remembered Calcutta's view of Burney's objectives had been radically different from Penang's.

Burney had now to wait in Calcutta for the return of the ratified copy of the treaty from the Governor-General. Then he was to travel, again by the Brig *Guardian*, which had brought him to Calcutta, back to the Malay Peninsula to exchange it with the Raja of Ligor's son for the copy ratified by the King of Siam. After that his next assignment was to be at Mergui, where he was to take charge of the administration of the southern part of the Tenasserim provinces ceded by Burma by the Treaty of Yandabo in February 1826. His knowledge of the Siamese language and

The Ratification

character was given in the minute recording this decision as the reason for this step.[1] One must bear in mind that Siam had held this territory since the end of the sixteenth century until it was reconquered by Burma less than three-quarters of a century before the British acquired it.

While waiting in Calcutta Burney was asked to read the despatches from Penang on Low's mission to Perak, and comment on them. The result was a long screed from him dated 29 December 1826. He began with a detailed statement of British relations with the king of Kedah, and referred to the difference between his own assessment of the Siamese question and that of the Penang authorities. Then he asked what the latter would have said if the Raja of Ligor had sent an agent to Perak and obtained a similar engagement to Captain Low's and directed against intercourse with the British. It does not seem to have occurred to him that it was not a valid comparison: Siam was seeking to establish overlordship over Perak, the British acted to safeguard Perak's independence. But he must have had bitter feelings, and they are not conducive to clear thinking.

Burney's next point was that there was no clause in the treaty—this was the term he used—providing for either ratification or rejection by the Government of India, yet it guaranteed the king of Perak's possessions against attack by either the Siamese or another Malay state. Surely, he said, this violated the East India Company's Charter Act of 1793, and was beyond the power of either the Penang Government or the Government of India to ratify without express orders from the Home Government.

On the Bunga Mas question, he said, when the king of Kedah had been ordered by Siam to bring Perak under subjection, he had excused his action to the Penang authorities on the grounds that up to the Burmese invasions of Siam Perak had acknowledged Siamese overlordship. When, however, the Penang government had urged the late chief of Perak, on several occasions, to send the Bunga Mas, he had rejected their advice saying that Siam had never had any authority over his country. This, said Burney, was not acceptable to the Raja of Ligor, and he went on to describe the situation leading up to his preliminary treaty with the Raja. In agreeing to that treaty he abandoned his preparations for a large-scale invasion of Perak and promised to keep no troops there. His

[1] BP, II, 4, p. 213.

own aim at Bangkok, he said, had been to preclude all Siamese interference in Perak in any of its many forms. In September of the previous year he had warned Penang that the Raja would continue to seek to maintain influence there by other means than that of open force. In Bangkok he had 'disproved' Siam's claims to overlordship, and when he heard that a small party of Siamese and Malays had gone to Perak, he had remonstrated with the Raja, telling him that it was a breach of the provisional treaty. It was only a small party, but, as Captain Low had pointed out, the king was weak, his chiefs divided, and his subjects open to bribery. The Raja of Ligor had denied that what he had done was in breach of the treaty; he had promised, he said, not to send *'any force with hostile intentions'*. The preliminary treaty, however, wrote Burney, had been only a temporary expedient to remove an impending evil, and keep the situation quiet while the Government of India was dealing with Burma. And it must not be forgotten that it had given Penang for the first time the right to interfere in Perak. Hence, he pointed out, he strongly disputed the opinion that had been expressed to the effect that it had opened the way for the furtherance of the Raja of Ligor's schemes. He himself, before going to Bangkok, had told the Governor of Penang that it was a pity that the agent he had sent to Perak and Selangor to negotiate peace between them had not 'raised up such a barrier against Siamese conquest to the Southward as might afford us a right and title wherewith to oppose the Siamese in case the Court of Siam refused to ratify my Agreement with the Raja of Ligore'. Unfortunately at Bangkok the argument brought up by the ministers was that the king of Perak and his principal chiefs actually favoured a connexion with Siam. Against that he had argued in vain.

Burney next went on to describe all the difficulties and arguments he had met with before securing agreement to the wording of the article in the Bangkok treaty dealing with Perak. Had he dealt with them all in his Journal, he said, it would have been ten times its actual size. A much simpler solution than the one devised by Captain Low could, he thought, have been adopted; all that was needed was for the Penang Government to assure the king of Perak of protection against Selangor. He would then have broken off relations with Siam. He himself had suggested to the Governor of Penang on his return from Bangkok that an officer should be deputed to Perak to obtain from the king a document declaring his determination to do so. 'I subsequently volunteered to proceed myself to Perak and obtain such a document, observing that I knew exactly what was necessary, but the Hon'ble the Governor decided that it was then too late, and stated that he would give Captain Low such precise instructions as would preclude all chance of misconception.'

Captain Low, Burney thought, had acted according to his view of the preliminary treaty without taking into account the fact that it 'merged' in the subsequent Bangkok treaty. He had reported that the King of Perak could neither free himself from Siam nor maintain peace and order in his state without British help. Had the methods used by Captain Low in Perak been put into effect in September 1825, Burney's own negotiations at Bangkok regarding Perak would have been shorter and easier. The Raja of Ligor's partisans in Perak, he went on, had kept him informed of everything that had happened there and had caused dissatisfaction at the Court of Siam. And when one bore in mind that these things were done on behalf of a chief with an income of barely twenty thousand dollars a year, the ablest critic of the Penang Government could not have shown more clearly than Captain Low had done, how petty, complicated and unprofitable was the policy of that government 'in taking the whole of the Malayan Peninsula under its protection', nor how far such a system of interference might draw it on.

On the other hand Burney was sure that there was not the slightest likelihood of this affair developing into a quarrel with Siam. He thought, however, that the Government of India should make the six ministers forming the privy council of Siam aware of its determination to maintain the independence of the king of Perak. The ministers should also be provided with the evidence brought back by Captain Low of the Raja of Ligor's interference in Perak after the signature of the preliminary treaty to show why the British had decided to extend their protection to the king of Perak.

Finally Burney offered some observations on the subject of relations with Siam.

Having concluded with that extraordinary people a treaty, [he wrote,] which appears to me to secure every object that is worthy the notice of the British Government and which it is manifestly the interest of the Siamese Government to keep and respect, I feel a natural, and I hope a laudable anxiety to see the relations which I have been the instrument of establishing, duly maintained and confirmed. On this service the Penang Government has expressed so decidedly its dissatisfaction at my proceeding, I cannot indulge a hope of being employed under its orders. But I earnestly intreat the Supreme Government, if that high authority shall determine to ratify the Treaty concluded by me, to order such measures as may not entirely leave the duty of seeing this Treaty maintained, confirmed and improved, in the hands of any officer to whom every alleged breach of it on the part of the Siamese will be a matter of triumph. I have already had occasion to bring to the notice of the Government the local feelings and prepossessions which exist at Prince of Wales Island as connected with the ex-King of Queda, and the Siamese once ventured last year to make an appeal on this point to the Government of Penang, but I only involved myself in a most unpleasant personal discussion, to which I regret to see some of the enclosures in the despatch from the Penang Government again refer.

The British Government, he contended, had nothing to fear from the Siamese. The Government of Siam, however, wanted to avoid all intercourse with the Government of Prince of Wales Island. It had embarrassed him by trying to write this into the treaty; this was the object of the fourth article in the original draft submitted by the Siamese ministers, and appearing as Appendix No. 32 to his Journal. Only after much pressure had he persuaded them to drop it by reminding them that the treaty would be made between the King of Siam and the Governor-General of India, so that all discussion regarding its provisions would be between those two authorities.

There was considerable delay in ratifying the treaty on account of the Governor-General's absence in the 'Upper Provinces', and early in February Burney, who had become worried about its possible effect upon Siamese minds, wrote to the Raja of Ligor's son to explain the cause of the delay. At last on 23 February 1827, Burney received, through the Vice-President in Calcutta the official pronouncement of the Governor-General in Council upon his mission. As he had already been given to expect, complete satisfaction was expressed with his conduct. Special praise was accorded to his handling of the matters arising out of the Anglo-Burmese war and to his success in securing the release of fourteen hundred Burmese captives. Their return home, the Secretary to Government informed Burney had had an excellent effect upon the Government of India's new subjects in Tenasserim according to Mr. Maingy's report. This would redound to the fame and reputation of the British Government.

Then, coming to the treaty itself, Burney was told that it received the sanction and approbation of the Government of India. Having said this, Secretary George Swinton proceeded to convey that government's comments upon each article in turn. On the economic clauses he wrote, its view was that Burney had obtained the utmost in the way of concessions that could be expected under the circumstances, and seeing that the original document was in the Siamese language, and was obviously to the advantage of the King of Siam to keep, there were grounds for hoping that these clauses would be respected; they might indeed lead to a great improvement in commercial relations.

Government regretted, he continued, the difference of opinion between the Penang Government and Burney concerning the local interests of the British settlements on the Straits of Malacca, but noted with approval that government's recognition of the wisdom of his policy of making concessions rather than quitting the Court on hostile terms. That he had been unable to obtain the restoration of the King of Kedah did not surprise the Government at all, for he had no equivalent to offer, and the Court of Siam was understandably outraged at the ex-King's overtures to Burma in 1824. Hence the employment of menace to enforce compliance with British wishes regarding the ex-King 'would have entirely changed the ground of negotiation and have been at variance with the conciliatory subjects of your mission'. Obviously, he went on, good relations between Penang and Siam could not be secured while the ex-king continued to reside in the settlement, and Government agreed with the Governor of Penang that every effort should be made to persuade him to transfer his residence to Malacca. This did not mean that the British would lose interest in their old ally should an opportunity arise of arranging with the Siamese for his restoration. He should be informed of this, but warned against expecting that any means other than friendly negotiation would be employed, and that while he and his family enjoyed a stipend from the British Government, he must abandon 'all designs and secret machinations calculated to give umbrage to the Siamese'.

The twelfth article dealing with Trengganu and Kelantan met with Government's complete approval, Burney was informed. One day if, as a result of the acquisition of Malacca, a change were to occur in the home authorities' views regarding the extension of British relations 'to the Eastward', it might be possible to grant British protection to these two states, as the Penang Government desired; in the meantime, however, in face of the Court of Directors' injunctions against intervention, Burney's cautious avoidance of any commitment 'to ulterior procedures' was to be approved. For the time being, the article provided all that was required for the intercourse of British subjects with those two petty states.

Government recognized the difficulties created for Burney with regard to Perak, he was told, through the relationship of the ruler and his chiefs with the Raja of Ligor, and the existence of a strong party under the heir apparent devoted to Siam. It noted with approval that the Penang government considered the fourteenth article satisfactory in that it confirmed Burney's preliminary treaty with the Raja of Ligor. Government agreed with the Penang Council that Captain Low 'had exceeded his powers and had moreover interfered in the affairs of Perak to an extent which was never contemplated or desired'. Therefore an extract from Burney's letter of 29 December last regarding Perak was to be forwarded to the Governor of Prince of Wales Island, and it was hoped that a document could be obtained from the king of Perak in the form suggested in that letter, and forwarded to the Raja of Ligor and the Court of Siam to satisfy them that he wished to discontinue his connexion with the Siamese. The fourteenth article, it was felt, should relieve Selangor from all further pressure on the part of Siam, for it should enable the Government of Penang to prevent the extension of Siamese conquest in the vicinity of Malacca. The hope was also expressed that the people of Prince of Wales Island and Malacca would take advantage of the valuable trade overland to the territory on the east coast of the peninsula that the tenth article offered them.

The Government of India, wrote Secretary Swinton, was aware of the immense contribution that Burney's mastery of the Siamese language had made to the success of the negotiations, and praised his zeal and industry in acquiring it; nor, in its view, he added, 'is the favourable effect to be overlooked which was produced in the mind of His Majesty when you personally addressed him on his own tongue'.

A further communication, wrote the Secretary, was to come later from the Governor-General on the subject of the general policy discussed in the papers received from the Penang Government;

but, [he went on], it will be satisfactory to you to learn that Lord Amherst has been pleased to express his concurrence with the Local Government in highly commending the zeal, address, temper and ability displayed by you during your negotiations with the Government of Siam, and had declared that he further considers that the results of your Mission have been in the main successful in placing the political and Commercial Relations of the British Nation and the State of Siam on a decidedly improved footing and that at all events the Treaty negotiated by you has in His Lordship's judgment secured every advantage that could have been expected under the instructions furnished to you by the Governor-General.

Finally the letter conveyed detailed instructions for the exchange of the ratified copies of the treaty and Burney's subsequent assumption of duty at Mergui. Should the Raja of Ligor himself be in Kedah while Burney was there, he was to do his best to persuade him to cultivate good relations with Penang, and to warn him against engaging in any secret design to disturb the peace of either Perak or Selangor.[1]

[1] BP, II, 6, pp. 100–111.

Chapter 9

Burney and the Raja of Ligor

BURNEY ultimately arrived in Kedah for the exchange on 14 May 1827. There he received a most friendly welcome from 'the Young Chief'. The Raja of Ligor himself had left Bangkok and Burney was invited to pay him a visit at the new settlement which he was developing about eight miles up the River Trang. While there he went by his host's permission to inspect Khuan Tani, where, according to Malay rumour, there was a large naval arsenal and depot, which no European was normally allowed to visit. He reported afterwards to Penang that he saw nothing to justify the rumour, and the Raja told him that Europeans were forbidden to go there because of his fear that if the defenceless condition of the place was known, the British might have been tempted to attack it. All this Burney seems to have swallowed easily, as also that the extensive exodus of population from Kedah was due to reports spread about by partisans of the ex-King of Kedah of an impending attack by Penang. He stayed four days with the Raja, and while his guest met the notorious Nakhoda Udin. The reports of this that he wrote to Penang and Calcutta strike one as surprisingly uncritical.

He told the Penang authorities[1] that in accordance with his instructions from Calcutta he had done all he could to interest the Raja in trade with Penang, which he assured him would be arranged in terms of complete reciprocity; he had also urged him to disprove the reports spread against him by his enemies that he was engaged in hostile preparations. The Raja, he said, declared again and again that mischievous reports of such a kind were bound to be circulated while the ex-King of Kedah continued to live in Penang. When Burney warned him against engaging in any secret designs against Perak or Selangor, the Raja, he said,

[1] BP, II, 6, pp. 161-8.

expressed great dissatisfaction with Captain Low's doings in Perak, and was 'most vexed' at his attack on Kurau; so vexed indeed that Burney had had to restrain him from going to Calcutta to submit his grievance to the British Government. Nakhoda Udin also wanted to go to Calcutta with the same object. 'The Raja of Ligore,' wrote Burney, 'maintains that Kurow is the last established boundary between Perak and Queda, and that this fact, as well as those of Nakoda Oudin having been made Chief of Kurow in the first instance by the ex-King of Queda, and of his having been confirmed only in that situation by His Highness of Ligore when the latter took possession of Queda, is very generally known in Queda and Perak. The Raja of Ligore therefore considers the attack on Kurow as a violation on our part of the Siamese territory, and an infraction of the 2nd Article of the Treaty with Siam.'

Burney then adumbrated further arguments adduced by Udin and the Raja's Malay adherents in support of his claims, and pointed out that in March 1825 John Crawfurd had stated that the Kurau River was the boundary between Kedah and Perak. But he went on to point out firmly that when Penang was founded [in 1786], Francis Light had reported that the River Krian, and not the Kurau, was the true boundary, and that this was shown in the chart of the coast made by Mr. Lindsay afterwards. The Krian therefore must be considered the boundary, and he had warned the Raja that if he sent anyone to the southward of it, he would displease the Government of Penang, and probably provoke a war between Britain and Siam.

That would have been unexceptionable had he not gone on to suggest that an appeal should be made to the Penang Government. The incident must be described in his own words:

After some trouble I persuaded His Highness to make Nakoda Oudin draw out a statement of his case and to refer it to the consideration and justice of the Government of Penang, and at the same time to request the Honble. the Governor to make enquiry and ascertain whether the Krean or the Kurow is the proper boundary between Perak and Queda, His Highness expressly engaging on this last point, to abide entirely by the decision of the Honble. the Governor. The Raja however insisted upon being allowed to make known to the Supreme Government what he termed the great concession which he is willing to make, in order to cultivate a good understanding with the Government of Penang.

That letter was dated 29 May. Two days later Burney enclosed a copy of it with his report to the Government of India concerning his mission to Kedah. In the latter he had more to say about the Perak affair. The Raja of Ligor, he said, had received detailed accounts of Captain Low's doings from a number of the king's [of Perak] officers, and had promised that on his return to Ligor he would send the original letters including some from the king himself. The Penang Government, he continued, had not reported that the king was 'a poor, weak, ignorant creature, scarcely able to read or write... the tool of all who may be near him'. While fully aware, he said, of the expediency of preventing the extension of Siamese influence over Perak, and indeed he had warned the Raja of Ligor of the danger of any interference in that state, he believed that the Raja was sincere in his assurances that he would accept his advice. He was convinced, however, that British interference there would be 'unprofitable, expensive and embarrassing to political relations'. The Government of Penang had advanced the King of Perak a loan of money and arms to a total of five thousand dollars. It was unlikely ever to be repaid; for one thing his agent had 'squandered a large portion of the money on the purchase of a clock, some jewels and other baubles' before leaving Penang. The active part played by Captain Low in Perak had led him 'into the questionable proceeding of attacking and destroying Kurow, a place which even if the Siamese had no claim upon it, is far inland and beyond our jurisdiction'. It had given the Siamese 'some cause to tax us with a breach of the Treaty'. And as to the question of piracy, Malays were such inveterate liars, where their own interests were concerned, that he would give no credit to the documents furnished to the Penang Government to prove that Nakhoda Udin aided and abetted pirates at Kurau. The latter's conduct in coming to Penang and engaging a lawyer to appeal on his behalf to the the Court of Judicature showed that he was confident of the justice of his case.

Burney hoped, he said, that the Government of India would approve of the terms to which he had persuaded the Raja to agree for the adjustment of his claims to Kurau and of Nakhoda Udin's complaint. There was an obvious advantage, he suggested, in persuading the Siamese to accept the Krian River rather than the Kurau as the boundary between Kedah and Perak since it was contiguous to the British mainland territory, Province Wellesley, so

Burney and the Raja of Ligor

that the Siamese would be more under the observation of Penang and hence less likely to interfere in Perak.

It is an unsatisfactory letter on all counts. 'It is difficult to understand Burney's conduct in this matter', comments Lennox Mills in his *British Malaya, 1824–1867*, and others have echoed the same view. The impression conveyed to Mills by the letter is that of a *volte face*: Udin was not a pirate and the Kurau was in Siamese territory. Careful study of both letters, the one to the Penang Government which must be read with the one to the Government of India, shows that this was not so. Rather was it specious pleading that things were not quite so simple as the pro-Malays of Penang thought and that the Raja had a case to be answered. There can be no doubt that the criticisms of his negotiations at Bangkok by the Penang people had cut Burney to the quick and attacks on him in the local press had rubbed salt in his wounds. Governor Fullerton's comments on paper must have echoed things he had said to Burney, more brusquely perhaps, in an interview, and one can well imagine the sort of hostility he had had to endure in his personal contacts in Penang. And like other Englishmen after him he had succumbed to the charms of the Siamese with their exquisite manners and careful diplomacy. He now saw the Raja as an honourable gentleman, and realizing that such an assessment might not go unchallenged even at Calcutta, he wrote that Mr. T. Miller of the Bengal Civil Service had been ashore with him at Trang and had visited the Raja daily, and Burney expressed the hope that since he was an impartial and independent witness, the Calcutta authorities would receive his evidence of the Raja's character and compare it with his own opinion based upon five years' acquaintance.

Before closing the letter Burney alluded briefly to two other matters. The Raja had asked him, he said, what the British Government intended to do with the territory on the Tenasserim coast ceded by Burma. He had replied that the expense of administration was so great that they were considering handing it back to Burma. The Raja he said, made no comment at the time, but after his return to the ship a letter from him came by express messenger asking whether what he had said was positive and could be reported to the king; and whether, should the Siamese want to recover these territories which once belonged to them, they would be given to them or not. 'And now my friend is going away in haste', the Raja had written, 'I have no time to think.' Therefore would he ask Captain Macfarquhar, when he took the ratified copy of the treaty to Calcutta, to write to him and keep him informed of whatever 'the great officers in Bengal' might say.

The other matter concerned the residence of the ex-King of Kedah at Penang. The Raja, said Burney 'expostulated much' that the British had not carried out their part of the conditions laid down in the thirteenth article of the treaty. He himself, he said, had carried out his part: he had released the ex-king's relatives, abolished the export duty upon grain, and ordered the immediate introduction of the stipulated commercial regulations into Kedah.

The Raja himself also wrote personally to the Governor-General. After expatiating upon his desire for Anglo-Siamese friendship to continue 'as long as the Heaven and Earth last', he went over the complaints reported by Burney, stressing the calumnies spread by the supporters of the ex-King of Kedah and calling for his expulsion from Penang. He suggested that perhaps the Governor-General did not know the recent history of Kedah, and proceeded to give his own version of the causes of the Siamese action against its ruler. He also mentioned his agreement with Burney that Nakhoda Udin's petition should be dealt with by the Governor of Penang, saying that he was forwarding a copy of the petition to the Governor-General so that he might be aware of what he, the Raja, had done by way of conciliation. 'My true heart sends this explanation with sincerity', he wrote.

Robert Fullerton's decision on the two questions referred to him by the Raja of Ligor was precise and uncompromising. He sent him a map prepared by Burney some two years earlier in which the Krian was shown clearly as the boundary between Kedah and Perak, and commented that ever since the British had been acquainted with that area the Krian had been shown 'in every map and account of those countries' as the southern boundary of Kedah. Kurau in Perak territory, he said, had been found to be a stronghold of 'daring marauders' with Nakhoda Udin as their chief. He not only set the authority of the ruler of Perak at defiance, 'but participated in the plunder, purchased the slaves, supplied the pirates with arms, ammunition and opium and in fact afforded every possible encouragement to the pirates residing with him'. It was indispensable to the security of native traders and subjects of the Settlement to disperse such a band of pirates. When the attack was made, Nakhoda Udin had fled, but subsequently he had had the audacity to come to Penang where he was arrested by the police, who had plenty of evidence against him, and was sent for punishment to the Raja of Ligor. 'I cannot consent to hold communication with such a person as Nakhoda Udin,' wrote Governor Fullerton. Furthermore, he added, another notorious robber, Fakir Saib, was reported to be in the Raja's confidential employment. A reward of one hundred dollars was offered for his apprehension. There were many serious charges against him. The Governor ended his note with the request that under the terms of the treaty Fakir Saib be seized and sent to him.[1]

His treatment of Burney's report of his talks with the Raja at Trang was equally crushing. Concerning the charge of scaremongering by adherents of the ex-King of Kedah, and its effects, he said, he could only express wonder that Captain Burney should make such a frivolous matter the subject of a public communication. The real intentions of the Penang Government were well known in both Kedah and Bangkok, and no attack was ever expected by the Siamese. That there was emigration from Kedah was indeed true; at least 16,000 of the inhabitants of Province Wellesley had come from that state. But its real cause was the severity of Siamese rule and the security afforded by British rule.

As to the statement that no warlike preparations were ever made in the Trang River, good care had been taken on Captain Burney's first visit there to prevent him from seeing the evidence of them. The Raja of Ligor was too good a carpenter to leave his tools and his chips lying about for Captain Burney to inspect. And it was lamentable that he should have allowed the Kedah boundary question to be raised, seeing that he had no authority to discuss it. Captain Burney had always professed to have an extensive knowledge of the geography of the Malay countries, and Penang had a map of his own making wherein the Krian was expressly shown as the boundary between Kedah and Perak. Now doubts were being expressed on this point, and it was not the first time 'when the past opinion of Captain Burney gave way to present objects'. Whether Nakhoda Udin had been first placed at Kurau by the King of Kedah, or whether that king had ever declared the Kurau River to be the boundary was of little consequence, since

[1] Letter of 12 July 1827, BP, II, 6, pp. 198–90.

these things were done by order of the Raja of Ligor when he forced the King of Kedah to attack Perak.

He himself would prefer, he said, to judge Nakhoda Udin by the evidence of the police files rather than by the assertion of the Raja of Ligor or the belief of Captain Burney. The Kurau pirates had infested the Penang coasts for nearly a year, plundering prows, junks and fishing vessels, and murdering and wounding their crews. Upwards of seventy of the inhabitants had been sold into slavery, being taken in the first instance to Kurau. All the papers dealing with this had been shown to Captain Burney, and he had therefore much to answer for in allowing Nakhoda Udin to lead the Raja of Ligor to think that a British government would ever parley with the murderer of its subjects. Yet it was obvious that the Raja did think so. Captain Burney should have closed the door to any such approach, instead of opening it for further useless and vexatious discussions.[1]

Strikingly different was the Government of India's reaction to Burney's report. On 6 July Secretary George Swinton wrote on behalf of Lord Combermere, the Vice-President, and the Council of Fort William expressing their satisfaction with his actions, and notably with the trouble Burney had taken to remove from the Raja of Ligor's mind the suspicions he had 'not unnaturally entertained' regarding Penang's hostile intentions in view of recent troop reinforcements from Madras. They approved also the advice he had given the Penang Government about the removal of the ex-King of Kedah to some other British territory, and his account of his meeting with the Raja of Ligor. In the matter of the Perak affair, the Kurau question and Nakhoda Udin's complaint they entirely approved his judgement in persuading the Raja to submit to the adjustment he had proposed. They agreed with him about the unwisdom of interfering in the internal affairs of Perak, and expressed their wish that no arms or money had been furnished to the king before informing them. They accepted Burney's view of the Kurau incident and promised to let the Raja and Court of Siam know that nothing was farther from their intention than any encroachment on Siam's possessions, or infringement of the treaty. The correspondence, including the Raja's letter, Burney was informed, had been forwarded to the Governor-General, and he would write directly to the Governor of Prince of Wales Island.[2]

[1] BP, II, 6, pp. 194–6.   [2] *Ibid.*, pp. 185–8.

On the same date Swinton wrote to Burney on another matter of a more personal nature. Since arriving back from Siam Burney had been the subject of scurrilous attacks in the press of Penang and Singapore and also of Bengal. One article in particular, which appeared in the official Penang Gazette of 17 April 1827, and described the treaty as a disgrace to the British national character, caused him to write a strong letter of complaint to the Government of India. The article was unsigned, but Burney reported that he had learnt that the author was a certain Captain Lake, who was in the service of the Penang Government. The Vice-President in Council decided that the article was 'highly objectionable', that Lake's conduct was reprehensible, and moreover, that the censor who had passed the article should be called upon to explain his reasons for doing so. The Governor of Penang was accordingly requested to take such notice as he might think proper of the conduct of these gentlemen. A first-class row thereupon broke out in Penang. Its story can be read in the Burney MSS in the keeping of the Royal Commonwealth Institute's library in London.[1] Lake was so incensed at Burney's criticisms of his handiwork in his report to Calcutta that he challenged him to a duel. Happily however the latter had left Penang and was serving under the Civil Commissioner of Tenasserim. So Lake's letter dated 20 July 1827 did not reach him until the following October. Burney at once penned a dignified reply justifying the expressions he had used in drawing Calcutta's attention to the article. Here is part of it:

I conceived that your short residence to the Eastward, your being unacquainted with the Malay or Siamese language, and your declaring in your observations upon the Treaty with Siam that the Siamese might lay claim to Tenasserim without any breach of it, justified the expressions I used in my report to the Supreme Government as to your "absolute ignorance" of all points connected with our relations to the Eastward and as to your observations being "inaccurate". You charge me in an official Gazette with having concluded a Treaty that "is a disgrace to our national character, that has bartered our national fame, etc.", and on my complaining of this to superior authority in such terms as a sense of your injustice and my wounded pride prompt, you take personal offence and make my official letter the grounds for engaging in a private quarrel. That letter contains no reflection on your character as a gentleman and a man of honour, and what complaint was ever yet made that could not be said to be "personally offensive"?

[1] D XIX, nos 7-24; D XXVIII, nos 2-4.

The Supreme Government has determined that the subject shall be dropped. I have already received one very severe reprimand from the Honble Governor of Pinang for attempting to found private discussion upon public documents, and how far I shall be justified in giving you the meeting you demand I propose to take the opinion of a mutual friend Mr Maingy, before whom I will place the whole of the papers and whose opinion he will probably be good enough to communicate to you himself.

And there the record ends. No 'meeting' took place.[1]

After that piquant little episode we turn back to the previous July, when the Governor-General, who was at Meerut, had before him Burney's report and the other Penang documents submitted to him by Lord Combermere and his colleagues in Calcutta. Lord Amherst appears to have accepted Burney's estimate of the situation in full. He told Governor Fullerton that there was no justification for hostile measures against the Siamese; their proximity to Penang was in no way dangerous, particularly now that the Treaty of Bangkok had placed Anglo-Siamese relations on a new basis. He noted with regret that in the Governor's correspondence with the Raja of Ligor he treated him as an 'inveterate foe' whose ambitious projects must be met with unremitting opposition. Any increase in Penang's military strength, he said, which caused alarm to its neighbours, was unjustified, and in the existing state of the Government of India's finances it was his 'absolute duty' to veto any expenditure that could not bear the most rigorous scrutiny. Military expenditure therefore must be cut down to the lowest possible scale, and the most effective way of doing so would be to remove the ex-King of Kedah from Penang to Malacca. The Siamese had carried out their side of the bargain and the British were bound in honour to carry out theirs. They could offer to increase the ex-king's stipend from six thousand dollars to ten thousand on condition that he made the move.

Over Perak, wrote the Governor-General, the actions of the Penang Government were strictly *ultra vires*. The fourteenth article of the treaty laid down an engagement regarding that state which was between the East India Company and the Government of Siam. It was therefore the Government of India's function to decide what should be done in the case of its infraction by the Raja of Ligor.

[1] The letter is dated 'H. C. Steam Vessel *Enterprise* off Rangoon, 11 October 1827'.

Yet the Penang Government had instructed Captain Low to pledge British assistance to the ruler of Perak in expelling the Siamese, and that pledge, as well as a promise of protection against Selangor, had been made to depend upon the ruler's maintaining his independence of Siam. And, moreover, the Secretary of the Penang Government had asked Captain Burney whether it was authorized to oppose by force any attempt, open or indirect, of the Raja of Ligor upon Perak or Selangor.

It was his duty, said the Governor-General, to remind the Penang authorities, that only the Government of India could determine such matters, though, of course, giving full consideration to the advice that they with their local knowledge and experience could afford. He had learnt, he said, of Captain Low's actions in Perak with sincere regret. They furnished 'just ground of offence' to the Raja of Ligor and the Siamese. Captain Low had effected a revolution in the government, placing in power a party which the Siamese must consider an English faction. Then he had negotiated a treaty with the ruler in which the latter 'engaged *to the British Government* to have no further political connexion with Siam, and in return was promised assistance and protection'. The Penang Government could not, of course, approve such an engagement, nor was Captain Low authorized to make it. And he had failed to procure, as desired by his instructions, a document to prove to the Siamese that the ruler desired independence of Siam. His conduct in Perak was 'improper and censurable', but his attack upon Kurau was 'still more deeply culpable'; all the more so since it infringed the second article of the treaty. There was evidence on record to show that the Kurau River had for some years been considered to be the boundary between Kedah and Perak, and that Nakhoda Udin was first settled there by the ex-king of Kedah, and subsequently received a commission from the Raja of Ligor. The proper way to deal with an accusation that he sheltered pirates would have been to address a remonstrance to his own government. If that had failed, the matter could have been the subject 'of grave consideration' by the Penang Government and the Government of India. But it was obvious that the real object of the attack of Kurau was to destroy Siamese influence in that quarter.

The Raja of Ligor's remonstrance, declared Lord Amherst, must not be disregarded. There must be a full enquiry 'into the proceedings of the officer who attacked Kurao, a place acknowledging the authority of Siam, without any sanction whatever from his own government', and he feared that a heavy responsibility would attach to Captain Low unless he could furnish a far more satisfactory explanation than the papers before him contained. Captain Low accordingly must be suspended from all political activity, and it would be inexpedient for the Penang government to depute any further political missions to the states of the Malay Peninsula.[1]

The truth of the matter, however, was very different from what the Governor-General had been led to believe. Captain Low, as might be expected, made a straightforward explanation of his actions in a letter to Governor Fullerton which must have played no small part in the process of the Governor-General's disillusionment. He admitted that there was an inadvertent omission of a ratification clause in his engagement with the King of Perak, but claimed that ratification was perfectly understood as a matter of course. He substantiated his estimate of the numbers of Siamese in Perak during Burney's talks at Bangkok by reference to letters written by the Raja of Ligor, or at his order, to the king. He claimed that they would have been quite equal to the task of subduing the state without additional aid, and further that the internal Siamese faction itself could have overawed the king. Open force on the part of Siam, he said, would have been quite unnecessary. The king, he declared, made strong and decisive expression of his hatred of the Siamese to him in the presence of two other European gentlemen. If he was dissembling, then he possessed greater powers of tact than Captain Burney had credited him with.

As to the charge of having exceeded his instructions, he said, he had been provided with a copy of Captain Burney's preliminary treaty with the Raja of Ligor, and it was his discovery of the infraction of its second clause that had caused him to act as he had done. He had been actuated by extreme solicitude to act up to the spirit of his instructions. He wanted to free the king from thraldom to a faction devoted to Siamese interests and to check the progress of Siamese conquest towards Malacca, an object considered important by the Government of India. He referred to Burney's letter of 29 December 1826, in which, speaking of Anderson's mission to Perak and Selangor, he said that he regretted that Ander-

[1] BP, II, 6, pp. 205–15.

son had not erected a barrier against the Siamese in case they refused to ratify his agreement with the Raja of Ligor. Anderson, said Low, would have exceeded his instructions, had he done what he himself was afterwards deputed to do. If the Raja of Ligor was as solicitous to avoid interference in Perak as Captain Burney represented him to be, he had only to inform his partisans there of the fact. He would serve his country's interests best by promoting the friendly relations established by the treaty.

The aspersions cast upon the king of Perak's character, he said, were quite untrue. He was a man of upright mind and most anxious to perform his obligations to the Penang Government. Captain Burney had spoken too hastily about the small loan that had been granted to him. He had been robbed by both the Selangorians and the Siamese, and hence needed a few articles of comfort; and his deputies had brought with them a quantity of tin and antimony, the sale of which was quite adequate to defray the cost of the petty supplies they purchased, but which Captain Burney apparently grudged them. Perak produced so much tin that his apprehensions about the repayment of the loan were groundless.

Captain Burney's charge of incapacity against the Perak ruler was based on hearsay alone, wrote Low. It was indolence, not incapacity, from which he suffered; it was the result of deprivation of power, and was the besetting sin of Malays. Captain Burney asked what guarantee had the British. The answer was that a weak state, surrounded by more powerful ones, tended, if left to its own free choice, to opt for the protection of the one able to defend it. It was fair to believe that Perak, now free of all foreign influence, would gradually gain its level among the Malay states of the Peninsula.

With regard to the Kurau incident, Low wrote, it was not at all surprising that the Raja of Ligor should be displeased with him, for the pirates there were countenanced by him, as was shown by his treatment of their chief, Nakhoda Udin. Those lawless and desperate characters were well placed to further the Raja's ambitions in the direction of Malacca, and when it was opportune to call upon their services, could supply at least a hundred well-armed and hardy pirates together with a fleet of boats. But, he continued, it was the last thing he would have expected of Captain Burney that after he had expelled a horde of dangerous pirates, too destructive of Penang's native trade to be any longer endured, and had received the thanks of government for doing so, he, Burney, should listen to any statement made by their leader, Nakhoda Udin. 'I must confess too', he wrote, 'that I cannot perceive how he could consistently with his public capacity take so active a part in a subject which, as it had reference to pirates in the Perak Country only, became thereby properly cognizable by the Rajah of that country alone, in communication, if he chose, with the Prince of Wales Island Government.' Even if the Kurau River had not belonged to Perak, but to Siam, it was the right of those suffering from these cruel depredations to adopt any means to stop them. Over a matter of years, he went on, remonstrances had been made to the Siamese authorities; he himself had on one occasion been the personal channel for one of these, but in his opinion the Siamese had neither the means nor the will to cooperate with the British in clearing the coast of pirates. Indeed, in his capacity as controller of police in Wellesley he had had to report that a notorious pirate Fakeersaib, for whose capture a reward was being offered, was living openly in Kedah ostensibly under the protection of its Siamese ruler.

As to the the Raja of Ligor's claim to the Kurau area, Low continued, if Kedah had ever occupied it, 'it was the result of superior power, not right'. And however much Captain Burney might hamper the question by doubts, the truth of the matter was clear from his own statements and his map, 'lithographically produced in Calcutta'. He poured scorn on the Raja of Ligor's duplicity in making the abandonment of an untenable claim appear as if it were an act of friendly condescension. He denied Burney's statement that the attack on Kurau had been made in order to help the King of Perak: his instructions, he said, were to root out pirates. Had Captain Burney consulted the Wellesley police files, regarding Nakhoda Udin, he would never have 'lent him his countenance' or have stated that he disbelieved the evidence against him because Malays were inveterate liars. The Nakhoda's own papers seized by him at his haunt bore ample witness to his delinquency. His son, who lived with him, was actually a worse pirate than his father, and a warrant for his arrest had recently been issued by the police office.

Low then went on to describe Udin's methods in directing piracy. He explained that since he remained outside the settlement's territorial waters, he could not be dealt with by the Penang

Court of Judicature. This, he said, would account for his audacity in coming to Penang, hoping for the intervention of the Raja of Ligor and Captain Burney on his behalf. His statement regarding his loss of property was worthless. The property taken in the attack consisted chiefly of arms and boats. Afterwards it had been sold at public auction and the proceeds divided among the sepoys and other combatants participating. Low had since learned, he said, 'that he deposited his most valuable effects in Penang and then encouraged his gang to hold out to the last'.

Low concluded his letter with a discussion of the rumours of military preparations by Penang which, according to Burney, had irritated the Siamese. They were the sort of thing, he said, that Kedah Malays, anxious for freedom from the Siamese, would fabricate. He believed, however, that whatever the Siamese might say, they were not really worried. It was significant that there had been no interruption in native trade between Kedah and Penang, and frequent exchanges of friendly correspondence passed between the 'Young Chief' and himself. Everything, in fact, wore a peaceful aspect.

The letter ended with a sting in its tail. Captain Burney, he said, had been the channel of very grave complaints made against him by a noted pirate; this action he could not reconcile with any 'just or recognized principle'. Hence he could only ascribe it 'to private feeling'.[1]

Private feeling seems also to have been strong among the pro-Malays on the Penang Council. On 27 August Governor Fullerton and Mr. Ibbotson the Resident Councillor directed a swingeing attack on Burney to Lord Combermere, the Vice-President of the Fort William Council at Calcutta, enclosing with it Low's letter. Captain Burney they said had magnified the fear of the Siamese caused by the rumours regarding Penang's hostile preparations 'with his usual object of making difficulties in order to ensure to himself credit for overcoming them'. The rumours they explained, had arisen because during the process of relieving the garrison there was an unusual number of troops in the settlement. The Penang Council thought it extraordinary, they said, that 'that gentleman' should have made so much of the supposed increase in Penang's military forces when not much earlier he had recommended their increase 'in the event (the very one he has been

[1] Letter of 17 August 1827; BP, II, 6, pp. 225–37.

instrumental in bringing about)' of the Raja of Ligor permanently annexing Kedah. And since he made that statement, the military power and political influence of the Raja had been much increased 'by the management of Captain Burney'. Captain Burney, they complained, had officially reported idle gossip fit only for a Bengal newspaper.

He had also, they claimed, misrepresented their relations with the ex-King of Kedah, implying that they had been dilatory in the matter. On the contrary, they had done their utmost to induce him to go to Malacca. Captain Burney himself with their full assistance had tried to do so, and failed. Hence it was deplorable that the 'loose assertions of such a person as Captain Burney' should be accepted rather than their own statements. The ex-king still expected British aid, and claimed that Captain Burney, when about to go to Bangkok, had promised to obtain his restoration.

Captain Burney, they wrote, had 'artfully' tried to connect Captain Low's actions in Perak with the Kurau River incident. There was no connection whatever. The attack would have taken place if Captain Low had never been to Perak. Captain Burney had called it a questionable proceeding which had given the Siamese 'cause to tax us with a breach of the Treaty'. Yet it was on his own authority that they had accepted the Krian River as the boundary, and they had never before heard a doubt expressed about it. Moreover, the attack took place in January, yet the 'Ligor man' made no complaint. In fact, no notice was taken of it until Captain Burney went to Kedah in April. Obviously therefore he himself 'through his ill-judged compliance with every wish of the Raja of Ligor', had given rise to the complaint. It was noteworthy, however, that since the incident there had been a complete cessation of piracy. It was indisputable that Nakhoda Udin was a professed pirate and the protector of the Kurau gang.

They had stressed these points, the writers said, because the Government of India had so readily accepted Captain Burney's unsupported opinions without offering them the means of explanation. Captain Burney, they went on, was constantly changing his mind, and to enumerate the 'endless contradictions and inconsistencies' in his writings would take up more of their time than could be spared. They went on, however, to quote some chunks verbatim from them to show that Low's actions in Perak had been 'all in strict, almost literal, conformity' with what Captain Burney had recommended in the passages quoted, as the only possible course to prevent the Raja of Ligor from gaining control over Perak. Indeed, on his return from Bangkok he had spoken to Governor Fullerton of the need to send someone to Perak to explain to the king how he stood under article fourteen of the treaty. They had asked him to go himself, they declared, but he had declined with the plea that he wished to go to Calcutta. So Captain Low was appointed to go. Captain Burney, they went on, had read Low's instructions in Governor Fullerton's presence, and had approved them. He had then expressed anxiety to go himself so that the Siamese might be expelled and the king left free to make up his own mind. Their account of this incident, it may be pointed out, does not tally with Burney's. Which was nearer to the truth? The obvious comment, however, is that surely Burney *had* to take the treaty to Calcutta for ratification as soon as possible. The Penang authorities were not in a position to depute him to Perak.

With regard to what Captain Burney had said about the impolicy of intervention, wrote Fullerton and Ibbetson, they fully agreed with him. Low's intervention in Perak, however, they claimed, had been undertaken in order to set the king free from the trammels of Siam, and having achieved its object had ended. It was rather unreasonable, they pointed out, for Captain Burney to claim all the credit for the preventive article in the treaty, and object to the measures they had taken 'which alone gave it effect'.

They then went on to devote much space to detailing the inconsistencies in the opinions expressed by Burney about the Raja of Ligor's character and to defend their own efforts to counteract his ambitious designs. There is a great deal of rather boring detail all aimed at illustrating Burney's inconsistency. Even his liberation of the Burmese captives is brought into the argument. Why did his humanity stop short of Kedah, they ask, where the most grievous exactions have been made, and the children seized and sent to Siam. He himself had admitted in his report, they declared, that with respect to the Burmese captives that had been free 'an equal number of Kedah Malays were consigned to slavery in exchange'.

Their final charge of inconsistency against him was that he had prematurely discussed with the Raja of Ligor the 'contemplated cession' to Siam of the Tenasserim provinces. In their opinion, they said, Captain Burney was the most unlikely person to bring such negotiations to a successful conclusion, for in a memorandum dated 3 May 1825 he had written on that same subject, 'the more territory we cede to the Siamese the more of human misery I fear we shall unavoidably create'. There the letter ended. It was easy to charge Burney with inconsistency: he had indeed changed his mind on a number of matters. But it was far from being a fair assessment of his views and there is a touch of scurrility about parts of it.

Governor Fullerton's reply to the Governor-General a fortnight later was much more sober in tone. He had perused the letter, he said, with regret and concern, mitigated, however, by the realization that it was based solely upon Captain Burney's representations. The Vice-President and Council in Calcutta had submitted these to the Penang Council, and an answer to them had already left before Lord Amherst's letter arrived. He deeply regretted that the opinions expressed therein were so much at variance with those of His Lordship. He described the letter that followed as a brief recapitulation of the points made in the earlier one, and some further comments.

He was at a loss, he said, to guess whence the reports of military preparations had originated. The explanation might be, he thought, that the replacement troops for the garrison had this time come from Madras, and not Bengal, and through a misunderstanding had arrived equipped as a field force instead of one for garrison duty only. The matter had been taken up with the Madras Government, he added. But the reported alarm among the Siamese was quite untrue. While the changeover of troops was in progress, an envoy arrived with a letter from the Raja of Ligor expressing his entire disbelief in the reports of warlike preparations. They had sent him a full explanation of what had happened. Moreover, official documents entirely disproved Captain Burney's statements about the cessation of trade and emigration. He entirely agreed with the Governor-General, he said, that Siam offered no threat to them: the British victory in Burma had removed any risk of trouble, and the idea of adopting a menacing attitude towards Siam had never even entered his mind.

He would judge the Raja of Ligor by his deeds rather than his words, he said; but, whatever his own private opinion of him, it would not interfere with the maintenance of the amicable relations required by the public service. He was disappointed that the ratification of the treaty had not put an end to irritating discussion; hence the new controversy raised by Captain Burney had caused him to use more asperity in his remarks than was perhaps necessary. He hoped that his recent letter to the Raja of Ligor would lead to the establishment of perfect harmony.

Then he turned to the fourteenth article of the treaty. He reminded the Governor-General that the restoration of the King of Kedah had been one of the objects of Captain Burney's mission to Bangkok; in other words, to push Siamese rule back to the distance from Penang at which it had originally stood. Failing that, it had to be prevented from expanding further southwards. This could be done only through Perak remaining independent. He had therefore considered himself warranted under the treaty to take the measure which appeared to be indispensable for that object. He could only repeat his regret, he said, that through his 'misconception' he had gone further in that direction than had been strictly intended. But Perak was now independent, and the benefits of this, the improvement of trade and co-operation in the destruction of piracy, showed what could be expected, were all the other Malay states of the Peninsula free.

There still appeared to be some misunderstanding about the attack on the pirates in the Kurau River. He must therefore repeat that it had no political implications. The depositions and papers he was now forwarding gave full details of everything. Captain Low acted on the express orders of the Penang Government. The attack was directed against the pirates, not against Nakhoda Udin individually. Udin himself was not actually engaged in any act of piracy, but supported, maintained and shared in the spoils of the principal pirates mentioned in the depositions. Kurau was originally under a Perak headman, and Perak's possession of it had been undisturbed until he was driven out by a Siak pirate. This man was later succeeded by another Siak pirate, Nakhoda Udin. The King of Perak was unable to expel him without Penang's aid. And, said Fullerton, they intended to carry on similar operations all along the coast. It had not occurred to him that the Raja of Ligor would lay claim to the Kurau area; otherwise he would have communicated with him as well as with the King of Perak. He had acted, he said, on the authority of a geographical sketch of the Siamese states made by Captain Burney, dated 10 April 1825 and signed by him as Political Agent to those states. In it the Krian was shown as the southern boundary of Kedah. And in a letter to the Penang Government as well as in a communication to the Raja of Ligor he had also made this quite clear. So it was strange that he should have described the attack on the pirates so many miles from the Krian as an infringement of Kedah's territory. It was a matter of the most serious regret to him, he said, that the Penang Government should have inadvertently afforded ground for the charge of infringment of the treaty, 'one of the very last acts we should be willingly guilty of'. Yet the police files told an indisputable tale of piracies which Nakhoda Udin and his principal, the Raja of Ligor, did nothing to stop. In fact the latter kept quiet about the whole business. 'It never certainly occurred to us', wrote the Governor, 'that the clandestine and unacknowledged establishment of an agent of Ligore within the territory of Perak could establish in the former any right over the country of the latter'. And it was very regrettable that Captain Burney, before adopting the views of the Chief of Ligor, and taking up Nakhoda Udin's cause, did not get in touch with the authorities on the island so as to obtain authentic information on the subject.

Captain Low, Governor Fullerton went on, was serving as an assistant to the Superintendent of Police. His post was non-political, but care would be taken that he should consult the Penang Government before doing anything that might cause offence to the Kedah authorities.

The injunction to abstain from deputing any further political missions seems to have touched Fullerton on a raw spot. He assured Lord Amherst that it should be scrupulously observed, and then went on to indulge in a lengthy apologia regarding those with which he had been connected in the past. He insisted that everything that he had done had been done with the sanction of the 'Supreme Authority' or in accordance with his own conception of the public interest. And he administered a passing kick at the doctrine of non-intervention. 'Had I found', he wrote, 'on the records of this government any decided opinions of the Home Authorities, such as would have satisfied me that they considered our interference a greater evil than the one apprehended in the extension of Siamese dominion, I would of course have adopted another line.' Now, however, he pointed out, the object of such missions no longer existed, and he gladly reverted to the strict observance of the principle of non-intervention. He would ever regret, he said, that his aberration from that principle had brought upon him the only censure from Superior Authority that he had ever met with in thirty-eight years of service.

It was an able statement, convincing, though not unfree from flashes of truculence. He had brought Siamese expansion on his side of the peninsula at least to a halt, and could therefore confidently face his critics. So confident indeed was he that without waiting for the Government of India's reply, he wrote to the Raja of Ligor that the Kurau River was within Perak's territory and that there was conclusive proof that Nakhoda Udin had engaged in piracy. Hence the Penang Government dismissed the case.

The Government of India accepted Fullerton's statement, and the Governor-General, who had returned to Calcutta, signed its letter of 16 November 1827 expressing its entire satisfaction that Nakhoda Udin was a pirate and that in the operation against him the Penang Government had taken the Kurau River to be inside the territory of Perak. It accordingly revoked the censure on Captain Low and his suspension from further political activities. The Government of India expressed regret that the evidence it now had before it, the police reports and the depositions, had not been forwarded earlier, and, moreover, that the Raja of Ligor had been afforded any plea to complain of aggression. It would have been better, Governor Fullerton was counselled, if before taking the extreme measure entrusted to Captain Low, his government had sent the Raja of Ligor the evidence it had against Nakhoda Udin, and informed him of the action it was about to take.

Furthermore, in the opinion of the Government of India the Raja of Ligor's claim to the Kurau, and its occupation for some years past as part of the Kedah state had to be examined. Captain Burney's map was based upon the best information he could procure at the time, but if the Raja of Ligor were to establish his claim, the British Government would be answerable for the error. Therefore the King of Perak must be asked to produce conclusive evidence that Kurau belonged to his state. At the same time the Penang authorities could impress upon the Raja of Ligor that it was the right of all nations to punish pirates wherever they might be found.

And so the matter ended. The Raja dropped his complaints; Nakhoda Udin drops into obscurity. And Henry Burney was in a new country learning a new language. Had he been as inconsistent as the Penang people claimed? Their cocksure, intolerant attitude towards him and his treaty when he returned from Bangkok must have galled him deeply, and his hurt feelings could have led him to show lack of judgement in reporting the Raja of Ligor's case to Calcutta. But there is no record that the Government of India considered him in any way culpable.

Rangoon in 1825

Part Three

BURMA

Chapter 10

Burma and the British

HENRY Burney's last and longest diplomatic appointment was as Resident Minister to the Court of Ava under the terms of the Treaty of Yandabo, which ended the Anglo-Burmese war of 1824-6. Through his study of the Siamese language he had been able to introduce some measure of mutual understanding into Anglo-Siamese relations, and his treaty, whatever view one may take of its place in Malay history, was for Siam the 'first step that counts' in the Chakri dynasty's dealings with the Western world whose expansion into South-East Asia was to assume such frightening proportions later on in the nineteenth century. Burney's achievement in persuading the rumour-racked court of Rama III to commit itself to such a step must not be underestimated. He was to have a far more difficult task in Burma, one indeed in which success in the ordinary sense of the word was impossible. But here again, although he finally left the country in despair, his achievement was considerable, and it sprang from just those qualities of character and intellect, patience and an ardent desire to understand, which he had shown in Siam. His mastery of the Burmese language and his study of Burmese chronicle writings enabled him to communicate with the members of the Court of Ava as no British envoy had ever done before. And the fact that, when the crisis of Tharrawaddy's rebellion occurred, the king and ministers turned to Burney for help and advice, is evidence of the special place he had come to occupy in their regard.

The kingdom of Ava, to which he was deputed in 1830, had a long history behind it, though not reaching quite so far back as the chronicles he studied would have us believe. In the year before Burney's arrival at Ava a committee of learned men had compiled the great record known as *The Glass Palace Chronicle*, and the ministers, with whom he was in daily contact were soaked in their country's history and traditions. The heartland of the kingdom was in the middle reaches of the Irrawaddy River, first settled by the Burmans in the middle of the ninth century A.D. coming down from the mountains of western Yunnan. They were a conquering people, bent on gaining the upper hand over the thinly-spread peoples of the land to which they were to give their name. Their first big achievement in this direction was the kingdom of Pagān which came into being in the eleventh century and ultimately controlled, directly or indirectly, all of present-day Burma save the mountain areas inhabited by the Chins, the Kachins, the Shans and the Karens.

Prior to its collapse at the end of the thirteenth century before the armies of Kublai Khan Pagān had produced a rich Theravada Buddhist civilization, the material remains of which still surviving today are as impressive as those of its contemporary Angkor, though less well known. To appreciate the glory of its architecture and sculpture during its first century of greatness, when Mon culture was the dominating influence, one must turn to the three masterly volumes of Professor Gordon Luce entitled *Old Burma— Early Pagan*.[1] The original Theravada influence had come from the old Mon kingdom of Dvaravati centred upon the lower Menam valley. It was revitalized from time to time by powerful influences from Ceylon beginning during the last quarter of the eleventh century, when Pagān acquired from Ceylon the complete text of the Pali Tripitaka.

The second half of the twelfth century saw the retreat of Mon artistic influence from Pagān and the triumph of Burmese styles. What this fundamental change betokened in social and political terms is largely a matter for guesswork. A rift developed between the Burmans and the Mons, and when Pagān was attacked by the Mongols, the Mons broke away to found their own independent kingdom, which under it capital Pegu maintained its separate existence till nearly the middle of the sixteenth century.

The Mongols failed to maintain their hold over their conquests in the centre and north of Burma, but in their wake had come Tai peoples looking for new homes in Burma. Shans the Burmans called them, and Shan leaders of military contingents played their part in freeing central Burma and the city of Pagān from the Mongol armies. They then made a strong bid to gain control over

[1] Published for *Artibus Asiae* and the Institute of Fine Arts, New York University as Supplementum 25, Locust Valley, New York, J. J. Augustin, 1969-70.

what was left of the Pagān kingdom. In the struggle Pagān ceased to be a capital city. After a period of chaos a new capital was founded in 1364 at Ava, many miles to the north at the confluence of the Myitnge and Irrawaddy rivers, which was to become a centre of Burmese culture, and of resistance to the Shans. Ava adopted the traditions of Pagān, including the ambition to unite all Burma under its sway. In this it failed, however, for it wasted its strength in futile attempts to conquer the Mon kingdom of Pegu before it had mastered the Shans. In 1527 it fell before the onslaught of a powerful Shan state.

Ava's fall turned out to be only a temporary setback for the Burmans. Leadership in the struggle to reunite all Burma under the Burmans was next assumed by the state of Toungoo, dominating the Sittang valley, which had come into existence much at the same time as Ava as a haven of refuge for Burmans escaping from Shan dominance, and when Ava fell received a large augmentation to its population. The Shans' congenital incapacity to unite made it possible for the Toungoo kingdom to conquer the rich Mon state of Pegu as a first step towards reuniting Burma and turning the tables on the Shans. It fell to the military hero Bayinnaung to accomplish this early in the second half of the sixteenth century. But he then frittered away his country's strength in attempt after attempt to conquer and hold Siam in subjection. By the end of the century Siam had regained independence and Burma was in chaos: all central authority had vanished.

The Toungoo dynasty, however, staged a comeback. It reasserted its authority over Burma and the Shan States, and even staged a counter-attack which made Chiengmai a vassal state. Then it transferred its capital away from the horribly devastated Mon area, which had borne the brunt of the struggles with Siam, to Ava far away up the Irrawaddy. There shut off from the outside world by difficulties of communications it pursued a policy of complacent isolationism which left its permanent mark. The palace was the centre of the universe, a Burmese one, to which foreigners were admitted only on sufferance and as humble suppliants.

In 1740 the Mons rebelled and re-established their kingdom of Pegu. They captured Ava in 1752 and brought about the final downfall of the dynasty. But this stirred up such a tremendous outburst of Burman resistance that they were driven headlong out of Upper Burma and thrown on the defensive. A new Burman leader, the headman of Moksobomyo, who called himself Alaungpaya, 'embryo Buddha', crushed Mon independence with the capture of Pegu in 1757 and reunited the whole country under his sway. The chief Mon port of Syriam was destroyed, and, in what might have heralded a breakaway from isolationism, Alaungpaya founded Rangoon, 'the end of strife', to take its place. But his own capital was at Moksobomyo, many miles north of even Ava itself, and his court reflected the time-honoured traditionalism of Upper Burma. His own ambition was to emulate the military exploits of Bayinnaung.

So for the second time in her history Burma engaged in half-a-century of further attempts to subjugate Siam, and with no greater success than on the earlier occasion. True, she captured and destroyed Siam's old capital Ayuthaya, in 1767. But this was a mere flash in the pan, for immediately afterwards she had to defend herself against a series of Chinese invasions, and lost hold of her prey. And Siam, as we have seen, staged a remarkable recovery under first Phraya Taksin and next General Chakri, the founder of Bangkok. Burma's military ardour, however, though unable to prevail against the new Siam, was stimulated by her success in withstanding the Chinese invasions, and further boosted by her conquest of the kingdom of Arakan on her western flank. Hence after the failure of her greatest attempt to subdue Siam in 1785–6 she turned her main attention to the states on her north-west frontier, regardless of the fact that her depredations became an intolerable nuisance to the expanding British dominion in India. Her treatment of the Arakanese, and later the Assamese, caused thousands of them to take refuge in British territory, whence they made attempt after attempt to recover their homelands. The English East India Company had not the means to cope with this situation to begin with, for it was faced with more urgent problems arising out of the Napoleonic wars and the maintenance of its position in India. So the situation gradually got out of hand until the Anglo-Burmese war of 1824–6 was the outcome. Before that war opened with the British seizure of the Burmese port of Rangoon in May 1824, hostilities had been in progress for some time in the frontier regions between Bengal and Burma. The Burmese had seized control over Assam and Manipur, and had begun to overrun Cachar, when the British decided that a stand must be made against further encroachments, declared that state to be a protectorate, and sent a force to withstand the invaders. On the Arakan-Chittagong frontier the Burmese had attempted to hold an island on the British side of the River Naaf. Then in January 1824 General Bandula, the supreme director of this forward policy, took charge in northern Arakan and began to threaten Chittagong. The British expected a move towards Calcutta. Hence war was declared, in March, and an expeditionary force was sent to seize Rangoon in order to compel Bandula to abandon his operations on the Chittagong frontier and turn his attention southwards.

Rangoon was taken almost without a blow, and the British-Indian force of 11,000 men should then have been at once launched on its way northwards towards the capital. But adequate transport was lacking and the monsoon rains were about to break. Hence it was tied down to Rangoon, for the duration of the rains, badly supplied and a prey to crippling casualties from disease.

Nevertheless it beat off major Burmese attacks so decisively that Bandula had to cancel his northern operations and made a forced march with 60,000 men to try to save the situation. His two attacks upon the British positions in December 1824 turned out to be the decisive battles of the war. Their defeat caused him to withdraw northwards to Danubyu, where in a further engagement he was killed on 1 April 1825 and his troops retired in disorder. Thereupon the British army, heavily reinforced, advanced to Prome and went into cantonments during the monsoon rains. When these ended in October, and the British advance up the Irrawaddy began again, the Burmese sought an armistice and peace talks. These turned out to be merely a cover for a surprise attack by the Burmese. It was beaten off, however, and the march on the capital was resumed. At Malun there was a further halt, at the Burmese request, for the discussion of peace terms. The British demands, however, so shocked the Burmese commissioners that again the talks were broken off. So again the march proceeded, with the British brushing off further Burmese attacks, and the Burmese commissioners coming back again and again to plead or haggle for better terms, but all in vain. At last on 24 February 1826 at the village of Yandabo on the Irrawaddy just three days march from the capital the Court of Ava accepted the British terms and ratified the treaty. The British advance was then halted.

This was the main operation of the war. There were, however, subsidiary operations on other fronts. Raja Gambhir Singh of

Manipur with some British officers as military advisers drove the Burmese out of his country and regained his throne. British Indian troops cleared Assam of its Burmese invaders. Further south Arakan was occupied during the early months of 1825, but a projected attack on the city of Ava across the Arakan Yoma had to be abandoned owing to the difficulty of transporting an army through the mountains. Lastly, though not in point of time, there was the occupation of the Burmese provinces along the Tenasserim coast from Martaban southwards, which figured so prominently in Henry Burney's negotiations in Bangkok. This was completed early in the war.

The war, as we have already seen, ended in February 1826 with the Treaty of Yandabo. Burma had to cede the kingdom of Arakan, which she had so recently acquired, and the southern provinces of Ye, Tavoy, Mergui and Tenasserim, which she had conquered from Siam in the middle of the previous century. She had further to yield all claims to Assam on India's north-east frontier, and abstain from any further interference in the states of Manipur, Kachar and Jaintia. Under Article 5 of the Treaty she had to pay the Government of India an indemnity of one crore of rupees, then equal to a million pounds sterling. The treaty also laid down, under Article 7, that in order to cultivate and improve friendly relations between the two governments 'accredited ministers' from each should reside at the 'durbar' of the other, and that a commercial treaty should be contracted for their mutual advantage.

During the negotiations the Burmese commissioners fought as hard as they could against Article 7. It was bad enough for the Golden Feet to have to sign a treaty with the Bangalamyosa, 'eater of the province of Bengal', a mere subordinate officer of the King of England, but to have to treat him as an equal by an exchange of resident ministers was an outrage. It was unprecedented in Burma's history, as also was such an instrument as a treaty; hence, no sooner was it signed than all the endeavours of the Court of Ava were directed towards rendering it of no avail.

The British were equally firm that such an engagement was essential for the maintenance of peace: they wanted no more trouble from Burma. They hoped that friendly relations could be cultivated, as they had been with Nepal 'under similar circumstances of defeat and humiliation and territorial cession' by the installation

of a Resident at Khatmandu.[1] They were to find the Court of
Ava bewilderingly different from that of Khatmandu. But they
should have known better. They had twice before in pre-war days
tried the experiment of maintaining a resident agent in Burma,
but after the failure of Hiram Cox's and John Canning's missions
it should have been obvious that the Court of Ava was fundamentally
opposed not merely to this method of carrying on relations but
to any other method than *ad hoc* missions which returned to base
when their business was concluded. A word of explanation regarding Cox's and Canning's missions must be interjected here.[2] The
Burmese conquest of the old kingdom of Arakan in 1785 had
brought them for the first time into direct contact with British
India, and owing to the flight of Arakanese refugees across the
frontier a dangerous situation arose which was embarrassing to the
Government of India which had all its attention concentrated
upon the Indian scene. The outbreak of war with Revolutionary
France and the possibility that French commerce-raiders would be
permitted to take refuge in Burmese harbours made Calcutta all
the more anxious to develop good relations with the Court of Ava.
Hence in 1795 Captain Michael Symes was sent to discuss matters
with King Bodawpaya's government and negotiate an agreement
whereby a Company's agent might reside in Rangoon. To this
the Burmese were agreeable and in due course Captain Hiram Cox
was deputed to reside on the Company's behalf in Burma. The failure of his mission was due primarily to his own unwillingness to
conform to the conception of his position envisaged in his instructions, and his refusal to accept the conditions imposed upon
him by the Court of Ava. He stirred up so much resentment that
the Government of India had to withdraw him and make what
amounted to an apology for his behaviour. Whether a more pliant
man would have succeeded is open to question. It wasn't just a
simple question of supervising trade and keeping an eye open for
French activities. The Court of Ava had become interested in the

---

[1] See Governor-General Cavendish-Bentinck's minute of 30 December 1829 quoted in Desai, p. 45.
[2] For the story of Captain Hiram Cox's residence in Burma in 1797-8 my edition of *Michael Symes; Journal of his Second Embassy to the Court of Ava in 1802*, Introduction, section vi, should be consulted. His own account, *Journal of a Residence in the Burmhan Empire* (London, 1821), omits vital parts of it. In my introduction to the 1971 reprint of the work (Gregg International Publishers, Ltd) I have indicated the nature and importance of the omissions.

breakdown of the Ahom dynasty's rule in Assam and was considering intervention. A British agent in Burma was bound to be regarded as a spy.

The Canning incident took place in 1803. To get into perspective we must go back to 1798 when another mass flight of Arakanese into Chittagong occurred, and Burmese incursion across the frontier in pursuit of them. The Burmese viceroy of Arakan went so far as to threaten war. The Government of India set in motion measures designed to render the control of the frontier more effective and sent Symes on his second mission to Ava to come to an understanding with the Burmese. The Calcutta authorities and Symes still believed that the only way to prevent ultimate war was to establish closer communications between the two governments. A British agent must reside in Rangoon. This time the plan was to send Symes's assistant, Lieutenant John Canning, there under his own direction, and not under the immediate control of the Government of India. It was hoped that through his personal friendship with the Viceroy of Rangoon Symes would be able to smooth out any difficulties that might arise. And Canning was not a stranger: he had been to Ava with Symes and was well liked. The experiment failed because of the feud between the viceroy and his deputy, the Yewun. The latter brought charges against his superior at Ava causing his recall and suspension. Canning arrived while this showdown was in progress at the capital. He was well received by the deputy head of the Rangoon administration. But shortly afterwards the Yewun returned with full authority, and at once issued an order for all Canning's correspondence to be opened. The object of course was to force him to return to Calcutta, and he did. Soon after he had gone, however, the Viceroy returned to Rangoon, having cleared himself of the Yewun's charges. When he discovered what had happened, he wrote off to Canning in Calcutta expressing his regret at his deputy's action and rescinding the order for correspondence to be opened. The Calcutta authorities on their part confirmed Canning's action in returning to base; they felt that there could be no guarantee against something of the sort happening again. So no further attempt was made to settle a resident agent in Burma.

The Court of Ava was equally against deputing a Burmese agent to reside in Calcutta. As to the exchange of residents at ministerial level, it was convinced that such a method was bound to lead to a loss of independence. Burma would be reduced to the status of an Indian native state.

And indeed how far wrong was this assumption? One has only to turn back to Michael Symes's report on his second embassy to the Court of Ava for light upon the British attitude. 'A paramount influence in the Court of Ava', he wrote, 'obtain it how we may, is now become indispensably necessary to the interest and security of the British possessions in the East.'[1] Burma was in the same position strategically in relation to British India as Ireland was in relation to Britain herself at that time, and strategic considerations dominated the minds of the British commissioners at Yandabo. The Government of India's view was that the treaty brought Burma into a special relationship with it as paramount power in India; the Court of Ava was shrewdly aware of the fact and determined to steer clear of the implications of the treaty. It could never for a moment accept Calcutta's version of its status. Furthermore, a British Resident would be a constant reminder of Burma's humiliation. He would also be a spy. Hence, when at last the Court did have to receive a Resident on a permanent basis, it was with the sole intention of using him as a channel for negotiations designed to whittle away the provisions of the hated treaty.

Such was the situation with which Henry Burney had to contend when he made his way up the Irrawaddy to Ava in 1830 as British Resident. And now we must take a brief look at the events leading up to his appointment to that office. The Bengal Secret and Political Consultations contain a notification dated 22 December 1826 to the effect that after exchanging ratified copies of the Siam treaty with the Raja of Ligor's son in Kedah Burney was to join the Civil Commission of the Tenasserim Provinces and assume charge of the southern portion at Mergui as Assistant to the Civil Commissioner.[2] There were at the time two commissioners, the Political Commissioner, Sir Archibald Campbell, Commander-in-Chief of the British forces in Burma, who was the senior, and the Civil Commissioner, Major A. D. Maingy, who had been sent from Penang in September of the previous year to introduce civil rule into the occupied Burmese provinces of Mergui, Tavoy and Ye under the supervision of the Governor of Prince of Wales

[1] *Michael Symes, Journal of his Second Embassy to the Court of Ava in 1802*, ed. D. G. E. Hall, p. 34.
[2] Document no. 13.

Island. The joint rule of Campbell and Maingy had been set up in September 1826 after the Burmese territories south of Martaban ceded under the Yandabo treaty had been consolidated to form the British province of Tenasserim. When this happened, the Governor of Prince of Wales Island ceased to exercise control, and the province was placed directly under the Government of India. This dual arrangement lasted until the end of the year 1828, when Maingy was placed in sole charge.[1]

Burney, who now began to learn Burmese with the same assiduity as he had shown earlier in acquiring other necessary languages, earned his new chief's warm approbation. In reporting on him to the Government of India Maingy wrote: 'It would be unjust in me not to take this opportunity of apprising the Supreme Government that the talents and resources of Captain Burney's mind, no less than his deep research and indefatigable zeal and exertions, place me on every occasion under very important obligations.'[2]

Meanwhile, not only did the Court of Ava make no move to appoint a minister to reside in Calcutta, but the British authorities also seem to have had second thoughts on whether the provision in Article 7 of the treaty was the best method of carrying on relations between the two governments. At last, after a delay of several months, John Crawfurd, Burney's predecessor as British Envoy to Siam and subsequently Raffles's successor at Singapore, was conveyed to the Burmese capital on the steamer *Diana*, and in September 1826 assumed his duties as Envoy and Resident Minister. His principal task was to negotiate the commercial treaty provided for in the Yandabo document. He was also empowered to discuss the adjustment of any boundary questions that might be raised by the Burmese, and, indeed, any other matters arising out of the treaty of Yandabo.

When he arrived, the British army no longer threatened the capital from the village of Yandabo, but had retired to Rangoon, where they were to remain until the second instalment of the indemnity had been paid. The Court of Ava therefore had recovered

---

[1] J. S. Furnivall, 'The Fashioning of Leviathan', *Journal of the Burma Research Society*, XXIX, i, April 1939, pp. 4–7.
[2] *Selected Correspondence of Letters issued from and received in the Office of the Commissioner, Tenasserim Division*, Govt. Printing Office, Rangoon, 1916, quoted by Furnivall, *op. cit.*, p. 11.

from the worst of its fright, and was prepared to treat him with all its customary technique of humiliation so familiar to pre-war British envoys. As in the csae of his earlier missions to Siam and Cochin China, Crawfurd later published a full account of his experiences in Burma in a book, which is also, like those of Symes, Cox and Yule, a storehouse of information about the country and its people.[1] He laboured under the disadvantage of inability to use the language, and possessed neither Burney's patience nor his charm of manner. But even the most complaisant of men would have been put out by the calculated insolence of his treatment at his official reception by King Bagyidaw, at which the Governor-General of India was described as making his submission to the Golden Feet and begging pardon for past offences. He had to endure weeks of intensive haggling over the outstanding instalments of the indemnity and the ceded territories, the object of which was the cancellation of the former and the retrocession of the latter. His proposals for the commercial treaty were for the most part rejected and he had to be content with an almost worthless document of four clauses, which in its Burmese version was shown as a royal order (*ameindaw*).

By the time this had been signed, Crawfurd had, in the words of Sir Henry Yule, been rendered 'weary, hopeless and disgusted'. He declared that his instructions did not permit him to make a final decision on the other matters, which must be left over for further negotiations, and on 12 December he left Ava and began the long tedious journey to Calcutta. He reported that it was in his view inexpedient to appoint a permanent Resident. Such an officer, he said, 'distant by a navigation of 1,200 miles (near 500 of it within the Burman territory, where every species of communication is placed under the most rigorous and vexatious restraint) from the authority he represents, and an object of perpetual jealousy to a Government indescribably ignorant and suspicious, could exercise little useful influence upon the counsels of that government, would have no means of furnishing his own with useful intelligence, and would, in a word, be placed in a situation amounting to little better than honourable imprisonment.'[2] He recommended that relations with Ava should be conducted through

---

[1] *Journal of an Embassy from the Governor-General of India to the Court of Ava*, London, 1829.
[2] *Journal*, 2nd edn., Vol. II, Appendix III, p. 26

the civil or military officer exercising chief authority on the Salween frontier.

The Government of India severely criticized Crawfurd's conduct of his negotiations: it was of opinion that he had interpreted his instructions too narrowly, and regretted that he had quitted Ava without first communicating with it. Lord Amherst himself, who was away from Calcutta when the report was considered by his Council, thought its tone of disapproval too strong, but agreed that, in the case of the points brought up for discussion by the Burmese ministers, he should have reported them to his government and awaited instructions. Crawfurd in a spirited reply made the telling point that far too much had been expected of him; the negotiations should have been opened before the British army left Yandabo: its withdrawal under a defective treaty drawn up by military men was a blunder. That was true enough, but the defects had not been discovered until after the army's withdrawal.

The Government of India now had to make up its mind as to whether to appoint another resident minister at Ava or a consul at Rangoon. Lord Amherst, writing in May 1827, came down strongly in favour of a consul at Rangoon to ensure the proper observance of the commercial treaty, and to act as political agent under the principal British authority on the Tenasserim coast.[1] He proposed Henry Burney's appointment to this post. It was not, however, envisaged as a permanent one. He thought that when Anglo-Burmese relations settled down, there would be insufficient employment for such an officer. This strange statement calls for explanation. It must be seen in terms of the fond hope, cherished by some at the time, that the new port of Kyaikkami, developed during the war for military purposes, and renamed Amherst, could supplant Rangoon as the chief centre for Burma's overseas trade. Events, of course, were to decide otherwise, and it is significant that Sir Archibald Campbell, on becoming Political Commissioner, established his headquarters at Moulmein, opposite Martaban at the mouth of the Salween.

Burney's views on his proposed appointment were quite different from Lord Amherst's, and in the following August he was deputed by his chief A. D. Maingy, to discuss matters personally with the Government of India. His argument was that there were two overriding reasons for the appointment of a Resident to the

[1] BSP, Vol. 346, no. 4, quoted in Desai, *op. cit.*, p. 52.

Court of Ava. In the first place because it was necessary to convey a proper impression of British power, and in the second place so that the Government of India might maintain direct communications with him. The Burmese version of the Yandabo treaty, he explained, used the term *ayashi*, meaning 'accredited minister', to describe the officer. As such he would not be amenable to Burmese law. The term 'consul', he said, was quite unknown to the Burmese, and there was a danger that unless his official position were not clearly defined, he would be treated as a mere commercial agent as Symes and Cox had sometimes been. He failed to convince the Supreme Government, however, and in January 1828 was sent back to Tenasserim and posted as Deputy Commissioner of Tavoy. It was decided to continue with the method of a Political Assistant in Rangoon under the authority of the Political Commissioner of Tenasserim. It was a much cheaper expedient than maintaining a resident at the capital and, incidentally, more in line with the very strongly held views of the Court of Ava. But it was far from adequate for the task for which the exchange of resident ministers had been envisaged by the British commissioners at Yandabo, and this events were to demonstrate.

It was the problem of the future of Tenasserim that, more than anything else, brought matters to a head. The cost of the new province's administration greatly exceeded its revenue. Added to this, the cost of the Burma war had embarrassed the East India Company's finances. Hence the Board of Directors began to toy with the idea of retrocession. But in 1827 there was a fairly considerable flow of immigrants from Burma, and Henry Burney urged that since they were Mon refugees, after the suppression of their rebellion against the re-imposition of Burmese rule after the war, retrocession must be ruled out. His suggestion was that the province should be offered to Siam in exchange for a consideration and subject to the overriding condition that such inhabitants as were unwilling to come under Siamese rule should have full freedom to quit. He advised that Britain should retain sovereignty over the off-shore islands and occupy one small well-fortified post as a commercial entrepot and port where vessels in distress might refit, and in case of another European war, to prevent any other power from settling there.[1]

[1] Note endorsed 'Fort William, Secret Dept, 6 July 1827' in Home Miscellaneous Series, Vol. 675; BP II, 4, p. 77-8.

This reads somewhat strangely in the light of the recommendations in Burney's report on his mission to Siam. What had made him change his mind? The answer seems to be that his experience in the Tenasserim administration had made him despair of the indigenous inhabitants. 'They are as averse as the Malays to labour,' he writes, 'and like the Malays they are content with cultivating a little paddy for their subsistence, and as one or two days' labour can supply them with the scanty means of subsistence they require for eight or ten days, they will work only for that short period.' The province, he was convinced, would never be of any commercial value unless 'an exotic race', Chulias or Chinese, were introduced, and that would be a long and expensive business.

Nothing came of Burney's proposal. It was quite impracticable, and indeed he realized that Siam was most unlikely to accept the British conditions. The Board of Control in London, however, decided to get rid of this 'undesirable possession', as its President, Lord Ellenborough, dubbed it in November 1828, when the decision was taken. But how to do so without incurring a considerable loss of face, was a question to which there was no ready answer. Siam was ruled out. So was the creation of an independent state. Retrocession was the only way to get rid of it. So the Government of India decided that the Court of Ava should be approached to see whether it would be willing to offer some consideration, the island of Negrais, or the Bassein district, or a sum of money, for the recovery of the unwanted province.

The sheer absurdity of this last proposal is an indication alike of Calcutta's abysmal ignorance regarding Burma and of its almost desperate desire to retrieve what it now saw as a most regrettable error. But this was not all: Henry Burney, who was selected for the task, was to go to Ava, not as the accredited representative of the Government of India, but as agent for the Commissioner of Tenasserim. By this time Sir Archibald Campbell had relinquished the post of Political Commissioner, and his colleague, A. D. Maingy, was in sole control. The latter was plainly horrified at the proposal: he was sure that the Court of Ava would regard it as an insult. He decided that the best way to persuade the Government of India of the unwisdom of its proposal was to send Henry Burney to Calcutta to explain matters. So thither at the beginning of the cold season late in 1829 went Burney to argue that no officer must be deputed to Ava save under the direct authority of the Governor-

General. He had apparently no difficulty in convincing Lord William Cavendish Bentinck, who in a minute of 30 December 1829 announced his decision to establish a permanent residency at the Court of Ava and to appoint Major Henry Burney British Resident.[1]

The Tenasserim question, however, was far from being the sole reason for this decision. A mere glance through Burney's instructions suffice to show how many other matters awaited his urgent attention. His first duty on arrival, he was told, was to remonstrate against the delay in the indemnity payments and against the frontier outrages; and he was further to make it clear to the Court of Ava that the Governor-General was determined to fix the Chindwin as the Manipur boundary with Burma, and to give support to its Raja Gambhir Singh by means of advisers and other aid. He was further to tell them that their claim to Moulmein could not become the subject of negotiations. These matters, therefore, must be briefly examined before we go further.

To do so we must go back to April 1827, when a Burmese deputation arrived in Calcutta, and was housed in a large house with an allowance for expenses, and a carriage, horses and palanquins. The two envoys, however, were not high-ranking officers, and at their official reception it turned out that far from being a delegation on a permanent basis, they were merely an *ad hoc* mission charged with discussing three urgent matters with the Government of India. Moreover they were not empowered to settle the matters at issue, but must refer them back to Ava. The Government of India therefore, somewhat disgusted, refused to deal directly with them, and referred them to Sir Archibald Campbell at Moulmein. So thither they went to a very unsympathetic reception by the Political Commissioner. Their most pressing request was for a delay of two to three years in the payment of the third instalment of the indemnity. The Mon rebellion after the British withdrawal, they explained, was the chief reason for their inability to pay. Campbell disbelieved their story, and in spite of their tears and entreaties all he would grant them was a slightly extended spreadover of payments, so disappointing that the Burmese ministers at Ava, when they learnt of it, concocted a more favourable version to report to the king. Only the fear of a British re-occupation of Rangoon caused the envoys to sign the new agreement.

[1] BSP, Vol. 357.

The other matters raised by the envoys concerned boundaries. They complained that Manipuris and some British officers had trespassed into, and occupied, Burmese territory in the upper Chindwin valley, and further that the British had occupied an area on the southern border of Arakan which had never belonged to that kingdom. They were told that these matters would have to be dealt with by commissioners appointed by both governments. Campbell, however, was instructed by the Governor-General to make it clear that the Raja of Manipur had the right to occupy the Kabaw Valley, the area claimed by the Court of Ava as Burmese territory, since it represented Manipur's ancient limits and had been recovered by the Manipuris before peace was signed with Burma. Moreover, as an independent ruler the raja had the right to employ British officers, and the Indian government the right to maintain a political agent at his court.

The British officers complained of by the Burmese were Major F. J. Grant, British Commissioner in Manipur, and Lieutenant R. Boileau Pemberton, his assistant. They had played leading parts in assisting the Manipuris to regain control of their country from the Burmese. The Manipuri claim to the Kabaw Valley, which lay between the River Chindwin and the Manipur mountains, was so hotly disputed by the Court of Ava, that next to the indemnity it had become the most urgent of the problems demanding a solution. After the departure of the envoys Campbell discussed it with the Governor of Rangoon, who held first class ministerial rank, that of *wungyi*, and they agreed that Burmese commissioners should meet Grant and Pemberton on the Chindwin in early February of the next year (1828).

The Burmese kept the British officers waiting until the end of March, and when at last they did turn up, they produced a map showing a large river called the Ningtee running to the west of the Kabaw Valley and this, they claimed, was the true boundary between Burma and Manipur. Pemberton, who had made thorough topographical surveys of the whole region, pointed out that there was no such river as the one shown in the map, which he pronounced a fake. The Ningtee, he said, was the local name for the Chindwin itself. This the Burmese categorically denied. Hence the only solution of the deadlock was to make a joint survey of the area. It was, however, too late in the dry season to start such an undertaking; the wet monsoon was approaching. So it was agreed to have a further meeting in the following January. But when that date arrived no meeting took place. The ministers at Ava sent a flimsy excuse for being unable to depute commissioners. They promised faithfully, however, to send them for a meeting in January 1830, and begged the Government of India not to settle the matter unilaterally. This is precisely what that government did do: it decided to let the Raja of Manipur retain the valley. Grant and Pemberton were accordingly instructed to fix the boundary on the western bank of the Chindwin. And when in January 1830 the commissioners of both sides had their promised meeting, it was useless for the chief Burmese commissioner, the Wundauk Maung Khan Ye, to declare that the Kabaw Valley had been in the possession of the kings of Burma for 2,000 years, for Grant and Pemberton carried out their orders by planting boundary flags along the Chindwin notwithstanding the vigorous protests and threats of the Burmese. At Ava the king and his ministers were shocked at the news. They adopted the line that the action of the two officers was unauthorized. By what casuistry they arrived at such a conclusion it is difficult to say, since the British Political Agent in Rangoon and the Chief Secretary at Calcutta had notified them of the Government of India's decision at the time it was made. Nevertheless they decided to send another deputation to Calcutta to complain of the conduct of the two officers. Then came news that Henry Burney had been appointed to reside at Ava as the Indian Government's representative, and the Court of Ava came to the conclusion that to deal with the matter through him would be better than to send envoys to distant Calcutta. And in the event they were to be proved right.

From the British point of view the situation on the Salween frontier was far more troublesome than the one described above. The Burmese claimed that the British had taken over part of their province of Martaban, and that the Moulmein district should be restored to them. This the British refused to consider: the Yandabo treaty had laid down that the Salween should be the boundary, and it was useless now to point out that part of Martaban's territory lay to the south of it. But what did seriously worry the British was that armed frontier affrays had become of almost daily occurrence, aided and abetted by the Burmese frontier officers, who were known to be sharing the proceeds of these 'dacoities'. Large parties of raiders were involved. A. D. Maingy took up the matter with the

Rangoon wungyi. Then in March the Governor-General himself, Lord William Cavendish Bentinck, came to Moulmein to examine the situation. He told Maingy to go in person to Rangoon to tell the wungyi that the British Government would use the principle of self-defence if the Court of Ava could not control its own subjects. His threat, however, was not taken seriously by the wungyi, and accordingly Maingy directed a long letter to the ministers at Ava. But to no avail: things got worse. Villages on the British side of the frontier were plundered and some of their inhabitants killed. The Moulmein police boats drove off a number of other attacks. An attempt was even made to land a force of sixty raiders a few yards away from the Commissioner's residence. Mr. Maingy, therefore, having obtained the names of seven of the ringleaders in the disorders, instructed Henry Burney, who was on his way from Tavoy to Calcutta, to stop off at Rangoon and tell the wungyi that they must be handed over. The Burmese Chief of Martaban, however, defied the wungyi's order to do so, and when Burney himself went to Martaban and warned him that if he did not hand them over the British would forcibly apprehend them, he kept up his defiant attitude, and Burney reported that he was obviously deeply involved. So there was nothing for it but to take action, and one early morning in November two companies of British troops landed at Martaban with orders to seize the dacoit leaders and the Chief himself. They found the stockades empty. The whole male population had decamped into the jungle, and although the troops advanced several miles beyond the town, they could make no contact with the fugitives. Meanwhile, behind them the outraged inhabitants of Moulmein set fire to the town and three villages nearby and burnt them to the ground, while the troops were out searching the jungles. The extraordinary, and significant, thing then was that neither Ava nor Rangoon took the slightest notice of the incident. In reporting it to Calcutta Maingy expressed his belief that the Court of Ava itself had been secretly behind the disturbances. He thought that 'the high tone Major Burney may be directed to take' when he arrived at the Burmese capital, would preclude such attacks in future. He was able to report also that he had arrested three of the culprits, and that the Rangoon wungyi had secured the other four. But it was the latter's turn now to drag his feet, and while negotiations for their surrender were in progress, news came that Henry Burney was to proceed to Ava as British

Resident. The negotiations were accordingly transferred to him. Meanwhile the Government of India fully approved Maingy's action at Martaban.

Burney's impression, after taking up residence at Ava, was that the raid on Martaban had performed a real service to the maintenance of peace, for the time being, on the Salween frontier. It had taught the Court of Ava that British threats to deal with insurgency must be taken seriously. From his talks with the ministers he was convinced that the bandit raids were inspired by Ava in the belief that the British had been financially ruined by the Burmese war and could therefore be pressured into restoring the lost territories. He made it his business to make the ministers aware of his suspicions, and they in response issued warnings to the frontier officers which, as he expected, were disregarded. In mid-1831 Commissioner Maingy accused the Martaban officer of harbouring robbers and sharing their booty. Burney accordingly went to the ministers with a threat of reprisals. They gave him their assurance that the Rangoon wungyi had already taken action in the matter. Mr. Maingy, however, went on to submit written charges for delivery to the Court of Ava. Then at last the combined pressure from Moulmein and the Residency proved effective: the Martaban officer was dismissed, and so for a time things settled down.

While Burney was engaged on this matter, complaints came also from the Superintendent of Arakan. The myothugyi of Kanaung was reported to be causing trouble by running an insurgency racket. Burney therefore went to the ministers and threatened reprisals similar to the action against Martaban. They in turn took the matter to the king, and as a result orders were sent to the Rangoon wungyi to investigate the charges. He summoned the offending myothugyi to Rangoon and summarily clapped him in jail. Then similar charges were made by Captain Dickenson, the Officiating Superintendent of Arakan against the myothugyi of Maphe. This time in response to Burney's representation the king sent one of his pages to conduct an enquiry. As a precaution Burney instructed Captain Dickenson to send the witnesses, who were to go before the Burmese commission, under the charge of a British officer. He added that even if they failed to make good their charges, it would teach the myothugyi to show more caution in future. When what he had anticipated turned out to be true, he went to the ministers and offered to reimburse the Burmese government for the full expense incurred by the commission. This, he believed, would be an insurance against their refusal to follow up any similar complaint he might have to make in future.

The next disturbance to arise on that particular frontier was of quite a different order. Thirty-two prisoners escaped from the Akyab jail and plundered a police post on their way across to Burmese territory. The Burmese authorities captured fourteen of them. To Burney's request that they be handed over to the British authorities in Arakan the ministers at Ava replied that they would readily do so if he would agree that in future all fugitives from either side should, on demand, be extradited. This placed him in something of a quandary. He tried to explain that among civilized states it was not the custom to surrender political fugitives; in fact, he said, hundreds of foreigners were living in England who had fled there because of differences of opinion with their own home governments. This evoked from the Shan atwinwun the impatient ejaculation: 'Your and our customs are so completely opposite on so many points. You write on white, we on black paper. You stand up, we sit down, you uncover your head, we our feet, in token of respect.'[1] Disregarding his outburst, however, Burney begged the ministers not to insist on the surrender of political refugees; it would give the British, he said, a bad impression of their intelligence. Nevertheless, he conceded that when the two countries were at peace, rebels who attacked one party and fled to the territory of the other might be punished by the latter, or handed over.

The ministers then proposed the mutual extradition of all accused of robbery or murder. Again, however, Burney was unable to agree. The British practice, he explained, was to surrender fugitives only if on examination of each individual case, they were convinced of the man's guilt. In the case of the Akyab escapees he submitted that their guilt had been amply proved. He warned that if they were not handed over, the consequences might be serious. Curiously enough, the basic fallacy involved in this threat does not seem to have occurred to him. What if the Burmese authorities were not convinced of the guilt of the escapees? The ministers, however, accepted his plea and the fugitives were handed over.

Disorders nevertheless continued on both the Arakan and Salween frontiers, in spite of prompt action by the ministers. When the king's health broke down it was feared that they might

[1] Journal, para. 626.

become worse. Burney accordingly suggested to the commissioner of Arakan that the British authorities there might adopt the practice of 'hot pursuit' of bandits into Burmese territory. To this the Government of India would accord only a strictly limited approval: no parties were to be sent into Burmese territory, it laid down, in search of fugitive marauders without its express permission.

As Mr. Desai points out, with such fundamentally different views on inter-state relations on the part of Calcutta and Ava respectively, their frontiers were bound to be troublesome. And, of course, it must be remembered that the Anglo-Burmese war had been caused by Burmese aggression on the frontiers of British India. Now the new frontiers imposed upon Burma as a result of that war and the loss of territory involved were totally unacceptable not only to the Court of Ava, but to every myothugyi whose circle touched them. These local chieftains, infused with messianic ardour, were out to try their luck in recovering what had been lost; for one never knew, one might be fated to become another Alaungpaya, a restorer of Burmese sovereignty, an embryo Buddha.

Chapter 11

Burney moves in

LORD William Cavendish Bentinck's minute of 30 December 1829 announcing Henry Burney's appointment as British Resident at the Court of Ava mentions the appointment of the British Resident at the Court of Khatmandu as the strongest precedent for his decision to carry out his part of the stipulation contained in the Yandabo treaty. He makes it very clear that the envoy's chief duty would be to cultivate friendly relations, remove jealousy and distrust, and improve communications between the two states. This point was also strongly emphasized in Burney's instructions. He was asked to do his best to convince the Court of Ava that his appointment had no other aim than the one expressed in Article 7 of the treaty, and to explain that the use of resident ministers to cultivate friendly relations was a principle of policy adopted by all civilized states. Should, however, the Court of Ava manifest 'an invincible repugnance' to a British Resident and behave in a way unbecoming to his situation, he might return to Rangoon; but in so doing he must not commit his government, or give 'unnecessary umbrage' to the Court of Ava.

With regard to his general methods, he was told to make no proposal, but encourage the Burmese to explain their views and make the first overtures, and he was to endeavour to gain influence. On the vexed question of Tenasserim he was informed that there had been a move from the Burmese side for the return of the province. It had come from the atwinwuns[1] through a Mr. Lane, a merchant at the capital. Burney should therefore endeavour to find out what were the real views of the Court. If a proposal was made, he was not to express any opinion on it, but enquire what equivalent the Burmese would offer for the province, or a part of it, and whether they would consider ceding either Negrais or Bassein. With

[1] Lit. interior ministers, i.e. those in closest attendance upon the king.

regard to his consular powers he was instructed to protect the interests of British subjects but not to interfere unnecessarily.

Thus instructed, and with official letters from the Government of India to the king and ministers in his keeping, together with presents to the king and chief queen, the new Resident left Calcutta early in February 1830 on the Company's steamship *Ganges*, accompanied by his family and servants and an escort of volunteers from the 38th Native Infantry commanded by his younger brother, Lieutenant George Burney. The escort consisted of an Indian officer, two havildars, two naiks, two drummers and thirty sepoys. There was also the mission's medical officer, Assistant Apothecary Bedford of the Madras Service. In addition, Burney was authorized on arrival at Rangoon to engage an interpreter, a clerk, a munshi (language teacher) and four peons (orderlies). The king's present included 'two brass 6 pounder guns complete for the purpose of Horse Artillery'. Burney was also authorized to spend up to 1,500 rupees upon a suitable present for the queen and 'certain small articles as Muslins, Penknives, Scissors and Essences' to be used as presents. To complete the picture it must be mentioned that as Resident he was granted the right to a salute of eleven guns.

The mission party sailed first to Moulmein, for Burney had to go on to Mergui to appear as a defence witness in a court martial at Mergui. Not until 18 March did they arrive at Rangoon. There they were given a very cordial reception by the Governor with whom Burney was well acquainted through his previous visits to the port. While there Burney was approached by the British merchants in the town with a complaint against the Yewun[1] the Governor's deputy. He was accused of taking bribes from arrested debtors to release them before they had come to an arrangement with their creditors. In response Burney obtained an interview with both the Governor and his deputy and with the utmost tact laid the complaint before them. Both of them promised to administer the law fairly and grant redress, and Burney without demur accepted their promises. In reporting the matter to the Government of India he said that no reliance could be placed on their promises; nevertheless the British merchants were pleased at his appointment as Resident: they thought it offered them their best chance of security in future.[2]

[1] literally 'water wun'.
[2] BSP, vol. 357, Burney's letter dated Rangoon 22 March 1830.

On his way up the Irrawaddy Burney noted the miserable condition of the people. He was inclined to attribute it to the effects of the war, but learnt that most of it was due to the oppressive behaviour of the local officials in collecting money for the indemnity. Only half of the proceeds actually went towards this object, he was told; of the remainder one half went into the pockets of the local officials and the other went in revenue to the queen, for many of the districts between Rangoon and Ava belonged to her *jagir*, as Burney terms it, using the Persian word normally employed in India for an assignment of land-rent. In the more picturesque Burmese phraseology she was the 'eater' of those districts.

The mission party arrived at Ava on the evening of 23 April, and on the following morning three officers of the Hlutdaw, or Council of State, a wundauk and two sayedawgyis, came to conduct them to the Residency, which Burney describes as 'a neat looking pucca built house close to the river side on the left bank'. He learnt that it had been purchased by the king for the accommodation of the mission from its owner, a Spanish merchant named Lanciago. But, having studied Crawfurd's report of his reception at Ava, he refused to step ashore unless officers of a higher rank than a minister of the second class and two secretaries were sent to receive him. Crawfurd had been received by a wungyi and an atwinwun, and, Burney intimated, equal honour must be accorded to him.

His stand caused something of a sensation, for it was reported to the king, who immediately ordered that due respect should be shown him, and a whole bevy of high ranking officers hurried down to the shore to welcome him. An atwinwun boarded his boat and invited him to land, while in the Residency a wungyi waited to receive him. Moreover, the wungyi broke precedent by enquiring after the Governor-General's health. In Crawfurd's case the ceremonial enquiry had been after the health of the king of England; the Governor-General had not been mentioned. Commenting upon this rush to be obliging Burney thought it arose from the Court of Ava's very real anxiety over the Kabaw Valley question: it wanted to gain his support for Burma's claim. He was favourably impressed by the behaviour of the Burmese officials: it was much better than that of the Siamese when he first arrived at Bangkok. On the other hand the contrast between the two capitals was overwhelmingly in Bangkok's favour. 'There all was bustle and animation, numerous boats and people passing to and fro.' At Ava, on the other hand, there was scarcely any traffic, many houses were unoccupied, and all was poverty and misery.

His early impressions of the court occupy much space in his Journal. Crawfurd had written a thorough account of the Burmese governmental system. Burney therefore did not have to explain institutions, but could concentrate upon personalities. He possessed unusual aptitude in describing the people with whom he came into contact. His character-sketches place the historian in his debt for they transform the lay figures of Burmese historical writings into real flesh-and-blood people. How reliable are his assessments it is not always possible to say, for he had strong personal feelings which show in his likes and dislikes—as in the cases of the Phrakhlang and the Raja of Ligor for example. By 1830, however, he had had many years of experience in South-East Asia: he had spent more of his life there than anywhere else. He had had no home leave since he returned to India in 1809 as a cadet in the East India Company's service. And he seems to have been quite indefatigable wherever he was in learning all he could about the country to which he was posted and in making himself proficient in its language. It is essential to realize, as I have written elsewhere, that in both Siam and Burma he was 'the first British envoy to either country for whom the formidable language barrier, preventing natural conversation and inviting misunderstanding, did not exist'. ('Burney's Comments on the Court of Ava, 1832.')[1] Those words are taken from my introduction to a paper written by Burney entitled 'Hints regarding the characters of the principal persons at the Court of Ava, and the conduct to be observed towards them' which he wrote for the private guidance of Captain H. Macfarquhar, when in September 1832 he took charge of the Ava Residency during Burney's absence in Calcutta.[2] It forms a useful supplement to what he has to say in his Journal about these people.

First there is King Bagyidaw, 'Royal Elder Uncle', the pampered grandson of his immediate predecessor, King Bodawpaya, 'Royal Great Grandfather', who had died in 1819, and was the youngest son of the founder of the dynasty to sit upon the throne. Burney describes him as 'a poor weak fool, incapable of comprehending any rational argument'. He writes that the king was much

---

[1] *Bulletin of the School of Oriental and African Studies*, vol. XX, 1957, p. 306.
[2] Royal Commonwealth Society's collection of Burney Papers, BXV, in Burney's handwriting.

under the influence of his personal attendants, who were nicknamed the 'Lubyus', 'Young Men', because they had been his companions from boyhood. They were said to be constantly urging him to recover the territories annexed by the British. Many British officers believed, he writes, that the king was a man of peace but that his ministers were very hostile to the British. This was quite untrue: the exact opposite was the case. 'More than any other man in his empire he feels and broods over the disasters of the late war, and of all his subjects that war has left the least impression of our superiority upon his mind'.

Subsequent events were to demonstrate the truth of the first part of that statement, when the king's melancholia turned to madness. But whether he was unable to learn the lessons of the war is open to doubt. It was a feature of Burmese royal arrogance to admit of no equal on earth, but Bagyidaw, notwithstanding the urgings of the *lubyus* and the boastings of the army leaders, which unduly impressed Burney, never showed any sign of really contemplating another war with the British. Burney, as we know, was a little too prone to think in terms of war. He was, of course, a soldier, but one who had seen very little active service, and that only in the distant past. One suspects that when his mind did turn in this direction it was a sign of physical exhaustion, for he did not enjoy robust health, and in Burma was never a fit man.

That the king was a spoilt child and his ministers cowards he says in so many words. He heard that on occasions when the ministers had to submit something disagreeable to him they would agree together to stand by and support each other in such a manner that he would not know which one to punish. Sometimes, however, he would become so enraged that he would hurl his spear at them. 'I am happy to say', wrote Burney in his Journal, 'that His Majesty has not thrown his spear at the Woongyees during the last four months.'[1] He might have added that he invariably missed his aim. Before the war the American Baptist Missionary, Dr. Adoniram Judson, had expressed a less devastating view of the King's character,[2] which, however, did not differ in fundamentals from Burney's when one bears in mind that the man Judson describes had not yet undergone the mortifying experience of defeat in war. They both agree on Bagyidaw's utter devotion to his chief queen, Mai Nu, and her immense influence over him. It was said that

---

[1] Para. 24.   [2] Quoted by Desai, *op. cit.*, p. 70.

when the ministers had something so unpleasant to report to the king that they feared the consequences, they would approach her with it first.

She was a woman of known low origin, and had a reputation for great avarice like her brother, the Salin Min, 'lord of Salin', generally referred to as the Minthagyi, 'Great Prince', who was the real head of the government. During the war they had both been leaders of the war party at Court. They disliked Westerners and all the innovations they brought with them. But, as Burney wrote for the guidance of his stand-in, 'You will have little to say to Her Majesty excepting to make a *salam* to her with your hand whenever she joins the King in your presence'.[1] He relates one extraordinary piece of gossip to the effect that the queen was an opium addict, and in consequence was unlikely to live long.[2] A couple of months later, however, when during a personal conversation with the king he had a better view of her, he had to admit that his first impression of her was completely mistaken. 'I had fancied her', he writes, 'to be a rather coarse, low-bred looking woman, whereas she really is the best looking Burmese woman of 48 years of age and showed much intelligence.'[3] On the other hand, R. B. Pemberton's impression of her, when he saw her at about the same time, was less flattering. 'Her countenance is that of a woman fast verging to old age, and its expression denotes an unamiable disposition.'[4]

Dr. Judson had dubbed the Minthagyi 'repulsive without one point to recommend him except some capacity for managing the affairs of Government after a fashion'.[5] Burney formed a rather higher opinion of him. In his 'Hints' he writes, 'You will see more of him than of any other prince, as he interferes in all business transacted at the Lhwottau, where you will sometimes meet him sitting in the middle of the Ministers.... He is avaricious, but civil and polite in his manners, and if his good opinion be gained much business will be facilitated at the Lhwottau'.[6]

The Hlutdaw, 'Royal Place of Release', to which he refers, was the supreme council of the realm and was composed of the

---

[1] Burney's Comments, BSOAS, XX, p. 307.   [2] Journal, paras, 42–3.
[3] *Ibid.*, para. 171.
[4] Hall, D. G. E. (ed.) 'R. B. Pemberton's Journey', JBRS, XLIII, ii, Dec. 1960, p. 43.
[5] Desai, *op. cit.*, p. 73 quoted from BSP vol. 341.
[6] Hall, *ob. cit.*, BSOAS, XX, p. 308.

wungyis, 'bearers of the great burden', who were the highest officers of state, controlling every department. Unlike their counterparts in Siam, there was no distribution of functions between them. Originally their number had been four, corresponding to the four Lokapalas of Hindu-Buddhist cosmology, the guardian deities of the four cardinal points of the universe. In Burney's day their number had grown to six, and included the governor of Rangoon. Each was normally known by the name of the appanage which he 'ate' prefixed to the title 'wungyi' or 'min', 'ruler'. Their normal procedure was to deliberate together on any matter referred to them by the king. There was a throne in their meeting-place, and the king himself, or the heir apparent, if there was one, might preside over their debates. Bagyidaw never did so, and although he had a son, the Sakya Min, he was never given the rank of Ein-shemin, 'Ruler of the Eastern Palace', accorded to the heir-apparent. He was the son of a deceased chief queen, and his step-mother and her brother excluded him from any share in the business of government. Although the Minthagyi took a leading part in the deliberations of the Hlutdaw, he was outside the normal ministerial pattern. Judson described him as 'Superintendent of Privy Councillors, acting Public Minister of State, *factotum* of the Empire'.[1]

Assisting the wungyis in the work of the Hlutdaw was a number of wundauks, 'props'. They were of ministerial rank and were employed in business of great public importance; but they sat in the chamber without voting. One of them was in attendance all night to receive royal orders. The decisions of this august body were recorded by a number of sayedawgyis, 'great royal secretaries'. Then there were thandawzins, 'heralds', whose main duty was to attend at royal audiences to note the king's orders and forward them to the Hlutdaw, and nakhandaws, 'royal ears', attached to it in order to report its doings to the king.

Another council functioned inside the palace, the Byedaik, 'bachelors' quarters', so-called from its situation in the palace. The six atwinwuns, 'interior wuns', who formed it in Burney's time, were of lower rank than the wungyis, but might exercise greater influence, for they relieved each other in close attendance on the king day and night, and were the immediate recipients of all his orders. Burney came in contact with two in particular, the Shan Atwinwun, named Maung Yeet, and the Kyiwun Atwinwun,

[1] Desai, *op. cit.*, p. 73.

named Maung Ba Yauk. He describes the former as 'dull of understanding, tenacious of his own opinion, and very vain', but because of his influence with the king he could 'rule' the rest of the ministers he says. This was largely because he was bolder in speaking to the king than anyone else in the capital.[1] Also he was keener on the Kabaw Valley question than any other minister. But he was 'very accessible to flattery' and his wife was 'the most conversible of all the ladies of the Burmese ministers'. The other had been one of the negotiators of the Treaty of Yandabo. 'He is very suspicious and capable of doing a great deal of mischief, and is therefore a fit person to be won over and quieted. His wife is a dull fat piece of humanity.'

Of the wungyis, the one who right from the start was in Burney's opinion head and shoulders above all the rest, and, indeed, anyone else at the Court, was Maung Sa, the Myawadi Wungyi, whom he describes as 'one of the most sensible, intelligent, liberal-minded men in the country.'[2] On further acquaintance, while continuing to hold the same high opinion of him, he noted for Macfarquhar's guidance that Maung Sa was now old, and becoming infirm in intellect as well as health. Because of the jealousy of the other ministers towards him, he was timid, and therefore not always as helpful to the Residency as he might have been. Between him and the Shan Atwinwun, indeed, there was such mutual jealousy, he told Macfarquhar, that it was advisable never to quote him to the latter 'as having said, or promised or done anything'. He had a reputation for rapacity, Burney noted, though he himself had never seen any sign of it. He was clearly a man of culture, acquainted with several languages, including Sanskrit and Portuguese; and he surprised Burney by singing some lines of a Latin hymn and 'displaying a fine ear for music'. Burney noted that he was 'very vain' about his accomplishments. They were to develop a mutual regard for each other that was greatly to enrich the Englishman's understanding of Burmese culture and history.

Two Europeans at Ava figure frequently in Burney's reports, the Spaniard Lanciago and the Englishman Lane. Both were merchants trading on their own account, but Lanciago was closely connected with the Court and was to become Collector of Customs at Rangoon. He attended on the ministers whenever they came to the Residency. He was connected by marriage with the king, for

[1] 'Hints', BSOAS, XX, pp. 301–2.   [2] Journal, para. 23; Desai, *op. cit.*, p. 75.

his wife was sister to one of the lesser queens. Lane, Burney reported, had, in the absence of a British Residency, been exercising the functions of a resident for the furtherance of his own commercial pursuits, and had done well for himself, notwithstanding that the king and court believed him to be a spy in the British service. Both men read the Calcutta newspapers and translated useful information from them for the king and ministers, and Burney soon discovered that they were fully aware of the Government of India's wish to return Tenasserim to Burma and of the reason for it. Lane was culturally somewhat above the usual type of English merchant trading to Burma. He was a close associate of the Mekkara Prince, uncle to the king, who delved deeply into Western science and philosophy. Lane had taught him logarithms, and together they were engaged upon the compilation of a Burmese-English dictionary which was nearly completed.

The first important business to be dealt with after Burney's arrival concerned the date and manner of his official presentation to the king. As usual in cases of this kind it gave rise to interminable and frustrating discussions in which the Burmese tried their hardest to make the resident and his suite submit to what they regarded, not without reason, as a humiliating procedure. Burney had carefully studied the reports of previous British envoys, notably Symes and Crawfurd on the subject. He had also his experience in Siam to go upon. There he had been permitted to keep his shoes on at royal audiences; in Burma therefore he was prepared to take his stand on this precedent. On 4 May he went in state to the Yondaw, the meeting place of the Hlutdaw, to discuss matters with the wungyis and atwinwuns. Some yards from the building he was met by a sayedawgyi who asked him politely to comply with Burmese custom by taking off his shoes. Ignoring the request, however, he strode into the assembly, wearing his shoes, and sat down on the floor among the ministers. Then, taking off his hat, he deposited it on the floor beside him, at the same time telling his interpreter to explain that he had kept his shoes on because most Englishmen considered it degrading to take them off at an official ceremony, but that he had uncovered his head, as it was his custom to do in the presence of the Governor-General of India.[1]

He was in an uncompromising mood. 'Do as the King of Siam did,' he urged. 'Allow me to appear before him [the king of Ava]

[1] Journal, para. 25, Desai, *op. cit.*, pp. 78–9.

in the same manner as I would appear before my own sovereign.' Maung Sa took him up on this with the remark that the Burmese did not care much for a country where the women took their lower garment between their legs and fastened it up behind like the men. To which Burney retorted that Siam was a very rich country which would have paid up the indemnity months earlier than the Burmese could have done. He was being deliberately provocative and was pleased to see the annoyance of his hearers. But, seeing how often this 'Shoe Question' cropped up between the British and the Burmese, one naturally asks whether British envoys to the Golden Feet were not making a mountain out of a molehill. Burney's explanation of his position, however, has much force.

My objection to removing my shoes, [he writes in his Journal] is formed on the fact that the Burmese require it not as the fulfilment of a mere custom, but as a means of exalting the King and gratifying their own pride and vanity by humiliating and degrading the British character. Besides, the Mussulmans of this place have persuaded the Burmese to carry the etiquette regarding the shoes of Europeans much farther than what it is, I believe, at any other Court in Asia. Even in the streets and highways a European, if he meets with the King or joins his party, is obliged to take off his shoes. Dr. Price [an American Baptist missionary] always walked and ran barefooted alongside the King's litter, and Mr. Lane on one occasion, when he was invited to see the ceremony of the King ploughing the land, which is annually performed here as well as in China and Siam, was obliged to remove his shoes and walk a mile or two over burning sand until he was quite lame. When Sir Archibald Campbell deputed Lieuts Rawlinson and Montmorency to this place in 1828, he prohibited them to take off their shoes, and they did not, therefore, see the King.[1]

This final sentence contains the heart of the matter. A royal audience was impossible without unshoeing: neither the monarch nor his ministers dared dispense with the custom. Even King Mindon, when confronted on the subject by the Government of India in the eighteen seventies dared not give way, and the loss of personal contact between the king and the British Resident which resulted was a prime factor in bringing on the war of 1885.

On 19 May the ministers resumed the contest: the wungyis and atwinwuns called on Burney at the Residency and there were three hours of argument. But the impasse remained intact. Two

[1] Para. 32.

days later the Royal Treasurer and Lanciago tried in vain to resolve it. Finally, after holding out for nearly a month, Burney offered to give in over the shoe question if his presentation did not take place, like Crawfurd's, on a Kadaw Day. This was the ceremony when the king's vassals appeared before him with presents to make their submission and beg pardon for past offences.[1] At once the clouds began to roll away, and on 2 June two wungyis and two atwinwuns appeared at the Residency to announce that the mission would be received by the king on 17 June and to assure Burney that under no circumstances would he be received on a Kadaw Day.

Burney felt the strain of all this acutely. During the deadlock he wrote in his Journal on learning that the Court of Ava intended to establish a residency at Calcutta, that he hoped they would be kept waiting as long as possible before being honoured with an audience of the Governor-General.[2] His hope was to be fulfilled in far greater measure than he could have dreamt of, for when the Burmese envoys, accompanied by his brother George, did arrive in Calcutta, the Governor-General was many miles away up country. Burney, however, was ill when he wrote that passage; so ill indeed that he contemplated returning to Rangoon. He went so far as to write to the wungyis asking for transport to be provided for the journey. But instead of boats the ministers sent two Burmese doctors who examined him, diagnosed an inflamed liver and prescribed raw citrons and coarse sugar. The treatment seems to have been effective; the plan to evacuate the Residency to Rangoon was abandoned; and it was at this point that the deadlock was resolved by Burney's surrender over the shoe question in return for the promise not to be received on a Kadaw Day. He consoled himself with the reflection that his acceptance of Burmese custom was seen as an effort to conciliate the king.

Agreement on the ceremonial to be observed proved easy. Burney learnt with pleasure that he was to be treated on the same footing as a wungyi: he was to be introduced as 'The Woongyee of the English *Min* who rules over India [Bengal] and the great countries to the westward [the rest of India]'. In his Journal he gives translations of the titles of the wungyis and the king to be used at the ceremony. The wungyis are called 'Those who bear his [the king's] two golden feet continually upon their heads like the germ of the lotus, and direct all important affairs of state, their

[1] *Supra*, p. 181.   [2] Para. 64.

Excellencies the Ministers of State and Generals'. The king is described as 'His Most Glorious and Excellent Majesty, who rules over all the white umbrella wearers and eastern countries within the empire of Thunaparanta [Golden Land] and Tombadewa [Copper Region], the King of the Rising Sun, Lord of the Celestial Elephant, and proprietor of all the White Elephants, Lord of Life, the Great and Just Chief'.[1] Thunaparanta was used to indicate the central part of the realm, and Tombadewa the region northwards of Ava.

Early on the morning of 17 June, before the procession started from the Residency, the Royal Treasurer arrived to take charge of the royal presents. He asked Burney to make the most of them, and accordingly they were borne to the palace by 24 ponies, a number of elephants and 150 coolies. Burney himself went in a sedan chair with four bearers. His suite and the escorting Burmese officials followed on about a dozen elephants. His brother George put on a pair of slippers under his stockings and shoes, and tried to persuade Henry to do the same; but he thought it would be too risky to do so.

In the audience chamber rugs were placed for him and his suite to sit upon, and he sat down with his hat on. The Tharrawaddy Prince and the Minthagyi were pointed out to him, and he rose, took off his hat and bowed to each. Then the king entered and took his seat upon the throne. Burney writes: 'He wore a crown resembling a Burmese war helmet richly set with jewels, and a gown of the same pattern as his officers, only of gold cloth and apparently studded with jewels.'[2] When he was seated the court Brahmans intoned a prayer and a song extolling the ever-victorious king. When it ended, two atwinwuns advanced close to the king and received from him in whispers the customary formal questions: when did the Envoy leave Bengal, how was the Governor-General when he left, and had the wind and rain been favourable? These he called out in a loud voice, and Burney made appropriate answers through his interpreter. Next a nakhandaw read aloud the Burmese translation of the Governor-General's letter followed by the list of the royal presents. That was all. The king then departed and the ceremony ended, to Burney's great disappointment, for his suggestion, made beforehand to the ministers, that the king should ask some 'sensible' questions, as the king of Siam had done, had been ignored. It was not the custom, he was told. Throughout the

[1] Journal, para. 116.   [2] Journal, para. 122.

ceremony the king maintained a completely impassive countenance, showing no interest in anything. That, Burney was informed, was the proper expression of royal dignity for such an occasion. He went away contrasting his Ava royal reception very unfavourably with his Bangkok one.

As in Siam, the royal reception was followed, after a discreet interval, by a round of visits to the highest personages, beginning with the king's son, the Sakya Min, the heir presumptive to the throne, but not yet recognized as heir apparent by the conferment of the title 'Ein She Min', 'Lord of the Eastern House', because of the opposition of the queen, Mai Nu, and as a result without political influence. He was so nervous, when receiving the members of the mission, Burney records, that he could not utter a word for some fifteen minutes.[1] In his 'Hints' he advises Macfarquhar when paying the prince a visit, to talk to his ministers and try not to notice his 'apprehensions or false shame'.[2] In complete contrast was his reception by the Tharrawaddy Prince, though he was kept waiting rather too long before his host deigned to appear. When he did, however, he was most affable and informal in his manner. He expressed the hope that permanent good relations would be established between Burma and the Government of India. Burney enquired whether he might consult him on any matters of business, but the prince replied that while he would always be happy to see him as a friend, matters of business must go to the wungyis. Burney made a similar request of the Minthagyi when paying his official visit to him; he went so far as to ask if his meetings with the ministers could take place in the Minthagyi's presence at his residence. The ministers had no power, he said, and were very timid. The Minthagyi's presence would greatly expedite business. The great man, however, refused to be drawn. He was afraid to take part in discussions, he said, since if a mistake were made, it would be more difficult to remedy than if he were not present. He also, like Tharrawaddy, was very affable. Burney noted that his house and menage gave evidence of greater wealth and importance than those of the two princes.

This first round of courtesy calls took place during the three days from 24 to 27 June. One other royal personage was included in it, the widow of the previous Ein-she-min, Bagyidaw's father, who had died in 1808. She had shown great humanity to the

[1] Journal, para. 142. [2] 'Burney's Comments', p. 308.

Europeans and Armenians who were imprisoned during the war. She received Burney very graciously, but unfortunately his visit was somewhat spoilt by the rudeness of a petty Burmese official at the entrance to her residence because he did not remove his socks as well as his shoes. Burney was attended by two officers of the Court, who acted as guides, not only to his destination, but also regarding the etiquette to be observed; and it had been agreed that they alone had the right to instruct him in such matters. He therefore disregarded the official's injunction and made his way into the audience chamber, causing quite a flutter by refusing to take a seat until the princess arrived, which she did almost at once, for her servants dared not keep the indignant visitor waiting. On Burney voicing his complaint against the official, she had the offender immediately put into the stocks. Then pleasantness prevailed, and Burney's only complaint was that he was sitting too far away from her. She attended to this one with the same alacrity as in the case of the first: she invited him to come and sit close to her.

The next round of official visits, to the ministers at their residences, did not begin until the end of July. In the interval, at the king's special invitation, Burney made two visits of special interest. The first was to the King's Monastery where he was received in state by its head, the Nyaungdaw Sayadawgyi, and a large body of sayadaws. It was explained to him beforehand that when visiting this monastery the king himself took off his shoes. Burney agreed without any hesitation to unshoe. He was glad to be able to show respect for the national religion, all the more so because he gathered that the lack of respect for it on the part of the Christian missionaries, both Catholic and American 'Anabaptist', and of some of the British troops during the war, had given the Burmese a bad impression of Westerners as being irreligious. He was given an exceedingly polite reception at the monastery and invited to converse with the monks on religious matters.

The other invitation was to the Elephant Palace on 26 July to meet the king himself when he went there to inspect newly captured elephants. His majesty was in a good humour and conversed affably with Burney about Siam and its white elephant, and Burney's own knowledge of the Burmese language. It was on this occasion that he revised his opinion of the queen's looks. He admits that he was out to create as good an impression as possible, and, according to what the Burmese officers present told him, he was very successful. Three days later he received permission to visit the ministers at their residences and at once availed himself of it to call on the Kyi Wungyi and, following him, the Kyiwum Atwinwun. Both received him with the greatest cordiality and introduced him to their ladies. He seems to have pleased them greatly by unshoeing before going into the domestic quarters and rather surprised them by the 'superior respect' he showed towards the ladies. They were not accustomed to European manners towards women. He was told that the queen would be much pleased to hear of this. As he continued with his ministerial calls he experienced the same cordial reception and introduction to the ladies, and he came to the conclusion that there had been mutual agreement among them on the subject. He called on the Myawadi Wungyi Maung Sa, the Padein Wungyi and the Atwinwun Maung Yeet in quick succession. He describes in some detail his visit to one officer of the palace below ministerial rank, who was among the king's boyhood friends and stood especially in his favour. He was Maung Shwe Lu, the Commandant of the Northern Gate of the Palace. During the war he had received Dr. Judson and the other prisoners into his house and given security for their good conduct, and now Burney took the opportunity to thank him on behalf of the Government of India. His house had what were then modern fittings such as hanging punkhas, i.e. fans, and he showed unusual urbanity for a Burman. It turned out that he had lived for some time in Rangoon and mixed with Europeans there. Burney comments in his Journal that all the Burmese officers who had spent some time in Rangoon were distinguished by good sense and lack of pride: Mr. Sarkies, he says, called Rangoon the Burmese university.[1]

To one of his calls there was strong opposition by the ministers. It was to the Rangoon Wungyi's wife, who was living in Ava while her husband was absent in Rangoon. He had asked Burney to call on her, and the lady herself sent him a gift of fruit and renewed the invitation. She browbeat the ministers into waiving their objections and, when he called, provided splendid entertainment. Her house also was furnished in European style.

Finally this round of visits at the end of July and the first few

[1] Paras. 183–4; Sarkies was leader of the Armenian community in Rangoon.

days of August led him to the Mekkhara Prince, Lane's patron and fellow-student. Burney himself was an unusually well-informed man, but the prince put him through his paces. The visit must be described in Burney's own words.

We found the Prince a very intelligent and inquisitive character. I was with him for upwards of an hour, and he put questions to me as fast as I could answer them, and then observed that he had not asked one-hundredth part of the questions which he wished to ask. He questioned as to the latitude and longitude of London, Calcutta, Ava and Bangkok, the cause of the polarity of the needle, the reappearance of the last comet, the properties of the Barometer and Thermometer both of which instruments were hanging in his room, and the nature of Algebra which science, he said, he much wished to learn. Indeed he surprised me with the extent of his knowledge and he seemed to comprehend and admit the correctness of our system of the Universe. We saw in a handsome bookcase with glazed folding doors his library books consisting of Rees's Cyclopaedia, Johnsons' Dictionary, the Holy Bible with Dr. Judson's translations, all of which, he said, he had read very carefully. On the whole he is certainly the most extraordinary man we have seen in this country. He sent lately to Mr. Lane translations from Rees's Cyclopaedia of two very scientific articles, one regarding the calculations of eclipses and the other regarding the formation of hailstones.[1]

Thus Burney's persistent campaign to build up the best possible relations with the chief personalities at the Court of Ava had begun to prosper beyond his initial expectations. He reported with great satisfaction to the Government of India that no foreign envoy had apparently ever been permitted to visit the ministers at their homes as he had done. He also met the king and queen again on 9 August at a dramatic performance of a story from the *Ramayana* at the palace. The king was very affable and presented him and his assistant with ruby rings; but they had to sit through the performance for nearly four hours with their legs tucked under them, and nearly lost the use of them. A song in praise of the king composed by Maung Sa was sung, but the melody, Burney thought, had been stolen from a hymn he must have heard sung by the Catholics. Burney himself was particularly anxious to cultivate the queen's goodwill, and with that object made some flattering remarks to some officers who were likely to report them to her. Two days later he received a 'very gracious smile' from her and knew his efforts had not been in vain.

[1] Journal, paras 208–10.

The upshot of all these efforts was that he was allowed to attend the king's morning levees, held every eight or ten days, with the ministers, and furthermore was granted the right to attend the Hlutdaw, whenever he had business to bring before it, and to request the presence there of the five wungyis and of two atwinwuns to discuss it with him.

Chapter 12

Tenasserim, the Kabaw Valley, the Indemnity

THROUGHOUT this early period of settling in there were urgent matters to discuss. The most urgent in the king's eyes, the Kabaw Valley question, was the least urgent in those of the Government of India. To the gentlemen in Calcutta the retrocession of Tenasserim and the completion of the indemnity payments were far more important. They regarded the Kabaw Valley question as settled; they had recognized the Raja of Manipur's occupation of it, and were in no mood to reconsider this decision. The Tenasserim revenue deficit, however, was expected to increase and the hope was that Burney could make a satisfactory deal with Ava and so save Calcutta's face. That, however, was not to be, as we know. The Court of Ava was fully apprized of the situation, any *quid pro quo* was out of the question, for it was confident that in due course the province would drop into its hands like ripe fruit. Before Burney's arrival, the atwinwuns had let Mr. Commissioner Maingy know through Lane that the King was quite prepared to take over the territory. They had rejected Lane's advice that they should make a specific offer. Burney accordingly reported to the Government of India that while the Court was in such a state of mind no negotiations were possible.

Furthermore, having seen lower and central Burma on his way up to the capital, he could now realize how the Court felt about Tenasserim. Tavoy and Mergui, he reported, were far more prosperous than any towns he had seen between Rangoon and Ava. Moreover, 'neither in the comfortable and decent appearance of the house or inhabitants nor in the cultivation of the country, nor in any one thing which raises man above the brute, is there a single place between Ava and Rangoon to be compared with even one of the second class villages in the province of Tavoy'. He excepted the pagodas, he said, but they were the work of an earlier age.¹

On 21 May Lanciago was sent to discuss the matter with him. He wanted an assurance that there was some hope of Burma recovering Tenasserim. Not without an equivalent, countered Burney, but he could see that the impression created by the reports in the Calcutta newspapers was stronger than anything he could say. Some weeks later, in July, Lanciago at the king's special request approached him again only to receive the same reply. Burney advised him to remove from the minds of king and ministers such a 'foolish notion' that they could have Tenasserim without an equivalent in exchange. No money and no cession of territory said the Spaniard and departed. A month later in conversation with the Myawady Wungyi and two atwinwuns his support for the Burmese cause was solicited: 'I was informed as a very great secret' that the king was very anxious about the matter. It was the atwinwun Maung Yeet who played this little game of taking the envoy into his confidence. He took him by the hand and led him into another room to enhance the effect. But Burney made exactly the same reply as he had done before to Lanciago. The ministers, however, had a further shot in their locker. Was it not true, they asked, that the Tenasserim provinces were held in pledge for the payment of the indemnity; so that when the expenses of the war had been paid by Burma, no more could be expected of her? To this Burney retorted that the indemnity represented not even a quarter of the British Government's expenses. He suggested that they should give the matter more thought and bear in mind that the Siamese wanted to gain possession of Tenasserim and would be willing to offer a consideration. What, they exclaimed, would the British sell the provinces to the highest bidder? And Burney laughingly agreed that they would. He wanted to shake them out of their complacency: it had become very tedious. So he aimed another dart. Before the British could restore Tenasserim, he said, a suitable asylum would have to be found for the Mon emigrants from Burmese territory and others whose connexion with the British during the war had rendered them obnoxious to the Burmese authorities. The ministers hastened to assure him that these people would on no account be molested, but he pooh-poohed their assurances, reminding them that the myothugyis of Prome,

¹ Journal, para. 38.

Henzada, Podaung and others had been put to death for helping the British. They denied this, of course, saying that these people had been guilty of other offences. Burney then cut the argument short by saying that he would be prepared to put up for his government's consideration any offer they cared to make either of money or of territory. There was still further discussion, with the ministers protesting that they had no money to offer and 'not a single inch' of territory, but without avail. They went away, as Burney puts it, looking 'woefully blank and disappointed'.[1]

On 25 October another fruitless discussion took place on the subject of Tenasserim. The ministers expressed their extreme dissatisfaction that the British should be prepared to sell their former dominion to Burma's enemy Siam; to which Burney replied that they had seized it from Siam, which had had earlier possession of it than Burma's. This, one may interpose, was only partly true, for the Burmese empire of Pagān had conquered and held Tenasserim for some two centuries, losing it only at the time of the Mongol invasions late in the thirteenth century. And without going into detail, it may safely be said that Siam never had firm possession of the territory until early in the seventeenth century. Burney does not record any reply from the ministers to his statement. After all, it was purely a matter of diplomatic give and take, not an academic discussion. He again proposed that the Court of Ava should offer some consideration, and if not money, the island of Negrais or some other territory. Atwinwun Maung Yeet, who could always be relied on to butt in with an absurd suggestion, said that the English could have Negrais if they would restore Arakan as well as Tenasserim, and when Burney explained as firmly as possible that the Government of India would never even consider such a proposal, went on to make an even more absurd one. When Burney laughed this off, he retorted that there would be no objection to Siam purchasing Tenasserim since the Burmese would soon reconquer it from her. Then suddenly Maung Yeet seemed to realize that he was attracting Burney's attention too much by the part he was playing in the discussions, he whispered to him to look in the direction of the wungyis when replying, 'since my addressing him alone so much had made them very jealous of him'.[2]

Thus the Tenasserim talks petered out. The Burmese hoped for

[1] Journal, para. 235.   [2] Ibid., 390.

the impossible. The Government of India on the other hand was becoming aware of growing opposition to retrocession among British officials in both Calcutta and London. Two views contributed to this. Firstly, there were much brighter hopes for the economic future of the province, and secondly, the belief that the Burmese would illtreat the people was a real deterrent. Accordingly, when Lord William Cavendish Bentinck read Burney's reports of his discussions, he found himself in disagreement with the line taken by the Resident: it seemed likely to encourage the Court of Ava to expect some concession on the part of the British. He therefore instructed Burney to discontinue the discussions. That was in February 1831; but it was not the end of the matter, so far as the ministers were concerned. In the following August Burney wrote that they still believed that a little patience was all that was required: they knew that hundreds of thousands of rupees had to be sent annually from Calcutta to meet the expenses of Tenasserim's administration, whereas it had previously yielded a revenue surplus to the king. A few months later they again raised the question of the boundary, claiming that the British were wrongfully occupying parts of the Martaban province and islands in the Salween. Burney gave them a written reply quoting the Yandabo treaty and the record of discussions leading to it, and asking the question why raise the matter again. This stirred them to make a written rejoinder strongly objecting to every point in his note, to which he in turn replied that there was nothing he could do about it without further instructions from Calcutta. Even then they refused to drop the matter. 'You hold our countries which we desire to get back,' they told him. That was the situation when in April 1832 he left Ava to go on sick leave to Rangoon. Ultimately the matter was clinched by the home authorities. The Tenasserim province, they instructed the Government of India, was to be retained permanently. Their decision arrived in Calcutta in March 1833.

Tension over the Kabaw Valley was building up to such a pitch, when Burney arrived at Ava, that an open rupture with Manipur was feared. The planting of boundary flags along the right bank of the Chindwin by Grant and Pemberton was such a challenge to the Burmese that only the opposition of the wungyis had prevented the king from ordering troops to remove them. To make matters worse the two British officers had followed up their action by issuing a proclamation that all Burmese subjects living in the disputed area must leave it by 25 June 1830 or be considered subjects of the Raja of Manipur. The news of this created consternation at Ava, and on 3 June the ministers urged Burney to take action to prevent the collision that they assured him must occur should the proclamation be carried into effect. Burney at once wrote off to the Government of India asking that either Grant or Pemberton should be sent to Ava to explain matters to the Burmese authorities; in addition he asked the wungyis to enable him to despatch a letter directly to the two officers in Manipur informing them of his action. He particularly requested that in the meantime nothing should be done that might exacerbate the situation.

The wungyis agreed without hesitation, and on 14 July at Thobal in Manipur, the usual point of departure for journeys to the Burmese frontier, Pemberton made the following entry in his Journal:

Two Burmese officers from Ava accompanied by two chapprassies of Major Burney, the Resident there, and a party from the Ningthee Raja, arrived at Langthabal on the 5th instant; they brought a letter from Major Burney inviting one of us to Ava, but recommending at the same time that we should not go until instructions had been received from the Governor-General on the subject.

He goes on to say that Grant and he thought that under the circumstances it was advisable for him to leave at once for the Burmese capital. So, having paid a farewell call on the raja and loaded his baggage on the necessary elephants, he started on his way at the head of a party of some seventy servants and sepoys. At the height of the wet monsoon it was a most difficult and dangerous journey. Yet he found time to maintain a detailed diary of his experiences which is one of the most fascinating documents of its kind in the whole range of the East India Company's records.[1] It is written with a gusto unusual in official reports, for such it was, and gives delightful descriptions of incidents and people, which display the writer's interest in everything he saw and his abundant sense of humour.

Pemberton reached the capital on 12 August to stay at the

[1] Two copies of it exist, one in volume 358 of the Bengal Secret Proceedings s.v. 19 November 1830, and the other in Volume 677 of the Home Miscellaneous Series. See my edition of it with introduction and glossary in *Journal of the Burma Research Society*, Vol. XLIII, Part II, December 1960, pp. 1–96.

Residency as Burney's guest, having had to leave most of his Manipuri escort at Kyauk-ta-lon, the nearest guard-post on the southern approach to the city by river, because of the embarrassment they caused to the authorities at the capital. On the 15th Burney and his brother George, at the head of a large retinue of servants and sepoys, took Pemberton to the palace to introduce him to the king. On their way they called at Maung Sa's residence, and there, among others, he met the Wundauk Khan Ye, with whom in March 1828 he had had the altercation concerning the accuracy of the Burmese map of the Manipur frontier. They shook hands, and the wundauk expressed pleasure at meeting him, 'but', writes Pemberton in his Journal, 'he evidently would have been much better pleased that I were at the bottom of the sea, as he knew that I should now be able to expose the falsehood he had indulged in. His countenance displayed the greatest anxiety, and, though he behaved with extraordinary arrogance to us at the Ningthee [Chindwin], I could hardly resist a feeling of pity on seeing his present very altered demeanour.'[1]

The king, who had been told by the wundauk that Pemberton was an out-and-out supporter of the Manipuri claim to the Kabaw valley received him with obvious aversion. When, however, Pemberton's present of 'a very handsome double barrelled fowling piece' was displayed to him, he gradually relaxed, and during the entertainment which followed the introduction he frequently asked Burney and Pemberton if they were pleased with it, and was gratified when they assured him that they were. The Resident's guard included a number of excellent wrestlers, and the king called upon them to show their prowess. He was delighted with their exhibition, 'but', writes Pemberton, 'immediately after the sepoys had retired, a party of Burmahs came forward and mimicked the wrestling and other feats of the sepoys with such humour and truth, that we all joined most heartily in the laugh, and the golden countenance quite lost its dignity in broad grins'.[2]

Then began a number of conferences with the ministers all of them reported in detail by both Burney and Pemberton. At the outset Burney sought to make it clear that Pemberton was not there as a negotiator, but to provide him with such information as he might need, and that he himself was not there to express an

[1] Hall, 'R. B. Pemberton's Journey', JBRS, XLIII, Part II, p. 42.
[2] *Ibid.*, p. 43.

opinion in the matter, but to hear what the Burmese had to say, and submit it, together with the documents they might produce in proof of it, to the Governor-General of India. Nevertheless they did their utmost to persuade him to admit the justice of the Burmese case. They even argued with Pemberton regarding the map which he had declared to be a fake, and, when he clearly pointed out their errors, they brought in a Manipuri for questioning. He, however, to their bafflement, merely confirmed Pemberton's statements; Maung Sa was so put out that he tried to argue that the man's pronunciation of the place names was incorrectly interpreted, but it was useless. The atwinwun, Maung Yeet, must needs complicate matters by introducing all sorts of irrelevancies. Burney had very firmly to show the absurdity of his suggestion that the Burmese and Manipuris should be left to fight it out. Undeterred by this, he then asserted that the Governor-General's letter to the king had intimated that he would not interfere in Manipur. Burney replied that there was no such statement in the letter. Then, as Pemberton puts it, 'he asked for the original letter to be brought', and, 'comparing it with the translation, which had been made by Doctor Judson, it appeared that the Attawoon had misrepresented its purport by omitting a word. The stupidity and rascality of this Attawoon, who is said to be high in the king's confidence, not only exhausted our patience, but that of the Woonghee Moung Sa, who said that he was quite disgusted. He read paragraphs of utter nonsense, and was with great difficulty prevented from continuing them.' Burney begged the ministers to dismiss from their minds any idea that the British would allow Manipur to be attacked by Burma.[1] Near the end of his record of this meeting Pemberton mentions that the Manipuri witness concluded his evidence by saying that although the people of the Kabaw Valley had been dependent upon Manipur in Chorjit's time,[2] his grandmother had told him that for seven generations before that they had belonged to Ava. This was much nearer to the point than the atwinwun's irrelevances which only served to create a bad impression of Burma's case. At the close of the meeting, when the British officers took their leave an amusing little comedy was enacted. It must be described in Pemberton's words. 'On

[1] *Ibid.*, p. 45.
[2] Chorjit had been Raja of Manipur from 1799 to 1813, when his brother Marjit had dethroned him with Burmese help.

going away I shook hands with the Woonghee, who is by far the most intelligent man among them, and was retiring, when the Attawoon called out, "Why don't you shake hands with me too?" Which I did, though I feel no partiality towards the fellow.'[1] Two days later, he tells us, when their next conference was due, but had to be postponed, Burney took the opportunity to have a private word with Maung Sa to suggest that he might use his influence with the Atwinwun 'to make him confine himself to the leading facts of the case'.

Whether as a result of his intervention or not, the discussions as recorded by both Burney and Pemberton tended henceforth to become more realistic and to concentrate upon the examination of such writings as were available regarding the valley. There were, of course, the Burmese chronicles, the last recension of which, the *Hmannan Yazawin*, 'Glass Palace Chronicle', had appeared as recently as 1829. There were also Manipuri chronicle writings, and in addition Pemberton had brought with him a Manipuri translation of an old Shan chronicle. At their second full meeting with the Burmese ministers these were examined and compared. Maung Yeet again made a nuisance of himself by insisting that Burney should be satisfied with copies made from the original chornicle, but Burney had had experience of Maung Yeet's methods and refused to look at anything but the original, much to the atwinwun's annoyance. The most intractable difficulty which arose lay in the great discrepancies between the dates assigned to the various events recorded. It caused an amusing little tiff between Pemberton and Lanciago, when the latter challenged him to give the date when the Manipuris first gained possession of the valley. Pemberton, who was engaged in discussing identifications of names with Maung Sa, tried to make him understand that that was not the subject of their discussion at that particular moment. This led to sharp words between them so that Burney had to intervene and tactfully suggest to his colleague that it be better for him to comply with the request. This he did, but his compliance failed to remove from the Spaniard's mind the impression that he had been deliberately stalling, and indeed in his journal Pemberton admits that he was unwilling to mention any dates because he suspected that the Burmese would make improper use of them.[2]

Burney's proposal, after this preliminary survey of the records,

[1] *loc. cit. supra.*   [2] *Ibid.*, p. 49.

was that he should make translations of them and forward them to the Governor-General in Calcutta using Pemberton as his emissary. This led to some further heat on the subject of Pemberton's fitness to report matters to the Governor-General. Lanciago was against entrusting Pemberton with the task: he thought he was committed to the Manipuri cause. The ministers asked him if he would promise to lay all the documents before the Governor-General and report everything that had been said. He replied that among European gentlemen such a question would be considered insulting. Finally it was agreed that the matter should be laid before the king. Before the ministers left the Residency, where the meeting had been held, Maung Sa sought to smooth Pemberton's ruffled feelings. He had heard, he said, that he was a partisan of the Manipuri cause, but he now believed him to be impartial. 'As soon as I saw you, I felt we must be friends.' Pemberton gratefully accepted his offer of friendship. He confided to his journal, 'I really feel kindly to this old man; he is the only one I have seen of the Ministers, who may be fairly said to have a head, and his intelligence saves a great deal of trouble'.

The king agreed to the proposal that Pemberton should travel with the documents to Calcutta by the shortest route, which was by the An Pass over the Arakan Yoma to Akyab. His majesty, however, was very displeased that Burney had persuaded the ministers to allow the matter to be referred to the Governor-General. When therefore on 24 September they came to a further conference at the Residency, ostensibly to check up on the originals of the documents to be submitted to the Governor-General, they were obviously suffering from the effects of the king's outraged feelings. Burney annoyed Maung Sa by lecturing him on his duty, which, he said, was 'to prevent the King from being misled by false hopes and flattering tales'. The old man was heard to mutter that it was very disrespectful to point out to him his duty as a wungyi. But he recovered sufficiently to joke with Pemberton about his being a Mueetuee Mucha, a Manipuri Lad; to which Pemberton laughingly agreed saying, 'and don't you like me better for being so?' The wungyi said he could not imagine how Pemberton could actually enjoy living in such a country. He himself had stayed there for twenty days, and that was quite enough.[1]

The conference came to an abrupt unpleasant conclusion over

[1] 'Pemberton's Journey, p. 51.

the treatment of Burmese subjects living in the valley. The ministers requested Burney to write to Captain Grant asking him not to molest these people. Burney denied that there was any interference with them and the matter was then referred to Pemberton who explained that the object of the Burmese was to establish themselves on the west bank of the Chindwin and that, of course, was impossible as matters stood. Maung Sa in rejoinder asked why two new *thannahs* (i.e. fortified posts) had recently been established there. This, said Pemberton, had been done with the sanction of the Governor-General, and in any case, he went on, he had declared that the land west of the Chindwin belonged to the Raja of Manipur so that they were free to establish as many *thannahs* as they thought necessary. But, objected the wungyi, the matter was not yet settled, and surely there should be no interference with people who cultivated in the valley before the Governor-General had considered the evidence that was now to be laid before him. Pemberton's reply to this was that so far as he and Grant were concerned the matter was settled; all residents on the western bank of the river were considered subjects of Manipur. Hence people living under Burmese authority on the east bank could not be permitted to come over and cultivate in Manipuri territory, unless they came across altogether and built their houses there; then they could cultivate as much as they liked. This answer displeased the ministers so much that they broke off the conference and left at once, 'with some rudeness', writes Burney[1] 'abruptly and rudely', comments Pemberton.[2]

The breach was quickly healed. The real trouble was, as Maung Sa told Burney later, that the king like a child was bent upon regaining possession of the valley, and if his wish were not gratified, would vent his wrath upon himself and the other ministers. Burney gathered that they were in truth frightened men. This conversation took place when together with Pemberton and the Wundauk Maung Khan Ye they went on an expedition across the Irrawaddy to visit the Kaunghmudaw Pagoda and see an inscription in which two places in the Kabaw Valley were mentioned as belonging to Ava. They were Sumjok and Kale, and copies were made for the Englishmen of the part of the inscription in which they were mentioned. Following this they were entertained by two young ladies who sang a number of Burmese songs. It was a

[1] Journal, para. 242.   [2] 'Pemberton's Journey', p. 52.

pleasant little party with everyone sitting under the shade of a large tree and enjoying what Pemberton describes as 'a great deal of desultory conversation'. Their Burmese hosts were in good form: they chipped Pemberton on being a bachelor, saying that he must marry a Burmese wife. He heartily agreed with them, but reminded them that he would have to take her away to Calcutta with him. No, they objected, that would never do; the wedding would have to be deferred until his business in Calcutta was concluded. But Pemberton told them that his plan was far more judicious since his Burmese wife 'would be devoted to their interests'. This made them laugh very heartily. Then the conversation turned to palmistry and Pemberton examined the Wundauk Khan Ye's hand and with great gravity told him that he would preserve the favour of his king and achieve the highest honours, which, he says, the minister construed rather as an expression of good will than as a prophecy likely to be fulfilled. He was to end his life in gaol at the strangler's hands when Tharrawaddy seized power.

A few days later Burney and Pemberton were the guests of the king at a regatta held at Amarapoora. Pemberton again provides a very colourful account of this, describing the procession of warboats with gilt umbrellas conveying the king and court and the way in which the boat races were conducted, with the king himself acting as judge. 'It was evident,' he writes, 'that this was a very favourite amusement of the King, for he showed great keennesss as the boats advanced, frequently jumping up and using gestures that denoted anxiety.' The myowun of Amarapoora sent them a tray of refreshments of which they all partook. As soon as they had finished Lanciago appeared unexpectedly with another feast sent over by the king, and with the injunction that they must make at least a show of eating it since his majesty was watching them through a telescope. They did their best, but, writes Pemberton, it was a penance. Not so, however, to Khan Ye, who made a second large meal as large as the first, though carefully ensconcing himself in a part of the boat where he was screened from the attention of the king's telescope. They divided the remainder among their boatmen who ate what they could and tied the rest up in their loin cloths.[1]

The final conference of Pemberton's visit took place on 1 September at Maung Khan Ye's residence. Burney describes it as

[1] *Ibid.*, pp. 55-6.

a very happy one. It was concerned entirely with the arrangements for Pemberton's journey via Akyab to Calcutta to lay Burma's case regarding the Kabaw Valley before the Governor-General and for the return of a part of his Manipuri following to their homeland by the route they had used on the outward journey. On the 6th the king accorded Pemberton a very cordial farewell audience, making him some valuable presents.

I fear, [he comments] that much of his condescension was exhibited with the intention of inducing the Resident and myself to make a report to the Governor-General as much in favour of his side of the question of the boundary as possible. Indeed, Major Burney was asked plainly by Moung Yeet, in a tone sufficiently loud for the King to hear, whether he had given an opinion to His Lordship in Council upon the subject, and translated the papers. The Resident replied that he had laboured assiduously at the translations to get them ready, and had arranged them with so much care that His Lordship would find no difficulty in forming an opinion on the question.[1]

Burney's covering letter, entrusted with the evidence to Pemberton for delivery to the Government of India is a model of diplomacy. He does not dispute the rightness of the Governor-General's decision in the previous January to award the valley to Manipur, but explains that he asked for the matter to be reopened because of the feelings of the king and ministers: his refusal to have done so would have destroyed all the confidence and goodwill he had been at such pains to build up. All the ministers were most anxious to avoid another war, but the king's mind was absolutely fixed upon recovering the valley, and a final decision in favour of Manipur would certainly bring about a collision. The ministers dared not contradict the king, 'and I see the personal safety and comfort of these poor creatures will be endangered by the unsuccessful issue of the negotiations. . . . It is difficult to describe and equally so not to sympathize in their extreme anxiety on this subject'. Both Lane and Lanciago, he goes on, had expressed their fears on the subject, and although he had always ridiculed the idea that the king would be ready to go to war over such a matter as the Kabaw Valley, they assured him that he would have done so at the beginning of the year, had not his own arrival in the country been expected.

This letter is dated 11 September. The reference to 'these poor

[1] 'Pemberton's Journey', p. 57.

creatures' is interesting: it reflects Burney's tendency shown earlier in Siam to develop feelings of sympathy for the people with whom he had had daily contacts over a period of time even though disagreeing with them on all sorts of important issues. In this case one has to take into account that three days earlier the ministers had done something unprecedented in Burmese history: they had dined with Burney at the Residency. He writes a detailed description of the dinner party in his Journal[1] and Pemberton also describes it, though in less detail, in his.[2] The guests were the Kyi Wungyi, the Myawadi Wungyi Maung Sa, Atwinwun Maung Yeet, Wundauk Maung Khan Ye and Messrs Lane, Sarkies[3] and Lanciago. Pemberton comments on how very well they succeeded in accommodating themselves to British customs and says that they seemed thoroughly to enjoy the food. They declined wine but ate well of the trifle which had a strong lacing of cherry brandy. 'The Ministers left us,' writes Burney, 'highly satisfied and overflowing with love and affection. So much so, indeed, as to lead me to fear that the cherry brandy, in the Trifle, of which they had all eaten heartily, without supposing it to contain any such liquor, had tended to exhilarate them not a little.' He felt that having persuaded the ministers to meet him in this friendly and informal manner was a tremendous achievement which was likely to ease his task 'to an eminent degree'. Did he suspect that it might have just as great an effect upon him as upon the ministers?

On 13 September Pemberton left to make his way down the Irrawaddy as far as Minbu, where he was to disembark and lead his party across the Arakan Yoma by the An pass to Akyab, whence he was to sail across to the Hugli and up to Calcutta. He made fairly detailed surveys of the land route from Minbu to Akyab, which he carefully recorded in his journal and the results of which found their way into a map which was being compiled on behalf of the Government of India. This he published in his book *Report on the Eastern Frontier of British India*.[4] He went to lay the Burmese objections to the Kabaw Valley award before the Governor-General. The matter was not considered urgent by the Government of India, and in any case a Burmese embassy had been deputed to Calcutta with the Kabaw question at the head of its agenda;

[1] paras 267–70.   [2] *Ibid.*, p. 59.   [3] See *infra* p. 256.
[4] Calcutta, 1835, a reprint of the book was issued in 1966 by the Department of Historical and Antiquarian Studies in Assam, Gauhati.

so further consideration was postponed until discussions with it could be held. Burney had strongly urged that the king should send a mission and that it should travel by the An Pass: he was extremely anxious to speed up communications between Ava and Calcutta.

The Burmese mission left Ava on 9 October. It consisted of two envoys, Mingyi Maha Sithu Maung Shwe, the senior envoy, and his junior, Mintha Nandagyawdin Maung Byo. Neither was of ministerial rank; Burney called them 'men of no influence'. He was deeply disappointed in their selection. Their instructions were to make four demands, in the following order: the return of the Kabaw Valley, the return of the part of Martaban district that was east of the Salween, the return of the provinces of Arakan and Tenasserim, and the abrogation of the seventh article of the Treaty of Yandabo providing for the appointment of resident ministers at the capitals of British India and Burma. The story of the mission, compiled by Burney, occupies 124 pages of the India Political Consultations.[1] For writing up his account Burney was able to use copies of the junior envoy's journal presented to the Ministers on the mission's return to Ava and of most of their reports sent from time to time from India. Some idea of the amount of material, all in Burmese, that he had to examine may be gained from the fact that during the first eighteen months of their stay in India the envoys sent home 105 reports.

The Burmese envoys were attended by Burney's younger brother, George, upon whom the king conferred the title Thiri Yaza Nawrahta, 'Excellent and Noble Son'. Their families and servants, who travelled with them, numbered 84 persons. To these must be added George Burney's servants and the sepoy guard, bringing the total number to well over one hundred. For such a miscellaneous crowd travelling on land was necessarily very slow; thus the journey from Minbu to Akyab took no less than forty-three days; Pemberton did it in only 12. They arrived in Calcutta by steamer from Akyab on 6 December. The Governor-General was away on an extended tour of the East India Company's possessions in northern India. Accordingly the envoys waited ten months in Calcutta for permission to meet him up country. They

[1] Range 193, vol. 79, Consultation of 6 July 1835. See W. S. Desai, 'History of the Burmese Mission to India, October 1830–July 1833' in JBRS XXVI, Part II, August 1936.

finally caught up with him at Agra and there on 23 November 1832 they were received in audience. Not until his return to Calcutta, however, in the following January was their business formally discussed with the Government of India, and to the discussions Henry Burney, Maingy and a number of other officers were summoned. Mr. Desai asks whether Burney's earlier treatment by the Court of Ava was one of the reasons for this extraordinary series of delays. But the detailed account of their proceedings provided by Burney shows that they themselves were mainly to blame, both for the long delay in Calcutta and for those on their journeyings in pursuit of the Governor-General.[1] They travelled in the most dilatory fashion, staying, for instance, a month in Benares, and sending home unbelievably fantastic reasons for their delays. The British, they said, were at war with Yanzitshein (Ranjit Singh) King of Peenja (Punjab) and Lahore, and they were being held as hostages to prevent Burma from joining him. Later they reported that Ranjit Singh had captured the Governor-General in battle, and that this was the reason for their inability to see him. When he came down from the hills to return to Calcutta, they reported that he had been released from captivity by Ranjit Singh in return for a ransom of fifteen lakhs of rupees, and had been recalled in disgrace by the British Government. On their way back to Calcutta after their reception by Lord William Cavendish Bentinck the envoys insisted on paying a visit to the famous Buddhist shrine at Buddhagaya, where the beloved founder of their religion had attained enlightenment sitting in meditation under the peepul tree which, according to tradition, was the very same one growing there at the time of their visit. For many centuries Burmese monarchs had sent presents to the shrine, and some had carried out repairs to the fabric of the temple. From the evidence of this and of the Burmese-type images of the Buddha there the envoys made the exciting 'discovery' that the kingdom of Burma had once extended right up to the Bodhi Tree itself. They therefore urged King Bagyidaw to become the protector of the sacred tree.[2] In his report on the mission Burney, while deploring the absurdity of the stories purveyed by the envoys to the Court of Ava, comments that the more intelligent ministers did not accept them, and says that the Rangoon wungyi had gone so far as to write to Ava

[1] Desai, 'History of the Burmese Mission to India', JBRS, XXVI, ii, p. 72.
[2] *Ibid.*, pp. 95–7.

castigating the envoys for listening to the lies of bad characters.

After the departures of Pemberton in September 1830, and of the Burmese envoys in October, the indemnity question became Burney's chief concern. His instructions, as we have seen, laid on him the task of remonstrating with the Court of Ava regarding the delay in the payment of the fourth, and final, instalment of the crore of rupees stipulated by the Yandabo treaty. Avoiding the wearisome details of previous negotiations on the subject let it simply be said that the Burmese had begun payments of this instalment in August 1828; there had been great delays; and when Burney arrived at the capital in April 1830, some twelve lakhs of rupees remained outstanding. That was according to British calculations, which Burney accepted as correct when he first took the matter up with the ministers. He asked that the whole sum outstanding should be paid off by the following October. The ministers in return asked for a further year's grace. When, however, he rejected their plea, urging that delay might prejudice their claim to the Kabaw Valley, or even lead to a British re-occupation of Rangoon, he found himself up against a brick wall of opposition. Reporting the situation to Calcutta, he said that unless drastic action were taken, the arrears would not be cleared up until February of the next year.

As Burney began to learn more about the country to which he had been deputed, he came to realize a basic fact of which the British commissioners at Yandabo seem to have been totally ignorant, namely that the payment of so large a sum of silver as was represented by the indemnity imposed a wellnigh intolerable burden upon the Burmese. Only an insignificant portion of the royal revenue was paid in money: most of it was paid in kind. Moreover, comparatively little silver was in circulation. Burney with his customary zeal collected all the information he could on the subject. He found for one thing that the ministers' difficulties in completing the payment of the fourth instalment were much increased by the fact that the queen had lent a vast sum of money from her own private fortune to enable them to pay the first instalment when the Yandabo treaty was signed, and was now pressing for repayment. He learnt also that pressure upon the people could be applied at only two periods of the year, just after the sowing of paddy in May or June, and when it was ripe for harvesting in December and January. At other times, if pressed, they would migrate to other parts of the country or simply take to the jungle. Maung Sa told him that every member of the government had had to make large personal contributions, he himself and the atwinwun, Maung Yeet, having been mulcted of 1,800 ticals each. What he learnt made Burney rather uneasy about the part he had to play in the matter, and he wrote in his journal that it was a pity that effective pressure could not be put upon the queen and her brother 'to force open their hoards', since the methods by which the poor were squeezed were a rich source of peculation to the subordinate local officials.

In November 1830, when only three very small payments had arrived in Rangoon, and the Government of India had made it clear that it was not prepared to apply military sanctions of any kind to induce the Court of Ava to pay up, the ministers quite unexpectedly confronted him with the contention that the whole indemnity had already been paid; indeed, according to their calculation 588 viss of silver had been paid in excess and must be returned. They had reached this conclusion by a re-examination of the wording of article 5 of the Yandabo treaty. The English version of the article stated simply that the Burmese king was to pay one crore of rupees, without even specifying whether the Madras or the Calcutta rupee was meant. Presumably the drafters had been unaware that there was a difference in silver content between the two. This, however, was not germaine. What was germaine was that the Burmese version of the article described the amount to be paid as 75,000 viss of good silver, and the question now raised by the ministers was what constituted good silver.

There were no less than 36 different qualities of silver current in the country, Burney discovered. He made exhaustive enquiries into the subject for the information of the Government of India, and as a result produced a valuable report entitled 'Observations on the Currency of Ava'.[1] In it he showed that where fairly large amounts of silver were involved, its quality was tested by the public assayer, called a *pweza*. In practice the commonest types were *dain* and *yowetni*. A hundred ticals of *dain* were considered to be the equivalent of 139 Calcutta sicca rupees and two annas. A hundred ticals of *yowetni*, on the other hand, were equivalent to only 126 Calcutta sicca rupees and eight annas. It was, however, the currency in which merchants kept their accounts, and was

[1] BSP vol. 360, Consultation of 15 April 1831.

usually known by Europeans as 'flowered silver'. Previous payments of the indemnity had been made in *dain*, but no actual stipulation to that effect would seem ever to have been made. Now it was the ministers' contention that *ywetni* was 'good silver', and that since they had already paid 68,716 viss of *dain*, and this was the equivalent of 75,588 viss of *ywetni*, they had more than discharged their obligations under article 5 of the treaty.[1]

Unfortunately for the ministers' argument, however, Lieutenant Rawlinson, the officer charged with receiving payments of the indemnity at Rangoon, had found the *dain* to be of an inferior quality; he had valued it at only 133 rupees per 100 ticals. Burney himself in a report on the subject in December roughly estimated that 750,000 ticals of *dain* was about as much above a crore of rupees as the same weight of *ywetni* was below it. He assured the ministers that the question would be referred to the Calcutta Mint, and if it were found that there had been an overpayment, this would be refunded in full. He forwarded their statement to the Government of India, warning them, however, that until the matter was settled, they must continue with the payments according to Captain Rawlinson's estimate. To his consternation he discovered that they had ceased collecting money on the assumption that he had accepted their case. To his strong protest the ministers replied in writing on 20 June (1831) that the indemnity had been paid in full and the Government of India should be informed accordingly.

This curt reply triggered off the biggest row Burney ever had with the ministers. It made him very angry. He sent a stiff rejoinder recounting the history of the indemnity negotiations and detailing their many unfulfilled pledges. Under the circumstances, he said, he must obey his orders, and if the ministers failed to resume the collection of money, he would remove himself and the whole residency to Rangoon.[2] The ministers returned an uncompromising reply claiming that the excess payment was no less than 336,116 sicca rupees, and telling him to write to the Bengal government confirming the correctness of their calculation. Burney of course refused to do anything of the kind.

So now it became a trial of strength. Burney was a very angry,

---

[1] For a fuller treatment of the subject see W. S. Desai, 'History of the Burma Indemnity, 1826–1833' in JBRS, vol. XXIV, Part iii, December 1934.
[2] Burney's letter of 9 August 1831 quoted in Desai, *British Residency*, pp. 119–120.

and a very determined man. For a whole month both sides were at loggerheads. On 6 August Burney went personally to the Hlutdaw and repeated his warning that unless indemnity collections were resumed he would leave Ava. Again his warning had not the slightest effect. He was told that the cause of the stolid refusal of the ministers to heed his warnings lay in a rumour reported by the Burmese envoys in India of an impending war between the East India Company and Ranjit Singh, the ruler of the Punjab. And although palpably absurd, as the ministers must have realized, Burney knew from his experience in Siam that it could be a useful diplomatic weapon. The ministers also, he was pretty sure, did not believe that when it came to the crunch he would actually carry out his threat.

This exceedingly difficult situation was made even worse by an incident at Kyauk-ta-lon, the nearest guard post on the Irrawaddy on the way southwards from Ava. A Moulmein merchant, Agha Saadat, travelling from Ava, was arrested for the breach of a regulation requiring all traders leaving the capital to declare the amount of currency they had with them. As he was a British subject his case came within Burney's consular jurisdiction. It turned out that the man had actually left Ava before the regulation was proclaimed. It was also a completely new departure in Burmese practice. One suspects that the whole affair was rigged as an act of defiance against Burney. He raised the strongest objections against the arrest and demanded Agha Saadat's release. He even addressed a letter personally to the king.

The ministers agreed to release the man, and to deliver the letter. They did neither. Burney therefore decided to carry out his threat. He started preparations for the complete evacuation of the residency. This shook the ministers out of their complacency. They released Agha Saadat and sent the wundauk Khan Ye to talk matters over. Burney, however, was intent upon a showdown. He told Khan Ye that the balance of the indemnity must be paid within one month of hearing from the Burmese envoy in Calcutta, to whom the matter had been referred. If not, he would remove the residency from Ava. On 13 August he went to the Hlutdaw and presented his demand as an ultimatum: unless they accepted his proposal he would leave on the following morning. When by 10 o'clock on the next morning 14 August no sign had come from either the Golden Feet or the Hlutdaw, Burney and the whole residency staff embarked on a flotilla of boats and began the journey downstream.

Consternation reigned at court when news came of Burney's departure. This he learnt later on from the Englishman Lane, who described the scene of confusion, with princes and ministers running to and fro with long faces. When the residency flotilla was no more than eight or nine miles on its way, it was overtaken by a fast warboat bearing the Treasurer and another officer, who begged Burney to accept a way out of the impasse, which he suggested. It was that he on his part should make a similar pledge to the one he had demanded of the ministers. In other words he was to promise that if the Burmese envoys in Calcutta reported that 'an overplus' had been paid by the Court of Ava, it would be repaid by the British in the same period of time, namely one month, that he had demanded of the Burmese, then the ministers would engage to do the same, should the balance be against the Court of Ava.

Burney naturally had no difficulty in accepting the proposal and at once wrote the required letter to the ministers. He promised to wait at his moorings until six o'clock the next morning for their reply. Well before the stipulated time the Treasurer returned with the required document. The row was over, and on 16 August Burney and his party were once again installed in the residency. Some days later he met all the ministers at the Hlutdaw. There were no recriminations; 'We became apparently as sincere and cordial friends as ever,' he reported.[1]

But, one naturally asks, had his journey been really necessary? The Governor-General thought not, and expressed his strong disagreement with Burney's action. He should not have taken the action he did, he wrote, without specific orders. He should have withheld all further communication with the Court of Ava until the matter had been referred to the Government of India for orders, rather than commit himself to a course of action involving retirement from the capital, which might have been difficult to retrieve.

Burney on his part had been convinced of the necessity for drastic action. He had carried out his decision realizing fully that it would involve him in personal loss; for he had to leave all his personal furniture behind with the prospect of losing it all, and

[1] BSP, Vol. 362, letter dated Ava, 28 August 1831 quoted in Desai, *op. cit.*, p. 122.

he had given away the contents of his wine cellar and other personal stores. Happily, however, when he returned, none of his furniture had been lost: the ministers had taken the precaution of placing a guard over it. Happily also his action had no serious consequences so far as his relations with the Court of Ava were concerned. Nevertheless, he had acted very unwisely: he had allowed his feelings of exasperation to take command. This was a pity, for he was a man of admirable character and immense ability subjected to almost unendurable strains, both physical and mental, and this breakdown of judgement may well have undermined the government of India's confidence in his capacity to deal with a serious crisis. It may indeed have had something to do with Lord Auckland's unreasonable and unfair treatment of Burney when, after Tharrawaddy's usurpation in 1837, he removed the residency to Rangoon without the previous sanction of the Government of India.

The subsequent history of the indemnity tends to confirm the Governor-General's view of Burney's action. The Court of Ava had for the moment been severely shaken and hence had been willing to give any undertaking which would secure his return. But quite soon the effects of the shock began to wear off, and ways and means were sought of avoiding the consequences of their pledge, especially when the Calcutta Mint Master reported that the value of the *dain* silver paid in was only 3.7 per cent above that of *yowetni* and not 10 per cent, as the ministers had claimed. When he demonstrated his methods of assaying the metal to the Burmese envoys, they said it was nonsense and his display of chemistry a trick. His calculations showed that out of the ten million rupees of the indemnity some 654,232 were still owing by the Court of Ava.

On 16 December (1831), under instructions from the Government of India, Henry Burney presented a formal demand for this sum to the Hlutdaw. When after more than a week no reply had been vouchsafed by the ministers, he appeared again before them. He warned them that if they did not pay up immediately, the British would have to charge interest on the sum outstanding. The atwinwun, Maung Yeet, declared that he would not hear of such a thing as paying interest. To this angry ejaculation Burney replied that there was a way of making people hear, with guns and muskets. This created an uproar and Burney was accused of losing his temper. When he could make himself heard again, he asked the ministers how they would feel if a private individual owing them money had continuously put them off with false promises for four or five years. Ultimately they agreed that the disputed balance was due.[1] On 6 January (1832) they handed Burney a document under the royal seal promising to pay the full sum demanded in 4,994 viss of *dain* within 300 days from 4 January just past, and to pay interest at 1 per cent per mensem on anything still unpaid at the close of that period. If on refining the *dain* the Calcutta Assay Master found it to yield a surplus above the stipulated amount of 654,232 rupees, it was to be returned with interest.

So the one month agreed with Burney as the condition for his return to the capital had now been stretched to ten, which evoked Calcutta's thunder of disapproval and a stern warning from Burney. Nevertheless, although serious efforts were then made to collect all the money due, and *dain* to the value of over 200,000 rupees was handed over in the following April, the total amount was not liquidated until February 1833. When the account was finally settled, Captain Rawlinson found that there was a surplus of 14,054 rupees to Burma's credit, and this was accordingly remitted to the ministers.

Mr. W. S. Desai expresses the opinion that but for the services of Henry Burney the East India Company would never have received the full amount of the indemnity.[2] This is indisputable, but what is perhaps more noteworthy is that notwithstanding the flare-up in the Hlutdaw, which has just been described, he managed to carry out his embarrassing and ungrateful task without seriously damaging the good relations he had so assiduously built up with the ministers. He understood the immense difficulties with which they had to contend in paying what was for Burma an unprecedented amount of silver. Yet as a British officer he had loyally to carry out the duties assigned to him by his government. Nevertheless the ministers sensed that he was a friend, just as, be it remembered, their predecessors at the turn of the century had done in the case of Michael Symes. Their consternation, when they learnt that he had indeed evacuated the residency, was a telling witness to their feelings about him. Fear of an adverse outcome of the Kabaw Valley negotiations only partly accounted for it.

[1] Journal, para. 870.   [2] *Op. cit.*, p. 125.

Chapter 13

Burney and the Court of Ava

HENRY Burney's record of his experiences at the Court of Ava, like his Bangkok Journal, shows literary style of no mean order. In both accounts, as one would expect, the king figures much less than his ministers with whom Burney had almost daily contact. King Bagyidaw, however, makes more frequent appearances in the record than Rama III. He had nothing like his Siamese counterpart's mental capacity nor his control over the administration of his country. But until incapacitated by illness, he appeared more frequently in public, and was a popular figure. His love of sport and enjoyment of his country's national festivals largely accounted for this. He also had acquired the reputation, uncommon among Burmese kings, of being averse to bloodshed. With little intelligence and no capacity whatever for hard work, he nevertheless could assert himself, and his ministers went in constant dread of him losing his temper. Burney therefore soon realized that it was essential for him to cultivate the goodwill of the king, and no less that of the queen. His Journal of his first stay in Ava contains a number of anecdotes about the king, on the truth of which he checked up with his usual care.

The King, [he notes on 20 August 1830] lost his temper today on being informed of the death of one of his female elephants which the Tsheng-Woon, or Superintendent of Elephants, had privately lent to some officer on the Tsagain [Sagaing] side of the river. His Majesty sent immediately for the Tsheng-Woon, and suspecting that the Atwenwoons had been bribed to conceal the man's fault, he ordered three of them, including Maung Yeet and Maung Ba Youk, the Tshan and Kyee Woon Atwenwoons, to be beaten! They were immediately seized by the head and dragged on one side by all the petty officers and people who were on the spot, and who eagerly strove to testify their sentiments of duty and devotion to His Majesty by beating the Atwenwoons most severely in the Burmese mode called *Thoung*, that is with the elbow and fist on the back. They were afterwards regularly flogged with a rattan.¹

Later on he describes an incident of quite a different type. His informant was the Awe Yauk, who had been telling him how during the king's illness eighteen men had been executed in a batch for highway robbery. Everyone believed, he told Burney, that had the king been well, he would not have permitted the executions.

The Awe Youk, [Burney wrote] also communicated to me an interesting anecdote of the King, showing that he possesses more true delicacy of feeling than we could have expected from him, and proving at all events the perfect sanity of his mind at present! In the course of this morning [22 January 1831] while the Burmese nobles were throwing lances at a target, in the presence of His Majesty, the old Kyauk Tshoung Woong-yee was thrown off his horse. The moment he fell the King turned away his body and pretended not to see the accident. All the spectators were enraptured with the gracious conduct of their sovereign, and attributed it to his desire of not increasing the mortification of the poor old Woong-yee.²

It did not take Burney long to realize that the fortunes of his mission did finally depend upon the king's will. One kind word from him and everyone's attitude towards the residency, from the highest to the lowest, at once improved. When he had got to know the ministers well, and could speak their language with ease, he was able to seize opportunities to appear in the royal presence. Late in September 1830, when he received another invitation to attend the boat races so much enjoyed by the king, and was summoned to the royal presence, he presented the king with a pair of pistols and asked for permission to see him every eight or ten days. The king granted his request. In the following December he was invited by the king to witness the laying of the foundation stone of a new monastery. On his arrival the king came forward to meet him and showed him where he and his party were to sit. Later on the king came up to him as if about to engage him in conversation, then suddenly checked himself, as if it would have been derogatory to his dignity to do so. Burney learnt that before the war he had made quite a practice of chatting with English merchants.

Attendance upon the king at public functions often entailed going without shoes at inconvenient places where the ground was

¹ Journal, para. 231.   ² Journal, para. 892; Desai, *op. cit.*, p. 163.

hard on the feet; it also tempted over-zealous officials to try to make Burney unshoe unnecessarily so that they might treat the public to the spectacle of the British Resident walking without his shoes. Normally he was a match for them, and would resume his shoes when he suspected a trap. But there were occasions when there was no escape from the full rigour of court etiquette. In September 1831, when E. C. Blundell, the deputy commissioner of Tenasserim, arrived in Ava to relieve Burney so that he might go for a time to enjoy the less exacting climate of Rangoon, they were both invited to the Elephant Palace to watch the separation of a wild elephant from the females used to decoy him into the trap. On arrival they were invited to the royal presence, and to get there had to walk without shoes on the top of the walls of the elephant trap, a most painful procedure for a European. 'I wished all who questioned the propriety of my endeavouring to evade this ceremony on my first arrival here could only come and try it in their own persons,' wrote Burney in his Journal.[1]

The king's propensity for chatting with foreign visitors did at last assert itself. In October (1830) at an audience accorded to Burney at the Hlutdaw they talked together on guns, painting, books and other subjects. The king spoke to him directly and not through the wungyis, addressing him as 'Bhauranee'. This new warmth in their relations caused him no little embarrassment, for the ministers now urged him to ask the king to confer an honorific title upon him. They brushed aside his very natural objections to this by saying that it was customary for the person whom the king wished to honour to make a formal request for the honour. A few weeks after his conversation with the king, when he was again in the royal presence, the Shan Atwinwun asked him to request the king to confer a Burmese title upon him and when he demurred, the wungyis mentioned the matter to his majesty, who at once ordered a title and the appropriate gold chain, the salwe, worn by the king and his highest officials, to be prepared for Burney. This sudden action took Burney so much by surprise that he failed to make an adequate show of gratitude; the king, apparently rather annoyed at his gaucheness, left the chamber somewhat abruptly. When, however, the time came for the presentation ceremony, his good humour was quite restored. A court herald ('Thandawzin') proclaimed the title in official sing-song, 'Maha

[1] Para. 856.

Zeya Raja Nawrahta', 'great victorious and noble son', and an atwinwun bound round Burney's head a thin piece of gold stamped with the words. 'His Majesty', wrote Burney in his Journal, 'smiled and looked gratified, and I was obliged to address him and say that I was highly sensible of the honour which he had conferred upon me.'[1]

The Governor-General, as Burney may well have guessed, disapproved of his acceptance of the honour. He reluctantly gave his consent for its acceptance, but ruled that in future no further Burmese title was to be accepted. He reminded Burney that in Europe a British officer might not receive any mark of honour from a foreign ruler without his own sovereign's express permission, which was granted only if he had performed some distinguished service. Burney expressed his humble submission to his superior's ruling, but at the same time defended his conduct with an array of precedents that must have been quite devastating. Captain Hiram Cox, he pointed out, when sent to Burma as East India Company's resident, was informed that the Supreme Government would have no objection to his accepting an 'honorary distinction', if offered one. Sir Archibald Campbell, the recent commander-in-chief of the British forces in Burma, John Crawfurd and various members of their suites had received titles from the king, when they visited the capital. 'I had never heard,' he continued, 'of any objection made to the Khelats [i.e. robes of honour], etc., which the King of Delhi bestows upon almost every officer introduced to him, and my mind had certainly never connected "distinguished services" with Asiatic titles.' His parting shot was that he understood that the British sovereign's permission had to be sought only if one wished to make use of a foreign title, since declining to accept one, when it was offered, might be impossible without causing offence to a foreign ruler.

The Governor-General cannot have realized what an overwhelming rebuttal of his arguments his well-informed subordinate could fling back. Burney's conscience was clear: under the circumstances he could not have refused the title. In actual fact, having received it, he found it of great assistance in furthering his business: his association with the ministers and other officials became more informal, and everywhere he was treated with greater respect. With the king his relations continued to thaw, even to the

[1] Para. 440.

point when the monarch could joke with him. When in the middle of December 1830 news came of the death of George IV, and the accession of William IV, Burney went formally with his suite to announce the change of rulers to the king. The latter, noticing their black armbands and gloves, asked why they did not blacken their faces also, and the whole court roared with laughter, 'as in duty bound', commented Burney.[1]

He had brought with him a Calcutta newspaper the contents of which the king asked him to explain. The various advertisements caused him great amusement, but he showed special interest in the news from France, where Louis Philippe had been placed on the throne as a result of the 'July Revolution'. Burney had to explain to him the relations between the new king and the Chamber of Deputies. On this occasion he presented the king and the queen with pairs of Indian slippers, rather expecting another joke about his own objections to unshoeing. It was not, however, forthcoming; both accepted the slippers with evident pleasure, and before leaving Burney saw the king trying on his pair.

Some time later the king conversed with Burney for the first time about his official business. He highly embarrassed the resident by constantly referring to the Governor-General as 'Myowun of Bengal', thus placing him on the level of a Burmese provincial governor. Burney in replying pointedly used the term 'Angleik Min', 'English ruler', when referring to the Governor-General. Later he complained to the wungyis and Maung Sa promised to correct the king's error, though Burney was certain that not even he would dare to do so. On this occasion the king granted Burney the privilege of using a gilt umbrella.

During these early months of his stay at Ava Bagyidaw's attempts to revive his military power, and their possible effects upon his relations with British India, gave Burney much food for thought. He came to the conclusion that the king was preparing for a war for the recovery of his lost provinces. He seems to have taken Burmese bombast rather too seriously. For instance, Atwinwun Maung Yeet's repeated ejaculations, echoed at times by individual wungyis, that Britain and Burma as firm allies could conquer the world, he was inclined to interpret as pointers in such a direction. On 13 December 1830 he summed up his ideas on the subject in a letter to the Government of India. The king and his

[1] Journal, para. 369.

advisers, he wrote, were manifestly dissatisfied with the situation; so much so that they listened eagerly to any absurd stories of British disasters in India. They were completely ignorant of the realities of British power there. Their history taught them that the disasters they had suffered at the hands of the Shans and the Mons had been far greater than their defeat in the war with the British. The Shans and the Mons had destroyed their capital and royal family, and driven the common people into the jungles and mountains. Yet the Burmans rose again and recovered their power, and everyone from the highest to the lowest believed that this would happen again, even the people of the Tenasserim provinces. Last time, they told him, it was Britain's turn to conquer; next time it would be Burma's. They regarded the Indian sepoy with contempt. European troops on the other hand had earned their high respect; in fact, a Burman officer had told him that he had never seen anything like the attack of the British troops upon the Burmese stockades. Burmese ignorance of British power, Burney continued, was in his belief the chief danger. On the other hand were the present king to die, there would be a succession struggle, and in the ensuing civil war the country would be divided into factions, and hence be less likely to trouble its neighbours.

This estimate of the situation was far from true. As Mr. Desai points out,[1] the king's warlike talk was due to 'temperamental excitement': fear of a further attack by the British was its real cause. Self-defence was the mainspring of the Court of Ava's military measures which Burney viewed with such uneasiness.

By the end of December large numbers of troops had assembled at the capital for military exercises, which Burney watched with professional interest. Early in January they were reviewed by the king dressed in gold brocade and riding on the royal white elephant, which he guided himself. Maung Sa gave him an account of the Burmese military organization, the gist of which he wrote down in his Journal.[2] The wungyi told him that similar training of troops was going on at Rangoon and in every other part of the country. From what he saw Burney confessed that he carried away a better opinion of Burmese 'power and finery' than he had previously had. His suspicions regarding Burmese policy deepened when shortly afterwards a relative of the queen was appointed myowun of Bassein and given a military rank. The same military

[1] *Op. cit.*, p. 176.   [2] Para. 487.

rank, he learnt, had also been conferred upon other provincial governors, and it looked as if the whole country were being placed on a war footing. The military powers conferred upon these local governors, he noted, enabled them at any time to call up the inhabitants of their areas. It was also, he discovered, a fruitful source of corruption through the collection of fines from those anxious to evade military service. Like Falstaff, he wrote, these officers took care to 'misuse the King's press damnably, press them none but good householders, yeoman's sons, and enquire them out contented bachelors'.[1]

The Court of Ava was undoubtedly out to impress Burney with all this military display and talk. At the same time, also a noticeable degree of hostility was displayed against *kalas* (foreigners) by the ordinary public. 'We never meet a drunken man,' Burney noted, 'who does not try to provoke us; and many disreputable characters among the lower orders often take an opportunity, when they can to do so with impunity, of throwing out abuse against the *Kalas*, as we pass in the streets.' He shut his ears, as he put it, to the abuse of petty offenders, for it was useless to complain to the ministers; they seemed to have a secret fear of the common people, who would accuse them, if they took action, of allowing the British Resident to dictate to them.

The boatmen and the city gatekeepers were the worst offenders, and finally Burney was goaded into taking action against a gatekeeper, who grossly abused him and his escort. He had him seized and taken before the Myawadi Wungyi. The latter, however, released him without examination on the specious plea that it was a Buddhist sabbath day. Burney sent his clerk, R. S. Edwards,[2]

---

[1] Para. 521.
[2] It is tantalizing that so little can be put on record about this remarkable man, who acted as Burney's clerk and interpreter throughout his service as British Resident at the court of Ava. British officers, who came into contact with Edwards, invariably praised his knowledge of the language and customs of the Burmese in the highest terms. He was a persona grata at the Court of Ava. He married a Burmese lady whose descendants today refer to her as a princess. He served as British interpreter during the Second Burmese War of 1852 and after the annexation of the province of Pegu became the first Collector of Customs at Rangoon. The first British Commissioner of Pegu, Major (later Major General Sir Arthur) Phayre, often availed himself of his services for special duties. He was on the reception committee to meet the Burmese mission led by the Dalla Wun which arrived in Rangoon en route for Calcutta in 1854, and together with Phayre accompanied it to Calcutta. In the following year he was a member of the British mission, led by Phayre, deputed by Lord Dalhousie to the court of King

with a protest to the wungyi, and when this was ineffectual, went himself only to be told to take the matter to the Hlutdaw the next morning. This he did, but the ministers then raised so many objections that he threatened to take the law into his own hands in future, and summarily punish anyone who insulted him. They then offered to punish the culprit in Burney's presence; but he found that they were about to make a scapegoat of one of the offender's subordinates, and accordingly refused to countenance such a farce. Then the gatekeeper tried to argue that he had not been abusing Burney at all, but someone else. Burney's command of Burmese, however, was too good for him, and his plea failed. Still the ministers refused to punish the culprit. Burney therefore prepared an address to the king asking him to order the ministers to punish the gatekeeper. The king, however, refused to take any notice of it. So finally Burney threatened the ministers that if no one else would punish the culprit, he would see to it himself. This was too much for them: they ordered the gatekeeper to be dismissed and placed in the stocks. And Burney took the precaution of going along to see that it was the right man whom they punished.

Mindon. This was the one that is the subject of Colonel Henry Yule's *Narrative of the Mission to the Court of Ava in 1855*, published in 1859, and reprinted together with Phayre's private journal and an Introduction by Professor Hugh Tinker, Kuala Lumpur, 1968.

During his stay at Ava as assistant to Henry Burney Edwards, like Burney, was on very friendly terms with the Myawaddy Wungyi, Maung Sa, who was later disgraced and cruelly treated by Tharrawaddy when he deposed his brother Bagyidaw in 1837. Surprisingly he survived and lived until 1853. In my *The Dalhousie-Phayre Correspondence, 1852-56* there is a letter dated November of that year from an Armenian named Jacob at the capital to Edwards in Rangoon in which he writes: 'Your old friend the Myawaddy Wungyi died the other day. He often asked for you.' (pp. 109-11) Edwards was also a personal friend of the Scottish merchant Thomas Spears, who as British Correspondent at Ava did so much to sweeten relations between the British and the Burmese during King Mindon's early years, and also so much behind the scenes to ensure the success of Phayre's mission of 1855. When the mission returned to Rangoon, before leaving for Calcutta, its members presented Spears with a gold watch with their initials engraved on it in recognition of his services. Among them are Edwards's RSE.

Thomas Spears went on a lengthy stay in Scotland in 1862 leaving his wife and family in a house in Phayre Street, Rangoon. He was away five years and during that period Edwards acted as his agent. He also lived in Phayre Street, and Spears's youngest son William, born in 1859, whom I got to know before his death in 1929, recounted to me how as a child he would often see Edwards returning from his early morning ride with his servant walking behind his pony and poking it with his umbrella if it showed signs of falling asleep. He is said to have come to Burma from Madras. See *infra* p. 427.

Burney could understand their reluctance to move in the matter: in the prevailing state of feeling in the country they dreaded being thought to favour *kalas*. 'No charge,' he wrote in his Journal, 'is more easily made, or more dreaded, or more likely to ruin a man in a moment here than the charge of being too partial to them.'[1] Not long after this tussle, when the Myolat Wun was paying him a call, Burney expressed the hope that now that the two nations were better acquainted, war between them was less likely. His visitor laughingly replied that only one more trial of strength was needed before that was possible, namely a war of revenge for Burma's defeat. In reporting this to the Government of India Burney remarked that the Burmese Chronicle defined revenge as a proper motive for going to war with another nation. He also noted down as significant an observation made to him by the Treasurer to the effect that in Britain only selected men were trained in the use of firearms, whereas in Burma almost every man was trained in their use.

Burney's reports on the war spirit in Burma had naturally to be taken seriously by the Government of India. The Governor-General himself wrote a minute on the subject dated 24 June 1831. It was very different in tone from Burney's reports. A fresh conflict, he said, was out of the question. What was necessary was to strengthen British military positions on the frontier so as to show the Burmese that the British were able and ready to deter aggression. Before those words were written, however, the situation in Burma had changed considerably as a result of the king's illness. By July his condition was reported to be serious, all talk of war ceased, and the minds of the ministers were fully occupied by the practical problems of how to carry on the government when the king was totally incapable of any participation in public affairs. Lanciago told Burney bluntly that the illness was mainly due to chagrin at the outcome of the war aggravated by the sight of a British Resident at his capital, and Burney accepted this as a reliable estimate.

At the first onset of the illness Burney was not a little worried about a possible collapse of the authority of the central government and its likely consequences. There was a notable upsurge of dacoity and, in addition, the fear of an attempt at usurpation by the Tharrawaddy Prince. In March (1831) therefore he addressed a

[1] Para. 765.

letter to the Government of India warning it of the possibility of a war of succession, and asking what he should do under such circumstances. The king's son, the Sakya Min, he explained was his rightful heir, but could not succeed without the support of the Minthagyi. One solution of the succession question that had been discussed was for the prince to marry the queen's daughter, but she was too young at present, and the Minthagyi might try to seize the throne for himself. If Tharrawaddy were to seize it, he would most certainly execute the Minthagyi. Burney's own prescription for the policy to be pursued in case of a struggle was non-interference; but, having in mind the instructions given by Lord Wellesley in 1802 to Michael Symes, when a succession struggle at Ava was believed by Calcutta to be imminent, he asked whether, if the occasion warranted, he should deviate from the rule of neutrality to seize a favourable opportunity, should one occur, to support the principle of legitimacy. He quoted from Symes's instructions the statement that a succession struggle would precisely constitute that crisis of affairs which was most to be desired for the purpose of establishing British influence.[1] And he went on to explain what in his view would precisely constitute such a situation. 'Were a party of the more respectable Ministers,' he wrote, 'to prefer their allegiance to the Tsakya Min, the rightful heir, it is possible that my joining them, upon certain conditions, might secure his right, and put down the opposition of his uncles.' Actually, he said, the king was in no danger; nevertheless, his condition was such that he, Burney, was very anxious to learn as soon as possible what the Government of India's wishes were.

Did Burney realize that Wellesley was looking for ways and means of bringing Burma into his system of subsidiary alliances or that this item in Symes's instructions was completely irrelevant to the realities of the political situation in Burma in 1802? If one may judge by the treatment of Symes's second mission to Ava in Dr. G. T. Bayfield's *Historical Review of the Political Relations between the British Government in India and the Empire of Ava*,[2] which gives a most misleading account of this particular mission, he apparently did not. One is tempted to wonder whether a less than firm loyalty to the principle of non-intervention inspired Burney to raise this matter.

[1] See Hall, *Michael Symes, Journal*, pp. lxxv and 115.
[2] See below pp. 251–3.

The Governor-General had no doubts on the proper action to be taken. He at once passed orders that the Resident was to be informed that he must preserve strict neutrality, and make it clear to all concerned that under no circumstances would he deviate from such a policy. If a succession struggle did break out, he was to announce that he would stay on at the capital and do business with whosoever should gain control there. He must also make it clear that under no circumstances would the Government of India agree to any alteration of the provisions of the Yandabo Treaty, and, moreover that that treaty was not made with King Bagyidaw personally, but with the nation, and was therefore perpetual. The Court of Ava on the other hand was to be assured that so long as its provisions were observed, it had nothing to fear from the British.[1]

Happily the expected crisis did not arise: no one at Ava seems to have been ready or anxious for desperate measures. For one thing also the king's health improved in June. Then when in the following month it deteriorated again, he was apparently persuaded by the Minthagyi and the queen to appoint a commission of three to represent him. It was composed of three of his brothers, the Tharrawaddy and Thibaw princes and the Bo Wun Min, together with the Minthagyi himself. How this strangely assorted group functioned we have no record. The dominating personality was the Minthagyi, whose ability and business capacity was easily above that of any other member of the Court. The king's health, however, soon improved enough for him to take part in public business. Indeed Burney, who was received in audience by him on 15 December, recorded that he seemed remarkably well.

The crisis, which Burney had feared to be imminent in 1831, did not occur for another six years. When it did, his estimate of the part he might be called upon to play was shown to have been sadly awry. There were features of the Burmese character which he had failed to take into account, notwithstanding his close acquaintance with all the leading personalities of the Court of Ava. And even in 1837, when the revolution broke out, it took what was for him a totally unexpected turn through the complete incapacity of the more respectable ministers, as he had described them in his letter of March 1831 to Lord William Cavendish Bentinck, to cope with the situation.

[1] Letter dated Simla 18 April 1831 in BSP Cons Vol. 361, Desai, *op. cit.*, pp. 191–2.

Chapter 14

Burney changes his mind: the Kabaw Valley, the Residency

WHILE the Burmese mission was ineffectively touring northern India in search of a Governor-General of whose very existence they came at one time to express doubts, Henry Burney had been studying the various writings available at Ava on the history of the Kabaw Valley. He had gradually arrived at the conclusion that the Burmese claim was a good one, and that the Government of India would be well-advised to reverse its judgement awarding the valley to Gambhir Singh of Manipur. His conversion to this point of view was announced to Calcutta in a letter dated Rangoon 2 June 1832. Before considering the arguments adduced in it, however, we must take a look at the background of his relations with the Court of Ava in the preceding period.

In the previous April Burney had departed from the capital for reasons of health to take up temporary residence in Rangoon. He had left his deputy Mr. E. A. Blundell in charge of the Residency, but continued in office himself as Resident. Before his departure his relations with both king and ministers had become extremely cordial; so much so that when in the previous September he had intimated to the wungyis that he was unable to stand the climate of Ava, and must go to Rangoon to recuperate, they had objected strongly to his leaving them, saying that if he went, 'they would have no one with whom to concert the necessary measures for keeping the two states in friendly relation'. He replied that he was willing to stay on at the capital for a few weeks longer so that they and the king could become reconciled to his departure. 'I laughingly added that upon my first coming to Ava many persons had said that the ministers would not agree to my remaining here for any time; but that now I see they will not allow me to leave them.' In the same spirit of banter he suggested that their real motive was to keep him there as a hostage for the good conduct of the British Government.¹ When soon afterwards Blundell arrived from Tenasserim, where he was Deputy Commissioner, Burney took him to the Hlutdaw to introduce him to the ministers, and found to his great relief that they took an instant liking to him. But for various reasons he was not to leave Ava for several months.

In the following December, as we have already noted, he had an audience of the king and found him looking extremely well and showing no signs of the mental illness from which he had been suffering. Afterwards he told Maung Sa and Maung Yeet that he would never forget the king's kindness and would always do his best to let the Government of India know his wishes. This they repeated with much pleasure to the king.

At his last audience on 10 March 1832 before leaving for Rangoon, he expressed the same sentiments in a complimentary address to the king, in which he promised that wherever he went he would report 'that I never heard of a more popular sovereign than the present King of Ava who is loved in a very extraordinary manner by all classes of his subjects'.² One is reminded of Fanny Burney's references in her diary to the 'dear king', George III, when she was Assistant Keeper of Robes to Queen Charlotte. The Burneys were prone to adoration of royalty. On this occasion both king and queen were looking strained and ill. 'I never saw a human being so full of ennui and melancholy, so tired of life and its cares, as the poor king struck me to be. I felt more pity for him than I can describe,' Burney wrote in his Journal.³ On hearing him express his sentiments in Burmese the king gave him a kindly nod of the head, and Burney had to admit that he was so deeply moved that he could almost have been persuaded to promise more than he could ever fulfil.

His farewell calls on the ministers at their houses were on the same emotional level. They all urged him to correspond with them, and to recommend to his government the Burmese claim to the Kabaw Valley. And, as if he suspected that his government might wonder whether he had overstepped the mark, he wrote in his Journal: 'I hope it will not be considered any weakness in me to own that I took my leave of them all with much regret, and with the kindest feelings in their favour.'⁴ The farewells culminated in a

¹ Journal, paras 608, 621; Desai, *op. cit.*, pp. 192–3. ² Journal, para. 922.
³ Para. 924.   ⁴ Para. 954.

dinner party at the Residency to the wungyis and atwinwuns, at which goodwill overflowed on both sides. They assured Burney that no British officer had ever been treated with such familiarity and kindness as he. He in response told them that they would gain great credit when he reported that, contrary to the belief then held in other countries, they desired to acquire a good name among other civilized countries.[1]

After all this outpouring of mutual regard one is not surprised to find Burney during his long trip down the Irrawaddy composing his letter to the Governor-General announcing his conversion to the Burmese cause in the matter of the disputed valley. 'Perhaps now that I have quitted Ava,' he wrote, 'Government will allow me to express with more freedom my sentiments with regard to the disputed territory of Kubo.' He had always, he continued, been in favour of the abstract right of the Burmese to the valley, but it had been his duty to try to reconcile the Court of Ava to the Chindwin boundary. He had done his utmost to accomplish this, but had failed. The Government of India therefore must decide whether it was worth while to maintain Gambhir Singh in possession of an unhealthy and depopulated strip of territory, divided from Manipur by a range of hills, through which communication was extremely difficult, and thereby disgust the Court of Ava and run the risk of another war. Everyone at Ava, he said, believed that if the Governor-General had any regard for truth and justice, he must decide in Burma's favour.[2]

Mr. Desai describes the Government of India as 'taken aback' by this letter. Nevertheless, it was prepared to reconsider the matter. Burney was requested to submit a clear statement of the grounds for the conclusion he had reached. This he did in a letter from Rangoon of 5 July. The Burmese ministers, he said, had made many untrue statements in support of their claim, especially the one maintaining that Burma had had uninterrupted possession of the valley for 2,000 years. But the fact remained that the Manipuris under Captain Grant and Gambhir Singh had expelled them from it before the peace of Yandabo was signed. He then went on to adumbrate the grounds upon which the British commissioners had awarded the valley to Manipur. These were firstly Symes's statement in his book naming the Chindwin as the boundary with Manipur, secondly the evidence of the old Shan royal chronicle of

[1] Journal, para. 957. [2] BSP Vol. 366, Desai, *op. cit.*, p. 203.

the Kings of Pong, thirdly the occupation of the valley by Manipur for twelve or fifteen years before the Burmese assisted Marjit to gain the throne in 1812, and lastly the Manipuri conquest of the valley during the Anglo-Burmese war.

Regarding the first point, wrote Burney, Symes obtained his information from Dr. Hamilton, the medical officer to his mission [then named Buchanan], who, however, had since published an article in the *Edinburgh Philosophical Journal*, together with a map, showing the Kabaw Valley as a part of Burma, and had since published further articles making the same point. On the second point Burney explained that the Burmese chronicle known as the *Mahayazawindawgyi* [later to be called by the British *The Glass Palace Chronicle*], which covered Burmese history up to 1821, showed that the valley had been in Burmese possession since 1370, though during the wars with the Shans in the fifteenth and sixteenth centuries it had been often overrun. There were also stone inscriptions supporting the Burmese claim. On the third point, he said, the ministers admitted that there had been times when the chief towns in the valley had thrown off the King of Burma's authority, even for as much as fifteen years. The most recent example of this was during the period previous to 1812. On the fourth point he said the Burmese had had undisputed possession of the valley for twelve years prior to the Anglo-Burmese war, and although during the war it had been conquered by the Manipuris, the stipulation in the treaty of Yandabo that the Raja of Manipur should recover his territories applied only to those which he had held before the war. He summed up by saying that he did not dispute the correctness of the statements made by the British commissioners in Manipur, but he believed that the evidence on behalf of the Burmese claim, which he now submitted, outweighed that upon which they had based their belief in Gambhir Singh's claims.

Finally he addressed himself to some specific questions which he knew counted heavily with the Calcutta authorities. Dr. Richardson, he said, as a result of a recent journey made by him from Ava to the Manipur frontier, had dissipated all idea of any British army ever venturing to march by that route against the Burmese capital. He had also expressed the belief that British protection was a far better safeguard to Manipur than a boundary line. Secondly, it was quite certain that to the Burmese the recovery of the Kabaw Valley was only a first step: once it had been achieved, some other claim would be advanced. Nevertheless, apprehension of further embarrassment of this kind should not prevent the British government from performing an act of justice.

Burney's advocacy of the Burmese case won the day. The Governor-General returned from his travels in northern India to Calcutta in January 1833, and soon afterwards Burney from Rangoon and Maingy from Moulmein were summoned to confer with him in Calcutta. The result of their discussion was a minute by the Governor-General dated 26 February dealing with all the boundary questions that had been raised by the Court of Ava. On the Kabaw Valley he said that the original decision awarding it to Manipur had not been erroneous. On the other hand expediency was, he believed, in favour of its concession to Ava; for in view of the anxiety of the Court to regain the valley, the humiliation of their pride, and the reduction of their power, it would be both generous and expedient to grant them this gratification. Accordingly, Burney was to return to Ava to tell the king that the Government of India still believed the Ningtee to be the proper boundary between Burma and Manipur, yet out of respect for his majesty's feelings, and in order to promote amity and goodwill between their two countries, the valley was to be restored to Burma and commissioners from both sides were to meet in the following November in order to fix the boundary line at the eastern foot of the Muring Hills, known as the Yoma Daung by the Burmese.

With regard to the Burmese claims to the islands in the River Salween, Burney was empowered to settle the matter according to universally accepted usage, assigning the islands to the right or left bank as determined by the course of the deepwater channel. This meant that Sir Archibald Campbell's rejection of the Burmese claim to Bilagyun Island, at the mouth of the river, must be upheld, since the deepwater channel ran round the northern extremity of that island.

That was at the end of February 1833. Some days later, after interminable delays, the Burmese envoys reached Calcutta. On 16 March the senior envoy received from the Chief Secretary to the Government of India that government's decisions on the points raised when the mission first arrived in India. The Kabaw Valley boundary, he said, was to be revised, but he gave no details. Secondly, the Salween was the true line of demarcation for

Tenasserim. Thirdly, the British Government would relinquish no territory ceded under the Treaty of Yandabo. Lastly, it rejected the Burmese demand for the abrogation of the seventh article of that treaty.

Burney's achievement in securing the return of the Kabaw Valley to Burma was on all counts a considerable one. It had entailed an incredible amount of work upon such materials as, for instance, Burmese palm-leaf chronicle writings, and no lack of courage in stating his views. But for him the Government of India would never have been moved to rescind its earlier decision in favour of Manipur. The Burmese envoys, however, had nothing to say in recognition of his efforts: quite the reverse. In their reports home they themselves took full credit for the return of the valley. Indeed, they went so far as to blame Burney for his government's refusal to abrogate the seventh article of the Yandabo treaty. 'Mazay Bhauranee', they wrote, 'follows one course present and another course absent; his words are not certain, and he is a man who is accustomed to deceive and delude, knowing truly that he had demolished the application which we made that no Resident should be fixed [at Ava].'[1]

This then was to be the next line of attack, the removal of the residency from the capital, and Burney was to be the scapegoat. 'We have reported thus,' they continued, 'that Your Majesty may bear it in mind when Mazay Bhauranee arrives at the Golden Feet.' And, looked at from the Burmese point of view, it was perfectly logical. The resident had been accepted by the Court of Ava purely as a means of wringing concessions from the Government of India aimed at rendering the Yandabo treaty nugatory. Both king and ministers had done their best to make this clear to Burney, and the affecting scenes just before his departure for Rangoon must be interpreted largely in the light of their anxiety to convert him to their cause. But he had failed them. That is how they would have interpreted the chief secretary's brief announcement that no further concessions would be granted. Hence there could be no further use for a British Resident at Ava.

The envoys themselves were in no hurry to return home. They spent several weeks in Calcutta collecting Buddhist relics and images for the king. When at last they did leave, in June, they took

[1] Burney's translation quoted in Desai, 'History of the Burmese Mission to India', JBRS, XXVI, Part II, p. 101.

with them a complimentary letter from the Governor-General to the king, and a number of presents which included a copy of Rees's Cyclopaedia in 45 volumes, and, what was far more important, a black marble image of the Buddha, which they had seen in the premises of the Asiatic Society of Bengal, and had specially requested might be included among the royal presents. When it arrived at Ava, it caused quite a sensation. The king and his court went down the river to meet it, and later the *Konbaungset Chronicle*, in recording the event, claimed that it had been worshipped by the Emperor Asoka.[1] The acquisition of this image brought the envoys far greater credit than any other act performed by them during their sojourn in India; so Burney reported when he arrived there later on.

That was in November 1833, and he found the ministers under no illusions as to the part he had played in the recovery of the Kabaw Valley for Burma. They received him with great kindness. He was, however, cold-shouldered by the king who was in a state of almost complete mental prostration, quite unable to take part in affairs of state. One may surmise that the news of the Government of India's total rejection of most of his envoys' demands was responsible for this. The minthagyi was now acting as regent.

On the subject of the Kabaw Valley award the ministers had strong objections to the new boundary line: they wanted one further to the west. To Burney therefore fell the thankless task of trying to persuade them that it was hopeless to expect any further concession in that direction. They remained obdurate, however, and when on 1 January 1834 the British commissioners, Grant and Pemberton, met their opposite numbers Wundauk Maung Khan Ye and Sayedawgyi Nemyo Chan Tha, at the new frontier at the foot of the Muring Hills to effect the transfer, the Burmese accepted it only under protest. They claimed that the British had wrongly identified the Muring Hills with the Yoma Daung further to the westward, and they asked to be allowed to appeal again to the Government of India. Further enquiry showed that they were right, but Burney managed to persuade the ministers to drop the matter, and write to Calcutta expressing their thanks for the restoration of the valley and for the good treatment accorded to their envoys during their stay in India.

Their next step was to propose the removal of the Residency

[1] Desai, *British Residency*, p. 214, f.n. 2.

from Ava to Rangoon, and the channelling of all diplomatic relations through the Rangoon Wungyi. This proposal, they informed Burney, was made at the express order of the king, who apparently was at least able to give vent to his feelings about the hated symbol of his failure. With this, contrary to what the Burmese envoys had reported, Burney was in thorough accord. In that same letter of 14 April 1832, composed during his journey from Ava to Rangoon, in which he had advocated the reconsideration of the Kabaw Valley question, he had also expounded his candid views on the subject of the maintenance of a resident at Ava. The ministers were reconciled to it, he wrote, and the people had come to accept it. The king, on the other hand, was absolutely opposed to it, and the fact that he was forced to entertain a British officer at his capital was undoubtedly a major cause of the continuation of his mental breakdown.

I am of opinion, [he continued,] that some officer, after he has had an opportunity of becoming personally acquainted with the members of the Court of Ava and with their modes of thinking and acting, should be fixed as the British Agent at Rangoon, which place he should make his headquarters, and that he should go up to Ava for 2 or 3 months only every year, pay his respects to the King, and transact any business which might occur. Such an arrangement would be most acceptable to the feelings of the King, and I think it might be made equally efficient with that of always maintaining a Resident at the capital.[1]

He further pointed out that it would lead to a great saving of expense, for by placing the agent under the general supervision of the Commissioner of Tenasserim as his first assistant, a great saving would be made in the matter of allowances.

Burney's scheme, one may remark, had much to commend it. It is easy to see now how much trouble in later Anglo-Burmese relations might have been avoided, had the Government of India been willing to listen to his advice. Undoubtedly his scheme, or some variation of it, would have removed from the Court of Ava the impression that its sovereignty was infringed by the presence of a British Residency at the capital, and not least that the Residency was a dangerous centre of espionage. The weak spot in the scheme lay in the key part to be played by the Rangoon Wungyi. When Burney made his proposal, the holder of the post was an enlightened

[1] Desai, *op. cit.*, p. 199.

and incorrupt man. Later, when he died, his successor was just the opposite, and the history of Anglo-Burmese relations amply demonstrates how much harm such a man could cause. The difficulty, however, was far from insurmountable, given that the British agent at Rangoon had established a good understanding with the ministers at Ava. The Government of India, however, totally rejected Burney's proposal; it was adamant on the necessity to maintain a resident at the capital. In its view this was the only way to maintain peace with Burma.

Now, soon after Burney's return to Ava in 1834, he had to raise the matter again, this time at the special request of King Bagyidaw. His letter is dated 15 April 1834, almost two years to the day from his previous one. This time he stressed with far greater emphasis the disadvantages of maintaining a resident at the capital.

Judging from my own experience, [he wrote] and from what has occurred during the last four years, I am inclined to believe, that until some changes take place in the state of affairs and the circumstances of the Residency at Ava, few British officers will be able to reside here uninterruptedly for more than two or three years. It is not really the hot weather although that is bad enough at a place where it seldom rains and where the thermometer often exceeds 100 degrees, and does not fall below 92 degrees before 12 o'clock at night, but it is the want of wholesome vegetables, of the means of taking exercise, and of adapting the house occupied by the Residency to the climate in the same manner as houses in India are adapted. It is these last mentioned circumstances, added to another I shall submit at the close of this paragraph, which renders a residence at Ava so irksome and trying to the constitution. The roads, such as they are, are impassable during the greater part of the hot weather owing to the overflowing of the Erawadi, and the spot of ground allotted to the Residency does not admit of being enlarged, although it has scarcely 10 square yards of open space, covered as it is with the huts of the Escort and servants and followers. But what ought chiefly to be mentioned, when any important event or discussion arises here, the consideration that there exists no certain means of communicating with your own Government, which possesses less knowledge of the real character and customs of this than of any other Indian Court, greatly enhances in such a climate and situation, near a crazy King and an ignorant and trembling set of Ministers, the mental anxiety which preys upon the health of a public servant holding a highly responsible office.[1]

[1] Desai, *op. cit.*, pp. 221–2 gives this quotation from BSP Vol. 380 in full.

Burney changes his mind

This almost agonized pleading, so terribly true in substance, failed to move the Government of India; it remained firmly committed to the maintenance of a British Resident at the Burmese capital, at any cost. And the appalling strain, which Burney had to endure, was ultimately to break him. He was instructed to convey to the ministers his government's total rejection of their proposal, and in future to discourage any further proposal aiming at the removal of the British Residency from Ava.

Burney's plea to be permitted to move the Residency to Rangoon was made when he himself was about to leave the capital a second time for reasons of health. This time he had spent only just over six months there. He never at any time indicates the nature of his illness. His mention of the lack of fresh vegetables at Ava makes one wonder if it was some sort of debility due to lack of calcium. Bad health dogged him throughout each period of his stay at the capital. As a European he had been far too long in the tropics without home leave. When he sailed for Europe in 1838 it was his first home leave in thirty years. The wonder is how he carried on as long as he did without a breakdown, working as hard and unremittingly as he always did. His is a sad story; yet with a little more understanding on the part of the Calcutta authorities it could have been so very different. The picture, which he gave in his letter of 15 April 1834, of the conditions under which he had to carry on at Ava, was not overdrawn. One can only wonder at the blindness which permitted the sacrifice of this supremely able and devoted servant.

Burney's departure from the capital in April 1834 was partly due to a worsening of the king's malady. He became so violent that the ministers kept out of his way and even the queen was afraid to be left alone with him. On one occasion he chased with a spear the atwinwun, Maung Yeet, who normally conducted Burney's business with him. On another, he turned all the atwinwuns out of the palace and forbade them to return. Again and again he would shut himself up in his private room refusing to see anyone or take any food. Under the circumstances therefore Burney hoped that his own absence from the capital would have a calming effect upon the king.

As his deputy he left the residency's medical officer, G. T. Bayfield who after four years in Burma, during which he had acquired some proficiency in the language, was anxious to be given political employment. Burney set him the task during this holding operation of writing up the history of British relations with the Court of Ava, and in this way there came into being Bayfield's 'Historical Review of the Political Relations between the British Government in India and the Empire of Ava up to the end of the year 1834', which, after revision by Burney, was published as a Supplement to Captain R. B. Pemberton's *Report on the Eastern Frontier of British India* (Calcutta, 1835). He seems to have been plentifully supplied with copies of records in the Calcutta archives for the period up to 1830.[1] The bulk of his compilation deals with the post-1830 period and is trustworthy. The same cannot be said of the earlier period. Copyists' errors abound and there are a few serious errors attributable to Bayfield himself. Worse still, however, is the evidence of his own prejudice against the Burmese which occasionally leads him to falsify the record in order to blacken the character of the Court of Ava. He goes out of his way to display his contempt for it.[2] Presumably Burney revised only the part of the work relating to the period of which he had personal knowledge. Only by careful comparison with the manuscript sources for the earlier period can one discover the nature and extent of Bayfield's mistreatment of them, and this Burney could not have done. Unfortunately, Bayfield's compilation has been much used by students of history, and a number of its misstatements are to be found in published works.

Much later on Burney was to realize that the Burmese disliked Bayfield as much as he despised them. But at the time with which we are concerned here he gives him high praise. On the strength of his performance as his deputy at Ava he recommended Bayfield for the political service, and the Government of India accepted the recommendation. In his letter of 31 December 1834 he wrote:

Since this gentleman has been serving under my orders he has applied himself very sedulously and successfully not only in acquiring a knowledge of the Burmese language, customs and manners, but in availing himself of the means which I placed before him for obtaining an acquaintance with all such historical and other information as might enable

---

[1] They belong to the series entitled *Bengal Political Proceedings* and *Bengal Secret and Political Proceedings* from 1794 onwards.
[2] On this subject see 'British Writers of Burmese History from Dalrymple to Bayfield' in D. G. E. Hall (Ed.) *Historians of South East Asia*, London, 1961.

Burney changes his mind

him hereafter to be useful to the public service of this country. His conduct also at Ava since I left him there in charge of the Residency has given satisfaction to the ministers at Ava as well as to myself. [And he ends with] I am aware of no person more capable of holding political employment in this country.

He was to change his mind on this subject also.

Where Burney lived while in Rangoon he does not say. His duties were almost entirely consular. With the Governor-General's refusal to heed any further Burmese request for the revision of the Treaty of Yandabo, and the long persistence of the king's illness, there was little of a political nature for Burney's attention. Between him and Maung Khain, the Rangoon Wungyi, there was an excellent understanding, and matters that cropped up were easily settled. A good example of this was the case of the *Young Rover* mutineers. She was an English schooner on her way from Moulmein to Bengal in September 1834 with a large sum of money on board. Eleven of her crew of Filipinos and Indians overpowered her captain and mate and those loyal to them, but navigated her so unskilfully that she ran aground on the Burma coast near Cape Negrais. There they set fire to the ship with their prisoners aboard, killed some of the passengers, and made off. The local Burmese officials, however, caught them and handed them over to the Rangoon Wungyi. Burney then requested that they be handed over to him so that he might send them to Calcutta for trial and punishment. There was nothing in the treaties between Burma and Britain to cover this sort of thing, and no precedent for the procedure invoked by Burney. The wungyi hesitated, and Burney himself wondered whether they ought not rather to be punished by the Burmese, but had his doubts whether due justice would be done. He seems to have overcome the wungyi's hesitation with the argument that under the law of nations the mutual surrender of criminals of this kind, was an obligation arising out of the common interest, and by promising reciprocal action in the case of mutiny on a ship flying the Burmese colours should the mutineers enter British territory. The criminals were handed over and sent to Calcutta for trial.

Arising out of this incident a quarrel between some Rangoon merchants caused Burney to seek the advice of the Government of India. William Spiers, a retired Royal Navy lieutenant, was sent by the Rangoon Wungyi to search for the place where the ship had been destroyed, and make a report. He discovered the wreck and reported that it had been looted. Two other Rangoon merchants thereupon spread a story around that Spiers had himself plundered the wreckage of two boxes of silver which he had removed to his house. They were respectively a British born trader named Staig who had fled from his creditors in Calcutta to Rangoon and renounced British citizenship, and Sarkies Manook, an Armenian resident of Rangoon. At Burney's request the wungyi held an enquiry into the allegations. This resulted in the acquittal of Spiers, who then brought a case for conspiracy against his two detractors. This was tried by the wungyi who, against Burney's advice, acquitted them. Spiers next presented a written appeal to the wungyi, but much to his disgust it was rejected. Burney believed that Spiers's case was a good one, but nevertheless advised him to drop the matter since the next step would have been an appeal to the Hlutdaw. He reported his action to the Government of India, asking its advice regarding any further action. He was instructed to take no further action.

It was presumably during this stay in Rangoon that Burney worked on his unfinished paper entitled 'Account of the Trade etc. of Rangoon' that is in the Royal Commonwealth Society's collection of Burney manuscripts. It is in his handwriting. Blanks have been left to be filled in later; parts of it are indecipherable, chiefly because of cross-writing, i.e. making an addition to a page by writing at right angles across the writing already there. It is a pity that he never completed it for it contains interesting material for the historian on such things as a master of a ship or a foreign trader coming to Rangoon for the first time would need to know about such subjects as navigation, pilots, anchorage, interpreters, landing formalities and so forth.[1]

Of Maung Khain, the Rangoon Wungyi, whom he describes as viceroy, he writes that the commander of a ship must call upon him. If there is a British officer residing in Rangoon, the commander should call him immediately upon landing. After putting him in touch with the King's Godown and Mr. Lanciago, the officer should introduce him to the wungyi. 'He is usually visible between 9 and 11, and 1 and 3, and notice of a commander's desire to visit had better be first sent to him. It is not necessary to take any present with you when you call on the Woongyee. An opinion

[1] Listed as document B XXVII.

existed at Rangoon among some of the English merchants, that the Woongyee did not desire to see commanders of vessels or strangers who might arrive; but such an opinion was very unjust to this chief, who is very inquisitive and anxious to converse with strangers and hear the news. But he did not wish to order all commanders of vessels and strangers to visit him, thinking that such an order might lead some of his subordinate officers to suppose that the commanders or strangers must bring presents with them. The Woongyee informed me himself that it always gives him great satisfaction to see English commanders and strangers if they liked to call upon him.' He had therefore ordered, he told Burney, that such people were not to be prevented from calling on him, but were to be given all assistance.

Burney writes also of the Spaniard Lanciago, supplementing what he has to say of him in his Journal with a further pen picture. Lanciago had been appointed akoukwun, or collector of customs, at Rangoon, and lived on the riverside to the westward of the wharf. Commanders of ships were advised to see him as soon as they had handed in a list of their cargo to the customs officers.

This gentleman, [he writes] although rather strict, and too anxious to please his royal mistress, the Queen, to whom he annually about the end of the year takes up all the customs and other duties he may levy, is still a gentleman of strict veracity, an uncommon [?thing] in Burmah, and one who has never been tainted with personal corruption. He speaks French like a native and is in fact more than half a Frenchman. He speaks English sometimes, not very intelligibly, but the commander will find much future comfort and fairness in his business if he gives this gentleman a favourable impression of himself. Mr. Lanciago will give very correct information to him as to the state of the markets, the vessels that sailed last or that are next expected. I recommend all commanders to take Mr. Lanciago's advice, should he be in a sufficiently good humour to give any.

Burney follows up these instructions with a brief account of the early history of Rangoon according to the traditions recounted in the Shwe Dagon thamaing, or pagoda history. He then passes on to a discussion of the population, its composition and numbers. He begins with the census ordered by King Bodawpaya (1782–1819) early in his reign and describes the methods used by the local authorities to keep the number as small as possible so as to bring it in line with their revenue returns to the Court of Ava.

King Bodawpaya, he tells us, on scrutinizing the lists of his first census, expressed the view that about one-third of the number of houses in each town had been suppressed. The method was to count houses and allow for from five to seven persons to each house. In the case of Tenasserim, Burney explains, the census taken by the British showed an average of five and a half persons to each house. The copy of the Burmese census in his possession, he said, showed that Rangoon with twenty villages dependent upon it had a total of 5,852 houses. Symes, when at Rangoon in 1795, was told that the number of houses was 5,000. 'Dr. Bayfield', he goes on, 'while he was residing with me at Rangoon in 1833, took several weeks in counting the number of houses in the town and suburbs and made them amount to a little more than 6,000, including of course many small houses which the Burmese officers would not include in their list. At the rate of $5\frac{1}{2}$ souls per house, the population of Rangoon may then be computed at 33,000 souls.' This was a considerable increase, Burney points out, on the census made by John Crawfurd in 1826, which gave only 1,570 as the number of houses in Rangoon and its suburbs. But even before the war there had been an appreciable decline in the number from that quoted to Symes in 1795. The great increase in the population to its 1833 number, according to Burney, was entirely due to the mild and prudent administration of the wungyi, Maung Khain.

The Armenians under the headship of Mr. Sarkies Manook were the largest foreign community in Rangoon, Burney writes, and they had their own church and priest. He describes Mr. Manook as a gentleman, honest and upright, and ready to befriend others. There was a Roman Catholic community of about 230 with a well-built church and a priest, Father Domingo Taroly, who was well educated, particularly in medicine, and had an excellent knowledge of the Burmese language and customs. There were also Jews and Parsees residing in Rangoon, but Burney leaves blanks in the manuscript for their numbers.

The largest and richest class of foreign traders, Burney writes, were the Moguls. Most of them were Persian and came originally from the Persian Gulf, but their connexions were now mainly with Calcutta and Madras. They imported chiefly English piece-goods, but only as agents for members of their community settled in Calcutta or Madras. They were great speculators, and some had

lost large fortunes, and so were unable to return home. The few
Burmese traders were chiefly women, but few of them were to be
depended upon. As to the Europeans, there were only three or four
respectable ones settled in Rangoon as traders. There were always
a few commanders of ships and officers dwelling there, but chiefly
persons who had lost their jobs, or their friends. He mentions no
Chinese, but since he says that the three daily bazaars in the city
were very badly supplied, especially with vegetables, evidently the
Chinese gardeners, who provided British Rangoon later with such
abundant supplies, had not begun to settle there. It is a pity that
Burney never finished this account of the Rangoon he knew, for
the glimpses he gives of it whet the appetite for more.

During this stay in Rangoon he took up with the Government of
India the matter of residency expenses. The practice in Burma's
case, as it had been in Siam's, was for the home government to pay
the salaries of its envoys and their suites, but for other expenses
such as those of travel, board and lodging to be the responsibility
of the host government. This imposed a heavy burden upon the
Court of Ava, which Burney estimated at round about twenty
thousand rupees a year. The Government of India also had been
put to considerable expense through the travels of the Burmese
envoys in India; so much so that the Court of Directors of the
East India Company in London had commented upon the subject.
Burney's suggestion that he should be empowered to negotiate
with Ava for a convention by which each government should pay
all the expenses of its own envoys was readily accepted by Calcutta,
and Bayfield, his deputy at Ava, obtained the immediate agreement
of the Burmese ministers. After all, they hoped to avoid sending
any more missions to Calcutta.

In August 1834 Burney applied to the Government of India for
permission to travel to Calcutta in order to proceed to England on
furlough. He had spent a quarter of a century in Asia without any
home leave. But now the special tasks for which he had been
appointed Resident at the Court of Ava had been completed, and
he must have hoped that the time had come when he could be
spared. His deputy had gained enough experience of the day-to-
day conduct of residency business at the capital for things to be left
in his hands. The Government of India gave immediate consent to
his application, but by some extraordinary ill-chance its letter did
not reach Burney in Rangoon until the middle of December. And

not until a month later was he able to leave Rangoon. When he arrived in Calcutta on 2 February 1835, he found to his bitter disappointment that by the time he would have completed all outstanding business with the Calcutta authorities, and equipped himself and his family for the long homeward voyage, the sailing season for Europe would have ended, and it would be, as he put it, hazardous to the health of his wife and young children, to sail out of season. There was nothing for it therefore but to cancel his furlough and return to the Ava residency. It must have been a harsh decision to take, for no family can ever, even in those days of long tours of duty, have needed home leave more than the Burneys.

So back to Burma they went, arriving in Rangoon in early April, when it must have been at its hottest, and remaining there until the wet monsoon broke in June. On 29 June they began the long journey by river to the capital, which was reached on 27 July. This time they were to stay there for almost two years. In Rangoon Burney received depressing news from Bayfield at Ava. The king's long illness had become worse; he was unable to attend to business and had not been seen in public for several weeks. The exactions of the Minthagyi and his party were causing grave discontent. The administration stagnated, it was difficult to get any business attended to at the Hlutdaw. On the most pressing matter, that of the Rangoon port charges negotiated by Burney before his departure for Calcutta, Bayfield said that he had completely failed to persuade the ministers to take any action. Burney had induced the Rangoon Wungyi to agree to a reduction in the port charges on British vessels as an experiment to see if it would attract more trade to the port. Just before his departure for Calcutta, however, the wungyi had told him that the old higher charges were to be restored. Bayfield had then taken the matter up with the ministers at Ava, but without success.

Burney's own feeling on returning to Burma was that it had become essential for a British agent to be stationed at Rangoon for the protection of British interests there. Before leaving Rangoon to return to Ava he penned a letter on the subject to the Government of India, saying that as soon as he reached Ava he would depute Bayfield to go to Rangoon as British agent. One can easily see in which direction his mind was running. He returned to the subject in a further dispatch written after his arrival at the capital. He reminded the Government of India of his much earlier proposal to substitute a Rangoon agency for the Ava residency which it had turned down on the score of the need to maintain the closest possible contact with the Court of Ava. He had accepted that decision as in duty bound, he said, yet he must again urge the absolute necessity that a British officer should be stationed permanently in Rangoon to give prompt and effectual aid and protection to the many British subjects, European and Asian, who resorted there. Hence he now 'earnestly requested' that a second assistant might be appointed to the residency to enable him to detach an officer to take charge at Rangoon.

The Government of India would have nothing to do with such a proposal. A despatch was sent post haste telling Burney in no uncertain terms that he should not have deputed Bayfield to reside in Rangoon without its prior sanction, and that he must suspend action, should the measure not yet have been carried out. Meanwhile, he was to write a much fuller explanation of his reasons for taking such a step, and state whether Bayfield's services could be dispensed with at Ava in both his political and medical capacities. Then, before there was time to have received his reply, the Government of India sent a further despatch summarily vetoing the scheme on the grounds of expense. Bayfield therefore was to take up again his medical duties at Ava. Since, however, he had not gone to Rangoon when the second despatch arrived, no practical difficulty was involved. But the request for further information elicited from Burney a reply which, in view of the circumstances leading to the second Anglo-Burmese war in 1852, has special significance. It was dated 11 January 1836. Burney writes:

My own opinions are so strong that a British officer ought always to be stationed at Rangoon, and that at that place, and not here [Ava] all the public business giving trouble or requiring attention now occurs in this country, that I have no hesitation in stating that the salary of the Resident ought to be reduced to pay for the expenses of an officer in Rangoon rather than that no officer should be stationed at that port.[1]

But no argument, however valid, could remove the bee from the Government of India's bonnet. There must be a resident at Ava because Burma was a possible source of trouble when the Government of India's attention was concentrated upon the Indian situation.

[1] India Pol. Cons., Range 194, vol. 6, quoted by Desai, *op. cit.*, 232–3.

It failed to grasp that what Burney was advocating was a far more effective way of preventing trouble from Burma than a residency at the capital, as subsequent events were to prove.

But more immediate ones also should have made only too clear the need for someone with consular powers to be on the spot in Rangoon in case of trouble. On 13 August 1835 the Rangoon Wungyi, Maung Khain, died. Burney had come to regard him as the most intelligent officer of rank in the country. He therefore did his utmost to persuade the ministers to appoint the best available man for this key position. Instead, however, a protégé of the queen and her brother was appointed, Maung Wa, a large, quiet-mannered, stubborn man, who had hardly ever been outside the capital, and was completely ignorant of the sort of conditions to be met with at such a place as Rangoon. Burney in Ava was soon bombarded with complaints from British merchants in Rangoon of extortion and molestation. One of the complainants, a ship's captain, prophesied that unless an officer were appointed to protect British interests, 'fearful consequences' would occur since no British seamen would tamely submit to be robbed at pleasure.[1] The Bengal Chamber of Commerce petitioned government to appoint a consul or assistant-resident to protect the persons, property, rights and privileges of British subjects at Rangoon. The Government of India accordingly wrote to Burney asking if the proper course would be to appoint a consul from among the British residents, and whether Spiers would be willing to undertake such a task in return for a remuneration of one hundred rupees a month.

In terms of the actual conditions prevailing in Rangoon, it was an absurd proposal, and Burney earnestly begged the Governor-General not to go ahead with it.[2] No merchant with consular powers, he wrote, could avoid using them to promote his own personal interests, and this would prejudice the British Government in the eyes of the Burmese. No merchant could carry on extensive trade without breaking the law of the land by smuggling specie out of the country; a consul-merchant therefore would be suspected of using his special position to facilitate his smuggling. This would bring endless disputes with the Burmese and bad feeling among his fellow-merchants. Even in such a simple matter

[1] Letter of 19 March 1836 quoted in Desai, *op. cit.*, 235.
[2] Letter dated Ava 8 June 1836.

as that of taking charge of public mails, he said, Mr. Spiers incurred the jealously of his fellows who contended that it conferred on him the influence of the British Government and gave him an unfair advantage over them. Moreover, it was often impossible to draw a line between commercial and political matters, and a consul could not avoid having to interfere in the latter. This rendered it all the more necessary that the officer in charge at Rangoon should be a covenanted servant of the Company, and he was so convinced of this, wrote Burney, that he would willingly forego a portion of his salary to meet the expense of maintaining a second assistant in Rangoon.

The truth of the matter, as Burney was only too well aware, was that the Calcutta authorities considered Burma an economic backwater. In an earlier letter he had written that there was a strong impression among both the English traders there and the Burmese officials that the British Government cared little either for the improvement of the trade or the well-being of the traders. He believed that not only should a British officer be stationed at Rangoon but also a Company's steam vessel or a Royal Navy warship should visit the port once or twice a year so as to inspire a proper feeling of respect among the Burmese officials and increase the Government of India's influence with the Court of Ava.

Before this array of cogent argument the Government of India gave way. It accepted the proposal to appoint Dr. Bayfield to undertake consular duties at Rangoon. When, however, this announcement reached Ava, he was not immediately available for the task: he had had to undertake a mission to the Assam frontier to confer with the British authorities there on an urgent situation that had arisen. It was to be many months before he was to assume his duties at Rangoon, and by then the whole Burma situation had undergone radical change. Meanwhile from Rangoon more and more complaints poured in regarding the treatment of British traders. The trouble culminated in a very unpleasant incident at the end of May 1836 when James Dorrett, the owner-commander of a schooner, was severely beaten up by a party of Burmese led by two local officials who then confiscated some three hundred and twenty rupees in silver in his possession. Burney in Ava did not hear of the incident until the following October. At his request the ministers at once sent down a commission of enquiry, which established the truth of the report, but could not assess the damages due to Borrett because he had left Burma long before the commission's arrival in Rangoon. What could be done, however, was to punish the two officials concerned, and this the Minthagyi agreed to without hesitation.

Chapter 15

The Assam-Burma Frontier

THE Court of Ava's explanation of Henry Burney's return in July 1835 after the cancellation of his furlough was that he had been entrusted with the task of persuading it to permit a British army to invade China across northern Burma. The Chinese, according to the purveyors of this rumour, had inflicted a great naval defeat upon the British at Canton, and in consequence the latter were preparing for war. One need not examine Anglo-Chinese relations for the explanation of the rumour; it probably arose out of the interest which British officers in Assam had been showing in trade routes to China across northern Burma. The late Miss Dorothy Woodman in her *The Making of Burma*[1] has drawn attention to this in terms of British expansionism. After the Anglo-Burmese war of 1824–26, she tells us, British strategists saw Burma as a door to a much wider area between India and China, and in such a context she interprets the impulse to exploration which came with the expulsion of the Burmese from Assam and the establishment of relations with the mountain tribal peoples, the Moamarias, the Khamtis and especially the Singphos, whose country lay on both sides of the new British-India border. In the same spirit therefore does she treat the part which Burney came to play in the affairs of that frontier in 1835-6.

After the establishment of British control in Assam, which had involved some minor military actions against the Singphos, some attention was given to the idea of exploring a route to Ava through the Hukawng Valley. Other matters, however, had to have priority, particularly the Hukawng Valley itself, for it was through it that the Burmese had invaded Assam, and after being driven out they had stirred up so much insurgency among the hill tribes of the area that Burney had been instructed to protest to the ministers at Ava.

[1] London, 1962, p. 83.

On the Burma side of the Assam frontier there were the provinces of Hukawng and Maing Khwan. The British officers in Assam knew nothing about them, and were uncomfortably aware of their ignorance. In November 1834 Captain Jenkins, the Governor-General's Agent on the North-east Frontier, reported to Calcutta that an important trade was carried on between Assam and the Burmese frontier districts. He asked how much authority the Court of Ava exercised over these areas, and suggested that reciprocal arrangements should be negotiated for the protection of traders and their exemption from imposts. He pointed out that the Mawari traders of Assam wanted to open trade relations with the Shan districts of northern Burma.

The Government of India referred the matter to Burney, asking for information. He replied in February 1835 that the Burmese ministers were very ignorant of the area in question; it included some Shan states and a number of wild hill tribes. These were under the jurisdiction of the Governor of Mogaung. Mogaung itself had once been a powerful Shan kingdom. Seven or eight days' journey from the town was Main Kon [Maing Khwan], the seat of the Shan chief of Hukawng. From Main Kon to the Burmese frontier post of Taban (known in Assam as Tapan) was a further twenty days' journey over very difficult country. The Burmese, he said, exercised very little authority over the Singphos and other wild tribes between Assam, Yunnan and Ava, and for that reason were against allowing foreigners into the area. The Singphos, he went on, would often attack Chinese caravans. They would murder a man just for his loin-cloth or his tinder-box. There was an impost of ten per cent on imports, and this, he warned, the Court of Ava would never give up: it had been fixed by their oldest code of laws. His advice therefore was that no approach should be made to the Court of Ava in the matter. If Assamese traders wanted to visit Burma, they should be given certified passes in English, Burmese and Shan, as provided for in the first article of Crawfurd's commercial treaty. Should traders meet with difficulties, a remonstrance should be sent to the Court of Ava and a request for an enquiry into the conduct of the local officers.[1]

But it was not a mere matter of trade regulation. In July 1835 tribal feuding suddenly disturbed the British side of the frontier. There were two rival Singpho chieftains, the Beesa Gaum, living

[1] Desai, op. cit., 239-40

in British territory, and the Daffa Gaum, in Burmese. The latter led a foray across the frontier, destroyed the Beesa Gaum's village and massacred everyone he could lay hands on. Then he set about occupying all his rival's lands, claiming them as his own. News of this was sent in all haste by the Government of India to Burney. He was instructed to tell the ministers that the responsibility for this frightful outrage lay with their government: it should keep its frontier tribes under control. When he reported this to them he found them quite ignorant of the occurrence. But a new governor was about to leave for Mogaung, he was told, and he would be instructed to restrain the Daffa Gaum.

This seemed to Burney to offer an excellent opportunity for him to send one of his staff to accompany the governor to the area and get in touch with the Assam authorities concerning the situation there. After some difficulty he managed to persuade the ministers to permit Captain Hannay, the officer commanding the residency escort, to go on the trip, and he and the governor left Ava towards the end of November 1835. Miss Woodman suggests that the Court of Ava had some grounds for suspicion regarding Burney's intentions, and quotes the following paragraph from his instructions to Hannay in support of her opinion.

It would be useful for you to ascertain as many routes as you can from Bamau [Bhamo] into China and from Mogaung into Assam. You will also take particular pains to ascertain how far the plan proposed by Captain Jenkins of establishing a regular route between Suddiya [Sadiya in Assam] and the Burmese dominions is likely to succeed, what are the difficulties of the overland route between Mogaung and Assam, and how they may be removed, what are the products and their prices on the Burmese side, what articles of British and Indian manufacture are in demand there, and the present rate at which they are selling, what duties are levied, and in what manner, what oppressions and difficulties traders are subjected to, and in short ascertain the present state of the commerce, and the best mode of extending and improving it, taking also every opportunity of pointing out to the Governor of Mogaung and other Burmese officers the great advantage and convenience to themselves of establishing a regular trade between their territory and Suddiya.[1]

The document seems to be concerned with commerce and to have no ulterior design.

Meanwhile the Assam authorities had taken action against the

[1] I.P.C., 6 Feb. 1836, no. 15, Woodman, *op. cit.*, p. 88.

Daffa Gaum. Major White, the Political Agent of Upper Assam, led a force of three hundred men against him, but finding him in a well-defended position, offered him terms. One reason for this was that it had been learnt that his treatment of the Beesa Gaum had been in retaliation for a similar action taken by the latter against him, the Beesa Gaum being the aggressor. But having accepted a settlement, the Daffa Gaum then broke it. Captain White accordingly stormed his stockades and captured them. The Daffa Gaum, however, got away, and although chased into Burmese territory, managed to make good his escape. That was in November 1835, but when the news reached Ava Captain Hannay and the Governor of Mogaung were far beyond recall. The ministers wished they had never listened to Burney's proposal for Hannay to go to the frontier; they now asked the resident to recall him.

Far away in the north he and the Governor arrived at Hukawng on the last day of January. There the Governor called upon the Daffa Gaum to surrender, and after some delay he did so, on 22 March. The governor and Hannay then returned with him to Ava, where they arrived on 29 May. The case was then considered by the ministers. Because the Daffa Gaum was adjudged not to have been the aggressor, but was simply taking revenge, they were against severe measures, but thought it best to give him an admonishment and send him home. And on consideration of all the circumstances Burney himself agreed that no further action was called for.

Not so the Government of India, when Burney made his report. It wanted no less than the surrender of the offending chieftain. Such a proceeding, Burney had to explain, was quite unrealistic. In order to hand him over the ministers would have to ask the king's permission, and because of the unstable state of his health no one, not even the Minthagyi, would dare to do so. They even suppressed all mention of the residency to him. To the ministers themselves, although agreeing with their treatment of the Daffa Gaum, Burney made it as clear as he could that the Government of India would hold the Court of Ava responsible for any further outrages on British subjects. When they were agitating for Hannay's recall, he had told them that it was obvious that even with an escort of a thousand men the Governor was afraid to go to the frontier. Hence, if there were further aggression into Assam, the Government of India would itself take action to punish the offenders without reference to the Court of Ava, and having done so would demand compensation for the damage suffered by British subjects and for the expense incurred in dealing with the matter.

Captain Hannay, as we know, had intended to go on to the Assam frontier to confer with British officers there, but with the surrender of the Daffa Gaum had had to return from Maing Khwan, where he had been at the time when this happened. He therefore sent a trusted sepoy with a message to them at Sadiya. The sepoy, on rejoining him, reported that his Burmese guides had taken him thither by a very difficult route, but that on his return journey he had discovered a much easier one, which could be made usable for wheeled traffic. This information, brought to Burney by Hannay on his return inspired him to write to the Government of India pointing out that the routes between Ava and Assam that had now been explored ought to be kept open. This could be done by sending an officer from Assam to Ava; trade might thereby be put on a better footing, he wrote, and the Court of Ava be led to remove its prohibition on traders going northwards from Ava to Bhamo or Mogaung, and thereby break the Chinese monopoly of trade in those areas.

Before anything was decided, however, Burney learnt that a letter had arrived from the Emperor of China protesting to the Court of Ava that it had permitted an English officer to investigate the route into China. The ministers denied that the letter had any such content, but Burney was convinced that it referred to Hannay's activities; all the more so when it came to his ears that the Chinese merchants at Ava had complained to Minthagyi after Hannay's departure on his mission, that their trade monopoly in northern Burma was threatened, and, as he pointed out to the Calcutta authorities, this included not only the entire trade of the area, but also the produce of the amber and jade mines there.

Ultimately in September 1836 he got hold of a copy of a Burmese translation of the imperial missive; it fully confirmed the report which he had received. Mr. Desai in the Appendix of his book gives Burney's annotated English translation of it.[1] The final paragraph contained the imperial complaint. It runs:

'Everything that occurs in Elder Brother's empire shall be made known to younger brother with respect to younger brother's empire. It is not proper to allow the English, after they have made

[1] *Op. cit.*, 471–3.

war and peace has been settled, to remain in the city. They are accustomed to act like the Pipul Tree.¹ Let not younger brother therefore allow the English to remain in his country, and if anything happens Elder Brother will attack, take and give.'

Needless to say, this accorded thoroughly with the sentiments of the Court of Ava. The Government of India, on the other hand, wanted all the information it could get on the routes used by Captain Hannay and sepoy Sirdar Singh. Burney was accordingly requested to send them to Calcutta, and on 20 October they left Ava for Rangoon on the first lap of their journey to Bengal. The Calcutta authorities planned to send them on to Assam with a scientist, Dr. Griffiths. Thence they were to make their way to Ava. On hearing of the plan Burney suggested that the whole route should be surveyed by a competent surveyor in company with Captain Hannay, and that Dr. Bayfield should be sent from Ava to the frontier with some Burmese officers to meet the party and accompany it back to Ava. Also, when at the frontier, Bayfield should confer with the British officials from Sadiya, regarding the feud between the Beesa and the Daffa Gaums in order to seek a settlement. He took this proposal to the ministers, and was successful in overcoming their objections to the expedition.

On 13 December 1836 Bayfield and his party left Ava. They were to join the Governor of Mogaung at Tingut and travel with him northwards towards the frontier. Burney's instructions to his assistant were to collect all the useful information he could about everything, and in particular about the extent and nature of the trade between Burma and China, and between them and Assam. He was also to enquire into the number of Assamese that the Burmese Singphos held in captivity, which chiefs they were serving and how to secure their emancipation or escape; he was further to gather all possible information about the Singphos and the means of stopping their forays into British territory. Together with the Burmese officers he was to confer with the British Assam officers regarding peace and trade, and the indemnity that should be paid by the Daffa Gaum.

Major White, the Political Agent of Upper Assam, went to meet

---

[1] Burney's note. 'Wherever this plant takes root, and particularly in old temples and buildings, it spreads and takes such firm hold that it is scarcely possible to be removed or eradicated. I believe Pipul does not grow in the northern parts of China, but the Burmese word Nyoung is applied to many species of Ficus.'

the party from Ava at the rendezvous in the Patkoi Hills, arriving there on 25 February 1837. He waited for them until 5 March; then had to leave because of shortage of supplies and a Singpho threat to the supply points in his rear. Before leaving he escorted Hannay and Griffiths safely across the range to await Bayfield's party which was close by. On that same day, indeed, the two parties met at Nouyang Paree and held a conference. But the sole business seems to have been the governor's objection to the frontier at the Patkoi Hills. He claimed that Burmese territory extended westwards beyond them. Hannay, however, replied that he had no power to discuss the matter; his instructions were merely to indicate the location of the boundary. Then came a further difficulty; no coolies were available to accompany Hannay and Griffiths to Ava. So Bayfield had to return to Ava without them. He arrived there in May to find a new king upon the throne and Burney contemplating the removal of the residency to Rangoon.

In his report to the Government of India Burney claimed that the mission had not been a complete failure, for Bayfield had helped Hannay to demonstrate to the Governor of Mogaung where the boundary-line lay. He had also managed privately to convey a message to the Daffa Gaum telling him the terms which Major White could offer him, should he decide to make his submission to the British Government. Long before the Ava revolution broke out in the previous February, however, Burney had experienced increasing difficulties with the ministers about the mission. They told him they had received a report that a British expeditionary force was in Assam preparing to occupy the whole country of the Singphos and Shans north of Mogaung. He was quite unable to allay their suspicions, even when he presented them with a declaration by the Government of India that its sole object was 'to promote a safe intercourse, beneficial to both sides, and to ensure efficient protection to the tribes under our authority'. The ministers remained unconvinced.

Chapter 16

The Coup d'Etat of 1837

THE Prince of Tharrawaddy, as we have already seen, had been one of the commissioners appointed in 1831 to act on the king's behalf while incapacitated by illness. The others were his halfbrothers the Thibaw Prince and the Bo Wun Min, and the King's brother-in-law the Minthagyi. In effect the three princes were cyphers; the Minthagyi controlled the government. The Tharrawaddy Prince was the only full brother of the king, and was warmly attached to him. Early in the year 1837 he gradually withdrew from all contact with the Minthagyi and the ministers. He increased the number of his retainers and collected arms with the object, should the king die, of preventing an usurpation by the Minthagyi to the detriment of the Sakya Min and the king's brothers. He lived close by the residency, and Burney described his followers as 'the most turbulent and saucy set of fellows in Ava'.

In due course information reached the ministers of Tharrawaddy's activities. It came from Maung Baya, a former chief of Pagān, whom Burney describes as a very respectable man. At first the Minthagyi advised the ministers against taking action. Maung Baya then made a second report, and this time the Wundauk Khan Ye urged the ministers to act. Tharrawaddy was said to be recruiting men with the help of certain notorious robbers. His sister, the Princess of Pagān, was also involved: she was said to be accumulating arms at her house in his support. The first step in the drama that was to follow was taken by the ministers on 21 February 1837, when they had her house searched. Some muskets and cannon were found, and during the operation a well known bad hat named Nga Ye was seen to escape. The princess, when questioned, declared that he was in Tharrawaddy's service. The ministers accordingly called upon the prince to surrender him, but he denied all knowledge of the man. Their next step was to summon the prince to the Hlutdaw, but he sent an excuse. The ministers thereupon collected troops and demanded that he should permit his premises to be searched. This he refused; he threatened to set fire to the city if they made any attempt to do so. He also sent a secret message to Burney on the following day asking him to intervene to prevent him from being molested without the king's knowledge. Burney replied advising him to inform the ministers of Nga Ye's whereabouts. He also went personally to see the ministers. He warned them that popular sympathy was with the prince, and that therefore they must show that they were acting with full knowledge of the king. They could do so, he said either by permitting him, Burney, to have an interview with the king, or by sending one of their number to call on Tharrawaddy with a suitable explanation.

Tharrawaddy and the ministers alike rejected Burney's advice, and on 24 February the ministers took what proved to be a fatal step. They arrested the prince's chief minister and sent a body of troops to search his premises. When the troops arrived, the guard at the gateway to the prince's compound fired on them, killing one and wounding two others. The remainder fled in disorder. Tharrawaddy at once set about evacuating his family and followers, some four hundred, all told, in boats across the Irrawaddy to Sagaing. In his article Burney declares that his clerk, R. S. Edwards, prevented some of Tharrawaddy's followers from setting fire to the city, but gives no details. From what one learns of Edwards from other sources at other times, this may well have been true. He tells us also that the crossing to Sagaing could never have been carried out had a determined attempt been made to prevent it; but nothing was done although the government had at its disposal between three and four thousand troops well provided with arms and ammunition. The ministers displayed a complete lack of energy or decision, as Burney puts it, and there was a state of alarm in the city.

The die was now cast and Burney expected a revolution. Right from the start he had done all he could to prevent an open rupture. To the prince's requests for intervention he had replied that he was under strict orders from his government to maintain absolute neutrality. On 23 February he had sent Edwards to the prince to ask how he could help to prevent a collision with the government, and the latter had asked him to point out to the ministers the indignity with which they were treating his sister and himself. At almost the same time he learnt that a rumour was circulating to the effect that he had joined Tharrawaddy and gone to his house. Accordingly he had gone to the Hlutdaw and tackled the Minthagyi on this point, and had elicited from him the lame admission that the information had proved incorrect. He then asked to see the king. His request was refused, but the ministers all made a great to-do of assuring him that the king was fully apprized of what was going on, but he had told them plainly that he believed they were acting without the king's knowledge. He had warned them that the measures they were taking against the prince and his sister were likely to have serious consequences. He had advised them therefore to send a principal minister to the prince to assure him that the measures he complained of were taken at the king's express orders. They had replied that they fully agreed with him, but had excused themselves from acting in accordance with his advice because there was no precedent for a wungyi to go to a prince's house.

Burney himself was an ill man at the time, preparing to go home to England on sick leave. Now, when he realized the seriousness of the situation and the unfitness of the government to cope with it, he warned all British subjects and foreign traders to leave the city and go to Rangoon; he also took charge of cash and jewels to the value of more than £100,000 belonging to those who left. As we know from the previous chapter, Dr. Bayfield and Captain Hannay were absent from the residency on tour when the trouble boiled up; Bayfield had with him five of the thirty sepoys of the residents' guard. With so tempting a prize for an attacking force in his keeping, Burney armed his servants and followers, and made the residency as defensible as he could. For the time being his own departure must be held in abeyance.

Tharrawaddy's next move was to begin to make his way up the river towards Moksobomyo, 'the town of the hunter chief', once the home of his great-grandfather, Alaungpaya, the founder of the dynasty. On modern maps it is shown as Shwebo, 'the town of the golden leader'. He and his followers travelled upstream in a vast flotilla of many hundreds of boats. This was the traditional sign of a challenge to the existing government, a bid for the throne. In effect he was now a *minlaung*, a 'pretender to the throne', though at this stage he did not claim it himself. On the way up he was sending out messages throughout the country announcing that the king was dead, the Minthagyi had usurped the throne, and he himself was resisting in order to maintain the rights of the lawful heir, presumably by this meaning the Sakya Min. He took a solemn oath publicly at a pagoda not to injure the king or his son: his quarrel, he said, was with the Minthagyi. Evidently his followers were aware that the king was not dead. Thousands from all sides went to join him. The ministers had at their disposal far more men, arms and supplies than the rebels. Burney was dumbfounded by their failure to intercept Tharrawaddy's force when it would have been an easy matter. The troops sent to deal with him never got within miles of it. Burney could only conclude that they were either panic-stricken or disaffected. Then, when a royal army was sent in pursuit of the rebels, it studiously avoided all contact with them, although far superior to them in strength.

When news of what was happening was broken to the sick king, he was given to understand by the Minthagyi that his brother had attempted a coup d'état but had been put to flight. Burney on the other hand learnt that Tharrawaddy's propaganda was proving effective in weakening the royal army in pursuit of him: most of it was said to have defected to him. Burney was acutely aware of the paradoxical situation in which the government with overwhelming military superiority seemed to be completely unable to act effectively. He tried to warn the ministers of the danger and advised immediate negotiations. He also advised them to marry the king's son to the queen's daughter and create him Ein-she-min, official heir apparent. When at last on 4 March he was summoned to a private audience with the king, he found him quite normal mentally and quite ignorant of the real situation. He tells us in his article that he offered his services as mediator with the object of bringing about a reconciliation, and that he repeated the offer several times. The ministers, however, totally rejected his advice and begged him not to mention it to the king. He would put them to death, they said, if they reported his plan to him.

Law and order had now begun rapidly to break down, and on 11 March a residency boat was attacked by insurgents. It had been up to Mogaung with despatches for Dr. Bayfield. The American missionary Kincaid was a passenger in it, and he and its lascars were severely beaten up by supporters of the rebel prince. Burney therefore asked permission to withdraw the residency from the capital. When, however, he started preparing to leave, he found it impossible to obtain the requisite number of boats, and had to abandon the project. So he strengthened the defences of the residency by building a stockade round it. The ministers were strongly opposed to his leaving: they said it would alarm the people.

From now on the situation deteriorated rapidly. Tharrawaddy's troops were seeking to isolate the city, and by 22 March, according to Burney, they had practically succeeded in doing so.

On the 21st Burney received a message from the Minthagyi saying that all was lost, and the English resident was the only person to whom the king and his ministers could look for advice and help. Next day Burney saw the king and the ministers twice. The ministers asked him to go to Moksobomyo to mediate. The *Konbaungset Chronicle* states that he offered to go, but this must refer to his much earlier offers to mediate. At that time he had believed it possible to bring about a reconciliation between the brothers, but his offers had been turned down. Burney's account gives no reason to suppose that he took the initiative now. He tells us that the ministers made the request, and that he said that he would agree subject to the release of all the members of the royal family who had been imprisoned because of their connexion with Tharrawaddy. The ministers consented to this and the release was carried out in Burney's presence. Those involved were the Princess of Pagān and her two sisters, and three of Tharrawaddy's male relatives, one of whom was Maung Shwe Za, a former governor of the province of Pegu. Burney now had no hope of bringing about a reconciliation, he tells us in his article: that was no longer possible. His object was to save the capital from the orgy of murder and destruction that would break out when Tharrawaddy's troops took possession of it, and, not least, to secure the residency against attack.

He left Ava on the evening of 23 March, crossing the river to Sagaing, and doing the rest of the journey on horseback. He had with him two sepoys of the residency guard and a party of royal troops, who were in such a state of panic, he writes, that it was difficult to prevent them from running back to Ava. He reached his destination on the afternoon of the 25th. In his long despatch of 24 May 1837 to the Government of India[1] he writes a vivid account of his journey. When he reached the headquarters of the

[1] IPC, vol. 41.

commander of the royal army, Prince Bo Hmu Wun, a full-scale attack on it by the rebels was in progress. He noted, however, that both sides seemed to be firing at an angle of 45 degrees so that little damage was done. Everyone he spoke to, he says, was in a state of most acute alarm. The officers were from the civil administration at Ava and were quite unused to military service which they hated. Their men were ordinary villagers called up for service at a moment's notice and without pay or provisions. When he got to the rebel lines, about a quarter of a mile away, he found 'a most remarkable contrast. Most of the officers . . . were bold, restless characters and notorious robbers and the private soldiers, although miserably armed, . . . full of confidence owing to the knowledge which they had acquired from numerous deserters of the state of panic of the Kings' troops.[1] Everywhere he saw the shocking evidence of burning and plunder by the brigands in Tharrawaddy's service, to whom the revolt was a heaven-sent opportunity to carry on their normal activities under the shelter of his authority.

The prince sent an escort of horsemen under an officer of high rank to meet Burney on his arrival at Moksobomyo, and received him with a great show of cordiality. During his visit hostilities ceased. As he had anticipated, when their first long conference began, it was at once evident that reconciliation with the Court of Ava was completely out of the question. Nevertheless he prepared a brief note urging it and stressing the misery the civil war had brought to the country. He asked how Tharrawaddy thought peace could be speedily restored. The prince took an hour to consider the note; then calling Burney in, he spent three hours, from 10 p.m. to 1 a.m., detailing all his grievances and blaming the queen and her brother for the misgovernment from which, he said, the country had suffered. Burney tried to remind him of the affection which he understood had always existed between him and the king, but he retorted that his brother had forfeited his right to reign by making a woman of low origin his queen. And when Burney went on to press the claims of the king's son to be created Ein-she-min, Tharrawaddy declared that his father, the previous holder of the title, had directed Bagyidaw to give him, Tharrawaddy, precedence over the king's son in the succession to the throne. On every subject raised by the resident at this interview

[1] Letter of 24 May para. 10

the prince was uncompomisingly opposed to a peaceful solution. He declared that he would sack and destroy Ava, and advised Burney to leave, offering him boats for evacuating the residency. Burney, however, explained that his assistant, Dr. Bayfield, and another officer, Dr. Richardson, were travelling in the interior of the country, and he must wait for them, and, moreover, all the British in the city, who were under his protection, must go with him.

As a result of that first interview Burney came to two clear conclusions, one that Tharrawaddy's aim was to seize the throne, and the other that he must confine his efforts to saving the city of Ava and safeguarding the residency. At subsequent discussions Tharrawaddy promised to issue orders for the safety of the residency and all connected with it. With regard to Ava itself he managed to obtain from the prince a guarantee that if the city were handed over to him without opposition, he would not harm the king or any ministers, he would put no one to death and would prevent his troops from assaulting the city or molesting its inhabitants. Finally he agreed that Burney should return and present his terms to the king and ministers, and in the meantime he would restrain his troops from approaching closer to Ava until he heard from Burney regarding the reaction of the Court to his terms.

Burney set out from Moksobomyo on his return journey at 4 p.m. on 26 March and hurried back to Ava, reaching it at 9 p.m. on the next day. He had ridden no less than forty miles during the heat of the day, and arrived completely exhausted. On the following day he reported to the king and ministers at the palace. After a full account of his proceedings at Moksobomyo, he gave them a frank warning against trusting Tharrawaddy. He said that as the prince was a Burman, 'he could not believe that he would ever keep to the full extent the engagement which he had made with the British Resident'. He advised them to obtain a fresh pledge from him through the Prince of Mekkhara, the king's uncle, whom he was about to send to Tharrawaddy at the head of a delegation of the chief Buddhist abbots of the kingdom. The king wanted Burney also to return to Moksobomyo to obtain a further pledge from his brother to carry out his promises. Burney, however, was not in a fit state to undertake two such exhausting journeys again. He therefore sent Edwards with a letter to the prince announcing the submission of the ministers, and advising him to come to

Sagaing as soon as possible to superintend the occupation of Ava by his troops. At his interview with the king and ministers Burney urged them in the strongest possible terms to man a sufficient number of boats with trustworthy adherents, and escape down the river to Rangoon. He offered to furnish them with letters to certain British merchants there who would arrange for their transport to Moulmein, where they would be safe. The king, he tells us in his article[1] favoured going ahead with the plan, but the ministers 'had not courage or energy sufficient to make the attempt.' The plan could easily have been carried out, as Burney learnt later. At Moksobomyo Tharrawaddy gave Edwards the assurance sought for in Burney's letter, but in the following words: 'Yes, I will keep the pledge I gave to Colonel Burney.' At their conference Burney had stressed the point that the promise was made not to him personally, but to the representative of the British government. The significance of the prince's phraseology does not seem to have escaped Burney: it provided an additional source of uneasiness.

To the Mekkhara delegation, which arrived after Edwards, Tharrawaddy made further stipulations: the queen must be removed from the king's presence and the Minthagyi, the Bohmin Wun, the Myawaddi Wungyi, three other ministers and seven principal military officers were to surrender to his son Htait-tin-byu at Sagaing. The Mekkhara Prince returned to Ava with this message on 6 April. In the meantime the royal army had evacuated Sagaing and the town had been occupied by Tharrawaddy's forces under Htait-tin-byu. Everywhere the advancing rebel forces were plundering and burning indiscriminately, and in desperation the king and ministers were considering defending Ava. Burney also, fearing for the safety of the residency, had sent a further message to Tharrawaddy by a trusted Muslim merchant of Ava urging him to come down to Sagaing and put a stop to the atrocities. Then came the Mekkhara Prince with his grim message and the ministers had to decide what to do about it. Their decision was to comply and trust the prince's pledge. Burney in his report to the Government of India wrote: 'At the time there were at least 7 or 8000 troops within the walls of Ava, infinitely better found in arms and ammunition than the prince's forces, and with a large number of guns of every description.'[2]

[1] p. 79. [2] Letter of 24 May, para. 21.

The Mekkhara Prince said he believed that Tharrawaddy would honour his pledge, but he requested Burney to accompany the little party of ministers and generals on its way to surrender at Sagaing. Burney did so, as, he tells us in his article, 'utterly dumbfounded by their credulity and suspecting some cruel treachery'. He writes a graphic account of the surrender. He himself crossed the river ahead of the party and obtained a promise from Htait-tin-byu that no harm should be done to them. The young prince provided him with an escort to go to the riverside to meet them and conduct them to him.

> On their way through the crowd assembled to see them pass, [he wrote] I was much pleased to observe that the populace, so far from showing any violence or insult, which I had apprehended, was perfectly silent and respectful. The ministers and officers were on foot. Menthagyeh manifested the utmost alarm, and seemed to have lost the faculty of hearing and speaking, but the whole demeanour of Prince Meng Myat Bo [the Bohmu Wun] excited my warmest admiration. He led the party with a firm step and a bold upright carriage, grave and serious, but evidently suffering much from feelings of indignation and wounded pride. Some of the military officers seemed to view the whole proceeding as an insulting degradation.[1]

Before leaving Burney made another strong appeal to the young prince on their behalf. Later in the day, however, Tharrawaddy's elder son Htait-tin-gyi arrived and placed two pairs of irons on the Minthagyi. That was on 7 April. On the following day Burney's special messenger returned to Ava and told him that Tharrawaddy had renewed the pledge he had given him at Moksobomyo. At the same time Tharrawaddy himself arrived at Sagaing, and the families of his confidential servants, who had taken refuge in the residency compound when their master had fled from the capital, now rejoined him. Their places were at once taken by women and children of some of the subordinate officers of the king's party, as well as some of the officers themselves.

Next day, 9 April, Tharrawaddy at Sagaing assumed sovereign powers, and, without consulting his brother, announced that he had abdicated the throne in his favour. He took the title of Yatana Thainga Konbaung Myo Ya Thaw Min, 'the king who rules over the city of Yatana Thainga Konbaung' (the classical name of Moksobomyo). His elder son Htait-tin-gyi with two thousand men then

[1] *Ibid.*, para. 21; Desai, *op. cit.*, p. 277.

occupied the Ava palace, King Bagyidaw was removed to a matting building south of the city, the queen and her daughter being taken from him and confined at Sagaing. The surrendered ministers and generals were placed in the common jail at Ava, their property confiscated and their wives and families tortured to reveal hidden treasure. Some twenty other ministers and state officials were also arrested and their property confiscated. Htait-tin-gyi then examined the chief ministers and forced them by severe treatment to testify that the Minthagyi had intended to put Tharrawaddy and the rest of the royal family to death and usurp the throne. In the city itself plunder and cruelty became rife.

Burney records that some days before his surrender the Minthagyi had sent a messenger secretly asking him to save his life and offering him ten thousand ticals. He promised to do his utmost, but refused the money. The messenger returned shortly afterwards offering double or even treble the amount; the minister had interpreted Burney's refusal of the money as indicating that it was inadequate. He was so horrified at the atrocities that as soon as possible he hurried across to Sagaing and obtained an audience of the new king. He describes him as surrounded by desperate characters. He begged him to behave in an enlightened and civilized manner, and so win the approval of the British Government. Tharrawaddy was full of excuses. He had never promised not to punish the guilty, he said; moreover he had put nothing in writing, and surely a king had the right to punish the guilty. In his report Burney commented: 'I soon saw that his head was turned by his extraordinary success and that he was a very different person from what he was two months ago.'[1]

Next day, 10 April, Burney went to visit the ministers in jail. He found them in a dreadful condition, in heavy irons and starving, since no one dared to feed them. He at once sent in food from the residency to them, and continued to do so daily while they were there. He also sent a very strong protest in writing to Tharrawaddy. The king read it carefully and then said to Edwards, who had brought it, 'Colonel Burney has not got my pledge in writing, and the 500 men in Parliament in England will laugh at it [i.e. Burney's protest] as no written paper can be produced'.

Three days later Lieutenant Beevor with a party of Madras sepoys arrived from Moulmein to relieve the sepoys of the resident's

[1] *Ibid.*, para. 24.

escort. He complained that at the Kyauk-ta-lon guard post six miles below Ava one of Tharrawaddy's general officers had stopped their boats, and when told that his party was on its way to relieve the resident's escort in accordance with the agreement in the Treaty of Yandabo, used threatening and insulting language, saying that his master and he did not recognize that treaty. The news caused Burney much anxious thought. He suspected that what the Burmese officer had said reflected Tharrawaddy's own views. In any case he had to send in a formal complaint about his behaviour; he decided, however, not to mention what the officer had said about the treaties. He hoped that when the king's excitement over the success of his coup had cooled down, he would drop the idea of repudiating the treaties. His suspicion turned out to be only too true. Not only was the offending officer not punished, but during the next few days report after report came in that the king was publicly abusing the British, running down the authority of the governor-general and declaring that he would get rid of the treaties made by his brother and of the presence of a British resident at his capital. Then one of the newly-appointed wungyis wrote an insolent letter to Burney regarding a trader who claimed British protection, saying that the new government would not recognize his rank as resident. Burney also learnt that the king's advisers were pressing him hard to expel the residency from Ava. The king let it be known that he contemplated moving his capital to Moksobomyo. He mentioned the subject in conversation with Burney, who replied that it would be his duty as resident to accompany the court thither. Tharrawaddy, however, said he would not hear of it: Burney could either remain in Ava or go to Rangoon until the building of the new capital city was completed.

While this situation was coming to the boil, fuel was added to the furnace by Dr. Richardson, who since 1829 had been exploring Moulmein's hinterland in the hope of developing its commercial possibilities. On 24 April Burney received a letter from him saying that he was held up in the Shan Hills, some seven or eight days' journey from Ava because his permit to travel to the capital had been granted by the previous government and was now invalid. On this journey he had visited Chiengmai in northern Siam, and then worked his way northwards through the Shan States to Yaung Hwe on the Inle Lake famous for its leg-rowers. He said that the country through which he would have to travel to the capital was infested with troops and plunderers. Burney went to Htait-tin-gyi, who was acting as governor of the city; but after being deliberately kept waiting for an hour by the prince's attendants, he left without seeing him. He then sent Edwards to the prince asking for an escort to be sent to bring Richardson to Ava. The prince apologized for the behaviour of his men when Burney called, but refused the request, saying that Richardson must return to Moulmein by the route he had used on his outward journey. Burney therefore went personally across to Sagaing to petition Tharrawaddy in the matter. The king, however, made the same reply as his son. Burney therefore took his stand upon Crawfurd's commercial treaty, whereat Tharrawaddy replied that the treaties had been made by his predecessor, and he refused to recognize them. This elicited from Burney the rejoinder that they were made with the Burmese nation, not with a particular reigning monarch. But Tharrawaddy brought the discussion to a summary conclusion with the remark that such might be the British custom, but it was not the Burmese one; the time had come, he said, for a new 'alliance of friendship'.[1]

On 27 April a message came from Sagaing summoning Edwards to the royal presence. He returned with a note dictated by the king personally, which Burney was asked to sign in order to obtain a permit for Richardson to come to Ava. It was in the form of a petition acknowledging that Richardson had trespassed in travelling from Moulmein by the route he had chosen, and saying that he now asked for pardon and promised never to trespass in Burmese territory again. Burney's feelings may well be imagined, but he kept them strictly under control. On the following day he sent Edwards back to explain that he could not sign such a document because Richardson was travelling not as a private person, but under the orders of the Commissioner of Tenasserim and the Governor-General of India, and, moreover, in accordance with 'the friendly alliance' between Britain and Burma. This description of the Yandabo treaty was probably an echo of the official description of it by the Court of Ava. Later the compilers of the *Konbaungset Chronicle* were to describe it in similar terms. The king's retort to Burney's message was: 'Well, if Colonel Burney will not write as I require, let him go to those with whom the English made the treaties.'[2]

[1] Letter of 24 May, paras 41, 42; Desai, *op. cit.*, p. 287.
[2] *Ibid.*, para. 42; Burney's article p. 51; Desai, *op. cit.*, p. 288.

On 30 April Burney was summoned by Htait-tin-gyi to the Hlutdaw for reconsideration of Richardson's case. He made a full statement of his position regarding the validity of the treaties. The British resident, he declared, had no right to be in Ava save under the authority of the Treaty of Yandabo. Some of the members of the council had been accorded protection in the residency when the trouble between Tharrawaddy and the previous government had broken out; they now promised their help to break the impasse. Burney was not surprised, therefore, when on 2 May the Hlutdaw informed him that the king would permit Dr. Richardson to visit Ava, but in future no officer from Moulmein might go to the Shan States. It was such an extraordinary climb-down on the part of Tharrawaddy that Burney asked the wundauk who announced the news to him whether the king had also changed his mind about the treaties. The wundauk begged him not to raise the question. Burney, however, reminded him that it was the king, and not he, who had raised it. The wundauk repeated that he hoped that Burney would not raise the question for the present; the very fact, he went on, that permission had been given for Richardson to come to Ava, even when Burney had refused to sign the letter dictated by his majesty, and that he himself continued to reside in Ava, should be taken as proof that the treaties with the British were considered to be still in force.

This incident, and the discovery by Burney just before it occurred that, notwithstanding the king's repeated pledges to hurt no one, the Wundauk Khan Ye and another high ranking officer had been secretly strangled in prison, gave him seriously to feel that he must have as little as possible to do with the king. In reply to his protest regarding the executions Tharrawaddy had replied loftily that it was his royal prerogative to have guilty persons executed. Burney realized that over Richardson the king had tried to bully him, but on thinking things over he came to the conclusion that for him to follow his personal feelings might exasperate the king. Hence on 3 May, the day after the announcement of his change of mind regarding Richardson, he paid a social call on him. He found him in a most affable mood. Tharrawaddy brought out some presents for Burney's children, enquired whether he had ever seen the interior of the Ava palace, and gave instructions for him to be taken over it. He also told Burney of his project for constructing a canal between Kyauk Myaung on the Irrawaddy and the new capital he hoped to build at Moksobomyo, and of another for the introduction of a regular coinage into the country. Laughingly he told the resident that his brother's government had been so stupid, when they entered into the war with the British, that they had appointed officers as governors of Bengal, Madras, Bombay and other parts of India before finding out whether they could beat them. As Burney told the Government of India, it was very difficult to do business with Tharrawaddy because of his unpredictable changes of mood. As a prince he had associated with dissolute characters, indulged in 'spirituous liquors' and gambled. The foreigners he employed were of notoriously bad character, and from them he had learnt to be cunning and plausible. He was also subject to fits of ungovernable rage, especially when he had had too much to drink and would then be cruel and bloodthirsty.[1]

What with anxiety over the treaty question and horror at the king's repudiation of the pledges he had given, before assuming the crown, not to hurt anybody, Burney was in a quandary regarding the wisdom of remaining in Ava. The strongest argument in its favour had been the need to restrain the king from wreaking vengeance on those he regarded as his enemies. The city of Ava had, so far, been saved by his efforts, but the dacoit *bos*, the leaders of Tharrawaddy's army, foiled of their opportunity to enrich themselves and their followers by indiscriminate pillage, were discontented, and were pressing the king to carry out more executions and seizures of property. On 8 and 9 May a series of unbelievably horrible executions of some of the most honourable and devoted servants of the previous régime shocked Burney beyond measure. The wife of one of the victims was beaten to death merely for imploring the king to spare her husband. At the same time the wife and two daughters of the Minthagyi were brutally tortured to force them to disclose the whereabouts of his supposed hidden wealth. Burney's protests were ridiculed by the king, who remarked to the officers in charge of the women, 'These hat-wearing people cannot bear to see or hear of women being beaten or maltreated.'[2]

Then the residency mails were intercepted and opened, and Burney decided that he must place himself where communications with his government were certain. Moreover, there was real danger

[1] Letter of 24 May, para. 50; Desai, *op. cit.*, pp. 289–90.
[2] Desai, *op. cit.*, p. 281.

of personal outrage, and this, under his original instructions, gave him a valid reason for withdrawing to Rangoon. A temporary absence from the capital would afford Tharrawaddy time to cool down, he argued and the Government of India an opportunity to make a vigorous demonstration that would bring him to his senses. So the decision was taken to ask the king for permission to withdraw the residency, as a temporary measure, to Rangoon, on the grounds of his own sickness, of which Tharrawaddy was well aware.

On 12 May Burney wrote in these terms to Tharrawaddy. The proposal, of course, suited the king admirably. He at once agreed to it, and issued orders for the necessary boats to be provided for transport to Rangoon. He mentioned also that Dr. Bayfield, who had gone to the Assam border, had crossed into British territory after hearing of the Ava revolution. This news turned out to be incorrect, since four days later Bayfield turned up at the residency. In his letter also Tharrawaddy pointedly remarked that the two countries, India and Burma, could remain friends without stationing officers at each other's capitals, and broadly hinted that it was up to Burney to make this clear to his own government. He was now all agog to induce Burney to leave as soon a possible. On 16 May in conversation he urged him to expedite his departure: he could return, he said, when conditions had become normal again. He said that Burney, while in Rangoon, should correspond with him.

Next day in open court the king announced that 'he had nothing to say to' the treaties made by his brother with the English. Burney was not present, and took no action when he heard of it. Ten days later, however, on 27 May during a conversation with the king on the subject of the customs duties at Rangoon, when Burney quoted Crawfurd's commercial treaty, Tharrawaddy repeated his refusal to recognize the treaties, and went on to exclaim petulently: 'Don't mention them; they are a matter of reproach and shame to the Burmese. The British frightened the Burmese officers into signing them.' Burney in rejoinder begged him to give the matter further consideration. His own function, he said, was to prevent any difference arising between their two governments. If his majesty disliked the treaties made by his predecessor, the proper procedure was to send an embassy to Bengal to propose a new treaty. On the contrary, urged the king, there was no occasion for any treaty at all; there were several articles in the Treaty of Yandabo over which he and the Calcutta authorities might quarrel. Hence, he said with a logic all of his own, it was best to have no written engagements at all. To which Burney replied, with some hauteur, one imagines, that among civilized states treaties were not cancelled by the death of a sovereign, and, indeed, the Burmese still recognized the treaty made with the Chinese in 1769. Yes, agreed the king, but that was a simple agreement, not a written one. On the contrary, replied Burney, according to the *Yazawin* [Burmese chronicle] it was a regular instrument drawn up and signed in the names of the principal Burmese and Chinese officers. Undeterred, however, by the resident's superior knowledge of his country's history, Tharrawaddy threw out another argument against negotiating a fresh treaty: treaties, he said, were only made after wars. But Burney was not to be dodged in this way. His majesty's ancestor, King Alaungpaya, he said, made a treaty with the British when there had been no war between them. But it was to no purpose: Burney realized that the king was paying little attention to the argument; he was resolved not to recognize Bagyidaw's treaties with the British; that was the simple fact of the matter.[1]

A brief explanation is called for here of Burney's reference to the Sino-Burmese treaty of December 1769, which stumped the king. It just happened to be a subject upon which he was particularly well-informed at the time, for he had been at work upon a paper entitled 'Some Account of the Wars between Burmah and China', which in that same year was published in the *Journal of the Asiatic Society of Bengal*.[2] It was composed entirely from Burmese sources, many of them being copies of the records of Burmese embassies to China since that treaty, supplied by his friend the Myawadi Wungyi, Maung Sa.

Shortly after this interview with Tharrawaddy alarmist reports came from the Rangoon Wungyi of the presence of a British man-of-war at the entrance to the Rangoon River. To calm the Court's fears Burney sent Edwards to explain to the king that she was paying a courtesy visit only. Edwards found Tharrawaddy in a swaggering mood. Of course the British man-of-war might visit Rangoon, he said. If as friends, then they were to be treated as

[1] Letter of 24 May, para. 65; Desai, *op. cit.*, pp. 292–3.
[2] Vol. VI, pp. 121–49, 405–51, 542–97.

friends; but if to fight, then they would find that the Burmese also could fight. He told Edwards to tell Burney that he, Tharrawaddy, had not been conquered; therefore he would not submit to dictation by the British. Unlike the King of England he had only the gods over him: he could issue any orders he pleased. He could put anyone to death at a moment's notice, and, as Burney sadly recorded, he followed this up by having Maung Boo, one of his brother's most respected and faithful officers, put to death in a most barbarous fashion. He was passing through a bad phase. A vile trick was at this time played upon the imprisoned Minthagyi and his colleagues. They were told that the king was about to release them. Some were actually set free, and their relatives thereupon collected the large sum of three thousand ticals which they gave to the Wundauk Maung Dout Gyi in anticipation of the release of the rest. The Wundauk pocketed the money and re-arrested those who had been freed. Burney learnt that when the story was related to the king, he thought it a huge joke.

On 6 June Burney together with Dr. Bayfield and Dr. Richardson had an audience of the king. There was some conversation about the Assam frontier, which Bayfield had recently visited; then the king delivered himself of a further denunciation of the treaties. Again Burney, with the greatest respect, advised him that his proper course was to send an embassy to Bengal. 'I will not send an embassy to Bengal', remarked Tharrawaddy, 'If I send an embassy, it will be to the king of England.' The governor-general, he went on to declare, was not a king. He should correspond with the Rangoon Wungyi. These insults stung all the sharper, since they were uttered in a tone of the utmost good humour. Tharrawaddy, it would seem, was indulging in the enjoyable sport of baiting Burney. It was pointless to reply. But Burney could not let pass such slurs upon the governor-general. The British parliament, he retorted, which controlled the king, also empowered the governor-general to make war and peace, and he corresponded with crowned heads. Burmese governors did not enjoy such powers. It would have been an excellent reply in a conference of statesmen, but on Tharrawaddy it had not the slightest effect: he was not in a mood for serious discussion. Then Burney, suddenly realizing that he was arguing with a king of Burma, an unheard of thing at the Court of Ava, apologized, asking Tharrawaddy not to be angry with him for arguing; to which Tharrawaddy replied: 'You may say whatever you like; I will not be angry with you.'[1] So Burney went on to preach a brief homily saying that if the Treaty of Yandabo were not recognized he himself could not reside at Ava. As for the governor-general, he continued, he was the tree, and he himself only the shadow. If therefore the king would not see the tree, it passed his comprehension how he could possibly see the shadow. This caused a roar of laughter in court in which his majesty also joined. Then he remarked: 'I will leave the tree alone. I want it to bear the same fruit as it did in my ancestor Alompra's reign. I am determined to place relations on the same footing as they were before the reign of the late king, who committed the blunder of going to war with the British. If I intended war, I would order you to leave Ava; but I will not tell Bayfield, or you, either to go or to stay. If you stay, I will make use of you; and if you want more officers, I will send for them; but you must all stay here not upon a treaty as a matter of right, but as dependent upon my will in the same manner as Colonel Symes and Captain Canning came to this country in the time of my grandfather.'[2]

At this Dr. Richardson ejaculated that the treaties could not be annulled in such a manner. But the king reiterated that he would not recognize them; he had not been conquered by the English, he had not made them. He rambled on, saying that the governor-general was responsible to five hundred men, their parliament. When he went out in state he was preceded and followed by bodies of troops. So too was a Burmese provincial governor. Burney then reminded him that his ancestor Alaungpaya had written in his own name to the governor of Bengal and received letters from him. 'True', replied Tharrawaddy. 'You know these things better than Burmese officers. I will not object to the governor-general writing to me in the same manner that Alompre was written to.' Which anyone familiar with the story of Anglo-Burmese relations in his reign will realize was a smart answer.

This was a farewell meeting; Tharrawaddy was preparing to transport his court to Moksobomyo, Burney to transfer the residency to Rangoon. He reminded the king that he had done his best to maintain friendship between his own government and that of Burma; he hoped there would be no rupture after his departure. When he reached Calcutta, he would inform the governor-general

[1] Letter to the Government of India, dated Rangoon, 12 July 1837, para. 12.
[2] Letter of 12 July, para. 12.

of the nature of the king's speeches and sentiments regarding relations with the British. Tharrawaddy replied to this with another long, repetitive speech. His brother's reign had been bad, he said, and his own desire was to remove the evils it had produced and bring everything back to the excellent state of affairs in the reigns of his grandfather and great grandfather. Bayfield could remain at Ava, he said, with a guard of sepoys. Later, when a site had been marked out at the new capital for foreign merchants, he could go up and live with them; but let it be quite clear that he would not acknowledge him as a public officer under the treaty. 'I will not acknowledge or grant anything to which you may found your right upon them,' he said, 'but in everything else you shall be treated much better than you ever were before.'[1]

The conversation finally touched on the subject of the Assam frontier. The king assured the three Englishmen that he did not wish to take a single inch of British territory, nor would he allow the British to take a single inch of Burmese territory. The *Yazawin*, he said, would show the correct boundary. Burney observed that the ancient history of Assam agreed with the present boundary fixed by the British. But the king refused to be drawn: histories, he said, were unreliable since they were compiled by human beings. He had a theory, he continued, about the Burmese frontiers; they were indicated by the inclination of the trees. Those on the Burmese side inclined towards Burma; those on the other side towards the other direction. Burney and his colleagues could find no suitable reply to make to this example of royal percipience, and the audience came to an end. The king bade them all a very kind and gracious farewell, as Burney put it, and presented each with a valuable ruby ring.

That was Burney's last meeting with Tharrawaddy. On 10 June the king and court and a large part of the population of Ava abandoned the city and embarked on an immense flotilla of boats bound for Kyauk Myaung nearly sixty miles up the Irrawaddy. The city was left under the Mindat Wungyi as civil governor. Burney described him as 'an imbecile old man' in his report to Calcutta. Associated with him as military commander was Maung Thaung Bo, 'a notorious protector of robbers'.[2] These two officers

---

[1] Letter of 12 July, para. 21; Desai, *op. cit.*, p. 300.
[2] Letter of 12 July, para. 1. Like the earlier one of 24 May it is in the form of a journal beginning with 27 May.

were to join the king at his new capital as soon as the guns and public stores had been removed from Ava. His majesty, wrote Burney, had expressed a desire to see Ava a heap of ruins, and there was much alarm, for he had threatened to burn the houses in order to compel the inhabitants to follow him.

Chapter 17

The End of a Diplomatic Career

A WEEK later Burney closed the Ava residency and set out with his family and household and the entire residency staff for Rangoon. Three American Baptist missionaries, Messrs Kincaid, Symons and Webb together with their families were also in the party. His intention was, as he told the Government of India, to establish the residency at Rangoon as a temporary measure. After the king's departure, he reported, no officer at Ava took the slightest notice of the residency. On his way downstream the provincial officers treated him with great lack of civility: everyone thought that the residency had been dismissed by the king, and that he would soon go to war with the British. At Rangoon, where his party arrived on 6 July, the acting-governor received him with proper respect. Soon afterwards the new governor, appointed by Tharrawaddy, turned up. He was Maung Shwe Min, an old acquaintance of Burney's, who treated him in a very friendly manner.

Burney's letter of 24 May telling the story of the Ava revolution, and of his decision to remove the residency to Rangoon as a temporary measure was dealt with by the Government of India on 3 July. The Governor-General, Lord Auckland, expressed very high approval of Burney's conduct throughout the emergency, praising his energy, judgement and humanity, but very strong disapproval of his decision to remove the residency, even temporarily, to Rangoon. He could contemplate no event, he said, with greater uneasiness than a rupture with Burma. In his opinion Burney had taken the new king's attitude towards the treaties too seriously, and had engaged in unnecessary discussion of them with him when he was so intoxicated with power as to be incapable of serious discussion. He recognized the special difficulties Burney had had to contend with, the king's cruelties in violation of his pledge, the unsettled state of the country, and the breakdown of trade, but thought they were likely to be aggravated by Burney's retirement from the capital. It was of the highest importance to the Government of India to receive accurate information of everything that occurred. Moreover, if the protection of the residency were removed, the interests of the English and others settled at Ava might materially suffer. Hence Burney must attach himself to the court, wherever it might be. If his health prevented him from doing so, then another officer must be appointed to do so. Meanwhile Dr. Bayfield was to remain with the king, or return to him, if on his way to Rangoon when this order arrived.

The letter conveying these sentiments and instructions reached Burney in Rangoon at the end of July. Long before it arrived he had despatched a further report, dated 12 July, detailing the course of events from 27 May onwards and including a full explanation of his action in evacuating the residency. In it he had answered effectively every point raised by Lord Auckland.

After obtaining the king's permission to withdraw the residency, he wrote, he had remained on at Ava in the hope that the situation would improve. But he lived in constant uneasiness that Tharrawaddy's faithless and savage treatment of the ministers and officers of his predecessor, the insolence of his followers and his own extravagant talk would bring him into personal collision with him, Burney. His own guiding principle, he said, was 'to do nothing that might tie the hands of the Government of India in choosing a course of action to meet with the altered conditions in Ava'. Even after coming to his decision to remove the residency, he said, fearing that the Government of India might consider such a measure premature, he was prepared to take advantage of the lack of boats to leave Bayfield and part of the residency at Ava. The king, however, had made this impossible by refusing to consider him an official agent appointed by virtue of a treaty. He had declared the treaties annulled, not once or twice and to him alone, but repeatedly and publicly. Hence Burney had decided to remove the residency as a whole from Ava without awaiting a reply to his despatch of 24 May.

In his many discussions with the king, he explained, he had never adopted the 'high tone' that he had had to with the previous king's ministers: that would have been fatal. 'I was told by many and I believe it, that nothing but his personal respect for me and his belief that I had done him some service during the late disturbances, restrained him from breaking all terms with me at once.' His disreputable followers were urging him to attack the residency, and rumours were current throughout the country that he had imprisoned all its members and put him, Burney, in irons. 'I earnestly hope then,' he wrote, 'that the Governor-General of India-in-Council will approve of ... my having avoided ... an immediate rupture with the King of Ava, and of my having withdrawn the residency on a fair and reasonable pretext with the full consent of the King without breaking with him or allowing him to suppose that I was departing with hostile intentions, and particularly without imposing upon our Government the necessity of adopting measures against His Majesty excepting at whatever time and in whatever manner His Lordship-in-Council may consider most advisable.'[1]

Two alternatives, he suggested, now lay before the Government of India. The first was to leave Tharrawaddy alone in the hope that he would recover his reason and good sense, and allow the residency to function on the same footing as in his brother's reign. The other was 'to decide at once to declare hostilities against His Majesty, and frighten or beat him into reason.' He himself, he acknowledged, favoured the second course. The late Government of Ava had accepted the Treaty of Yandabo under duress, and always hoped to release itself from its engagements under that treaty. Notwithstanding his own efforts to create good will, there were frequent disputes with the ministers over frontier matters which produced in them a sense of degradation. 'I was considered not only as a spy but as a dictator set over them.' The present king and his party had accused them of yielding too many points to him. Moreover, the present generation in Burma had forgotten the lessons of the late war. They believed strongly in fate, and confidently looked forward to different results in another war. Tharrawaddy himself had told him that they had lost the last war because of the unpopularity of the Minthagyi and his sister, the queen. 'One universal impression therefore exists, not only at Ava but throughout the country, that the present King has determined to declare war against us for the purpose of recovering the territories ceded by the Treaty of Yandaboo and restoring the Empire

[1] Letter of 12 July, paras 41–2.

of Ava to its former extent of power and dominion.'[1] Burney did not think, however, that Tharrawaddy intended to declare war at once, but merely to refuse to acknowledge the treaties; yet at the same time pretend not to have dismissed the British residency, telling its officers they might stay or go as they pleased.

All this of course was written before the arrival of Lord Auckland's letter strongly disapproving of the removal of the residency from Ava. To this Burney replied on 1 August pointing out that had he, or, failing him, Bayfield remained in Ava or followed the king to Kyauk Myaung, the Government of India might conceivably have been kept in touch with events in Burma, but it was most likely that the king would have ignored him, and, in addition, would have made it impossible for him to stay because of difficulties over food supplies, housing, mails, and so on. Then the governor-general would have to withdraw the residency. Rather than face this kind of thing, he himself had chosen to withdraw honourably. This decision, he emphasized, was supported by Bayfield and Richardson, as well as by Blundell, the Commissioner of Tenasserim, Adoniram Judson, the American missionary and Sarkies Manook, the last two having an unrivalled knowledge of the Court of Ava.

Burney's arguments regarding the removal of the residency were not merely unanswerable, but prophetic, for he indicated exactly the methods that were to be used by Tharrawaddy in forcing the final withdrawl of the residency some three years later. In a later letter Burney reported that in accordance with the governor-general's instructions he had written several times to Tharrawaddy informing him of the proposal to send Bayfield to reside at his new capital but his letters had been completely ignored. He had also suggested that Blundell might pay Tharrawaddy a friendly visit; but the king had replied that he would neither invite him nor stop him from coming: he might come if he wished. He or any other English officer might come in the same way as they used to come in the time of his grandfather. The inference was, of course, that no question of treaty rights was involved. Hence, Burney reported, he had not sent Bayfield to attach himself to the Court: he feared that he would not be treated properly.[2]

[1] *Ibid.*, para. 43.
[2] India Secret Consultations, Vol. 8, Burney's letter of 25 August 1837.

Burney had made a fatal mistake in counselling the Government of India to adopt a policy of coercion towards Tharrawaddy. It caused the attention of the Calcutta authorities to be concentrated so much on the question of war that their judgement of the immediate question, that of the impossibility of maintaining a resident at the Burmese capital, was affected. Lord Auckland and two members of his council expressed their unanimous and unequivocal opposition to a war with Burma: no advantage was to be gained from it; it would be an unmitigated evil. Moreover, as Lord Auckland himself pointed out very pertinently, Burney had parted on friendly terms with the king, and had removed the residency voluntarily. The government's view was that Tharrawaddy was not anxious for war immediately: his chief object was to set aside the Treaty of Yandabo without a positive breach of it. The governor-general recognized that after the revolution Burney's position had become very difficult, but thought he was to blame for raising unpleasant topics with the king at a time when he was excited by the success of his coup. He was thus to some extent responsible for the king's provocative speeches. Lord Auckland said he did not attach much weight to the king's unguarded expressions: he felt that Burney should have shown greater reserve, discretion and quiet firmness. Moreover, some of his reports of the king's strong language were secondhand ones transmitted by his clerk Edwards. It was undesireable to send a clerk to confer with the king.

All this was conveyed to Burney in an official letter of 1 September from the Government of India. He was informed that Government unequivocally and decidedly rejected his suggestion of war. He was to avoid any action which might cause the king unnecessary excitement, and refrain from raising questions regarding frontiers. If they were raised by others, he was to insist upon the maintenance of their integrity. Thus he was to avoid controversy unless it was forced upon him. In his communications with the king he was cautioned not to provoke collision, though at the same time to make it clear that the British Government would uphold its rights and resist aggression, but in language 'free from offensive menace'.

This was very severe censure, but was it fair? The governor-general himself apparently had second thoughts on the subject, for in his minute of 29 August he wrote:

The End of a Diplomatic Career

Whilst I remain, on the whole, unsatisfied of his conduct in his communications with the Court, and yet regret that the Residency should have been wholly removed from Ava, still in his firm and active endeavours to check violence and to save life I see much to praise, and (especially upon first and uncertain impressions) I own that I am never disposed to exact a severe responsibility from officers fairly acting (as I must presume Col. Burney to have been) in strange and hazarding dilemmas to the best of their judgement, because my judgement of what was feasible does not entirely co-incide with theirs. I would not therefore, upon the present information, although pointing out the instances in which his proceedings seem to have been obviously injudicious, repeat the strong censure that was conveyed in our former dispatch (dated 1 July) as applicable to the removal of the residency by Col. Burney in the state of things which is in these papers reported to have there existed.

Lord Auckland also, while deprecating war, was not entirely convinced of Tharrawaddy's pacific intentions. He followed up his minute of 29 August by a memorandum dated 8 September providing for the strengthening of the British garrisons along the whole length of the frontiers with Burma from Sylhet in Assam to Moulmein. The king was not to be trusted, he wrote. He was a savage surrounded by the worst of his own subjects, and was strengthening his army and defences. The governor-general therefore greatly feared, he said, that a rupture might be forced upon the Government of India. So the frontier garrisons must be kept ready for both defence and offence.

The irony of the situation is clear. Each side feared an attack by the other. In a later letter Burney mentioned that in September in conversation with him the Rangoon wungyi had said: 'You are all wrong in supposing that the king is going to attack you immediately. He has plenty to do just now in settling his kingdom; but in two or three years hence, when we are better prepared, we shall either ask you to sell us the Tenasserim provinces back, or fight you like men and try to recover them.'[1]

Earlier on, when troop reinforcements were reported to have arrived at Moulmein, the wungyi had written to Burney on the king's instructions asking for reassurance regarding the Government of India's peaceful intentions. He had reported to the king he said, that the troops at Moulmein were intended purely for defence. 'Do not let me fall into an error,' he pleaded, 'but write

[1] ISP, Vol. 8, Cons. of 8 Nov. 1837, no. 5, Burney's letter of 30 Sept.

me a letter and let me know the truth.'[1] In face of reports of this kind, and there were more of them in due course, Burney remained firmly convinced of the need for a policy of intimidation. In his letter of 30 September he repeated his strong recommendation that military action be taken to establish British influence in the country on a more extensive scale. The moment was opportune, he urged, and if the opportunity was missed, the effort would be ten times more difficult and expensive later on. The king should be made to recognize the Treaty of Yandabo, the authority of the Governor-General of India and the British right to have a resident permanently stationed near him. 'To intimidate him and his Court into terms just now', he went on, 'would be most easy when compared with what it will be when the king has reconciled his subjects and increased his means, and when he may take advantage of any occupation which some other power may give our armies in Hindosthan.'

The reference to northern India shows that Burney was aware of the plans to interfere in Afghanistan which exerted such a dominant influence over Lord Auckland's strategic outlook at the time. And his renewed advocacy of military action was made in full awareness of the governor-general's expressed view in his letter of 1 July that he could contemplate no event with greater uneasiness than a rupture with Burma. How then could a man as intelligent as Burney come up with such a proposal at such a time? He must also have known that the experience of the war of 1824–26 exerted a powerful deterrent effect upon Calcutta's thinking about Burma, that the Government of India labelled that war a disaster from the point of view of its cost in lives and money, and that a government with its eyes upon the north-west frontier of India in those days of exceedingly slow transport, would avoid like the plague any risk of getting bogged down again in that unhealthy country. He was, we know, a sick man. In any case he had been far too long in monsoon climates without a break. He had also passed through frightful experiences such as would break most men's nerve, with the residency and its occupants, including his wife and young children, in constant danger of attack. He had had to bear the gibes of the unbalanced, yet still shrewd, Tharrawaddy against the India establishment which he invested with an aura of near-sanctity. His schoolmasterly attempts to

[1] *Ibid., loc. cit.*

bring the Court of Ava to a proper awareness of British greatness and power had been unceremoniously flouted. And in his heart of hearts he must have felt that Tharrawaddy's sins must not go unpunished. He must be made to eat humble pie. Thus the desire to intimidate the Court of Ava must have become an emotional obsession with him. But to continue to advocate it against its complete rejection by the Government of India was the height of unwisdom.

Burney had asked permission to go to Calcutta with the further object of proceeding on furlough to England. This was granted in the Government of India's letter of 4 September. At the same time he was instructed to send Dr. Bayfield to Kyauk Myaung in his capacity as acting-resident. Instead, however, he withdrew the residency to Moulmein leaving Bayfield at Rangoon as officer in charge of British interests there under the authority of the Commissioner of Tenasserim. He explained to the Government of India that he had taken this step because Bayfield was disliked by the king and ministers.

Then having made these arrangements Burney boarded the ship *Mermaid* and sailed for Calcutta, arriving there on 1 November. By the time of his arrival the Governor-General had left Calcutta and was on his way towards the north-west. Burney accordingly was ordered to go to Allahabad to confer with him.[1] Most unfortunately, he was unable to do so; he was too ill to travel. He had to undergo an operation in Calcutta, and when he had recovered from it, the chance of a meeting had been missed. Had he been able to discuss matters with Lord Auckland face to face, one feels that, notwithstanding their difference of view on a number of matters, the misunderstanding which had arisen between them could have been removed. As it was, instead of an interview with Lord Auckland Burney had to explain his position, and defend his actions in writing. And, as we shall see, this was not the way to remove fixed impressions from his lordship's mind. But before coming to a consideration of it there are other matters to be discussed.

In the first place Burney's relations with the Government of India were not improved by the letter he wrote to it soon after his arrival re-iterating the view that 'the most certain mode of persuading the present King and Court of Ava to become safe

[1] ISP, Vol. 8, Cons, 8 Nov. 1837, no. 13.

and friendly neighbours to us, is by intimidating them by a military demonstration, and crippling their power.'[1] But this was not all. While in Rangoon Burney had written to the ministers at the Court of Ava urging them to receive a British officer there. In Calcutta he received their reply which he interpreted as an invitation for him himself to return. The Government of India, however, on receiving his translation of their missive, took strong exception to the tone of his own original letter to the ministers because he had asked them to accept a British officer as a matter of personal solicitation. This, he was told, was unbecoming in the light of the stipulation in the Treaty of Yandabo which entitled the Government of India to make such a demand as of absolute right. It does not seem to have occurred to the Calcutta authorities that to have couched a letter in such terms would have been utterly ineffectual, as Burney had already tried to explain.

They also objected strongly to Burney's action in withdrawing the residency to Moulmein and placing it under the authority of the Commissioner of Tenasserim. Bayfield, they said, should have been left in specific charge of it at Rangoon. They therefore proceeded to annul Burney's arrangement and appoint Bayfield acting-resident under the direct authority of the Government of India. Burney was instructed to inform the ministers of this arrangement and explain to them that the state of his own health would not permit him to resume his duties at the Court of Ava. He was also to tell them that by coming to Calcutta he had ascertained that the views of the British Government were pacific; yet, owing to the reports reaching Calcutta it had become necessary to strengthen the frontier military posts so as to be prepared for any event, and they would remain at this strength until confidence was restored. It was up to the ministers therefore to move the king to testify by acts that he wanted peace to continue.[2] Amid so much hostile criticism of his conduct Burney may have gained at least some small comfort from the reversal in this letter of the previous order that Bayfield was to proceed to the Court of Ava. That was abandoned; as assistant-resident he was to stay in Rangoon. Burney had won that point.

On yet another matter of possible major importance he even received the Governor-General's approval. It was over his rejection of feelers put out by ex-King Bagyidaw asking for British

[1] ISP, Cons. 15 Nov. 1837, No. 2.   [2] ISP, Vol. 8, Cons. 6 Dec. 1837, No. 10.

intervention to replace him on the throne. The first approach to Burney had been made towards the end of May, while he was still in Ava. He had ignored it, hoping to discourage any further approach. The second came after his arrival in Calcutta in the form of a letter from a certain Shwe Dwat, a Burmese Muslim, who had held important offices under the Minthagyi, with whom he had been associated in commercial transactions. Burney turned the matter over to the Government of India enclosing with his report an English translation of Shwe Dwat's letter. No further action was recommended, or taken.

We come now to Burney's answer to the criticisms of his conduct made by Lord Auckland. It was given in a long personal letter to his lordship dated 21 November 1837.[1] 'Unable to proceed immediately to the presence of your lordship,' he begins, 'I beg leave most respectfully to lay before you several circumstances and explanations connected with the late events at Ava and my proceedings there, on which your lordship appears to me to require information such as no one at Calcutta or near you could supply. I would not repair to Calcutta on board His Majesty's ship *Pelonees*, fearing that my departure [from Rangoon] on board a vessel of war might increase the excitement at Ava, which you seemed to deprecate, but I took the first opportunity afterwards of proceeding to Moulmein, and after consulting with Mr. Blundell the Commissioner, and other officers of local experience, hastened to Calcutta. It has been a source of very great disappointment to me, that I did not arrive here before the public service obliged you to proceed to the Upper Provinces. Many points can be explained and impressed on your lordship's attention much better by means of a personal communication, than by official correspondence. I am now lying on my bed from the effects of a surgical operation, and as I know not when I shall recover sufficiently to proceed to the presence of your lordship, which I still most ardently desire to do, I entreat permission to address this letter to you.

Your lordship seems inclined to decide that I provoked and irritated the King of Ava, and that I repeatedly mooted questions of a most unnecessary and impolitic character. I can produce witnesses of the most unimpeachable testimony to assure your lordship that I never once provoked or irritated His Majesty, that I bore with the insolence of his followers and with his own

[1] ISC, Cons. 24 Jan., 1838, no. 4.

remarks, insulting to our Government and Nation, more than most British officers would or could have done, and that in every conversation I had with him, he never displayed anger or personal insult, but was good humoured and even kind, although most firm and determined. On one occasion only, on the evening of the 25 April, he was a little warm from the effects, I believe, of liquor, but even then there was no disposition on his part to be angry with me, or to treat me with personal disrespect. I heard for several days that the present king, after his return from Tsagain, was daily holding forth, in open *durbar* before hundreds of persons, abusing our Government and Nation, avowing his determination to repudiate our treaties, and to have no British Resident near him. Several of his hearers were encouraging him in these opinions, and none dared even hint an objection. I was the only person who could do so. I was requested by his own uncle, the Prince of Mekkhara, to wait as often as I could on the King, as the best mode of preventing the success of mischievous counsels, and I considered myself bound to *seek* for opportunities of teaching him and his Ministers what no one else dared to do, of pointing out to them the impolicy of his language, the irrevocable nature of our treaties, and I did so with prudence and discretion, never, as I said before, provoking and irritating the king, but keeping him always good humoured and willing to hear all that I had to say. Lord William Bentinck on one occasion observed to me that I must go to Ava and act as 'schoolmaster' to the King and Ministers. Surrounded as the King was by a set of violent, reckless and ignorant characters, I always was fearful that from words he might be very easily led into action, and I must submit that there could not have been a more judicious, and politic course of preventing this than that which I adopted.'

Burney dealt next with the criticism of his action in communicating with the king through his clerk Edwards. The interpreter, he said, had always been the recognized organ of communication with the king and ministers. For instance John Canning in 1812 had used his interpreter for this purpose. Edwards, a native of Madras, had been known to him for nineteen years, and as his clerk received a salary of three hundred rupees a month. The Burmese government employed men of much lower status to bring messages to him, Burney. Moreover, Edwards was a great favourite with the king, and for this reason certain young English merchants

The End of a Diplomatic Career 301

were jealous of him, and, he thought, had sent unfavourable reports of him to Calcutta. He was, however, absolutely trustworthy.

Burney then went on to describe the extreme danger the residency was in during the revolution. 'Those who directed that the British Residency should remain at Ava during the progress of a revolution there', he wrote, 'little know, I fear, anything of the history of these Indo-Chinese states. What do these races know or care about the sanctity of an ambassador's character?' And he proceeded to give a number of historical examples of the massacre of foreign missions. 'I was aware of all these historical facts', he commented.

His justification for the removal of the residency to Rangoon must be quoted in full.

I beg your lordship to remember, [he wrote] that *before* I applied to the King for permission to return to Rangoon on account of my health, he had not only expressed his determination to desert the city of Ava, but had distinctly rejected my offer of accompanying him to his new capital, he had publicly denied the substance of the treaties concluded with us in his brother's reign, he had openly broken a solemn promise engaged to me as the representative of the British Government, he had been putting to death in the most cruel manner, and in the immediate vicinity of my house, the most respectable of his brother's officers, who and their friends were all looking to me for protection which I was unable to afford, and there was no law or Government, but all was torture, confiscation and plunder, under the direction of his violent followers, who moreover were openly treating me with insult, and who, to my knowledge, were maliciously instigating the King against me. All the traders entitled to my protection had some weeks before been earnestly advised by me to remove to Rangoon. My presence was no longer of any use in protecting any one of them, if the King desired to injure him as was afterwards seen in the case of the trader Ally Khan.

Then, after quoting his original instructions to leave Ava if treated in a manner unbecoming to his situation, he continued:

Mr. Blundell and other officers, who have visited Ava and possess an intimate knowledge of the language and character of the people, have frankly averred to me that they think that I remained at Ava *too long* and that in my situation they would have quitted it at the commencement of the revolution, as my own judgement and opinions had urged me at the time to do. All the foreign traders also at Rangoon and Ava, with the exception of three or four only who were previously offended with me, have expressed to me their unqualified approbation of the whole of my late proceedings up to the date of my departure from Rangoon. I remained in Ava, however, for more than a month after I had obtained the King's permission to retire, and I am sure, all that passed during that interval proved, that as the King was daily increasing in arrogance, and pretensions until he worked himself into using grossly insulting language towards your lordship, it would have been infinitely preferable for me to have retired from his presence at the period I first intended.

Your lordship also disapproves of my having removed the whole of the Residency from Ava. But I intreat your lordship to recollect that I did not adopt this measure until after the King had again and again openly expressed his determination not to acknowledge our treaties, until after he had denied to have a Resident near him, and had refused to acknowledge your lordship's authority, or the official designation of those accredited by you, and until after he had dictated that no reference should ever be made either to our treaties or to your lordship's name. He had further distinctly refused to acknowledge my Assistant as a public officer, or to allow him to accompany the Court to Kyauk Myaung. He had gone off also with the whole of the Court and public officers 60 miles above Ava, leaving the British Residency to shift for itself at the deserted city of Ava, in which he had just before told me, that he would not be responsible for the safety of any individuals who continued there after his departure. I cannot describe to your lordship the derogatory and undignified situation in which the British Residency was placed at Ava after the King's departure. Not a soul took the slightest notice of us, and all that quarter of Ava in which the Residency was placed was uninhabited and very broken down. Maung Thoung Bo, the officer who was in military charge of Ava, was a notorious robber and bad character. Mendet Men, the officer in civil charge of the town, although he was under the greatest obligations to me, having been released from gaol and six pairs of irons by the late government at my intercession, yet dared not even send me so much as a civil message. My very followers and servants asked me if I, who was known to be of high rank and character, whom the Burmese had known so long, and were under such obligations to, received such treatment at Ava, what could I expect would be the situation and treatment of my Assistant, Dr. Bayfield, if I left him, an officer less known and respected, and of so much lower rank than myself? And here it becomes my duty to avow to your lordship that Dr. Bayfield appeared to me to be personally obnoxious to the King who repeatedly spoke of him to me in a disparaging manner, and who, as well as many of his followers often contemptuously styled him *Tshethema* or Compounder of drugs. Dr. Bayfield with many good qualities is inclined in his conduct towards natives to be proud, and in his too great desire to be considered as a political officer and diplomatic character, he is apt to forget that he is also a Medical officer, and he has been complained of to me as disobliging and unwilling to afford medical aid and attendance to those not belonging to the Residency. Hence he was unpopular with many near the present King, and a tale was even told me of his having once, when in charge of the Residency at Ava, treated the King with slight and *hauteur*. He had also, when I proposed leaving him at Ava, made a remarkable observation to some of my followers, which had excited a great deal of alarm among many of them, and which, although he afterwards said it had been made in jest only, was still a most injudicious and improper speech, calculated to render me yet more unwilling to leave one who could pass such a foolish joke at such a time by himself at Ava. He had observed that I was going to leave him behind to have his throat cut. I really could not have been responsible for his safety from outrage, and had I left him at Ava, and had any outrage been afterwards committed upon him or the Residency, I feel that I should have had a most heavy charge to answer, for your lordship and to my country.

I grieve to learn, since my arrival at Calcutta, that your lordship also disapproves of the terms of my last address to the Ministers at Ava dated 28 September. Your lordship, having given it as your opinion, that you saw little ground to apprehend any serious misunderstanding with the present King of Ava, and having not only condemned in strong language the measure of my removing the Residency from Ava, but distinctly ordered me to send Dr. Bayfield back thither, I naturally considered it was my first duty to try and replace an officer near the King. For the reasons above stated, however, I doubted whether an officer would be able to reach the King or would be suitably treated by him, unless I previously obtained His Majesty's permission to send one up; and indeed, as the Errawadi between Prome and Rangoon had since July become much infested by robbers, who had attacked and plundered several boats and killed an Armenian trader, I could not be responsible for the personal safety of any officer who might attempt to proceed to Ava without the previous consent of his Majesty. When therefore the Burmese Ministers wrote to me to continue to keep the two countries on terms of peace and friendship, I thought an excellent opportunity was afforded to me of accomplishing the object which I desired, and in my reply I told them to 'solicit' the King to allow some English officer to go up and wait upon him, pointing out the obvious advantages of such a measure. The word 'solicit' was the proper one for me to use to the Ministers in requesting them to speak to the King; they themselves would apply to such a communication a far more humiliating term. If however my letter was indiscreet and indiscreetly worded, it was my own, and could not compromise the dignity of your lordship, and perhaps you will consider it of still less importance when you, as I have just learnt, [hear?] that there are grounds for believing that the letter never reached the King.

I have thus, my lord, performed a very painful duty in submitting to you explanations regarding my late proceedings which you condemned upon what I humbly conceive to have been imperfect information. Mr. Blundell has apprised me that his letters from Calcutta stated that your lordship had received opinions at variance from mine from some men of authority at Calcutta. If such is the fact, I entreat your lordship to do me the justice to enquire whether such 'men of authority' possess one tenth of my knowledge and experience of the Burmese character, or whether their competency to form an opinion regarding the present King of Ava could for one moment be compared with mine I assure your lordship that whatever bias I had, was, as all at Ava knew, in favour of the present King, until he broke his faith and assumed the tone of defiance and utter disregard of all engagements with respect to us. He little expected that I should have come under your lordship's displeasure, for he not only offered me a high Burmese title as a reward for my exertions in preventing a rupture between the two countries but sent me word, in reply to my last message, that he was certain I should receive very great credit and honour from your lordship for the whole of my conduct during the late revolution and up to the time of my departure from Ava. So far from expecting that your lordship would have supposed me to be guilty of irritating and provoking the King, I had been apprehending (recollecting the tone of the despatches which I had received immediately before the late revolution, wherein I was censured for not appearing to pursue the Duffa Gam with more rigour, and repeatedly ordered to tell the Court of Ava, that it would be held responsible by the British Government for the acts of that wild chief) that your lordship would have conceived my demeanour towards the King as too lame and conciliatory.

I feel that I am not at present honoured with your lordship's confidence, and with this feeling I know not how I can offer the continuance of my services. My own earnest desire is to return home to Europe on furlough, not only on account of the impaired state of my health, but for some family reasons, and one object of my hastening to Calcutta was to solicit your lordship to send up immediately for Mr. Blundell, Dr. Richardson and other officers of judgement and local knowledge, and examine them and me, for the purpose of collecting substantial materials on which you might safely decide the best course to be adopted with regard to our future relations with Ava. The decision and all the responsibility for it now rest with your lordship. Let me conclude this letter by soliciting your attention to one point only. The present King of Ava is a restless, intriguing character without any proper principle. He occasionally exceeds in liquor, and he is surrounded by a set of reckless and ignorant soldiers of fortune, who are offering to recover Assam, Munipore, Arracan and Tenasserim for him. If in a moment of exhilaration he consents to the proposition of one of these military chiefs, the first we shall hear of it will be the intelligence of an inroad into our territory and the destruction of the lives of a good many of our subjects. The presence of an officer on our part near the King would not prevent such a catastrophe or give us timely notice to prevent it. Few at Calcutta know with what ease the King and Court of Ava always prevented the Resident from gaining intelligence regarding any measure or proceeding of theirs which they desired to keep secret from him. The foregoing observations however are intended to press on your lordship's notice the fact that we cannot for an hour be certain of peace with the present King and Court of Ava. Do not let your lordship believe that the King's remark that his predecessor had committed a blunder in going to war with the British Government, and that his reduction of the shipping duties at Rangoon by a sum of 200 rupees may be taken as proofs of his unwillingness to go to war with us, and of his desire of conciliating us. The remark was understood at the time by Dr. Richardson and Dr. Bayfield, as well as by myself, as intending to condemn the late government for having undertaken a measure which it was incompetent to carry through; and at the very time the King was ordering a reduction in the Rangoon duties he pointed out the circumstance to me as an additional proof of his opinion that the Commercial Treaty was at an end, for, as he pretended, had its provisions still existed, he would have been debarred from making any change at Rangoon. Your lordship also needs to be informed that by the custom of the country the King of Ava remits the whole of the duties for the first year after his accession to the throne. The late king remitted the customs duties at Rangoon for a period of three years after his accession to the throne.

To this appeal Lord Auckland replied through his secretary, H. T. Princep, and in terms of cold formality. In his letter dated 15 December 1837 Princep wrote:

I am directed to state that there is nothing in your present communication to induce the Governor-General to doubt the general correctness of the opinion which he had already formed relative to the transactions in question. His Lordship still thinks it would have been better to have refrained from so readily removing the Residency, and that it would have been more consistent with the resolution which you had formed to part in terms of friendship with the King had you more studiously avoided irritating topics of discussion.

His Lordship is by no means satisfied that you could not with propriety have done so, nor is he aware of any good effect which the spontaneous introduction of such topics could produce. You state that you 'won some of the Kings' more respectable followers who were at first very unwilling that I should touch on these topics, fearful that I should irritate and provoke the King, but who afterwards fully admitted that my representations had done great good.' This, however, I am desired to observe, is not easily reconcilable with what follows, where you state 'I remained at Ava, however, for more than a month after I had obtained the King's permission to retire, and I am sure all that passed during that interval proved that as the King was *daily increasing in arrogance and pretensions until he worked himself into using grossly insulting language towards Your Lordship*, it would have been infinitely preferable for me to have retired from his presence at the period I first intended.

The grounds you assigned for asking permission to repair to Rangoon and for taking the Residency along with you were detailed in your letter of the 24 May last and recapitulated in the 9th paragraph of your letter of the 3 July. The new grounds, which you now assign, chiefly consisting of personal objections to Dr. Bayfield, cannot (whatever weight they may intrinsically possess) at all affect the accuracy of the judgement which was founded upon your original statement.

His Lordship does not deem it necessary to enter into any discussion of the arguments which you have now advanced. Difference of opinion will naturally arise in negotiations of a protracted nature, and His Lordship is always willing to place the best possible construction of the actions of his agents when placed in difficult and embarrassing circumstances. In your own case His Lordship has not failed, while pointing out what he considered might have been a more desirable course of proceeding, to give you ample credit in other respects.

With reference to what is stated in the 7th para. of your letter, I am desired to observe that the Governor-General would be unwilling to interfere with your earnest desire to return to Europe for the reasons assigned, and he wishes me to express his regret that this step should have become necessary partly by reason of the impaired state of your health.

The letter ends with the curt observation that Burney's letter should have been addressed to Mr. Princep.[1]

It was a shabby reply. One wonders how much of Burney's epistle his lordship had bothered to read. Some of it, at least, because of the reference to Burney's remarks about Bayfield. Mr.

---

[1] *Loc. cit.* no. 5.

The End of a Diplomatic Career

Desai has rightly described Burney's arguments in his letter as 'unanswerable'.[1] Obviously the residency could not have remained at derelict Ava. Burney knew Tharrawaddy well enough to realize that the move from it was final. He would soon find that a new capital in the Shwebo area was utterly impracticable and abandon the scheme. But he would never return to Ava. Hence it was useless for the residency to remain there. Equally it would have been useless to attempt to follow Tharrawaddy, for the reasons detailed by Burney. Where else then but to Rangoon could it have gone? Short of war, and that was out of the question, Tharrawaddy held all the best cards. But Lord Auckland was too ignorant of the Burmese scene to realize the force of Burney's arguments.

Burney, however, must bear some of the blame for the position in which he was placed. It was the height of unwisdom to advocate the use of force, and even the threat of it, to bring Tharrawaddy to his senses, and when the proposal was summarily turned down, to continue to harp upon it, and warn the Government of India that the king would one day attempt to recover his kingdom's lost provinces. Even as late as 16 January 1838 he wrote another letter of warning to the Government of India, claiming that its overwhelming desire to keep the peace with this ambitious and self-sufficient ruler offered no security for the continuance of friendly relations, and that the office of resident at his capital would be unenviable and useless. He said that he had studied Tharrawaddy and knew him to be 'one who entertains opinions and harbours designs that may one day render him a very formidable and troublesome neighbour to us'.

There was some truth in this. Indeed, the history of the subsequent attempts to re-establish the British Residency show his words on that score to have been prophetic. But did he take Tharrawaddy's intentions too seriously? Was the king as dangerous as he suggested? In the light of subsequent events the answer must be in the negative. For all his brave words, Tharrawaddy was to show that he was much too aware of British power ever to challenge Calcutta to another trial of strength. Nor did he send embassies either to Calcutta or to London to denounce the treaties. But this did not prevent him from indulging in every trick of brinkmanship that would keep the British authorities constantly on the alert. Throughout his reign war with Burma was anathema to the

[1] *Op. cit.*, p. 324.

Government of India; he may have realized this and traded upon it. A time was to come, however, when his incompetent son, Pagān Min, was to play into the hands of those who believed, like Burney, that a showdown with Burma had become essential, and careful study of Lord Dalhousie's minutes on Burma in 1852 shows that it was not merely what happened to Captains Lewis and Sheppard that made him decide on one. That was merely the last straw, though, while this explains, it does not justify his action. So far as Burney was concerned, it seems pretty evident that the Governor-General's fear of having trouble with Burma on his hands when his whole attention was directed elsewhere, was the overriding reason for his grossly unfair treatment of a brilliant and devoted servant of the East India Company. Yet with a little more diplomacy on Burney's part in his dealings with Calcutta, how different the result could have been. One feels that, as in the case of his relations with Governor Fullerton of Penang, he was a little too schoolmasterly in his attitude. He seems to betray the arrogance of the one who feels he can speak with authority towards the ignorant. It was a pity, for he must have been horribly hurt by the treatment he received. He deserved so much better.

Epilogue

BURNEY the orientalist.
So ended Burney's diplomatic career. On 8 March 1838 he relinquished charge of his office as resident and left for England on the Barque *Cornwall*. In England he lived at a house in Hamilton Terrace, St. John's Wood, London. While he was on furlough his aunt, Fanny Burney, Madame d'Arbly, died on 6 January 1840. He had been appointed her executor and attended her funeral. In April 1842 he returned to Calcutta and resumed military duties as general officer to the 28th Native Infantry. In the following year on 23 March he was transferred as general officer to the 5th Native Infantry. Soon afterwards his health broke down and he was given sick leave. On his way home to England he died at sea on 4 March 1845 on the ship *Maidstone*. He was 53 years old.

A very warm appreciation of Burney's services to oriental studies was presented at the anniversary meeting of the Royal Asiatic Society in London on 16 May 1846 and subsequently published in the Society's *Proceedings* for that year. Strangely enough, it begins with a curious geographical error: it refers to his excellence in several oriental languages, 'particularly those of the Eastern Archipelago, where on account of his peculiar qualification he resided during the greater part of his Indian service'. The writer might perhaps be excused if, without consulting a map, he assumed that Prince of Wales Island was in the archipelago, but to include Siam and Burma in the same category is somewhat confusing, though not quite inexplicable when one remembers that the stock joke, when referring to Burma fifty years ago was that most people confused it with Bermuda. On the subject of Burney's mission to Siam the article comments on his remarkable achievement in securing the liberation and repatriation of 1,400 Burmese captives from that country, but has nothing to say about his treaty. The hope is expressed that his account of his mission would be soon published, since 'no account could be more authentic or more comprehensive'. One wonders whether the writer of the article knew of John Crawfurd's book on his own mission to Siam. He writes that the Society's Council had resolved to make enquiries 'in the proper quarter' to ascertain what the situation was with regard to publication, and to offer any help within its power towards that object. The Burney MSS in the keeping of the Royal Commonwealth Society contain an autograph letter of 11 November 1841 to the Court of Directors of the East India Company from Burney asking permission to publish his Journal together with such commercial and other information as he thought might be of interest to the public. 'I shall take every care to commit no breach of diplomatic confidence', he writes, 'but the time which has elapsed since that mission took place leads me to believe that it would not be possible for me to make any disclosures that could now inconvenience the public service in any way.'[1] Permission was granted, but the book was not published; nor did anything come of the Royal Asiatic Society's move. Examination of the Siam papers in the collection suggests that too much editorial work remained to be done when Burney died for publication to be put in hand. Besides a MS copy of the Journal there are uncollated notes in good number in Burney's handwriting, but no indication of the use he intended to make of them.

The R.A.S. article next describes Burney's connexion with Burma, first as Deputy Commissioner in the Tenasserim Provinces, and later as British Resident at the Court of Ava. 'During this period,' it says, 'it devolved upon him to discuss with the Burmese Government many delicate and important points, in all which he won the confidence and esteem of that Government, as well as of his own, by a conscientious and firm, though conciliating, advocacy of the just pretensions of either.' The chairman of the meeting, it is worth noting, was none other than the Earl of Auckland, who was the Society's President at the time. Was his advice sought concerning the wording? Then the article proceeds: 'Nor was his attention restricted to his official duties; with his characteristic zeal he instituted and promoted various inquiries into the history, geography and antiquities of the Kingdom of Ava, by which our knowledge of that Kingdom, and of the countries lying between it and Bengal, has been greatly improved, and he was an industrious contributor to the Journal of the Asiatic Society of Bengal.' And this is followed by a list of his contributions. The article gives no inkling of the fact that Burney had been in effect dismissed the Company's political service.

Burney's earliest publications were in a journal entitled *Gleanings from Science*, which appeared monthly in Calcutta during

[1] Listed as D XXIX in the catalogue.

the years 1829–31. They were in fact extracts from his official despatches passed on to the journal for publication by George Swinton, the Chief Secretary to the Government of India. They include two notes on the climate of Ava published in vol. II and III respectively, the second of which contains a meteorological diary kept by him from 25 June 1830 to 8 March 1831. There are also notes on fossils and minerals found in Burma, specimens of which he had forwarded to the Government of India,[1] a note on the spelling of the names mentioned in Dr. Richardson's account of his journey from Moulmein into the Laos country,[2] and an account of the Chinese caravans which annually visited northern Burma.[3]

In January 1832 *Gleanings from Science* was superseded by the *Journal of the Asiatic Society of Bengal*, and in the first number of the new journal there was an announcement that Major Burney had presented the Society with a further supply of minerals from Burma. The descriptive list includes his notes on the Burmese methods of assaying silver and of washing for gold dust in small streams. On 6 March of that year a paper by him entitled 'Some Account of the Lacquered or Japanned Ware of Ava' was read at a meeting of the Society's Physical Class.[4] With it he submitted specimens of the ware and of the materials used in making it, fifty-two items in all, which were placed in the Society's museum. His paper contains explanations of the many Burmese technical terms employed in the industry. Included also in the first volume is an extract from one of his letters published under the title 'Memoir of Giuseppe d'Amato'. It tells the story of a missionary belonging to the *De Propaganda Fide* Society, whose acquaintance he had made at Ava, and offers valuable information about Catholic missions in Burma. Thus it describes the group of *Bayingyi* (Bur. for *Feringhi*) villages in Dibayin district, near Moksobomyo, where dwelt the descendants of the French captives taken by King Alaungpaya at the capture of the Mon port of Syriam in 1756, when engaged upon the reduction of the Kingdom of Pegu.[5]

Of perhaps greater interest to the historian are the two notes in this volume relating to the Burmese chronicles. One deals with an outbreak of cholera in the city of Ava in 1706 as recorded in 'the

[1] Vol. III.   [2] Vol. II.   [3] Vol. III.
[4] Vol. I, pp. 169–82. and in *Transactions* of the RAS Vol. II.
[5] See D. G. E. Hall, 'The Tragedy of Negrais', Supplement to *Early English Intercourse with Burma, 1587–1743*, second edition, London, 1968, pp. 322–3; and G. E. Harvey, *History of Burma*, pp. 145–6.

21st volume of the Burmese History'; the other records that at the Society's meeting on the 7 November 1832 parts of a letter from Burney on the subject of Burmese historical records were read. What he had to say about them is not mentioned. The Royal Asiatic Society's obituary article tells us that he 'first brought to notice the existence of voluminous records of Burmese history, one extending to thirty volumes, and another revised and continued by order of the reigning prince in 1839'. The reference must be to U Kala's *Maha Yazawin* (Great Chronicle) compiled in 1724, and to the *Hmannan Yazawin*, (Glass Palace Chronicle), compiled by order of King Bagyidaw in 1829, not 1839, as stated in the article. In his book on his mission to Ava published in 1829 John Crawfurd had drawn attention to the fact that Burma possessed historical writings. In his chapter on Burmese history he writes: 'The Burmese are not absolutely destitute of historical compositions, and I am indebted to translations of some of their narratives for a few of the details about to be given.' The translations were made for him by Dr. Judson, and the chief document used, 'a long scroll of paper folded zig-zag', had been captured by British troops in a Burmese stockade during the war.[1] But from what he has to say about Burmese history it is doubtful if he was aware of the chronicles themselves; and he knew no Burmese, unlike Burney. The latter indeed right from the outset of his stay at Ava was faced with the need to search for evidence regarding the Burmese claim to the Kabaw Valley, and we may be sure that his friend Maung Sa would have shown him where to look for it.

In volumes IV, V, and VI of the *Journal of the Asiatic Society of Bengal* Burney went on to publish further articles based upon his researches into the chronicles. One in Vol. IV is entitled 'Notice of Pagan the Ancient Capital of the Burmese Empire'. This is a translation with introduction and notes by Burney of the account in *The Glass Palace Chronicle* of the Tartar conquest of Pagān at the end of the thirteenth century. With the paper, we are told, was submitted a drawing of the city by Mrs. Burney showing the famous Ananda Temple, but unfortunately for the lack of space this could not be reproduced.

In Vol. V is an article entitled 'Discovery of Buddhist Images with Devanagari inscriptions at Tagaung, an Ancient Capital of the Burmese Empire'.[2] The images were discovered by Captain

[1] 1832 edn, vol. II, pp. 272-3.   [2] pp. 157-64.

S. F. Hannay, the officer commanding the resident's escort, while on his mission to the Burma-Assam frontier in November 1835 with the Burmese Governor of Mogaung. These were received at a meeting of the Society on 6 April 1836, and Burney's paper, giving the chronicle account of the history of Tagaung, was read. In the report of this meeting there is a note as follows: 'A drawing of the full size of the sculptured impression of Gautama's foot in Ava was presented by Ensign Phayre, with a description of the several compartments'.[1] Many years later in 1883 Sir Arthur Phayre, long retired from the Chief Commissionership of British Burma, was to publish the first full-scale history of Burma in the English language. It is based mainly upon the chronicles, and in his Preface Phayre quotes Burney's opinion that they 'bear strong internal marks of authenticity'.[2] On the other hand he gives pride of place as the discoverer of their existence and value to Dr. Francis Buchanan, who accompanied Michael Symes on his mission to Ava in 1795, and at one time contemplated producing a translation of the *Maha Yazawin*, 'The Great History of the Kings'. Phayre tells us also that Raffles's friend, Dr. John Leyden, had drawn attention to the importance of the chronicle writings of both Burma and Arakan. Nevertheless, through the extensive use he made of them, Burney may fairly claim to have been the real pioneer in the exploration of the chronicles. He was the first to give practical demonstration of their importance.

His article entitled 'Some Account of the Wars between Burmah and China' is by far his weightiest contribution to the Journal.[3] He traces the history of Sino-Burmese relations from the earliest times to the exchange of embassies in 1833-4. From the middle of the eighteenth century he treats the subject in detail, with many translations of original material. His account of the Chinese invasions of Burma in the years 1765-9, based on Burmese sources, is in striking contrast to the Chinese version of the war written by the Kuomintang propagandist T'eng Tch'ong in his *Ming te* and translated by Siguret in the second volume of his *Territoires et Populations des Confins du Yunnan*.[4] Burney's story of the peace negotiations at Kaungton on the upper Irrawaddy at the end of that war, and his verbatim translation of the *Hmannan Yazawin* account of the agreement concluded there on 31 December 1769

[1] p. 190.   [2] pp. v-vi.   [3] Vol. VI, pp. 121-49, 405-51, 542-59.
[4] Peiping, 1937, pp. 144-52.

by the generals of both sides is of special interest for in the discussions between Britain and China arising out of the Anglo-Burmese war of 1885 the Chinese claimed that Burma was a vassal state pledged to offer tribute to Peking every ten years. The Burmese ministers of the Hlutdaw at Mandalay, on the other hand, when their opinion on the subject was sought by the British, denied categorically that Burma had ever been subordinate to China or had ever paid tribute. They took their stand upon the Kaungton agreement, which, they claimed, was one of friendship only. And they pointed to the fact that no mission bearing the customary letter and presents to the emperor of China, as laid down in the agreement, was ever sent except in response to one from China. Burney's translation of the operative part of the Kaungton agreement runs: 'And suitably to the establishment of the gold and silver road, as well as agreeably to former custom, the princes and officers of each country shall move their respective sovereigns to transmit and exchange affectionate letters on gold, once every ten years.'[1] And in Phayre's *History* of 1883 the agreement is described in almost identical terms.[2]

Burney's accounts of the missions between Ava and Peking after the Kaungton agreement begin with his translation of the record in 'the 33rd volume of the Burmese chronicles' of the reception on 3 April 1787 of a Chinese embassy by King Bodawpaya.[3] This is followed by 'a free translation' of the journals and routes of the Burmese missions to Peking in 1787, 1823 and 1833. Each, he shows, was sent in response to a mission from China. He provides English translations of the official correspondence between the two monarchs. He tells us that in the case of those from the emperor of China he has used the official Burmese translations made by a group of Chinese and Burmese interpreters. The emperor refers to himself as 'elder brother' and to the king of Burma as 'younger brother'. The king, after a tremendous parade of his own titles, addresses the emperor by name, and, in Burney's words, 'besides not acknowledging the fraternity claimed by China', styles him simply 'royal friend', and deliberately omits the customary respectful particle 'ba', although employing it in the Burmese translation of the imperial missive.

Burney's translations of the journals kept by the Burmese envoys are of unusual interest. 'I have procured copies of the

[1] JASB VI p. 147.   [2] p. 202.   [3] Vol. VI. pp. 408–13.

routes', he writes of the missions of 1823 and 1833, 'and of most of the reports submitted by each to the king'; and of the 1823 mission, 'Two or three years ago, at my request, the ministers of Ava kindly made the subordinate envoys draw up an abstract of the report they had sent in, and I now give a translation of it.' The envoys put down not only the details of their journeys but much else besides. 'When you reach Pekin', run the instructions to the 1833 envoys, 'observe and record everything carefully and unreservedly. You must note and bring back with you, after making enquiries secretly and ascertaining, what the Emperor of China worships in order to obtain *Neibban*; what he practises and worships in order to obtain the advantages in this world; as well as an account of his queens, concubines, kinsmen, children, nobles and officers, and of their equipage, dress and ceremonies, with a map and description of China and Tartary.'[1] And their reports show that they carried out the task meticulously.

This study, like most of Burney's other publications, was made possible through the co-operation of the ministers of the Court of Ava. They afforded him every possible assistance in the collection of his research materials. Another impressive example of this, mentioned in an earlier chapter, may be recalled. The East India Company's *India Political Consultations* contain a document entitled 'Account of the Burmese Mission, which resided in Bengal from December 1830 to July 1833, compiled from the reports made by the envoys to the Court of Ava and other Burmese documents by Lt. Col. H. Burney, Resident in Ava'. It is dated Rangoon 17 September 1834, and runs to no less than 124 folio pages.[2] Since the great bulk of the records of the Court of Ava has been lost, these faithful compilations of Burney's are of unique value to the historian. His own splendid collection of Burmese manuscripts, which he presented to the East India Company's library, contains a large proportion of writings on Buddhism. He himself became much interested in Burmese Buddhism as the extensive and scholarly notes on the subject in his own handwriting in the royal Commonwealth Society's collection of his papers bears evidence. The India Office collection also includes the Burmese materials which he used in his study of the Kabaw Valley question, with much annotation and translation in his handwriting.

Bagyidaw's court produced *The Glass Palace Chronicle*, one of

[1] *Ibid.*, pp. 544–5.   [2] Vol. 79, Cons. of 6 July 1835, no. 18.

the great works of Burmese literature, and the Burney papers provide much evidence of its high standards of scholarship before Tharrawaddy's barbarities summarily removed its best men, including the Myawaddy Wungyi, Maung Sa, from the scene. The Royal Commonwealth Society's Burney collection contains a note from the distinguished Sanskrit scholar, Horace Hayman Wilson, asking Burney to procure for him a Pali grammar and vocabulary from the Court Brahmans, 'if possible,' he writes, 'transcribed into Bengali or Nagari characters'. And there is one from Dr. Adoniram Judson recommending a Pali dictionary, which, he says, is 'the only one that has ever obtained currency among the learned of this country', and, he explains, 'it is precisely the Sanscrit Amera Kosha, adapted to the Pali dialect and written in the modern Burman character. This work could be of inestimable use to any Sanscrit scholar, who should desire to investigate the Pali language through the medium of Burman.' Presumably an adaptation of this work is the one referred to in the Royal Asiatic Society's obituary article wherein we are told: 'A Dictionary of Pali, with explanations in Sanskrit and Bengali, was also compiled by his desire a copy of which is now [1846] deposited in the Bodleian Library at Oxford.' Mention has been made earlier of Dr. Bayfield's 'Historical Review of the Political Relations between the British Government in India and Ava', which was published as a supplement to R. B. Pemberton's *Report on the Eastern Frontier of British India* (Calcutta, 1835) and of the fact that the compilation was undertaken at Burney's suggestion. The obituary article, it may be pointed out, wrongly attributes the authorship of the work to Burney himself with Bayfield's aid. Reference has been made above[1] to the nature of Bayfield's 'Historical Review' in so far as the pre-1830 period of Anglo-Burmese relations is concerned, and obviously, Burney in examining the document before publication, was in no position to check up on Bayfield's treatment of his source material for this period. Unfortunately, however, his errors have shown notable powers of persistence.[2]

Lastly, two entries in volume VI of the *Journal of the Asiatic Society of Bengal* record the Society's acceptance of Burney's recommendation that it sponsor the publication of the English-

---

[1] pp. 357–8.
[2] On this point see my *Michael Symes, Journal of his Second Embassy to the Court of Ava in 1802*, Introduction, Section 1.

Burmese dictionary which was in course of preparation by the Mekkhara Prince and the English merchant, Charles Lane, when he first arrived at Ava.[1] In 1836 the prince, a man of unusually wide learning, was elected an honorary member of the Society.

The journal *Asiatic Researches*, published in Calcutta, contains an article by Burney entitled 'Translation of an Inscription in the Burmese Language discovered at Buddha Gaya in 1833'.[2] The inscription had been discovered by the Burmese mission to India whose adventures in search of the Governor-General Burney describes in his account of the mission referred to above.[3] It was fixed upside down in a wall. They took facsimiles of it and brought them to Calcutta, where they were studied by James Princep among others. He published an article on them in the *Journal of the Asiatic Society of Bengal*, 'Translation of an inscription in the Pali character and Burmese Language on a stone at Buddh Gia in Behar'.[4] It was then taken to Ava and examined by the Burmese scholars who had compiled *The Glass Palace Chronicle*. The results of their labours have been summed up by Gordon Luce in his paper 'A Century of Progress in Burmese History and Archaeology.'[5] He writes: 'A fair measure of agreement about the general sense was reached with considerable error of interpretation; but the Burmese Envoys and the Ava scholars insisted on reading the dates 467 and 468 Burmese Era, while Ratna Paula and Princep read them 667 and 668. The correct reading is 657 and 660.'

It was to be a long time before further progress was to be made along the lines so enthusiastically laid down by Henry Burney. Arthur Phayre was to be his closest successor; but his pioneer *History of Burma*, based upon the chronicles, did not appear until 1883. The biggest expansion and progress in Burmese studies came only after the annexation of Upper Burma in 1886. In 1910 the Burma Research Society was founded by J. S. Furnivall and U May Oung to bring Burmese and British scholars together in common efforts for the advancement of learning. Its founder members were inspired by the same spirit of enquiry as had actuated Burney some three-quarters of a century earlier, when he had made the Ava Residency a veritable centre of research. His links with Adoniram Judson, the lexicographer, the Mekkhara Prince

[1] pp. 78, 705. [2] Vol. 20, pt 1, 1836 pp. 161–189. [3] p. 450.
[4] Vol. III, no. 29, May 1834, pp. 214–15 and Plate XVI.
[5] JBRS, Vol. XXXII, Pt 1, Dec. 1948, pp. 79–94

and the Myawaddy Wungyi, today famous for his contributions to Burmese literature and music, could have been immensely fruitful under happier circumstances, had not the Ava revolution of 1837 with all its woeful consequences brought such activities to a sudden stop and Burney's connexion with Burma to an end.

A century later another cataclysm, the Japanese invasion of 1942, brought a temporary halt to the scholarly activities of the Burma Research Society in close co-operation with the University of Rangoon, which had been founded in 1920. Under the joint aegis of these two bodies, notwithstanding the opposition of the growing nationalist movement to the British connexion, Asian and Western scholars in co-operation achieved great advances in cultural studies relating to Burma, and notably in the fields of language studies and archaeology. The Burmese dictionary project, launched by J. A. Stewart and C. W. Dunn, both of the Indian Civil Service, is a striking illustration of this point, involving, as it has done, the co-operation of no less than 150 Burmese scholars, and today under the direction of Professor Hla Pe of London University's School of Oriental and African Studies. In archaeology even more striking results have been achieved which have revolutionized the study of Burma's distant past and vastly expanded our knowledge of it. In this connexion one thinks especially of Charles Duroiselle, U Mya, U Lu Pe Win and Gordon Luce, to name only the more prominent researchers in the field. But these are only a couple of examples out of many of the revival of the Burney spirit during the last days of British rule in Burma.

During his furlough in England after relinquishing the post of Resident at the Court of Ava, Burney produced one further study based upon Burmese materials. On 4 December 1841 he read a paper entitled 'On the Statistics of the Burmese Empire' to the Royal Asiatic Society. This was followed in January 1842 by an article entitled 'On the Population of the Burman Empire' in the *Journal of the Statistical Society* Vol. IV, pp. 335–47. Just under a century later this was reproduced in facsimile in the *Journal of the Burma Research Society*, Vol. XXXI, part 1, 1941 January, pp. 19–33 with a brief introduction by the late G. E. Harvey. For it he used Burmese records deposited in the Palace archives at Ava, copies of which, secretly transcribed, he had managed to obtain. They relate to King Bodawpaya's census of 1783 and the one ordered by King Bagyidaw in 1826. Burney discusses the methods used in compiling each census, comparing them with those used by the British in Tenasserim after its annexation, and their results with the various estimates made by Symes, Cox, Canning, Crawfurd and Malcolm, none of whom, of course, knew Burmese. It is a very valuable piece of work and offers what must be the closest estimate possible under the circumstances.

Bibliography

ANDERSON, John, *Political and Commercial Considerations relative to the Malayan Peninsula and the British Settlements in the Straits of Malacca*, Prince of Wales Island, 1824. Facsimile reprint with Introduction by J. S. Bastin, JRASMB XXV, iv, Dec. 1962.

ANDERSON, John, *Mission to the East Coast of Sumatra in 1823*, Edinburgh, 1826.

BEGBIE, P. J., *The Malayan Peninsula*, Vepery, 1834. Reprinted Kuala Lumpur, OUP, 1967.

BIGANDET, Bishop, *An Outline of the History of the Catholic Burmese Mission, 1720–1887*, Rangoon, 1887,

BOWRING, Sir John, *The Kingdom and People of Siam, with a narrative, of the Mission to that Country in 1885*, 2 vols., 1857.

The Burney Papers, reprinted from the originals in the India Office, Bangkok, Vagiranana National Library, 1910–14.
— Reprinted with an Introduction by D. K. Wyatt, 5 vols., Farnborough, Gregg International Publishers, 1971.

CADY, John F., *A History of Modern Burma*, Ithaca, New York, 1960.

COWAN, C. D., 'Early Penang and the Rise of Singapore, 1805–1832', JRASMB, XXIII, 2 (March 1950).

CRAWFURD, John, *Journal of an Embassy from the Governor-General of India to the Court of Ava in the year 1826*, London, 1829; Second edn, Edinburgh, 1833, 2 vols.

CRAWFURD, John, *Journal of an Embassy from the Governor-General of India to the Courts of Siam and Cochin-China*, London, 1828.

CRAWFURD, John, *History of the Indian Archipelago*, 3 vols, Edin., 1820.
— *A Descriptive Dictionary of the Indian Islands and Adjacent Countries*, 2 vols, London, 1856.
— *The Crawfurd Papers: a Collection of Official Records relating to the Mission of Dr John Crawfurd sent to Siam by the Government of India in the year 1821*, Bangkok, 1915.

DESAI, W. S., 'History of the Burma Indemnity, 1826–1833', JBRS XXIV, Dec. 1934.
— 'The Rebellion of Prince Tharrawaddy and the Deposition of Bagyidaw King of Burma, 1837', JBRS, XXV, iii, Dec. 1935.
— 'The History of the Burmese Mission to India, 1830–1833' JBRS XXVI, ii, August 1936.

— *The History of the British Residency in Burma, 1826-1840*, Rangoon. 1939; reprinted Gregg International, Farnham, 1972.

DHANI NIVAT, H. H. Prince, 'The Old Siamese Conception of the Monarchy', JSS 36, 2, 1947.

— 'The Reconstruction by Rama I of the Chakri Dynasty', JSS 43, 1955.

FINLAYSON, G., *The Mission to Siam and Hue*, London, 1826.

FYTCHE, Albert, *Burma Past and Present*, 2 vols, London, 1878.

GRAHAM, W. A., *Siam*, 2 vols., London, 1924.

HALL, D. G. E., *A History of South-East Asia*, 3rd edn, London, 1968.

— 'Henry Burney's Comments on the Court of Ava', BSOAS, XX, i and ii, 1957.

— 'Henry Burney, Diplomat and Orientalist' JBRS XLI, Dec. 1958.

— 'R. B. Pemberton's Journey from Munipoor to Ava and from thence across the Yooma Mountains to Arracan (14 July-1 October 1830)' JBRS XLIII, ii, December 1960.

HARVEY, G. E., *History of Burma*, London, 1925.

KENNEDY, J., *A History of Malaya*, London, 1962.

The Konbaungset Chronicle, Mandalay, 1905.

LUCE, Gordon H., 'A Century of Progress in Burmese History and Archaeology', JBRS, XXXII (1948).

— *Old Burma, Early Pagan*, Locust Valley, 1969-70.

LAURIE, W. F. B., *Our Burmese Wars and Relations with Burma*, London, 1880.

MALCOLM, Howard, *Travels in South-Eastern Asia*, 2 vols., London, 1839.

MARSHALL, Lieut. John, R.N., *Narrative of the Naval Operations during the Burmese War in the years 1824, 1825 and 1826*, London, 1830.

MILLS, L. A., *British Malaya 1824-1867*, JMBRAS, III, ii, 1925.

— *British Malaya, 1824-67*, edited for reprinting with a bibliography by C. M. Turnbull and with a new introductory chapter on European influence in the Malay Peninsula, 1511-1786 by D. K. Bassett, Singapore, 1961 (JRASMB, XXXIII, 3, 1960).

NEWBOLD, T. J., *British Settlements in the Straits of Malacca*, with an Introduction by C. M. Turnbull, 2 vols., Kuala Lumpur, 1971.

PEARN, B. R., *Judson of Burma*, London, 1962.

PEMBERTON, R. B., *Report on the Eastern Frontier of British India*, with a supplement by G. T. Bayfield, 'Historical Review of the Political

Relations between the British Government in India and the Empire of Ava ... to the end of the year 1834', Calcutta, 1835. Reprinted, Department of Historical and Antiquarian Studies in Assam, Gauhati, 1966.

PEARN, B. R., 'Felix Carey and the English Baptist Mission in Burma', JBRS, XXVIII, 1938.

— *A History of Rangoon*, Rangoon, 1939.

PHAYRE, Sir Arthur P., *History of Burma*, 1883.

QUARITCH WALES, H. G., *Siamese State Ceremonies, their History and Function*, London, 1931.

— *Ancient Siamese Government and Administration*, London, 1934; reprinted New York, 1965.

RICHIE, A. I., *Lord Amherst and the British Advance Eastwards to Burma*, Oxford, 1909.

SCHOLES, Percy A., *The Great Doctor Burney*, 2 vols., London, 1948.

SIGURET, J, *Territoires et Populations des Confins du Yunnan*, Peiping, 2 vols., 1937, 1940.

SKINNER, William S., *Chinese Society in Thailand*, Ithaca, N.Y., 1957.

TARLING, N., 'British Policy in the Malay Peninsula and Archipelago', JMBRAS, XXX, 3, 1957.

VELLA, W. F., *Siam under Rama III, 1824–51*, Locust Valley, N.Y., 1957

WAYLAND, F., *A Memoir of the Life and Labours of the Rev. Adoniram Judson, D.D.*, 2 vols., London, 1853.

WENK, Klaus, *The Restoration of Thailand under Rama I, 1782–1809*, Tucson, Arizona, 1968.

WILSON, H. H., *Documents Illustrative of the Burmese War with an introductory Sketch of the War and an Appendix*, Calcutta, 1827 (N.B. The Appendix contains Burney's despatches from Bangkok).

WINSTEDT, Sir R. O., *A History of Malaya*, Singapore, 1935.

WOOD, W. A. R., *A History of Siam*, London, 1926; Bangkok, 1933.

WOODMAN, Dorothy, *The Making of Burma*, London, 1962.

WYATT, David, 'Family Politics in Nineteenth Century Siam' JSEAH 1968.

YULE, Sir Henry, *A Narrative of the Mission to the Court of Ava in 1855*, London, 1858.

— *A Narrative of the Mission to the Court of Ava in 1855 together with the Journal of Arthur Phayre*, with an Introduction by Hugh Tinker, Kuala Lumpur, O.U.P., 1968.

INDEX

INDEX

Index

Akyab, 190, 220, 221
Alaungpaya, King, 1752-1759, 67; 'embryo Buddha', 191, 272, 287
Amarapoora, 84; regatta at, 219
American Baptist Missionaries, 273, 290
Amherst, Lord, Gov.-Gen. of India, 117, 157, 164, 182
Amherst (town), 182
An Pass, in Arakan Yoma, 217
Anderson, John, 20, 28, 129-31, 158
Anglo-Burmese War 1824-1826, 20, 21, 23, 50, 62, 64, 86, 119, 131, 133, 171, 174, 191, 263
Anglo-Chinese relations, 263
Arakan, 174, 175, 176, 177, 186, 189
Armenian community, 256
Assam, 174, 176, 263, 264, 287, 288
Atwinwun, 192, 194, 198, 201
Auckland, Lord, 229, 290-8; letter to Burney, 305-306
Ava, capital of Burma, 173, 176, 178-9; saved by Burney, 283, 288-9, 291, 302
Ava, Court of, *ix*, 54, 71, 84, 171, 183
Ayuthaya, capital of Siam 1330-1767, 33, 57, 67, 81, 122, 174

Bagyidaw, King, 190, 195-6, 198, 207; his titles, 203, 223, 231-2; confers title on Burney, 234; Burney converses with, 235; his military measures, 235-7; illness March 1831, 239; popularity, 242, 250, 275, 278, 285, 298, 299, 312
Bagyidaw and Rama III compared, 231
Balmain, Major, 24
Bandula, Maha, 175
Bannerman, Governor of Penang, 6, 10
Bayfield, Dr G. T., 251, 252, 253, 256, 258-61, 276, 284, 286, 287, 291-306
Beesa Gaum, the, 265, 266
Bentinck, Lord William Cavendish, 185, 188, 192, 212, 223, 241, 300
Blundell, E. A., Commissioner of the Tenasserim Provinces, 242, 293, 298-301, 304

Bodawpaya, King of Burma, 4, 32, 177, 195, 255-6
Bo Hmu Wun, Prince, 275, 277
Buddhagaya, 223
Buddha image presented to Bagyidaw by the Government of India, 248
Buddhism, Buddhist Order, 33, 35, 117
Buddhism, Theravada, 36, 54, 64, 66; influence of Ceylon, 172; Pali *Fripitaka*, 172
Bunga mas, 4, 12, 28, 77, 81, 85, 100, 102, 109, 111, 130, 131, 135
Burma Indemnity, 176, 194, 224-30
Burma's silver currency, 225
Burmese deputation to Calcutta, 1827, 185
Burmese embassy to Calcutta, 221ff.; Burney's account of, 222, 242, 246-8
Burney, Fanny, Madame d'Arblay, 242
Burney, Lieutenant George, 193, 202-3, 222
Burney, Henry, *Passim*, *Seriatim*; Phases in career, *ix*; private papers, *x*; Siam and Ava journals, *x*; 'Observations on the Currency of Ava', *x*; 'Report concerning the Commerce of Siam', *x*; 'Account of the Burmese Mission which resided in Bengal from December 1830 to July 1833', *x–xi*, 315; 'Memorandum regarding the Singphos', *xi*; 'Hints regarding the characters of the principal persons at the Court of Ava', *xi*; 'Account of the Trade, etc., of Rangoon', *xi*, 254ff.; 'Account of Ava revolution of 1837', *xii*; early connexion with Penang, 6; marriage, 6; family background, 6-7; birth, 8; arrival in India, 9; reticence regarding private life, 9; Military Secretary at Penang, 6, 12; in Calcutta, 1825, 23; mission to Siam proposed, 25; appointed Political Agent to the Siamese States, 21; official presentation to Rama III, 42ff.; treaty proposals of, 85-6, 89, 94, 102; 'abandons'

Index

Kedah, 99ff.; literary skill, 110; farewell audience of Rama III, 121-2; leaves Siam, 124-5; defends treaty with Siam, 132ff.; comments on Low's activities, 141ff.; visits Raja of Ligor, 148; *Penang Gazette* attacks him, 165; Capt. Lake challenges him, 155; accused of 'private feeling', 162; joins Civil Commission of Tenasserim Provinces, 179; appointed Resident at Ava, 187; his instructions, 192; contrasts Ava and Bangkok, 194-5; character-sketches of personalities at Court of Ava, 195ff.; comments on 'shoe question', 201; reception by King Bagyidaw, 203-4; sick leave in Rangoon, 212; his 'Observations on the Currency of Ava', 225-6; evacuates the Residency over indemnity question, 227-8; His literary style, 231; receives honorific title from King Bagyidaw, 233; correspondence with Governor-General regarding it, 234; announces death of George IV to King Bagyidaw, 235; asks Governor-General's advice in case of a succession struggle at Ava, 240; comments on Bagyidaw's popularity, 242; advocates retrocession of Kabaw Valley, 244-6; advocates removal of Residency to Rangoon, 247-51; abortive attempt to go to England on furlough, 258; proposal to post Bayfield to Rangoon, 259-61; instructions to Captain Hannay, 265-9; translation of the Emperor of China's letter, 267-8; meeting with Tharrawaddy at Moksobomyo, 274-6; account of the ministers' surrender, 278; saves Ava from destruction, 283-9; removes Residency from Ava, 290; recommends hostilities against Tharrawaddy, 292-3, 296-8, 307; arrives in Calcutta, 297; answer to Lord Auckland's criticisms, 299-305; Lord Auckland's reply, 305-6; returns to England, 309; resumes military duties in India, 309; death, 309; Royal Asiatic Society's tribute to him, 309-10; his contributions to *Gleanings in Science*, 309-10, and to the *Journal of the Asiatic Society of Bengal*, 311-15; articles on the Burma census, 318; the Burney spirit, 318

Burney, Janet, wife of Henry, niece of Governor Bannerman of Penang, 6, 312

Burney, Richard, 'Bengal Dick', father of Henry, 7; dies in Rangoon, 8

Burney, Mrs Richard, Jane Ross, mother of Henry, 8

Burney, Richard, elder brother of Henry 8

Bye daik, 198

Campbell, Sir Archibald, 24, 50, 63, 65, 179, 180, 182, 184-6, 201, 234, 246

Canning, Captain John, 177, 178, 319

Chakri, Chao Phraya, Rama I, 46, 48, 52, 171, 174

Chiangmai, Chiengmai, 50, 51, 173, 280

China, Burmese embassies to, 285; embassies to Burma, 314-15

China trade, 5, 264, 267

China, Emperor's letter to King of Burma, 267-8

Chindwin River, 'Ningthee', 212

Chinese at Bangkok, 80; invasions of Burma, 174

Chittagong, 174-5, 178

Chula, Phraya, 47, 48, 79

Chumphorn, 22, 24, 40, 58, 61, 97

Cox, Hiram, 177, 319

Crawfurd, John, 15-18, 23, 24, 37, 42, 81, 117; his chart, 96, 120, 136, 149, 180-2, 194-5, 256, 264, 269, 312, 319

Daffa Gaum, the, 265, 266, 267, 269

Dalhousie, Lord, 308

Deportees, Burmese, 49, 54-62, 63, 68, 97, 121

Desai, W. S., *ix*; tribute to, *xi, xii*; 223, 230, 236, 307

Dhonburi, Taksin's capital, 31

Dupleix, Josef, 67

Dutch, the, Convention of London 1814, 10, 12, 80

Index

Dvaravati, pre-Siam kingdom, 24, 50, 91, 172

East India Company, 9–10, 112, 115, 116, 174; Court of Directors, 257
Edwards, R. S., 237, 271, 276–7, 281, 294, 300–1
Ein-she-min, Heir apparent, 204, 273, 275

Feet, Golden, 176
Fenwick, Captain, 65, 97
Frith, Major, 63
Fullerton, Robert, Governor of Penang, 19–20, 23, 25, 26, 28, 110, 111, 112, 118, 125, 129, 136–8, 151–3, 158, 161, 163, 164, 308

Gambhir Singh, Raja, 175–6
Ganges, H.C. Steamship, 193
Glass Palace Chronicle, 216
Grant, Major F. J., 186, 187, 212, 213, 218, 244–5, 248
Guardian, the brig, 36, 38, 60, 83, 94, 95, 97, 99, 100, 123, 124, 140

Hannay, Captain, 265–9, 312–13
Harris, Sub-Assistant-Surgeon, 36, 61, 74, 96
Hlutdaw, the, 'Lhwottau', 197, 208, 225–7, 229, 230, 233, 258, 271, 281
Hsinbyushin, 'Lord of the White Elephant', 4, 29
Hukawng Valley, 263, 264
Hunter, Robert, 37, 39, 46

India, Governor-General of, 85, 89, 90, 95, 117, 118, 123, 132, 152, 154, 194, 200, 202, 203, 218, 234; minute on Burma's military preparations, 239; rejects Burney's proposal to transfer to Rangoon, 250, 286–7
India, Government of, 103, 106, 120, 144; praises Burney's conduct of mission to Siam, 144–5, 149, 150, 156, 167, 168, 182, 183, 189, 204, 207, 259–61, 264, 266, 298
Irrawaddy River, 172, 175, 194, 282, 303

Jenkins, Captain, 264
Judson, Dr Adoniram, 196, 197, 206, 293, 312, 316, 317
Junkceylon, Ujong Selang, 14, 21–2, 25

Kabaw Valley, 186, 212ff., 221–2, 230, 242–9, 315
Kachin people, 172
Kadaw day, 202
Kalahom, Akka Mahasena, 46, 48, 52, 61
Karen people, 172
Kaunghmudaw Pagoda, 218–19
Kedah, Malay State, 4, 18, 27, 76, 77, 80, 81
Kedah, Sultan of, 4, 12, 13, 19, 25, 28–30, 82, 83, 86–88; Burney's abandonment of, 102–7; 'ex-king', 113, 129, 134, 137, 148–50, 152–6, 165
Kelantan, Malay State, 4, 76, 77, 87, 88, 100, 102, 129, 145
Khatmandu, Nepal, 177
Kinkaid, Rev., American Baptist missionary, 273
Kra, Isthmus of, 22, 23, 32, 98
Kray Kosa, Phraya, 61
Krian River, 149, 150, 152, 153, 155
Kublai Khan, 172
Kurau River, 149, 151, 157, 167
Kurau incident, *xii*, 139, 149, 154, 158, 160, 165
Kyauk-ta-lon, 214, 227
Kyi Wungyi, 206

Lanciago, Mr, 199, 202, 210, 216, 220, 254, 255
Lane, Charles, 192–3, 199–200, 209, 220, 228
Leal, Mr, 36, 61, 65, 74, 96–8
Lhwottau, see Hlutdaw
Light, Francis, 149
Ligor, Raja of, Chao Noi, Chao Phraya Sithammarat, *xii*, 13, 17, 19, 21, 26–30, 36, 46, 48, 68, 71, 74–6, 82, 83, 88, 89, 90, 97, 101, 103, 104, 107, 109, 112, 115, 117, 120, 124, 125, 129, 130, 131, 132, 137, 147, 148, 150–3, 156–9, 160–4, 166, 168
Low, Captain James, 131, 137–9, 148–9, 150, 156–61, 163, 165–6

328 Index

'Lubyus', Bagyidaw's associates, 196
Luce, Gordon H., 172, 317, 318

Macfarquhar, Captain Hugh, 36, 52, 58, 85, 89, 106, 158, 195, 204
Maha Yotha, Chao Phraya, 41, 42, 50, 61, 64, 65, 69, 82, 84, 91, 92, 94, 106
Maingy, Major A. D., Commissioner of Tenasserim, 39, 40, 55, 56, 61, 65, 103, 179–80, 187, 189, 209
Malacca, 3, 77, 145
Malcolm, Rev. Howard, 319
Mandalay, 67
Manipur, 174, 176, 244, 245
Martaban, 22, 24, 41, 42, 50, 51, 65, 68, 70, 71, 97, 176, 180, 188, 189, 212
Maung Baya, 270
Maung Ba Yauk, Kyi Atwinwun, 198–9, 206
Maung Khan Ye, Wundauk, 214, 219, 227, 248
Maung Sa, Myawaddy Wungyi, 199, 206, 207, 210, 214–17, 225–7, 242, 277, 285, 313, 316, 318
Maung Yeet, Shan Atwinwun, 198, 199, 206, 210, 211, 215, 216, 225, 235, 242
Mekkara Prince, the, 200, 207, 276–8, 317
Mergui, 21, 40, 41, 57, 62, 63, 69, 70, 71, 83, 98, 140, 147, 176, 179, 193, 209
Mills, L. A., *ix*, 10–11, 151
Minthagyi, Salin Min, 197–8, 204, 241; becomes regent, 248, 258, 262, 266, 270, 273, 274, 277, 279, 286
Mogaung, 264, 265, 266, 269, 273
Moksobomyo (Shwebo), 272, 280, 282, 287
Mon people, 23, 24, 62, 70; in Siam, 91, 92, 172
Mongkut, Prince Chaota, later King, 34, 96
Moulmein, 182, 185, 188, 193, 295, 298
Muang Mai, 58, 61
Muring Hills, 246, 248
Myawaddy Wungyi, see Maung Sa

Nakhandaw, 198
Nakhorn Sithammarat, 4
Narai, King of Siam, 86
Nguyen, Hué dynasty, 31
Nyaungdaw Sayadaw, 205

Padein Wungyi, 206
Pagān, Burmese capital, 1044–1287, 20, 172, 312
Pagān, Princess of, 270, 271, 274
Pagān Min, King of Burma, 308
Pakchan river, 23
Paklaat, 60
Paknam, 37, 60, 77, 112, 124
Pangnga, Governor of, 21–2, 25
Pantanaw, 69, 133
Pattani, 4, 20, 28, 132
Pegu, city, Mon state, 25, 50, 64, 66, 67, 68, 71, 84; Pegu project, 91, 172–3
Pemberton, Captain R. Boileau, *xii*, 186, 187, 197, 212, 213–20, 221, 248; *Report on the Eastern Frontier of India*, 252, 316
Penang, Prince of Wales Island, Government of, 4, 5, 12–14, 23, 77, 83, 99, 112, 125, 129, 132, 134, 135, 140, 146, 149, 154, 155, 162
Perak, Malay State, tin trade of, 12, 26, 27, 77, 87, 88, 125, 131, 137, 138, 149, 150, 158, 164–7
Perak, Sultan of, 12, 108–10, 150, 156, 157, 158, 159, 165
Phayre, Sir Arthur, 9, 317
Phillips, Governor of Penang, 14
Phrakhlang, The, Dit Bunnag, 34, 37–42, 47, 48, 56, 58, 59, 60, 69, 72, 74, 78, 82, 89, 90, 91, 95, 96, 100–2, 105, 107, 108, 110, 112, 114, 123, 124
Portuguese consul, 37, 56, 119
Prinsep, H. T., 305, 306, 317
Prince of Wales Island, see Penang
Prome, 68, 175

Queen Mai Nu of Burma, 194, 196–7, 204–6, 279

Raffles, Sir Stamford, occupies Singapore, 10; 16
Rama I, King of Siam, General Chakri, 4, 31, 35, 101
Rama II, King of Siam, 35, 46

Index 329

Rama III, King of Siam, Prince Chetsadabodin, 11, 25, 34–6, 37, 95, 96, 113, 116, 120–1, 122, 123
Ram, Phraya, 75
Ram Khamheng, Phraya, 75
Rangoon, 174, 175; Burney's description of, 254–7; census, 242, 256, 260, 261, 272, 283, 284, 290, 297, 298, 305
Rangoon Wungyi, Maung Khain, 186–9, 223–4, 249, 250, 253–5, 258, 260; succeeded by Maung Wa, 260, 285, 295–6
Ratchasethi, 'Radsithi', 47, 48
Residency, transfer question, 247, 249–51
Richardson, Dr D., 276, 280–2, 286–7, 293, 305
'Ron Rov', see Maha Yotha
Ross, Jane, wife of Richard B., mother of Henry B., 8

Sagaing, 277–9, 281
Sakya Min, the, 204, 241, 273
Salween River, 187, 246
Sam Roy Yot, 61
Sarkies Manook, Mr (usually referred to as Mr Sarkies), 206, 256, 293
Sayedawgyi, 198
Selangor, Malay state of, 76, 77, 87, 88, 131, 158
Selangor, Sultan Ibrahim of, 19, 27, 77
Shans, the, 172, 263–9
Shan Atwinwun, see Maung Yeet
'Shoe question', 201
Siam, southward expansion, 3; conquered by Burma, 1767, 4; liberated by Taksin, 4; governmental set-up, 33–4; China trade of, 35; relations with Malayan states, 102, and the Tenasserim provinces, 211
Siam treaty conference, first session, 99ff.; second session, 103f.; third session, 106f.; fourth session, 113ff.; sealing ceremony, 119
Singapore, 82, 85, 125
Singphos, the, 263
Si Phiphat, Phraya, That Bunnag, brother of Phrakhlang, 47, 52, 55–9, 73, 82, 83, 90–4, 99, 100, 101, 121
Snow, Lt.-Col., 20
Spears, Thomas, 238 fn.

Spiers, William, 253–4, 260, 261
Surin, Krommamun, 47, 48 99; houses treaty conference, 101ff., 104, 121
Sutherland, Captain George, 36, 60, 124
Swinton, George, Secretary to Government of India, 145, 154
Symes, Michael, 177, 179, 319

Taksin, King, 4, 11, 31, 174
Tavoy, 21, 24, 25, 40, 41, 70, 71, 176, 179, 193, 209
Tenasserim provinces, 20, 21, 23, 24, 25, 52, 86, 91, 148, 176, 180, 183–4, 188, 209, 211
Thandawzin, 198
Tharrawaddy, Prince of, King of Burma, *xii*, 120, 171, 204, 270–89, 290–308 *passim*
Thaton, 66
Thiphákorawong, Khan Bunnag, chronicler, son of Dit, 96
Toungoo, city, 50; dynasty, 66
Trade, Regulations at Bangkok, 77–80, 81
Treasurer, Royal, 202, 203, 233
Treaties, Anglo-Dutch of 1824, 6, 10; Anglo-Burmese of 1826, see under Yandabo, 176; Bangkok Treaty of 1826, 118, 150, 156, 157; Crawfurd's Commercial Treaty with the Court of Ava (1827), 181
Trengganu, Malay State, 4, 36, 76, 77, 81, 87, 88, 100, 102, 110, 125, 129, 145

Udin, Nakhoda, 138, 139, 148, 149, 151–4, 157, 160, 167

Vella, Walter, 95

Wangna, Maha Uparat, 22, 34, 37, 46; his 'party', 48, 56, 84, 86, 95, 96, 116, 122, 124, 133
Wellesley, Arthur, Duke of Wellington, 5
Wellesley, Province, 5, 13, 14, 111, 134, 153

White Elephant, royal, 46
White, Major, 266, 269
Wilson, Horace Hayman, 316
Wisset, Phraya, 49, 52, 54, 57
Woodman, Dorothy, 263
Wundauk, 'prop', 198
Wungyi, 'Bearer of the Great Burden', 194, 196–8, 201, 202
Wyatt, David, *x*, *xii*, 18, 23

Yandabo, 62, 69–70, 73, 94, 108, 133, 171, 175, 180, 183, 199, 224–5, 245, 247, 294, 296, 298
Ye, 21, 69, 70, 176, 179
Yewun, the, of Rangoon, 178, 193
Yoma daung, 246, 248
Yondaw, the, 200
Yule, Sir Henry, 181
Yunnan, 172

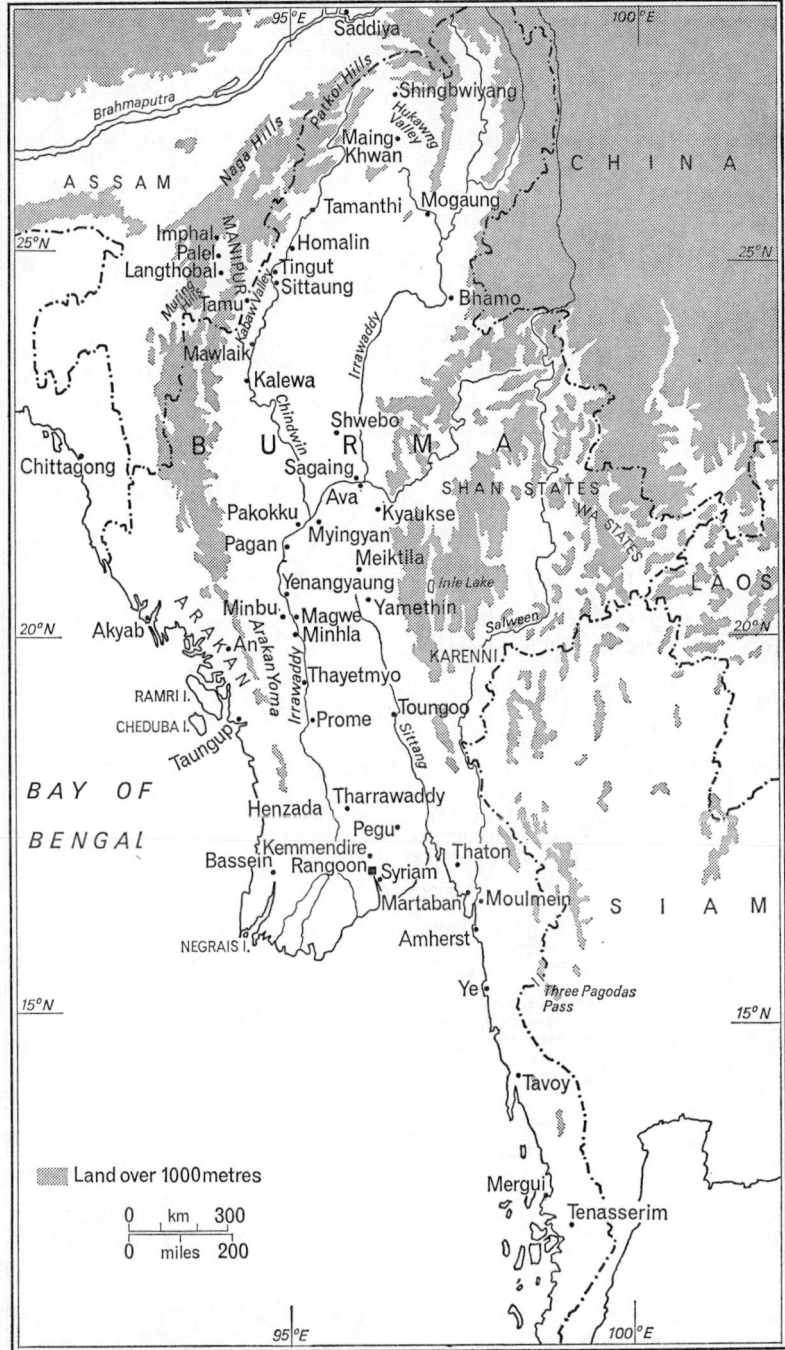

Burma

Siam and Malaga